FEASTING AND FASTING

Feasting and Fasting

The History and Ethics of Jewish Food

Edited by Aaron S. Gross, Jody Myers, and Jordan D. Rosenblum

With a Foreword by Hasia R. Diner and an Afterword by Jonathan Safran Foer

NEW YORK UNIVERSITY PRESS
New York

NEW YORK UNIVERSITY PRESS

New York
www.nyupress.org

References to Internet websites (URLs) were accurate at the time of writing. Neither the author nor New York University Press is responsible for URLs that may have expired or changed since the manuscript was prepared.

A previous, modified version of Chapter 15 was published as "Loving the Stranger and the Fall of Agriprocessors" in *Jewish Ethics in a Post-Madoff World*, by Moses Pava, published in 2011 by Palgrave Macmillan. Reproduced with permission of SNCSC.

Library of Congress Cataloging-in-Publication Data

Names: Gross, Aaron S., editor. | Myers, Jody Elizabeth, 1954– editor. | Rosenblum, Jordan, 1979– editor.
Title: Feasting and fasting : the history and ethics of Jewish food / with a foreword by Hasia R. Diner and an afterword by Jonathan Safran Foer ; edited by Aaron S. Gross, Jody Myers, and Jordan D. Rosenblum.
Description: New York : New York University Press, [2019] | Includes bibliographical references and index.
Identifiers: LCCN 2019015755 | ISBN 9781479899333 (cl : alk. paper) | ISBN 9781479827794 (pb : alk. paper)
Subjects: LCSH: Jews—Food—History. | Jewish cooking—History. | Jewish ethics.
Classification: LCC TX724 .F3715 2019 | DDC 641.5/676—dc23
LC record available at https://lccn.loc.gov/2019015755

To the Jewish Community

CONTENTS

FOREWORD

HASIA R. DINER

Food matters. Without it, pure and simple, there can be no life. Because it matters so profoundly, it informs human behavior and concern about it—including the material details of getting it, preparing it, and consuming it—infuses every aspect of all human cultures. Food provides a, or possibly the, key to understanding each and every social and cultural system that ever existed across time and place.

Wherever human beings lived, they concerned themselves first and foremost with food. Their societies took their shape around the tasks of satisfying peoples' daily needs for something to sustain their bodies, whether by hunting and gathering, fishing, farming, or laboring to purchase the food they needed. Wherever human beings have lived, they fretted over the innumerable physical and material matters of eating, concerning themselves with ingredients, modes of cooking, and decisions as to who got to eat what, when, and with whom. Their pots and pans, cutlery and plates, meal formats, and so many more minutiae of the day-in and day-out aspects of their food worlds defined them. All human beings worry about food, consume it as they must, and build their daily, weekly, monthly, and yearly calendars around it.

All of human history can be considered in light of how changes in technology, in the environment, and in lived economic relationships impacted the human-food equation. Did these changes—migrations, wars, the enclosure movement, industrialization, and on and on—provide women and men with more and different foods, or did these events jeopardize their chances of getting enough to eat? Droughts and insect infestations, floods and earthquakes made access to food difficult, if not impossible. How did such historic happenings complicate and leave their marks on the ways women and men in a particular place at a specific time literally got their "daily bread"?

Food's influence, though, extends far beyond the mundane and material. All human beings also make sense of themselves through the foods they eat and do not eat. They all do so differently but do so nonetheless. Food defines the boundaries of the group at the same time that it serves as a bridge between people, often individuals thrown together through circumstances beyond their control. Whether boundary making or bridge building, food historically went hand in hand with transformative shifts in peoples' lives and with their quest for order and identity.

Not surprisingly then, food has always existed in the realm of the religious, rendering forks and plates, spoons and tables, fruits and vegetables, meat and fish, feasting and fasting as not just ordinary items and acts but props in a vast, sacred drama. Food and religion—all religions—cannot be disassociated from each other. Since food constitutes the core of life and religion seeks to imbue meaning to life, a deep and inextricable bond must bind what we humans eat with our understanding and engagement with the sacred.

Women and men have variously sacrificed food, prayed to it for rain and dew to ensure an ample harvest, and defined some foods as inedible and as an affront and other foods as worthy of blessing. The connection between food and religion, performed everywhere and at all times, involved such matters as thanking their god or otherwise displaying gratitude for the food about to be consumed, eating or abstaining from special foods at holy times, or symbolically breaking bread with other members of their community under the shelter of their many "sacred canopies" (to borrow a phrase from religious studies scholar Peter Berger).

The twined relationship between food and religion surely deserves study, and no relationship can be said to be more important, richer, or more complicated. The range of these different relationships and the similarities between them lurking under the surface can give scholars of religion and scholars of food much to think about together.

The subject of food and—or in—Jewish traditions provides one such place to stop and think together about food as an engine that propelled the Jews through history. Indeed, scholars of food claim that the deep and complex history of Jewish food served as the springboard for nothing less than the creation of cultural anthropology. Both Mary Douglas and Marvin Harris, pioneers in this field of study, began their academic work by trying to parse out the cultural origins of kashrut, the biblical and Jewish dietary laws that segmented the universe into the pure and polluted, the edible and the inedible. These anthropologists sought to understand how these laws began and how Jews dealt with transgressions of the sacred binary of kosher and *treif*.

Wherever Jews lived, on whatever continent and in whatever era since ancient times, food defined them. As a people who entered the world with a compendium of sacred texts, the Hebrew Bible and its authoritative interpretations and then the Talmud with its multiple subsequent commentaries and responses to questions, they recognized at a visceral level the importance of food, a topic that never strayed far from their minds.

The first of these works, the Hebrew Bible, known to rabbinic tradition as the written law, might be read as a long origins story that went from food story to food episode as it described how the Jews' forebears concerned themselves with eating, sacrificing, and dividing the world into the edible and the forbidden. The later rabbinic compilation of the Mishnah and the Gemara, what they called the oral law, provided intricate and exquisite detail as to how Jews should actually conduct their lives and structure their communities in relationship to food. Later works by rabbis and other commentators devoted much time and energy to the task of further elucidating food matters.

More than symbolically, the 1563 code of Jewish law authored by Joseph Karo, considered to be the most authoritative compilation of the many details as to how Jews should live and fulfill their obligations, appeared under the title of the *Shulhan Aruch*, literally translated as the "set table." In Karo's book, Jews everywhere could penetrate the complex web of rules and regulations, the strictures decided by centuries of rabbinic disputation, as to what to do and what not to do, and its author made "the table" the central image that conveyed this knowledge.

Karo's book, and the many others that both proceeded and followed it, shaped the ways in which Jews and Jewish communities constituted themselves. The Jewish enclave, the *kahal*, existed in a dazzling array of places for most of history until the modern era as a self-governing entity that could control the lives of its constituents. Often recognized by the larger, non-Jewish state as the sole authority in the lives of the Jews, it could decide who had the requisite credentials to slaughter the animals, sell the meat, bake the Passover matzah, feed the Jewish wayfarers, and provide wine for religious purposes. Food matters, like so many others, lay in the hands of duly recognized rabbinic authorities who could, and did, use their power to discipline the Jews under the jurisdiction. Social pressure in these relatively closed communities also led to punctilious and probably nearly universal acceptance of the system.

While we have no evidence that all Jews at all times and in all places followed the absolute letter of the law when it came to eating, for the most part, we can say that what went on in Jewish communities tended toward conformity. The unselfconscious following of the law as defined by the local religious leaders constituted the norm. Jewish women and men in their homes scrupulously patrolled the pantries and shelves of their kitchens, inspected their chickens for flaws that might render them inedible, turned inside and out the pockets of their clothing before Passover to remove offending crumbs of bread, and when confronted with, for example, the abhorred mixing of meat and dairy, subscribed to purification rituals to render their spoons and pots, forks and dishes usable and newly reborn as kosher.

Yet the long history of the Jews involved much more than law inherited from the distant past. Their food history took much of its complexity from the Jews' constant migrations, from in and around the Mediterranean basin to Europe, the Americas, parts of Asia, the Antipodes, and elsewhere. Whether they migrated because of persecution and expulsion or if they relocated because of the beckoning of economic opportunities in one newly accessible place or another, they carried with them their sacred texts, religious practices, and their recognition that they were what they ate.

Wherever they went, they confronted three food problems. They had to, as they believed, attend to their dietary laws and continue to conform to this integral part of *halakhah*, a legal system they knew to be obligatory, yet they also had to deal with the reality that in each new place, they had to create from the ground up new communal structures to provision themselves with acceptable (kosher) food. Additionally, each new place—Spain, Poland, Morocco, Yemen, England, Italy, Germany, North America—exposed them to new ingredients and to previously unknown styles of cooking. In each one of these places, and so many others, they saw, smelled, and often tasted unfamiliar, sometimes tantalizing, novelties. While they lived for the most part exclusively with and among themselves, they met non-Jews in the marketplace and in other settings and thus were exposed to previously unknown foods. How, they asked themselves, could they eat the new good stuff while maintaining their personal and communal commitments to the sacred system? They essentially, in each locale, went through a process of figuring out how to face these three challenges.

While some elements of this conundrum confronted them everywhere, the peculiarities of different time periods mattered much as well. The connections between food and Judaism cannot be understood independent of the tectonic shifts in the social, political, and cultural histories that the Jews lived through. The first four chapters that follow, composing the first of the three parts that constitute this volume, begin by telling this story in a chronological fashion, setting the table (so to speak) for the case studies that constitute the second part and the ethical reflections that constitute the book's third and final part. Each era provides a particularly dramatic canvas upon which to think about food in Judaism. But the epic transformative impact of modernity, which continues to the present moment, deserves a special mention here, for it most directly shapes the present food-Judaism complex.

Modernity, whenever it began and when it actually struck the Jews and their communities, can be said to have exerted a powerful and disruptive impact on the food-Judaism connection. While historians debate the contours of modernity as well as its timing, all agree that it elevated the individual to a kind of quasi-sacred status. Individuals, especially men, emerged in the modern period as the ones who decided, on their own, how to lead their lives, follow their fortunes as they wanted, and define their values. No longer as restrained by the heavy hand of the past, they could move around the world as possibilities opened up, change their identities, reconsider ethical positions, and participate in institutions and decision-making processes once limited to the elites. Political, religious, moral, and cultural authorities could now be toppled, replaced by those who agreed to respect the "consent of the governed."

The Jews who lived through the modernization process, as well as the generations of their offspring who experienced other historically specific confrontations between tradition and personal choice, experienced opportunities unavailable to their progenitors. They could decide on their own, variously, where to live and how, how to make a living, what to read, whom to befriend, how to spend leisure time, whom to marry, how—or how not—to be Jewish, and, yes, what to eat.

They, individual Jew by individual Jew, as well as the Jewish communal institutions that they *chose* to participate in, had to decide how much the inherited Jewish religious food practices they wanted to keep, modify, or reject. How much, they asked themselves, person by person, family by family, did the observance of Jewish dietary law hamper them from accepting the opportunities of modern life, and how much did those traditions represent deep, beautiful, and meaningful connections to the group, its values, and its traditions? How to reconcile them? Why reconcile them? All these questions ran through Jewish communities as women and men decided, debated, and disputed among themselves—and they still run through Jewish communities today.

While modernity for the most part severed the deep, state-sanctioned bond between Jewish religious authority and the food choices of individual Jews, the tight ties between food and Judaism hardly disappeared. Rather they took new forms, involved novel decision-making processes, and created new kinds of institutional practices. As such, the connection between food and Judaism persists in the twenty-first century. The terms of the contemporary discussion about food's connection to Judaism and Judaism's relationship to food contain both echoes of the past and new dimensions of thinking that reflect diverse ethical stances and the sensibilities of postmodernity.

The subject of food and Judaism has a future that will play out in ways unimaginable to us in the present. It has a deep, rich, complex history that, as the chapters in this book will show, provides much to think about. And it has an open future that will shape Jewish communities and the values those communities embrace in consequential ways. Taken as a whole, this book also offers models of how the important histories of other religious communities and traditions and their ongoing relationship to food might be explored and contributes to a larger project of understanding the relationship between food and religion. In that sense, this book also issues a call for scholars of religion, perhaps historians especially, and scholars of food to meet together and examine the many ways in which we need each other.

Introduction

A A R O N S. G R O S S

Why Food and Religion

What are the advantages of attempting to understand a religion through the apparent detour of food? One reason is that food's location at the intersection of nature and culture invites us to think about religion from the perspective of multiple disciplines and in a more integrated way. Food is most obviously a necessity fixed by both biological requirements and cravings, but it is simply wrong to imagine that food is *only* a vehicle to provide nutrients to the body and satisfy appetites. If I enjoy a potato latke with a festive Hanukkah meal, it is not as if I first experience a certain caloric need being met and a certain sensual satisfaction, and then, after those needs and desires are fulfilled, I additionally experience a second-order sense of connection to Jewish traditions and community. We can analytically separate the nutritional and communal benefits of a potato latke, but in my experience of eating one—or serving one to my niece or nephew, for that matter—the satisfaction of biological needs and cultural connections are impossible to disentangle. "Food is culture, habit, and identity," as Jonathan Safran Foer put it,[1] or as Hasia Diner explains, "Talking about food is a way of talking about family, childhood, community," and more.[2]

Whatever material impacts food may have on the world—by providing nutrients, influencing immune systems, effecting longevity, shaping the lived-in environment, setting up particular human-animal interactions, and more—are invariably altered, slowed, amplified, or even obfuscated to generate diverse systems that construct identity and meaning. Food also provides a wieldy symbolic field that is called upon to construct sex and gender, social status, racialized identities, and even the line that distinguishes humans from other animals.[3]

This book explores food in Jewish communities and texts while also attending to these more universal features of food as a vehicle for human

1

meaning making—that is, food as a vehicle for *religion*. Food is not important in only some cultures; food is important in all cultures. The kind of creature we humans are simply requires that food be a vehicle for meaning making. From the perspective of food studies and religious studies, humans eat the way they do for complex reasons that are never simply the result of nutritional drives or taste preferences. Despite the fact that some individuals or religions explicitly embrace food as part of their identity and others claim that their food habits are essentially pragmatic, scientific, "healthy," or simply unimportant, from this scholarly perspective, food is a constitutive part of the hardware of human meaning making. The person who says "I'll eat anything" is making a statement of meaning as much as the person who follows a highly restrictive food regime (and likely the person who says "I'll eat anything" doesn't mean that literally in any case). Religion and food are always intermixed, and examining this intermixture in any one tradition, Judaism in the case of this book, can provide some insights into a more or less universal human process of making meaning *via culinaria*.

Bread Is More Than Bread Alone

The way in which human foodways both create and reflect different forms of human society, religious and otherwise, can be brought into sharp relief by considering the possibly immense impacts of very basic, fundamental features of human diets generally taken for granted—like the fact that humans now function as apex predators (i.e., at the top of the food chain). In his one-volume history of Homo sapiens, the Israeli historian Yuval Noah Harari speculates that much of what we consider uniquely human in comparison to other now extinct members of the genus Homo boils down to a change in our eating (and being eaten) patterns. Harari argues that a key to understanding humanity lies in understanding Homo sapiens' ecologically unusual leap to the top of the food chain about one hundred thousand years ago. According to Harari, data suggest that no previous hominid species had risen beyond the middle of the food chain despite two million years in which hominids had "large brain[s], the use of tools, superior learning abilities and complex social structures."[4] Harari ultimately suggests that if we thought big brains made humans unique, they might not be as important as our location in the food chain. The leap from the middle to the top of the food chain, argues Harari, "is a key to understanding our history and psychology. . . . Other animals at the top of the pyramid . . . evolved into that position very gradually, over millions of years. . . . In contrast, humankind ascended to the top so quickly that the ecosystem was not given time to adjust. Most top predators of the planet are majestic creatures. Millions of years of dominion have filled them with self-confidence. Sapiens by contrast is more like a banana republic dictator."[5]

Harari goes on to suggest that this prehistoric shift in food patterns was the first of several key changes around food that have continued to shape our species. He even goes so far as to suggest that the leap to the top of the food chain that is roughly concurrent with the rise of Homo sapiens as a distinct species can account for some wars and ecological problems visible today. "Having so recently been one of the underdogs of the savannah," Harari theorizes, "we are full of fears and anxieties over our position, which makes us doubly cruel and dangerous. Many historical calamities, from deadly wars to ecological catastrophes, have resulted from this over-hasty jump."[6]

A perhaps unlikely ally of Harari in his case that being at the top of the food chain had profound repercussions for humanity is the Romanian historian of religions, Mircea Eliade, generally considered a founding figure of religious studies as a contemporary discipline. Eliade speculates in his most mature work of scholarship that one of the fundamental roots of religion was that "man is the final product of a decision to kill in order to live. In short, the hominians succeeded in outstripping their ancestors by becoming flesh-eaters."[7] This decision to kill, Eliade theorizes, ultimately leads to the production of gender differentiation and the structure of sacrifice and helps constitute religion itself.[8] We need not further unfold let alone agree with the details of the ultimately unprovable speculation Eliade makes—he takes more than one thousand pages to make his case—to agree with the more basic assumption that features of Homo sapiens' diet have shaped humanity at a fundamental level. Even assuming that food practices are not important in the *precise* ways that Eliade or Harari speculate, it seems improbable that such enormous changes as Homo sapiens moving from being a prey species to an apex predator would not ripple through the generations in some way, shaping human religions while also being shaped by them.

Perhaps even more intriguingly, it turns out that nonhuman primates, at least some other social mammals, and some bird and fish species also organize their societies in part around the shared procurement and distribution of food and often do so in regionally distinctive ways that are passed generationally from parents to their offspring rather than simply being encoded in genes.[9] And if food is already this complex outside the human species, it becomes clearer why it is a safe assumption that bread is always more than bread alone.

Food and Being Human

As a way of arguing for the importance of giving foodways serious scholarly attention, an earlier generation of food studies scholars confidently asserted a (still often unchallenged) break that absolutely separates animal "feeding" from human "eating." This volume, while concurring with the general conclusion that food is important, will, for reasons that will become clear, avoid such grand attempts to separate human and animal. "All animals feed but humans alone eat," reads the opening line of Farb and Armelagos's seminal book *Consuming Passions: The Anthropology of Eating*, which has shaped food studies since its publication in 1980.[10] "A dog wolfs down every meal in the same way," Farb and Armelagos continue, "but humans behave in a variety of ways while eating."[11] In the details of their arguments, which include meaningful engagement with the scientific literature on animal behavior, even Farb and Armelagos do not try to defend the absurd assertion that animals consume "every meal in the same way," but they do try to defend an absolute line between human and animals even while acknowledging considerable complexity in animal "feeding." At stake in all the scholarly effort they expend to defend the human/animal binary in relation to food is less the actual data about ways that various animal species, including humans, actually eat and more their attempt to overcome a cultural bias that suggests that the consumption of food cannot possibly be interesting enough to merit study and reflection if it has anything in common with animal behavior. That is, in separating animal feeding and human eating and announcing that they are studying the latter and not the former, Farb and Armelagos are saying, in one manner of speaking, that human eating is filled with meaning.

Farb and Armelagos have to go out of their way to make a compelling case that food is important in part because the dubious cultural logic of their opening line and its absolute demarcation between animal feeding and human eating suggest that careful observation of most forms of animal eating can be totally explained by simple, predictable mechanisms, which would indeed tend to make the study of food rather pedestrian. This way of thinking about food as basically mechanical and unimportant is one of the major biases that often leads people to think that food would not be a rich lens into a topic like religion. If eating in animals—especially those closest to humans, like other primates—was all but mechanistic, scholars would have good reason to think that much of human food behavior could be explained as a simple fulfillment of biological drives, and there would be good reason to be skeptical of a book like this that wants to connect a religious tradition intimately with the culinary traditions of its practitioners.

As it turns out, far earlier than the appearance of humans on the evolutionary tree, food procurement and consumption became a more interesting and complicated affair than Farb and Armelagos's opening line implies. And when we realize this long evolutionary imbrication of food, social formation, communication, and even culture making, it becomes clearer why it makes all the sense in the world to examine a religious tradition in connection with food. For example, the primatologist Craig Stanford points out that "as far back as the 1960s, the American primatologist Geza Teleki proposed that the predatory behavior of the Gombe chimpanzees [who hunt particular monkey species] had a strong social basis. The Dutch primatologist Adrian Kortlandt suggested that hunting was a form of social display, in which male chimpanzees revealed their prowess to other members of the community. . . . [And] Richard Wrangham . . . noticed that certain aspects of their hunting behavior could not be accounted for by nutritional needs alone."[12] It is now a matter of consensus among primatologists that the only way to explain chimpanzee behavior in relation to hunting and some other food-related practices is to assume that they, like us, have cultures (in the sense of extrabiological information transmitted generationally). And as

Stanford goes on to reflect, if this is true, then we can also conclude that "the role of hunting in the lives of the earliest hominids [the evolutionary ancestors of Homo sapiens] was probably as complex and politically charged as it is in modern chimpanzees. . . . When [for example] we ask the question, 'when did meat become an important part of the human diet?' we should look well before the evolutionary split between apes and human beings in our own family tree."[13] If Stanford is right, food, perhaps meat especially, as discussed in this volume in the chapter I author, does not come to humans as simply a blank slate serving a pure animal-biological mandate but is already shot through with layers of socially constructed meanings, some perhaps forged before humans were humans. Even Farb and Armelagos are ready to admit on the force of evidence like this that "the human tendency to switch to animal foods whenever these become available is apparently a legacy from primate ancestors."[14]

From the perspective of this volume, it is simply not important to distinguish between features of human foodways that are "a legacy from primate ancestors" and ones that are products of cultural "refinement." Ironically, instead of helping us understand universal features of human behavior, the entire project of producing knowledge about humanity by dividing the human—or dividing human foodways—into allegedly unimportant animal parts that can be explained by neuroscientists and primatologists and allegedly more refined uniquely human parts that require the special tools of the social scientist and scholar of the humanities to explain is itself hopelessly wed to a culturally specific way of understanding that belongs to the Western intellectual tradition. This way of thinking is, for example, foreign to the worldview found in the Hebrew Bible and parts of other Jewish texts that simply lack anything like the kind of human/animal binary familiar to many later Jewish texts and to contemporary ears. For purposes of this volume, foodways are interesting as such; we do not need, like Farb and Armelagos, to first prove that a food practice is uniquely human—untainted by "primitive," "biological," "animal" forces—to find its study intellectually enriching.

The human construction of foodways perhaps may be best understood by ceasing to subdivide this process into cultural bits and noncultural bits (human-cultural aspects versus biological-animal aspects of foodways) in the manner Farb and Armelagos encourage. Like the process of critically understanding the workings of race and gender in contemporary society, the critical understanding of foodways today is at its best when it looks skeptically at our commonsense division of the world into us and them, male and female, culture and nature, human and animal, Jewish and non-Jewish, or, for that matter, features of food-ways that are "uniquely human" and those that are part of our "primate legacy," a division that usually ends up imagining the "human" on the model of a white, masculine, Eurocentric ideal.[15]

Fortunately, there are more intellectually fruitful paths into food studies. Consider, instead, attending to the numerous intertwine-ments among the construction of foodways, the construction of gen-der, and the construction of communal and often racialized borderlines. Eating certain foods may be encoded as particularly masculine or feminine—contrast the different gender associations with barbecue and salad in contemporary America. Decades of studies have explored what the American feminist scholar and animal advocate Carol Adams has called the "sexual politics of meat"[16]—the way in which eating meat can be encoded to reinforce structures that oppress women. Religious food laws can amplify such gender distinctions or be a source of relative egalitarianism. Who prepares food and who makes economic decisions over a family's food purchases is also gendered; consider in this volume Rachel Gross's discussion of Procter & Gamble's targeted marketing of Crisco to Jewish women as part of a campaign to convince Americans that they wanted to buy hydrogenated vegetable oil.

Especially relevant for a consideration of Jewish traditions, food may be claimed by often competing ethnic, national, or religious communi-ties. Consider debates about whether hummus is Israeli, Lebanese, or pan-Arab[17] or the use of falafel to help construct "the power struggles and moral dilemmas, the negotiation of religious and ideological affili-ations" in modern Israel.[18] In this volume, Katalin Rac's discussion of cholent charts its transformation from a specialty dish served on the Jewish Sabbath to a secular Hungarian favorite. Particular foodways may be embraced as a part of cultural identity or forcibly associated with a particular group in a process of racialization, such as colonial depic-tions of Indians as weak because they ate lots of rice and little meat,[19] racist American stereotypes portraying black people as obsessed with chicken,[20] or in this volume, the often anti-Jewish association of Jews and garlic discussed by Jordan Rosenblum. In a variation on this process discussed in this volume by David Freidenreich, some foods that rabbinic tradition had deliberately associated with Jewish ritual, like the use of unleavened bread (matzah) on Passover, were avoided by some medieval Christians out of fear they might acquire the negative characteristics they associated with Jews by contagion. Examples could be almost endlessly proliferated. In sum, food is a central node in the nexus of influences that shape the kind of creatures humans are today: gendered, stratified, divided into different groups on the basis of concepts like race and ethnicity, committed to different values, and attached to particular religious identities.

Food and Jewish Traditions

So what does it mean to be a book about these important aspects of food *and Judaism*? On the one hand, this book is about Jewish traditions, and food functions as the focal point for examining different forms of Judaism, different "Judaisms."[21] As its chapters progress, the book considers the history of Jewish foodways; studies in food and culture exploring how Jewish communities have been imagined alongside garlic, schmaltz (rendered chicken fat), and other foods; and finally how Jewish communities and texts engage the ethical questions raised by food. In this sense, this is a book about how the making of different Judaisms and the making of Jewish meals have been intertwined throughout history and in contemporary Jewish practices.

On the other hand, this book is also a study of what we might call the *religious dimensions of food*, and the case of Judaism serves as an exemplum in a wide-ranging scholarly discussion of how we might best think about the intersection of food and religion. This book deals with not only Jewish studies but also both religious studies and food studies—interdisciplinary fields that deal respectively with the nature of religion and food. As its chapters progress, the book examines how particular human communities, in this case Jewish communities, move through history, construct identity, negotiate modernity, define authenticity, draw social boundaries, and enact their ethical lives—that is, how they make meaning—through food. In this sense, this is also a book about how human beings make meaning and thus organize society through food, activities that are often best described as religious.

This book does not presume a single definition of religion or Judaism, but it does challenge certain commonsense ideas that can weaken our ability to accurately perceive the phenomena of religion generally and Jewish traditions in particular. Against the view that food is a secondary concern for understanding a religious tradition, this volume suggests that no major historical development in Jewish life can be fully understood without reference to food. Against the view that religion is primarily about beliefs, this volume uncovers a robust intertwinement of the culinary and the processes of meaning making in the Jewish case. And against the view that food is an apolitical, personal matter, this volume shows that in the Jewish context, questions about food—and, as we will see, especially about animal food—are sites of both important ethical consensus and disagreement.

The book's three parts respectively include four chronologically arranged historical overviews by period specialists[22] (first part), six studies in food and culture built around particular foods and theoretical questions (second part), and seven chapters addressing ethical issues (third and final part). The first part, edited by Jody Myers, provides the historical and textual overview that is necessary to ground any discussion of food and Jewish traditions. The first chapter by Elaine Goodfriend covers foodways during the thousand or so years before the Common Era as indicated by the Hebrew Bible, Apocrypha, and historical sources. The second chapter by David Kraemer describes the crucial changes in foodways during the first nine centuries of the Common Era as expressed through classical rabbinic literature such as the Mishnah and Talmud. The third chapter by Jonathan Brumberg-Kraus focuses on developments in the ninth to the fifteenth century as they appear in medieval Jewish legal (halakhic), liturgical, and mystical (kabbalistic) writings. Taking us up to the present moment, the fourth chapter by Jody Myers surveys the effects on Jewish foodways wrought by the sweeping changes during the last five centuries associated with migrations and modernization. Myers's chapter in particular provides a counterweight to presently popular versions of Jewish food history that often function simply as "a celebration of kosher food's increasing acceptance among food manufactures and appeal to a largely non-Jewish population"—a narrative that historian Roger Horowitz demonstrates has been "relentlessly promoted" by business interests and taken at face value by a range of popular books and articles.[23]

The second part, edited by Jordan D. Rosenblum, provides case studies of the religious dimension of foods in different Jewish contexts, including garlic (Rosenblum), wine (Freidenreich and Susan Marks), Crisco and schmaltz (R. Gross), peanut oil (Zev Eleff), and cholent (Rac). This part deals with a range of time periods, and each chapter addresses not only a particular food but also a theoretical issue of broader interest in the study of religion, including chapters that explore food as a metonym for religious identity (Rosenblum), food and industrialization (R. Gross), and food and authenticity (Eleff). If the first part documents how food has been essential to Israelite and Jewish cultures historically, the second part demonstrates this at a closer range while also providing additional examples for reflection.

Three chapters in the second part give special weight to the processes by which food creates and erases cultural borders (Freidenreich, Marks, and Rac). David Freidenreich provides a wide-ranging study demonstrating how ideas about Jewishness play important roles in the construction of Christian and Islamic identity, especially in relation to wine. Susan Marks also focuses on wine to reconsider received wisdom about just how strict ancient Jewish communities were in separating themselves through drinking practices, finding more common ground than previously thought. While Freidenreich's and Marks's chapters provide grounding on how a highly regulated food, wine, was used to construct Jewishness (and by extension Christian and Islamic identity), Katalin Rac explores how a dish once associated with Judaism became secularized into a contemporary Hungarian favorite.

The final part, which I edited, focuses on moral and ethical questions generated by and answered through Jewish engagements with food. This part includes two chapters dealing with gardening, farming, and Jewish ethics (Jennifer Thompson and Adrienne Krone); three chapters dealing with ethical issues as they appear in connection with kosher food both in the Bible (Daniel Weiss) and today (Elliot Ratzman and Moses Pava); and two chapters that provide additional novel approaches to everyday eating and Jewish ethics in the contemporary period, including the ethics of consumption amid plenty (Jonathan Crane) and the ethical treatment of farmed animals (myself).

Overcoming Resistance to Studying Food and Religion

To take food seriously in this way is relatively new in the Western academy. The influential American scholar of food studies Warren Belasco argues that the field of food studies is "inherently subversive" and that "to study food often requires us to cross disciplinary boundaries and to ask inconvenient questions."[24] Belasco and other founders of food studies like American scholars Sidney Mintz and Marion Nestle—all three of whom are, perhaps not incidentally, Jewish—swam against the tide to establish the study of food as a major area of both academic research and serious discussion in the public square. In his groundbreaking studies of sugar's massive sociopolitical influence, Mintz builds on the work of anthropology pioneers like Claude Lévi-Strauss to argue that sugar and the commodity market that arose with it was "one of the massive demographic forces in world history," shaping the slave trade, colonialism, and global capitalism.[25] In his now classic book *Sweetness and Power*, Mintz defended the study of foods, arguing that "just such homely, everyday substances [as sugar] may help us to clarify both how the world changes from what it was to what it may become, and how it manages at the same time to stay in certain regards very much the same."[26] Following the lead of these scholars but focusing specifically on religion and Jewish traditions, this book resists powerful currents in contemporary Western thought that suggest that the kind of meaning that counts as religious is found in the contents of holy books but not the contents of soup.

Influential voices within Western culture have created a set of associations in which religion—or at least the "right" kind of religion—is associated more with belief than with ritual, more with ideas than practices, and more with the often male-dominated world of politics than the often female-dominated world of cooking. All this functions to make it difficult to see the way that producing and consuming of food intersects with the processes that many of us would want to associate with religion: creating human identity, building communal boundaries, structuring the human relationship with life, and discerning ethical ideals.

If food is as central to understanding religion as this book argues, why is it that both common sense and scholarship have suggested to us that food and religion have little to do with one another? It turns out that neglect of food in the study of religion has a particular relationship to the way Christian communities who have shaped the Western academic study of religion have imagined Jewish traditions. Following a bias especially strong within some streams of Protestant Christianity and early Reform Judaism that have tended to diminish the importance of dietary practice, scholars of religion, including many scholars of Jewish studies, have historically gravitated toward sacred texts, narratives, social history, law, belief, and philosophical systems as the most profound vehicles through which to explore religion. Food was inevitably mentioned in the course of addressing these allegedly more important matters but was not itself seen as an important locus of meaning. As the New Testament books of Mark (7:15) and Matthew (15:11) had suggested, what went into people's mouths seemed far less interesting than what came out. However true it may be from a certain theological vantage that food is of little importance to ultimate matters like salvation, this volume disagrees with Mark and Matthew insofar as it insists that food and dietary practices are a major location for meaning making. Indeed, this book suggests that it is perhaps only in recognizing the descriptive fact of how profoundly food does shape religious phenomena that one might come to recognize the full significance of theological claims like those of Mark and Matthew.

Jewish Foodways and Academic Scholarship

At the risk of oversimplifying a long and often violent history, certain streams of Christian polemic against Judaism and, later, Christian polemics against Islam cast food practices as a lower-order form of religion. In this often overtly hostile narrative, rabbinic traditions were viewed as so preoccupied with food rules—and with rules and law more generally—that Jews were blind to the true spiritual truth realized in Christianity. In this reading, Jews related to food akin to the way that Farb and Armelagos imagined animals relating to food: Jews slavishly followed the dictates of outdated laws in the same way animals were condemned to slavishly follow the dictates of their biology. This basic form of critique was voiced in some streams of early Christianity against Jews and was repeated in the medieval era by Protestant Christianity against not only Jews and Muslims but also Catholic and Eastern Orthodox forms of Christianity, and as documented by Myers, in the modern period, it has even been repeated by Reform Judaism against more traditional forms of Jewish observance.

These polemics did not totally disavow the religious importance of food but set the importance of food inside supersessionist narratives in which Judaism (or Islam, Catholicism, Eastern Orthodoxy, or more traditional Judaism) and its food laws represented a lower-order revelation superseded by a later and allegedly more mature religious insight. Thus Jews were racialized through food in a manner parallel to the way that European Christian colonial powers racialized defeated populations by attributing the success of their conquest to the allegedly superiority of their meat-heavy diets. As one nineteenth-century doctor put it, "The rice-eating Hindoo and Chinese and the potato-eating Irish peasant are kept in subjection by the well-fed English. Of the various causes that contributed to the defeat of Napoleon at Waterloo, one of the chief was that for the first time he was brought face to face with the nation of beef-eaters, who stood still until they were killed."[27] Within this large frame that often denigrated non-European, non-Anglo-Saxon, or non-Christian food practices, diverse forms of anti-Judaism imagined Jewish food practices as decadent. For example, Claudine Fabre-Vassas shows how French Christians articulated anti-Jewish ideologies by, ironically, associating Jews themselves with the animal their dietary prohibitions forbade them from eating: the pig. Not only were Jews associated with a slew of negative characteristics associated with pigs, but, Fabre-Vassas explains, "and this is the great contradiction of their [Jewish] destiny—since they deprived themselves of this meat, they were constantly seeking the closest substitute, the flesh and blood of Christian children."[28] That is, Fabre-Vassas concludes that one of the most influential of all anti-Jewish ideas, the "blood libel"—the hateful accusation that Jews used and consumed Christian blood for ritual purposes—was perpetuated in part as a peculiar Christian interpretation of the dangerous effects of Jewish adherence to religious dietary law. Again, a parallel is found in the attitudes of European colonial powers toward conquered populations, who were often and inaccurately described as cannibals.[29]

The legacy of this theological suspicion about the religious relevance of dietary practices has today been secularized into a broad attitude that food and religion are distant domains. Religion might be viewed as appearing in, say, a blessing that is *added onto* an act of food production or consumption like a blessing made over wine, but only to the extent that the blessing moves beyond the physicality of the meal itself into the realm of beliefs. Food, meals, and the embodied intra- and intercommunal social contexts that are woven together with them are, on this view, just not that important to understanding a religion. Instead, this volume will also move in the other direction, as, for example, in Marks's chapter on rabbinic libation practices, which uses the study of blessings to help reflect on the complex, lived social reality of Jewish participation in "a common banquet tradition" in which Greeks, Romans, and Christians also participated. In ways like this, the present volume resists a long scholarly and "commonsense" tradition that has ignored and hidden the importance of food.

Although there are academic scholars who have been interested in food, many of them manifest a related bias that this volume also hopes to overcome. For example, anthropologists and other scholars interested in religion who studied nonwhite cultures have historically paid considerable attention to food practices, but at least some of the time, this was precisely because they considered these human communities inferior to European societies (again, more like Farb and Armelagos's picture of animals). The racist bias went like this: if you are studying sublime religions like Christianity, food is relatively unimportant, but if you are studying "primitive" peoples, then food will be important since their culture has not yet gone beyond (superseded) a preoccupation with materiality. In this way, anti-Judaism and racism were part of a broader worldview in which meaning making through food was derided.

A focus on food was seen as a focus on the "animal" aspects of humanity, and scholars of religion have virtually without exception placed—arguably incorrectly—religion in precisely those aspects of humanity that distinguish humans from animals.[30] That is why it was seen as more legitimate to analyze the blessing over wine than, as this book will also do, reflect upon the lived reality of drinking wine in community. How could, the logic went, studying human physical ingestion of various species possibly add to our understanding of the most uniquely human of activities, religion? Studying food practices was what one did to study primates and primitives—and Jews, Hindus, and other racialized religious communities—not the great world religions.

It turns out that the religious phenomenon itself was divided in two—world religions versus ethnic or national religions—in part on the basis of food. Still to this day, it is common to categorize religions in a twofold manner: on the one hand, we have the invented category of "world religions," traditions in which food practices are allegedly not that significant.[31] The second category consists of all the rest of the world's religions, which are in this problematic way of thinking lumped together and called "ethnic" or "primitive" religions, what we today might call the religions of traditional peoples.[32] In primitive religions, so the logic went, food practices were still crucial, owing to their generally closer approximation of an animal state. Judaism (and Hinduism) were, notably, not originally considered world religions and were only later added to the list.[33] Instead, they were seen as "ethnic" or "national" religions, tied to particular places and bound up in arcane laws—like the anachronistic practice of biblical food laws (or rules against eating cows)—that were evidence of their inferior state.[34] This othering of non-Christian religion also had a temporal dimension. The communities that were labeled "primitive" were, of course, the living contemporaries of the scholars who studied them, but early scholars viewed them as arrested at an early stage of development as if they were caught in some distant past while only Europeans had moved on to modernity. That is, the study of religion was once imagined in evolutionary terms, an idea now discredited. The notion was that what we now call religions of traditional peoples were representative of early religions that evolved to look like what we still call the world religions. This implied, again erroneously, that the further back one went in human history, the more important food would be in the life of any given community. This kind of thinking is part of the legacy this volume seeks to overcome.

Biblical Dietary Laws and Judaism

All these attitudes converge in explaining why the only truly massive exception to the rule that scholars of religion have neglected food is the study of biblical food law. "More thought has been given to the origins of the ancient Hebrew dietary law than any other religion-related food topic," writes food studies scholar Jeffrey Pilcher in a review of food and religion scholarship.[35] And this interest is not strictly academic; the editors' experiences have been that if we share with a friend or colleague that our scholarship focuses on "food and Judaism," common responses go like this: "You mean the biblical separation of milk and meat?" or "You mean sacrifices in the Bible?" as if no other intersection of religion and food of consequence had occurred in the Jewish fold since biblical times. It is important to clarify here that the Hebrew Bible does not depict or represent Jewish traditions any more than it does Christian traditions. Both traditions, of course, have a special relationship with the Hebrew Bible, but only the biblical text interpreted through the lens of Jewish or Christian interpretation makes it a Jewish or Christian book. On its own, the Hebrew Bible describes a religious tradition distinct from both Judaism and Christianity that we could (somewhat confusingly) call "ancient Judaism," but that might be better thought about simply as "ancient Israelite religion."[36]

Returning to the enormous amount of scholarship and popular imagination that has been given to biblically rooted food practices, we can see that multiple biases have converged in making visible the significance of food practices in the biblical period. Judaism generally was understood as a religion of law, especially nonrational laws like food laws; thus, the association of Judaism and the Bible made it feel natural to see food practices as important in it. Moreover, from some, though by no means all, Christian theological perspectives, the biblical food laws were prior to Jesus's revelation and thus belong to an earlier period of religion in which God was still actively commanding obedience to the food laws for his followers; this too made it feel natural to see biblical food practices as important.[37] After all, a Christian scholar might reason, there was some explanation why God commanded them. This theological bias had a counterpart in the allegedly nontheological study of religion where some scholars argued for the developmental view of religion discussed earlier. This bias made it feel natural to see food practices as important when studying an ancient text while still diminishing the ongoing importance of food to religion. Again, this is a way of thinking that this volume seeks to overcome.

"Jewish food" in modernity or the contemporary period is equally saturated with meaning as it was in the days when meat was obtained from the sacrificial altar in Jerusalem. The meanings are different, but food did not become a site of meaning or cease being one. To eat is to become involved in a social world and a symbolic world. Just as eating shapes the world materially whether we will it to or not or pay attention to it or not, eating also proliferates religious meanings whether the eater wills them or not and whether scholars pay attention to them or not.

Defining Jewish Food

Viewing food as a general site through which humans make meaning has a correlate: it is not obvious what food should count as specifically Jewish. If we accept the notion that food plays an important role in the processes by which all humans make meaning, it suggests we need to work hard to determine which aspects of food's interplay with meaning deserved to be called "Jewish." Is a bagel Jewish because it is associated with Jews in the popular imagination even if there is nothing in Jewish law that makes a bagel particularly Jewish?[38] Is food Jewish only when it is produced in concert with rabbinically recognized norms like the laws of kashrut? Is a food Jewish if it is also eaten by non-Jews? Just what is Jewish food?

For the editors of this volume, the most palatable understanding of "Jewish food" would identify it with what food studies scholars would call "Jewish cuisine." In everyday speech, "cuisine" may refer to elite and fancy foods, but in food studies, it is widely viewed that all human communities have cuisine in the sense that all human communities make meaning through food. Following Farb and Armelagos, Belasco understands cuisine as "a shared set of 'protocols,' usages, communications, behaviors, etc." that is akin to language.[39] Cuisine provides "a system of communication that is inculcated from birth, if not before, and is hard to change or learn once you are grown."[40] Cuisine, in this understanding, prioritizes certain food as basic staples, dictates ways of eating or "manners," preferences certain modes of preparation and seasoning, and much else.[41] So whatever we call it, how do we define Jewish food?

The first thing we can note is that "Jewish food" is not a category indigenous to traditional Judaism like the category of kosher food. Classical Jewish law does indeed include robust laws dealing with food—most famously the kosher laws that define what foods are fit to eat—but defining a food as "kosher" does not make it "Jewish." Indeed, a food may meet kosher requirements but be eschewed by Jews for a whole range of other halakhic, moral, or aesthetic reasons. And of course, beyond kosher law—which only a minority of Jews in America and a slight majority of Jews in Israel today claim to observe—a whole range of cultural factors shape what most Jews eat today far more profoundly than traditional law. As is the case with most cuisines, Jewish cuisine is shaped by the same three factors that food studies scholars see operative in virtually all human contexts: personal identity, convenience, and to a lesser extent, concerns with questions of responsibility—questions about supporting local businesses, sustainability, animal welfare, public health, and so forth.[42]

Jewish Food as Kosher

These limitations notwithstanding, there are still several important distinctions in Jewish dietary practice that are frequently applicable across many Jewish populations. First, we can note the enduring influence of the prohibitions associated with kosher law. In a limited but important sense, "Jewish food" can sometimes be fruitfully defined as food shaped by kosher regulations. During much of the premodern era and still today, many Jewish communities have been out of principle or because of social habit more or less observant of these laws as interpreted by rabbinic tradition in textual compilations like the Talmud and subsequent law codes. These religious dietary laws forbid the consumption of certain animals, require Jews to slaughter animals in a specific manner, and prohibit mixing meat and dairy in foods. The "distinctly Jewish" aspects of the diets of Jews would be most discernable, then, in lands where foods eaten by non-Jews were shunned by Jewish law. For example, pork, prohibited for Jews to consume by kosher law, was the meat of choice among Eastern European Christians but forbidden to Muslims, so Jewish dietary distinctiveness was more obvious when they lived in, say, Catholic Poland compared to Islamic Morocco. Among the poor everywhere, for whom eating meat was a luxury, differences between Jews and gentiles would not appear as great.

Jewish Food as Holiday Food

Second, "Jewish food" might also be fruitfully used to refer to food-stuffs associated with Sabbath and holiday foods. If not entirely different from everyday fare, such foods might appear different because they were shaped by symbolic meanings or prepared according to the unique requirements of Jewish law or custom. *Haroset*, for example, a Passover Seder fruit relish consisting of chopped apples, wines, and nuts (a European Jewish recipe) or chopped dates, raisins, almonds, and sesame (a recipe of the Jews of Yemen) has multiple symbolic meanings connected to the biblical Egyptian slavery narrative. Another example is the warm, hearty stew, typically made with meat, known as *hamin* or cholent, discussed in the chapter by Katalin Rac. It is to be eaten mid-day (Saturday) in order to enhance the joy of the Sabbath, and while its ingredients may be similar to the stews eaten by non-Jews, the Sabbath stew must be prepared before the Sabbath, kept warm until the next day without violating religious prohibitions on kindling a flame on the Sabbath, and contain ingredients that would still remain tasty after so many hours of heat.[43]

Jewish Food as Ethnic Food

There are also factors totally unrelated to kosher law or holiday practices that have shaped understandings of "Jewish food." There have been foods with no ostensible religious meaning that Jewish immigrants brought to their new lands, which became signs of Jewishness because they were unknown to the native non-Jewish population. Similarly, "Jewish food" might be distinctive independent of kosher and holiday practices for including nonlocal or uncommon ingredients. Jews have tended to have had a more cosmopolitan diet than their non-Jewish peers due to their exposure to foreign foods through their occupations in trade or urban settings, from their connection to the network of Jews worldwide, and from their immigrant and refugee origins. For example, in mid-nineteenth-century Britain, only Jews may have known about the Dutch food *waflers*—in their later, American context, these were called waffles—because of the Jewish immigrants in their midst who had previously lived in the Netherlands.[44] Another example is the secular American Jewish enthusiasm for Chinese food, dating to the beginning of the twentieth century and arising from Jews' exploration of ethnic immigrant enclaves in their cities.[45]

Finally, another source for distinctive Jewish eating outside of kosher and holiday practices is the communal and family-centeredness of Jewish culture that finds expression in serving distinctive foods passed down from previous generations. One might be able to discern in this practice and in these specific foods some hints of Jewish geographical origins, religious traditions and values, and nonreligious ethnic practices. Thus a discussion of Jewish food must be wide ranging, encompassing behaviors connected to Jewish religious practice as well as those indicative of Jewish cultural identity, sentimental toward the Jewish past, or that are transgressive, such as consuming bacon wrapped around a matzo ball.[46]

This volume will not assume any single normative definition about what constitutes Jewish food just as it will not assume any single normative definition about what constitutes Judaism. Instead, to the extent that a given Jewish population can be clearly discerned at all, the scholars in this volume ask about its distinctive cuisines and, working from such population-level analyses, sometimes try to make more general observations that are valid across multiple Jewish populations.[47]

Food and Jewish Culture in America Today

While this book provides a comprehensive consideration of food and Jewish traditions, it is the editors' hope that it also will better equip contemporary Jews who wish to engage their Jewish values or Jewish community through food to do so with greater understanding. As such, readers will notice we have given extra attention to the contemporary North American context. Jews in the contemporary Americas continue to make meaning through food in the traditional ways noted earlier, but today they are also metareflecting on food and Judaism as a source of meaning in ways that are more novel. For around a decade, American Jews have been talking about a "Jewish food movement"—a phenomenon that is only beginning to receive focused scholarly examination but that is evident to anyone looking at recent rosters of events at mainline Jewish institutions. The chapters by Thompson and Krone touch upon this movement, which now includes explicitly food-themed events, festivals, and even an annual multiday conference that gathers Jews explicitly in the name of Jewish food to do everything from arts-and-crafts-style workshops on pickling techniques to social justice workshops that call for Jewish institutions to buy their food according to ethical guidelines that consider Jewish approaches to issues like animal welfare, environmental impact, and the treatment of workers.

This attention to food coincides with the related rise of working farms that are simultaneously nodes of Jewish community life—what are called Jewish community farms—an important phenomenon documented in this book in the chapter by Krone. Whether on Jewish community farms or in conventional Jewish spaces like synagogues, community centers, and summer camps, much of this new attention to food and farming takes place alongside a focus on being outdoors, experiential education, and concern for the environment. Giving attention to the outdoors, food, and the environment in tandem is common enough in institutional American Jewish life today that Jewish funders and nonprofits have given it a name, JOFEE (Jewish Outdoor Food and Environmental Education), and issued a substantial report evaluating the success of this genre of Jewish education.[48]

The first part of the book helps provide a historical context for these contemporary North American engagements with food visible today; two chapters in the second part build upon this history to frame key issues especially relevant in the North American context. R. Gross considers how the larger phenomenon of industrialization changed the very substance of Jewish food, exploring how remaking foods—specifically changing the cooking fat of choice from traditional schmaltz to Crisco—remade aspects of American Judaism. While R. Gross shows how larger historical processes from without impact the meaning of Jewish food, Eleff provides us a case study of the special food laws that surround Judaism's most widely observed holiday, Passover, to consider how these internal and external forces converge to determine questions about what food practices will be considered authentically Jewish and valid according to Jewish legal authorities. Finally, the third part on ethics includes both descriptive and prescriptive (normative) chapters to provide a robust platform from which to engage contemporary food issues from the perspective of Jewish values. All but the thirteenth chapter focused on the biblical text include a greater or lesser focus on ethical issues widely discussed in North America today.

Conclusion

Altogether, these chapters provide a rich opportunity to reflect on the universal process of humans making meaning through food in the specific context of Jewish traditions. The first historical part provides a uniquely comprehensive grounding that allows one to understand how Judaism and Jewish foodways have changed together over time. The second part adds to this broad historical understanding by sharpening our understanding of food and culture, including theoretical issues like how food functions as a metonym for Jewish identity and by providing case studies of specific foods. The final part invites readers to reflect on how past and contemporary Jewish communities have brought Jewish ethics together with Jewish eating and provides resources allowing contemporary Jews to better engage ethical questions surrounding food from a Jewish perspective. Throughout, the volume seeks to keep open the question "What is Jewish food?" just as it keeps open the question of what constitutes Judaism itself. Finally, the volume provides enough examples speaking out of or to the contemporary North American context to make it of special value to American Jews as they seek to understand their heritage and as they participate in the processes that constantly and inevitably remake diverse Judaisms. Taken collectively, it is the editors' hope that this book heightens our appreciation about how the most familiar act of eating is also one of the most profound acts of meaning making.

NOTES

1. Foer, *Eating Animals*, 259.
2. Diner, *Hungering for America*, xv.
3. On racialization, see Omi and Winant, *Racial Formation in the United States*; HoSang, LaBennett, and Pulido, *Racial Formation in the Twenty-First Century*.
4. Harari, *Sapiens*, 11.
5. Harari, 11–12.
6. Harari, 12.

7. Eliade, *History of Religious Ideas*, 4.

8. Eliade, 5. For discussion, see Gross, *Question of the Animal and Religion*, chap. 3.

9. Evidence of this complexity in social mammals is extremely widespread. For a more general discussion with further citations to scientific literature on fish, see Brown, "Fish Intelligence, Sentience, and Ethics"; for birds, see Ackerman, *Genius of Birds*.

10. Farb and Armelagos, *Consuming Passions*, 3.

11. Farb and Armelagos, 3.

12. Standford, "Chimpanzee Hunting Behavior and Human Evolution," 256.

13. Standford, 261.

14. Farb and Armelagos, *Consuming Passions*, 44.

15. Jacques Derrida has named this tendency to understand the human subject in this manner "carnophallogocentrism" to emphasize the intertwined creation of a subject that idealizes meat eating ("carno"), maleness ("phal" for phallus), and Western-European Christian identity ("logos"); for discussion, see Gross, *Question of the Animal and Religion*, 141–44. Also see Aph and Syl Ko, *Aphro-ism*.

16. For discussion, see Adams, "Very Rare and Difficult Thing"; Adams, *Sexual Politics of Meat*.

17. Ariel, "Hummus Wars"; Gvion, *Beyond Hummus and Falafel*.

18. Raviv, *Falafel Nation*.

19. For discussion, see Adams, *Sexual Politics of Meat*, 52–55.

20. For discussion, see Williams-Forson, *Building Houses Out of Chicken Legs*.

21. Hahn Tapper, *Judaisms*, 1–11.

22. These four chapters constitute the first attempt to produce a comprehensive history of Judaism and food written by specialists in their respective time periods.

23. Horowitz, *Kosher USA*, 3.

24. Belasco, *Food*, 6.

25. Mintz, "Plantation as a Sociocultural Type," 49.

26. Mintz, *Sweetness and Power*, xxv.

27. As quoted in and discussed by Adams, *Sexual Politics of Meat*, 54.

28. Fabre-Vassas, *Singular Beast*, 7.

29. For discussion, see Adams, *Sexual Politics of Meat*, 54–55.

30. For discussion, see Gross, *Question of the Animal and Religion*, chap. 3.

31. For discussion, see Masuzawa, *Invention of World Religions*.

32. For discussion, see Smith, Green, and Buckley, "Religions of Traditional Peoples."

33. For discussion, see Smith, "Matter of Class."

34. Smith.

35. Pilcher, *Oxford Handbook of Food History*, 417.

36. For discussion, see Rosenblum, *Jewish Dietary Laws in the Ancient World*, chap. 1.

37. For discussion, see Rosenblum, chap. 1.

38. For discussion, see Balinska, *Bagel*.

39. Belasco, *Food*, 15. Belasco draws especially on Farb and Armelagos, *Consuming Passions*.

40. Belasco, *Food*, 16.
41. Belasco, 16–18.
42. For discussion of the triad "identity, convenience, and responsibility," see Belasco, chap. 1.
43. For discussion, see Cooper, *Eat and Be Satisfied*, 66–68.
44. For discussion, see Cooper, 88, 140.
45. Tuchman and Levine, "New York Jews and Chinese Food."
46. Kaminer, "Gorbals' Ilan Hall Talks Treyf."
47. I am especially indebted to my coeditor, Jody Myers, for the taxonomy and example used in the "Defining Jewish Food" section, which draws in part on Claudia Roden, who defines "Jewish food" as food marked by the rules of *kashrut*, holiday foods, foods associated with Jewish immigrants, and foods transmitted through Jewish families as emblems of family culture. See Roden, *Book of Jewish Food*, 10–11.
48. Informing Change, "Seeds of Opportunity."

BIBLIOGRAPHY

Ackerman, Jennifer. *The Genius of Birds*. New York: Penguin, 2016.

Adams, Carol J. *The Sexual Politics of Meat: A Feminist-Vegetarian Critical Theory*. 20th anniversary ed. New York: Continuum, 2010.

———. "'A Very Rare and Difficult Thing': Ecofeminism, Attention to Animal Suffering, and the Disappearance of the Subject." In *A Communion of Subjects: Animals in Religion, Science, & Ethics*, edited by Paul Waldau and Kimberley Patton. New York: Columbia University Press, 2006.

Ariel, Ari. "The Hummus Wars." *Gastronomica: The Journal of Critical Food Studies* 12, no. 1 (2012): 34–42.

Balinska, Maria. *The Bagel: The Surprising History of a Modest Bread*. New Haven: Yale University Press, 2008.

Belasco, Warren James. *Food: The Key Concepts*. Oxford: Berg, 2008.

Brown, Culum. "Fish Intelligence, Sentience, and Ethics." *Animal Cognition* 18, no. 1 (2015): 1–17.

Cooper, John. *Eat and Be Satisfied: A Social History of Jewish Food*. Northvale, NJ: Jason Aronson, 1993.

Diner, Hasia R. *Hungering for America: Italian, Irish, and Jewish Foodways in the Age of Migration*. Cambridge, MA: Harvard University Press, 2001.

Eliade, Mircea. *A History of Religious Ideas*. Vol. 1, *From the Stone Age to the Eleusinian Mysteries*, translated by Willard R. Trask. Chicago: University of Chicago Press, 1981.

Fabre-Vassas, Claudine. *The Singular Beast: Jews, Christians, & the Pig*. Translated by Carol Volk. New York: Columbia University Press, 1997.

Farb, Peter, and George J. Armelagos. *Consuming Passions: The Anthropology of Eating*. Boston: Houghton Mifflin, 1980.

Foer, Jonathan Safran. *Eating Animals*. New York: Little, Brown, 2009.

Gross, Aaron S. *The Question of the Animal and Religion: Theoretical Stakes, Practical Implications*. New York: Columbia University Press, 2014.

Gvion, Liora. *Beyond Hummus and Falafel: Social and Political Aspects of Palestinian Food in Israel*. California Studies in Food and Culture. Berkeley: University of California Press, 2012.

Hahn Tapper, Aaron J. *Judaisms: A Twenty-First-Century Introduction to Jews and Jewish Identities*. Oakland: University of California Press, 2016.

Harari, Yuval N. *Sapiens: A Brief History of Humankind*. New York: Harper, 2015.

Horowitz, Roger. *Kosher USA: How Coke Became Kosher and Other Tales of Modern Food*. Arts and Traditions of the Table: Perspectives in Culinary History. New York: Columbia University Press, 2016.

HoSang, Daniel, Oneka LaBennett, and Laura Pulido. *Racial Formation in the Twenty-First Century*. Berkeley: University of California Press, 2012.

Informing Change, comp. *Seeds of Opportunity: A National Study of Immersive Jewish Outdoor, Food, and Environmental Education (JOFEE)*. Jim Joseph Foundation, Leichtag Foundation, Morningstar Foundation, Rose Community Foundation, Schusterman Family Foundations, UJA-Federation of New York, Hazon, 2014. https://informingchange.com/seeds-of-opportunity-a-national-study-of-immersive -jewish-outdoor-food-and-environmental-education-jofee/.

Kaminer, Michael. "The Gorbals' Ilan Hall Talks Treyf." *Forward*, October 9, 2014. http://forward.com.

Ko, Aph, and Syl Ko. *Aphro-ism: Essays on Pop Culture, Feminism, and Black Veganism from Two Sisters*. New York: Lantern, 2017.

Masuzawa, Tomoko. *The Invention of World Religions: Or, How European Universalism Was Preserved in the Language of Pluralism*. Chicago: University of Chicago Press, 2005.

Mintz, Sidney. "The Plantation as a Sociocultural Type." In *Plantation Systems of the New World: Papers and Discussion Summaries*, edited by Research Institute for the Study of Man and Pan American Union, 42–50. Washington, DC: Pan American Union, 1959.

———. *Sweetness and Power: The Place of Sugar in Modern History*. New York: Viking, 1985.

Omi, Michael, and Howard Winant. *Racial Formation in the United States: From the 1960s to the 1980s*. New York: Routledge & Kegan Paul, 1986.

Pilcher, Jeffrey M. *The Oxford Handbook of Food History*. Oxford: Oxford University Press, 2012.

Raviv, Yael. *Falafel Nation: Cuisine and the Making of National Identity in Israel*. Lincoln: University of Nebraska Press, 2015.

Roden, Claudia. *The Book of Jewish Food: An Odyssey from Samarkand to New York*. New York: Knopf, 1996.

Rosenblum, Jordan D. *The Jewish Dietary Laws in the Ancient World*. New York: Cambridge University Press, 2017.

Smith, Jonathan Z. "A Matter of Class: Taxonomies of Religion." In *Relating Religion: Essays in the Study of Religion*, edited by Jonathan Z. Smith, xv, 412. Chicago: University of Chicago, 2004.

Smith, Jonathan Z., William Scott Green, and Jorunn Jacobsen Buckley. "Religions of Traditional Peoples." In *The HarperCollins Dictionary of Religion*, edited by Jonathan Z. Smith, William Scott Green, and Jorunn Jacobsen Buckley, 1087–98. San Francisco: HarperCollins, 1995.

Standford, Craig. "Chimpanzee Hunting Behavior and Human Evolution." *American Scientist*, May–June 1995. www.americanscientist.org.

Tuchman, Gaye, and Harry Gene Levine. "New York Jews and Chinese Food: The Social Construction of an Ethnic Pattern." *Journal of Contemporary Ethnography* 22, no. 3 (1993): 382–407.

Williams-Forson, Psyche A. *Building Houses Out of Chicken Legs: Black Women, Food, and Power*. Chapel Hill: University of North Carolina Press, 2006.

PART 1

History

Introduction to Part 1

JODY MYERS

The chapters in this part describe Jewish foodways as a dynamic cultural phenomenon. Practices are lost and added over the centuries and layered upon each other, intertwined, and continually shifting. Biblical food laws and ceremonies form a starting point. Food—or more often, the perils of food scarcity—is crucial in stories of creation, settlement, exile, and potential redemption in the core literature of the Israelites and the later Jewish people. Especially when they move to lands dominated by people of other religions, when the priestly sacrificial system ends, and when commonly available foods are different than those their ancestors ate, Jews adapt their modes of food production and eating and also leave their visible mark on the foodways in their new lands. The frequent reference to biblical texts in Jewish prayers, ceremonies, and religious law conveys the impression that Jewish foodways have changed little from biblical times. In truth, the ancient practices would be merely a shell without the substance supplied in the rabbinic, medieval, and modern eras. The intricate rules for keeping kosher, the meanings ascribed to foods, the liturgies and ceremonies added to home-based eating, and the food markers that became signs of Jewishness were barely present in the earliest phase of Jewish history; they emerged and then were continually reshaped in the centuries after the Hebrew Bible was composed. Like a recipe, these four chapters explain the steps taken that produced today's Jewish foodways in their multiple variations as well as the characteristically modern ways of rejecting these behaviors and beliefs and supplanting them with others.

Chapter 1, "Food in the Biblical Era" shows the importance of the ecology of the ancient Land of Israel in Israelite religion. The Bible insists that God rewards Israel's obedience to divine laws with necessary rain and ample harvests and punishes its disobedience with drought and scarcity. Foods central to Israelite worship and celebratory meals are the ones most plentiful in the Mediterranean climate and dry terrain, and these are the ones permitted for profane consumption; foods plentiful at certain seasons become essential to seasonal holiday practices. Yet religious factors account for the prohibition of some readily available edible foods such as animal blood, amphibians, and insects. The challenging natural environment and the closeness of ancient Israelites with their animals provide the basis for later food ethics, especially the rules of charity and laws mandating respectful treatment of nature and animals. The six chapters on food ethics in part 3 of this volume demonstrate that biblically based principles still provoke creative ethical thinking today.

Chapter 2, "Food and Eating in the Rabbinic Era," describes the crucial practices developed in the second thousand years of Jewish history, until about 1100. With the cessation of sacrificial worship and the dispersion of Jews throughout the Mediterranean region, religious scholars known as rabbis constructed an alternative means for Jewish women and men to express their relationship to God through food. The formation of Judaism and the making of Jewish meals were connected. The rabbis significantly expanded biblical prohibitions, provided details for animal slaughter and food ceremonies only vaguely recounted in the Bible, and transferred the locus of worship to the home and synagogue by creating domestic table rituals and devotion by way of Torah study. Rabbinic writings such as the Talmud include food blessings and rituals for daily, Sabbath, and holiday observances as well as *kashrut*, the Jewish dietary laws that restricted food choices, combinations, and foods prepared by non-Jews. By the last centuries of the first millennium, most Jews lived integrated within Muslim- and Christian-dominated societies but also followed these rabbinic practices, albeit with regional and class variations. Jewish distinctiveness in eating become the norm from the rabbinic era onward, creating the concept of "Jewish food" and "Jewish ways of eating" illustrated in the six case studies in part 2 of this volume.

Chapter 3, "Food and Jewish Culture during the Medieval Era," describes foodways during the eleventh to the sixteenth century, when rabbis, influenced by the cultures of the Muslim and Christian empires where they lived, interpreted and adapted earlier Biblical and Talmudic food traditions for the Jews living under their authority. Despite interreligious collaboration in food preparation and trade, religious leaders—Jews, Christians, and Muslims—used food to mark their religious identities. Rabbis strengthened and extended the food laws to more rigorously define kosher food preparation and eating. Jews attributed new meanings to their foods, regarding them as symbols of their relationship to God. They created food-centered ceremonies and liturgies that fostered love for and loyalty to communal values. Rabbinic innovations helped Jews preserve their distinctiveness at a time when they were pressured, sometimes quite harshly, to accept the religious views and practices of their non-Jewish neighbors. Unique Jewish foodways enabled Jews to regard themselves as more elevated and refined in comparison to the surrounding majority cultures, and in the process, the rabbis found an outlet for their own pious expression and their sense of self-importance relative to ordinary Jews.

Chapter 4, "Food and Jewish Culture in the Modern Era," describes how the six Jewish global migrations during the sixteenth to the late twentieth century influenced Jewish cuisines in Europe, the Middle East, and the United States. Although Jewish religious law was codified and widely disseminated at the start of this era, the political changes implemented by "modernized" governments severely lessened rabbinic authority and the power of religious law. New religious denominations appeared, each offering different interpretations of the dietary laws and different ways of honoring or rejecting separatist Jewish food preparation, eating, and food-based rituals. Defining "Jewish food" becomes difficult in the modern context of migration, modernization, and globalization. As Judaism becomes less important to many Jews, or where antisemitism wanes sufficiently so as to lessen the boundaries between Jews and non-Jews, distinctive "Jewish food" and "Jewish eating" becomes increasingly relegated to the more insular Jewish religious communities. Furthermore, when food was no longer prepared locally but produced in factories distant from home, religious Jews created systems of checking and marking the kosher status of processed foods and meat. Kosher certification plays an important role in differentiating Jews from each other, determining whether they may eat together, and it has created new ways of interpreting religious law and new religious professions. The deleterious effects of industrialized food production on the natural environment, animals, and food workers prompted the emergence of a food movement offering new ways of applying older Jewish ethical principles to food preparation and food commerce.

1

Food in the Biblical Era

ELAINE ADLER GOODFRIEND

The Garden of Eden was filled with fruit trees "pleasing to the sight and good for food," according to the Hebrew Bible's account of the first phase of human history. God allowed Adam and Eve to eat from all the trees in the garden except one, and when they ate from the prohibited tree, they were punished, exiled, and required to grow food laboriously by the sweat of their brows. This biblical story foreshadows the logic of the dietary rules later transmitted by Moses. God permits the consumption of animals easily available in and native to the natural environment but forbids, with no explanation, some commonly available animals and food mixtures. Those disobeying these decrees would be punished by bad harvests and exile. The reward for obedience—the dream—was living in a land in which one could effortlessly find and enjoy a bountiful supply of food. The present chapter shows not only what the Hebrew Bible and postbiblical apocryphal literature, in addition to archeological evidence, reveal about the actual foodways in the society known as "ancient Israel" but also how food was used to demonstrate the Israelites' unique relationship to God, to the land, and to each other. For the thousand years beginning in the Iron Age (1200 BCE) and extending to the Hellenistic era (approximately the second century BCE), the Israelite diet appears to be shaped by ecological pragmatism—that is, by what would be available in a challenging environment—and yet religious and cultural factors intervene to mark some edible animals and food mixtures as taboo.

The ancient foodways, especially as they are expressed in the Hebrew Bible, provide the template for later ways of considering and consuming food. First, the Pentateuch, or first five books of the Hebrew Bible—often referred to as "Torah" by Jews—presents food as the subject of divine law commanded by YHWH, Israel's God, and says that God will reward or punish Israel according to its adherence to these and the rest of God's laws. Belief in the need to eat in conformance with God's laws is passed down the generations. Second, the Torah commands that Israelites offer gifts to God from their produce and livestock, a practice abandoned in the postbiblical era but symbolically performed in later Jewish worship, ritual, and study. Third, food in the Hebrew Bible serves as a means to celebrate sacred occasions and probably also major life events. In the postbiblical era, the celebratory function of food continues, and the centrality of food to Jewish culture survives through the modern era even as religious observance declines. Fourth, whereas the Hebrew Bible alludes to the social function of food laws in distinguishing or separating Israelites from other peoples, in the postbiblical era, this theme is expanded into a central element of religious practice. Fifth, these Jewish food traditions influence the formation of Christianity and Islam, whose leaders rejected or adapted them for their unique forms of religious expressions.

Finally, although the food laws are described as vehicles for making ancient Israel a holy nation, they address ethical ideals fundamental to world religions and moral philosophies. Implicitly or explicitly, biblical food-centered texts teach concern for animal suffering, the need for careful stewardship of the earth, the importance of hospitality to strangers, and the obligation to feed the poor. The actual historical context of these ancient foodways shows how ethical ideals were inculcated—and could be today, something explored in part 3 of this book—through daily routines and weekly and seasonal celebrations and commemorations.

Certain limitations in our knowledge of ancient Israelite food practices must be admitted from the outset. The Hebrew Bible, the major source of information for life in ancient Israel, is an anthology of literature that covers more than one thousand years and includes many mostly anonymous authors, the chronological context of whom is widely debated by modern scholars. While knowing the authorship of a literary section would help us understand the writer's context and agenda and provide greater data about the evolution of foodways, this knowledge is hard to establish. Another limitation of the Hebrew Bible as a source is that it does not offer a complete snapshot of the Israelite diet, partly because of its focus on the royal and priestly segments of society. Further, we cannot be sure when and to what extent biblical laws were imposed or practiced. Our knowledge of how food was processed and who produced it is also limited. Therefore, the evidence offered by the Hebrew Bible must be supplemented. Archeology offers unwritten materials such as artifacts and structures that tell us how food was processed and stored, or it reveals animal bones that offer insight into which animals were consumed. Other sources of information include written documents about food supplies; comparative data from other cultures of the ancient world, such as Egypt, Mesopotamia, or Greece; and information offered by modern anthropology regarding traditional cultures in the region.[1] Finally, the land's geography and ecology were of paramount importance. Ancient Israelites—only by the end of this era is the designation "Jews" used—resided in the center of the Fertile Crescent. The Hebrew Bible called it Canaan and then "the Land of Israel." Its ancient borders coincide approximately with the borders of modern Israel, with the addition of the land immediately east and west of the Jordan River. It shares the same climate as other regions in the Mediterranean basin, with its mild, wet winters and warm, dry summers. The Land of Israel consists of three vertical parallel zones from west to east: the coastal plain, the central hill country, and the Jordan River valley (containing the Sea of Galilee, Jordan River, and Dead Sea), with its eastern Transjordanian plateau. The central hill country—known as Judah and Samaria—was historically the most important, as it constituted the heartland of biblical Israel. Because of its limited water resources, hilly spine, and thin and rocky topsoil, this area is best suited for olives, grapes, sheep, and goats; the cultivation of grain is more tenuous. Israelites practiced "dry farming"—that is, reliance on rainfall with no artificial irrigation. This stands in contrast to its neighbors Egypt and Mesopotamia, which are both river valleys and flood plains and therefore could serve as food sources for Israelites in bad times.[2] Even with all these sources of information, the modern scholar's understanding of the ancient reality is still somewhat speculative.

Basic Foods and God's Blessings

The biblical text repeatedly indicates that the supply of three basic foods was synonymous with the divine blessing that would be earned by obeying God's laws: "If, then, you obey the commandments that I enjoin upon you this day. . . . I will grant the rain for your land in season, the early rain and the late. You shall gather in your new *grain* and *wine* and *oil*."[3] Grain (wheat and barley), olive oil, and wine are known as the "Mediterranean triad" because of their prevalence in the Mediterranean basin. This often-repeated triad, usually in the poetic form of *dagan* (grain), *yits-har* (freshly pressed olive oil), and *tirosh* (grape juice before fermentation), formed the basis of the daily diet, and all three were fundamental elements of festive meals.[4]

Grain provided most of the calories consumed by Israelites on a daily basis, and wheat was the preferred grain. Cultivated in the fertile coastal and inland valleys, wheat cost twice as much as barley, which could tolerate a more hostile environment—less rain, poorer soil.[5] Both grains were consumed in various forms: raw and unprocessed, boiled into porridge, roasted, or ground into flour for bread. Bread was so important to the Israelite diet that the word for bread, *lehem*, frequently signifies food in general in the Hebrew Bible. Bread also plays a prominent role in the official religion of Israel in the guise of the "showbread," the twelve loaves of unleavened bread that were placed weekly on the table inside the Tent of Meeting. Further, grain donations could be made to the Sanctuary as an independent sacrifice or to accompany an animal offering.[6]

The making of bread was a time-consuming daily task. Wheat berries were ground in a large concave stone basin with a smaller convex upper stone, and for a family of five, this could take as many as three hours per day.[7] Water or oil and salt were added to the flour, and the mixture was baked usually without leavening, akin to today's pita bread. Leavening was not allowed when bread was made for sacrificial purposes.[8] Men prepared the bread sacrifice in the cultic context, while reference is made to a "Bakers' Street" (masculine plural) in Jerusalem in the sixth century BCE. Otherwise the Bible indicates that women were responsible for grinding grain and baking bread for the family; the Hebrew Bible offers no other information about gender distinctions in food production.[9] Biblical texts and archeological and iconographic evidence indicate that women worked cooperatively in food production. Large ovens, fueled by wood or animal dung, were often situated in courtyards between houses so that baking became a cooperative enterprise and opportunity for social interaction.[10] Often several sets of grinding stones are found in a single dwelling unit, indicating that two or three women were grinding grain at the same time.

The second component of the Mediterranean triad was olive oil. Olives were too bitter to be eaten raw, and techniques that make the olive edible were not known until the postbiblical era. Oil was produced by crushing olives by foot, by pounding them with a mortar, or on a larger scale with a mechanism called a beam press. Oil was most important as an ingredient of bread and as a dip for bread and other foods. It served an important function in religious life as an additive to sacrifices and as the fuel for the menorah or candelabra, which illuminated the Tent of Meeting.[11] Also, it was used for anointing priests and kings, an indication that the person anointed was God's chosen.[12] In a profane context, applying oil to one's head was an indication of joy.[13]

The third component of the triad is wine. With its hot, dry summers and wet, cool winters, the Israelite climate is ideal for viticulture. Grapes required little water for growth and gave juice without tapping into limited water resources.[14] Grapes were consumed fresh or dried, as juice or vinegar, but most importantly as wine. Because fermentation occurred quickly in Israel's warm climate, wine was more available than grape juice. It may have been occasionally mixed with water and other ingredients. Wine was the principal drink of ancient Israel, although water supplied hydration to travelers in the wilderness and workers in the fields.[15] The importance of grapes appears in the biblical narrative, when Moses sent out spies to reconnoiter the land and they brought back one cluster of grapes too heavy for one man to carry.[16] Wine's status as a staple of the Israelite diet is evident in the book of Lamentations, a poetic response to the siege and destruction of Jerusalem in 586 BCE: young children "keep asking their mothers, 'Where is bread and wine?'"[17] An Egyptian text expresses the perception that ancient Israel "had more wine than water."[18] Wine also served a religious function as a liquid sacrifice and as a central component of sacred feasts.[19] Many biblical texts associate wine with joyful occasions.[20] Despite the importance of wine and its association with happiness, however, many biblical texts warn of the dangers of drunkenness.[21]

Ancient Israelites found evidence of God's blessings in other foods as well. The Land of Israel is often called a "land flowing with milk and honey." Honey in this context, the Hebrew *devash*, refers mostly to date syrup and less often to bees' honey.[22] Goats, and not cattle or sheep, were the animals associated with milk. Milk and other dairy products have obviously positive associations in the Bible. Fresh goat milk is not available year round in traditional societies because goats birth on a seasonal basis during December and January, wean their young in March and April, and only after that are milked solely for human consumption through the summer months. Drinking milk is mentioned only in Judges 4:19, and so it appears that more commonly, milk would be consumed in other forms, such as soured milk, loose yogurt, or cream and butter from cow's milk. In the warm Mediterranean climate, milk quickly sours and has to be processed or preserved for those months when nanny goats gave no milk. Soured milk could be turned into cheese by allowing the water to drain and evaporate, with salt added during the process.[23] As for the abundant fertility of the Land of Israel, Deuteronomy 8:7 references seven fruits of the land and idealizes its blessings: "For the Lord your God is bringing you into a good land, a land with streams and springs and fountains issuing from plain and hill; a land of wheat and barley, of vines, figs, and pomegranates, a land of olive trees and honey; a land where you may eat food without stint, where you will lack nothing; a land whose rocks are iron and from whose hills you can mine copper."[24] Modern scholars are skeptical that this lavish description accurately represents the actual Land of Israel. Rather, the Bible's praise serves a theological purpose: God would clearly not promise or reward a less-than-perfect land to His covenant people.

Foods as Daily and Holiday Offerings

It is not surprising, then, that ancient Israel's cult—that is, its official system of rituals as reflected in the Hebrew Bible—gives food a central role. Sacrifice is the primary mode of worship. Whether the explicit purpose of the sacrifice is to express gratitude, enact expiation, request interventions, or other reasons, it demands the donation of a variety of foods. Scholars of religion have suggested many different interpretations of sacrifice, particularly animal sacrifice, and various functions of this richly symbolic act can coexist. Jacob Milgrom leans toward seeing animal sacrifice as a gift to induce the assistance of the deity and at the same time views the dedication of the animal as a way to rid the giver of the guilt resulting from its death.[25] In this sense, it is the sacrifice (the ritual dedication of the animal's blood and fat at the altar and the setting aside of portions for others) that enables the giver and his family to consume the meat in celebration without culpability.[26] Further, since food abundance is YHWH's gift for obedience to Israel's covenant, recipients—or seekers—of His bounty bring food offerings to the local or central cult site and its staff. The sacrifice of livestock was accompanied by offerings of grain, oil, and wine, so a meal devoted to God resembled the ideal human meal.[27] In addition, Israelites were expected to give tithes (one-tenth), firstfruits, and firstlings of all produce and livestock. Sources differ as to the recipients of these contributions. While Deuteronomy allows the giver and his family to joyfully consume the offerings in the holy place, presumably Jerusalem, Leviticus and Numbers demand that the Levites (the tribe designated to serve at the Sanctuary) receive the donations as compensation because they received no landed property in Israel, and the poor would receive some as well.[28] Farmers participated in a ritual when they brought their firstfruits for acceptance at the altar: they declared God's great acts of salvation in Israelite history and offered thanks for the gift of a land "flowing with milk and honey."[29]

Although we cannot be sure to what extent altar or Temple rituals were mirrored by domestic customs, it is likely that Israelites celebrated Sabbaths, new moons, and other festivals with special meals and familial and communal gatherings.[30] Israelites were obligated to participate in three pilgrimage festivals each year so that celebrations would have taken place at the local or national altar.[31] The Pesach or Passover sacrifice was entirely consumed by the family (or extended family) unit. Passover was also commemorated by a complete ban on leavening for seven days, and Israelites were enjoined to eat unleavened bread, matzah, for seven days to commemorate the Exodus from Egypt. Following Passover, another ritual that had reverberations in the home was the waving of the omer, the first sheaf of the spring barley harvest. Until this offering was made, no part of the new grain crop could be eaten in the home or elsewhere. Seven weeks after the omer offering, a second festival—today known as the holiday of Shavuot—was celebrated with its prescribed sacrificial offerings. The third festival, Sukkot, occurred at harvest time, at the end of the summer, and biblical texts describe it as being marked by feasting in huts erected in the harvested fields as well as a pilgrimage including sacrificial offerings.[32] In the postbiblical and post-Temple era, Jewish texts describe at great length the Sabbath and holiday practices that included home-based feasting and fasting.

Eating Animals

For the Torah, the eating of land animals is more circumscribed by rules than any other food. The Bible equates humans and animals in a surprising array of passages: land animals are created from the soil on the sixth day of creation as humans are;[33] they, like humankind, are God's covenant partners in the aftermath of the flood;[34] animals are subject to the death penalty for bestiality and homicide;[35] and the illicit spilling of animal blood is likened to human bloodshed.[36] This tendency to liken land animals to people is in part a function of their important role in daily life. Furthermore, both land animals and humans have copious amounts of blood, which in the Bible is the substance of life and thus forbidden for human consumption. Based on the Bible's testimony, we can assume that virtually all meat eating in the preceding centuries of Israelite history started as a sacrificial ritual at the local holy sites, and this included a specific way of treating the animal blood. Eating the meat of domestic animals without the ceremony at the altar was, in some biblical passages, sanctioned only later in the biblical era after King Josiah of Judah initiated a reform that eliminated all altar sites except for the central Jerusalem Temple.

A fundamental starting point for understanding the Torah's restrictions on the eating of animals is found in the story of creation, when God expresses the intention that humankind consumes seed-bearing plants and fruit, while animals eat green plants for food. Humankind is entitled to "rule" over animals (a reference to their domestication and/ or the use of their by-products) but not to kill them. According to the Torah's narrative, after God responds to violence on the part of both humans and animals by flooding the world, He ushers in a new order with legislation intended for humanity as a whole: human blood must not be shed, and although people are now permitted to consume an animal's flesh, they must not consume its blood. The life fluid of the animal must be drained into the earth.[37]

Since the biblical narrative teaches that eating meat is only allowed after humankind has proven that their nature is irredeemably evil, many modern interpreters conclude that eating meat is a concession to humankind's violent nature and therefore vegetarianism is an ethical ideal (a topic explored in some detail in the last chapter of this volume).[38] There is no explicit statement of such an ideal, however, or evidence that many Israelites voluntarily adopted vegetarianism. Yet the consensus of modern scholars is that meat was an infrequent item in the Israelite diet because they assume that the farmer would be reluctant to deplete livestock, which gave wool or milk or the muscle to pull the plow. They argue that meat eating would occur at the annual clan celebration or pilgrimage festival or for the fulfillment of a vow.[39] Further, they suggest that meat was only consumed when there were enough people present to eat the meat within a few days; they suggest that this was due to the lack of refrigeration and that perhaps the commandment to discard the meat of a sacrifice after the second day was in reference to the meat's growing unpleasantness.[40] The archeological record, however, and information about livestock utilization suggest more frequent meat consumption. It may be that primarily the elite—priests and royalty and their circles—consumed meat, as reflected in texts that suggest considerable donations of livestock to the priesthood. The abundant supply of meat available to royalty is reflected in the menu at King Solomon's table: "ten fattened oxen, twenty pasture-fed oxen, and one hundred sheep and goats besides deer and gazelles, roebucks and fattened geese."[41] Even if meat eating was not a rare event, it may not have been a staple for most Israelites' diet.

Dietary Laws and Animals

The Hebrew Bible includes food laws, but these are not presented systematically as a daily food regimen detailing food choices, preparation, and food mixtures—such a system, later known as *kashrut*, was developed in the postbiblical rabbinic, medieval, and modern eras (described further in this volume's upcoming chapters). The biblical dietary laws focus primarily on permitted and prohibited foods. Obeying these was considered essential to being God's holy nation. Because they focus so much on animals, these laws indicate not only food choices but also beliefs about how animals should be treated.

The Torah offers two chapters of detailed legislation regarding the consumption of animals, but no laws restrict the eating of some plants as opposed to others.[42] Leviticus 11 and Deuteronomy 14 differentiate between permitted and prohibited animals of all categories: land animals, birds and insects, sea animals, and amphibians. These restrictions are accompanied by God's demand that Israel be "holy" and dedicated to Him. Permitted mammals have "true hooves, with clefts through the hooves, and that chew the cud."[43] The divided hoof of permitted animals such as goats and cows can be contrasted with the singular or solid toe of a horse or donkey or the paw of a lion or dog. Animals that chew the cud are ruminants, which refer to herbivores equipped with a four-chambered stomach; after the animal chews and regurgitates plant material several times, the nutrients can be absorbed through digestion. These criteria also apply to wild animals, so deer, gazelle, antelope, and ibex are permitted. Pigs are prohibited because while they do have split hooves, they are not ruminants.

The Torah does not explain its choice of permitted animals. Over the centuries, many theories have been proposed, but just four will be mentioned here as the most commonly suggested as indicative of ancient perspectives. The first is the health/hygienic theory, which assumes that the forbidden animals are carriers of disease or have a deleterious effect on health in general. However, no such health association is alluded to in the Bible, and there is no evidence to support a health-related theory for the dietary restrictions.[44] The second is the view that the criteria are arbitrary and have no intrinsic value: they are decrees meant to instill self-restraint and demonstrate obedience. This is arguably implied by the Torah itself, which offers no explanation other than conformity with God's will. A third family of theories suggests that the permitted animals, or their unique characteristics, are symbolic of desirable traits. An ancient Jewish philosopher named Philo Judaeus writes that the split hoof represents the ability to distinguish between right and wrong and chewing the cud symbolizes a person's mental rumination—that is, mastery of knowledge through "continued exercise of memory."[45] Other scholars look at the common biblical metaphors of Israel as sheep or flock animals and conclude the permitted animals represent qualities that should be emulated. Israel "was to be like that which she ate"—that is, loyal and peace loving.[46]

The fourth family of theories can be termed *religioethical*. Building on the scholarship of Milgrom, who ties God's demand for holiness with ethics and reverence for life, Israel's dietary laws are viewed as a means to limit access to the animal kingdom and reduce the Israelite's choice of flesh to just a few animals that are the main domestic species kept by pastoralists.[47] This ethical theory is compatible with ecological pragmatism in that a pig is raised solely for meat and is therefore an economic drain, while other livestock, such as cattle, sheep, or goats, had other useful functions.[48] Another variation of the religioethical theory is expressed by Baruch Levine. He points to the Torah's blood prohibition as an underlying principle of the prohibited species and suggests that permitting only herbivorous ruminants will ensure that foods forbidden to the Israelites will not have been consumed by the animals they were going to eat. Carnivorous birds are likewise forbidden, as are crustaceans (crabs or lobster) with their claws (as opposed to permitted "peaceful" fish with their fins). Levine writes that method of locomotion is the second factor. Only an animal with truly cleft hooves was regarded as domesticated, but "paws were bestial and so forbidden." Regarding the pig, he writes that there is nothing in the dietary codes or the Bible to indicate that it was singled out as an abomination; rather, it is mentioned in Leviticus 11 because it is a borderline case, possessing a fully cleft hoof without chewing its cud. Like Milgrom, Levine points to the vegetarian ideal of Genesis as the underlying rationale for the dietary laws. He regards blood, the substance of life, as the principle element in the dietary laws: humankind may not consume blood, but Israel may not even eat animals that eat blood.[49] Another example of religioethical interpretation is found in Daniel Weiss's chapter in this volume.

Because the consumption of blood was forbidden, the means of slaughter was dictated by the concern to ensure the easy removal of blood from the meat. A specific procedure intimated by the Hebrew verb *shahat*—the slitting of the animal's throat—permitted the blood from the major blood vessels to fully drain.[50] If the animal was sacrificed at an altar, the blood would be thrown against its walls, but if the animal was slaughtered in a nonsacrificial context or through hunting, the blood would be poured on the ground and covered with dirt.[51] The same applied to birds.[52] An extension of this law against consuming blood was the prohibition of eating the carcass of a clean animal that was not slaughtered—that is, animals that died of disease or old age or animals torn by other animals. In Exodus 22:30, God decrees, "You shall be a people holy to Me: you must not eat flesh torn by beasts in the field; you shall cast it to the dogs." Based on the same concern for holiness, Deuteronomy 14:21 adds that any animal that has died a natural death must be transferred to and consumed by a non-Israelite. (Later Jewish kosher slaughter preserves and expands upon these principles.)

Although hunters and their techniques and tools are mentioned occasionally in the Hebrew Bible, and it is permitted to eat certain animals killed by hunting as long as their blood is drained, it is unlikely that hunting contributed much to Israelite subsistence.[53] Biblical texts mention hunting birds with nets and traps, and the references to the use of pits suggest that Israelites sought bigger game too.[54] Some animals that pose a threat to people and their flocks, such as lions or bears, may have been hunted but not eaten.[55] Wild animals that were cloven-hooved ruminants, such as deer or gazelles, could be eaten as long their blood was poured out on the earth and covered with soil in accordance with the Torah's blood prohibition.

While the blood prohibition applies to all animals, the prohibition of *helev*, the fat attached to the stomach and intestines, applies only to animals that were sacrificed.[56] Genesis 32 records the Israelite taboo of the sciatic nerve. This prohibition is explained by the story of Jacob wrestling with an angel who wrenches his hip at its socket: "That is why the children of Israel to this day do not eat the thigh muscle that is on the socket of the hip, since Jacob's hip socket was wrenched at the thigh muscle" (v. 33). Nowhere else in the Hebrew Bible is this prohibition mentioned, and archeological evidence cannot affirm whether it was obeyed. (Later Jewish law mandates the removal of both the *helev* and the sciatic nerve from animals slaughtered for food.)

Finally, a notable element of the Bible's dietary laws is the thrice-repeated commandment "You shall not boil a kid in its mother's milk."[57] In its simple biblical sense, this enigmatic rule prohibits the cooking of a young goat in its own mother's milk. The goat is mentioned here either because it was the main source of milk in ancient Israel, because it was the most commonly owned type of cattle, or because goat meat is most in need of tenderizing through cooking in milk.[58] It is possible that the clause intends to include sheep and large cattle, but evidence for the generalization of this prohibition to a complete ban of combining dairy and meat appears only in the later rabbinic period. (This becomes a major principle of *kashrut*, the Jewish dietary laws, as the next chapter will show.) While the Torah offers no reason for the prohibition, some later commentators suggest that it is grounded in sensitivity to animal life, so that an animal's young not be destroyed by the fluid meant to sustain it.[59] We have no evidence that biblical people honored this dietary restriction.

Ecological Pragmatism and Prohibited Animals

The Torah's disqualification of whole classes of animals from Israel's diet must be considered from an ecologically pragmatic approach—that is, whether it was a useful response to environmental considerations. The most common domestic animals in ancient Israel and the wider Near East were goat, sheep, and bovine, and so from the ecologically pragmatic approach, the permissibility of cloven-hooved ruminants makes sense. Yet from that same perspective, the prohibition of the pig, which was raised all over the ancient Near East, cannot be explained. Pig and dog bones are present in ancient Egyptian and Syrian animal remains, even though both animals were urban scavengers and sometimes the object of disgust.[60] While pig rearing was practiced at sites along Israel's coast that were settled by the Philistines, a people of Aegean origin, pig bones are notably absent farther east in the Iron Age (1200–1000 BCE) settlements where the people of Israel emerged.[61]

In contrast to the archeological record, the textual evidence for the observance of the food taboos is weak for the early period of Israelite society. The Hebrew Bible refers to Israelites who refused unclean food without explicitly mentioning prohibited animals.[62] Later sources are more explicit: for example, Isaiah 66:3 and 66:17, passages that are considered to be recorded after exile of 586 BCE, condemn the sacrifice of dogs, mice, and swine—indicating both great respect for and rejection of the taboos. Hellenistic Jewish literature (notably 2 Maccabees 6–7), however, tells of Jews who become martyrs rather than eat pork.

Some scholars suggest that this abhorrence of pork, which was carried into later Jewish foodways, was the result of the dietary laws mentioned in the Pentateuch. Alternatively (or at the same time), some suggest it may be the consequence of more complex cultural considerations, such as the contempt for urban living—of which pigs were characteristic—held by pastoralist Israelites or those who recalled their past as desert nomads, or perhaps it reflects the antagonistic relations of Israel with the nearby foreigners who ate pig. Another suggestion is that the problem with pig rearing is that it demands too much water from Israel's dry climate. Yet there could have been ecological and economic benefits for pigs in Israel's village and city life. Pigs are omnivores and therefore eat garbage and human feces, turning both into edible meat. (They play this role in garbage collection and waste disposal, as an "edible sanitation service," in both ancient and modern Egypt and in many other geographical and historical contexts.[63]) Pigs have much larger litters than cows, sheep, or goat and a much faster growth rate, and they can be exploited for their lard, skin, mineral-rich waste, and bristles.[64] In sum, Israel's pig taboo, whatever its basis or bases, was unique in the ancient world and resists an explanation based on economic and ecological considerations.[65]

Fish, Birds, Eggs, and Insects as Food or Taboo

The consumption of marine life is included in the Torah's laws on animals: only those creatures that have fins and scales may be eaten. The prohibition excludes from Israel's diet aquatic animals such as crustaceans or mollusks.[66] No specific species are mentioned; indeed, eating fish is mentioned only four times in the Hebrew Bible, and the only species of fish named is a mythical sea monster.[67] Israel's geography would suggest that fish were seldom eaten in ancient Israel because the heartland of its population lay in its hilly interior, which had few perennial rivers, natural harbors, or lakes. Fish go unmentioned among the "clean" animals suitable for sacrifice, perhaps because they do not have copious amounts of blood, the substance used in sacrificial ritual. On the other hand, other data indicate the consumption of fish and familiarity with fishing in ancient Israel. The specialized gear used for fishing, including hooks and various kinds of nets, is mentioned in the Hebrew Bible,[68] and archeological research, specifically the science of paleozoology, has uncovered significant consumption of fish during the Iron Age.[69] The fish consumed probably came from nearby freshwater sources, such as the Yarkon and Jordan Rivers and the Sea of Galilee. Saltwater fish would have originated in the Mediterranean and perhaps the Red Sea. Nathan MacDonald suggests that because of the long distance involved, consumption of fish would have been restricted to elites in urban areas and to those who lived along the rivers.[70] In this case, the findings of archeology have modified assumptions made on the basis of Israel's geography and evidence from the Hebrew Bible.

The Torah's legislation shows a great familiarity with species of birds, in contrast with its references to fish. While those permitted are not named, Leviticus 11 and Deuteronomy 14 list twenty-one species of forbidden birds. These include eagles, vultures, falcons, ravens, crows, various kinds of owls, hawks, ospreys, storks, herons, hoopoes, and bats (a mammal, or course, but Leviticus categorizes animals by means of locomotion). The common denominator regarding forbidden birds is their identity as raptors—that is, consumers of carrion or live prey.[71] Clearly these birds were available as food, but religious and cultural factors prevented them from being considered acceptable. The frequent mention of fowling (hunting wild birds with nets) indicates that permitted wild birds were consumed.[72] Some birds were probably domesticated and kept in cages, and their eggs were probably eaten. The eggs or fledglings of wild birds were also eaten, and the Israelite was required to shoo away the mother bird before taking these, a biblical law enshrined in later Jewish practice.[73] Leviticus mentions turtledoves and pigeons as sacrifices acceptable from poor people, which suggests that these birds were inexpensive and plentiful.[74] One issue of contention among scholars is whether ancient Israelites kept the domestic chicken: the archeological evidence is ambiguous.[75]

While Westerners generally view eating insects with disgust, Israel and other ancient Near Easterners had a more tolerant attitude to consuming locusts, crickets, and grasshoppers. Leviticus 11:20 declares, "All winged swarming things that walk on fours shall be an abomination to you," but then enumerates four species of locusts that are permissible. Within the Hebrew Bible, no explicit mention is made again of the consumption of these insects, although in the New Testament, the Jewish ascetic John the Baptizer ate locusts and wild honey.[76] Milgrom suggests that locusts and grasshoppers were made exceptions to the blanket prohibition on insects because this practice recalls Israel's past as pastoral nomads, who feast on locusts to this day.[77] Locusts are known otherwise in the Hebrew Bible for their catastrophic invasions. It is possible that the Torah's permission to consume locusts is ironically a consequence of these periodic calamities, as having no other source of food, the people collected and ate the invading insects!

Other Foods: Vegetables, Pulses, Fruit, Spices, and Condiments

Ancient Israelites probably consumed various kinds of fruits and vegetables in addition to the Mediterranean triad. However, archeological evidence for their consumption is lacking because they leave no trace, unlike bones for the consumption of meat or olive presses for oil. Legumes and pulses, which include lentils, broad beans, chickpeas, and vetch, were valuable supplements to their diet. They served as a source of protein in the absence of meat and could be easily dried and stored for times of food shortage.[78]

The Hebrew Bible offers contradictory attitudes to eating vegetables. 1 Kings 21 notes that the king of Israel, Ahab, desired land for a vegetable garden, and Numbers 11:5 records that the Israelites longed for the cucumbers and leeks they ate in Egypt. Other texts suggest that vegetables were generally undesirable or considered unhealthy to ancient Israelites.[79] Proverbs 15:17 advises, "Better a meal of vegetables where there is love, than a fattened ox where there is hate." The narrative in Daniel 1 suggests that eating a vegetarian diet normally would make one look sickly. Vegetables, therefore, may have been a desirable addition to a meal centered on animal-based foods (meat, eggs, fish), but a solely vegetarian diet was considered undesirable. The need for nutrition in a limited environment means that eating meat, which is denser in nutrients, fat, and calories, would be favored for providing more effectively for periods when food was scarce. In addition, the association of meat eating with celebration is in opposition with the idea that there is a general biblical religious and ethical vegetarian ideal.[80]

Fruit plays a prominent role in the Hebrew Bible. In Genesis 2, it constitutes the first food of humankind in the Garden of Eden. Fruit was associated with sensual pleasure; fruits are mentioned twenty-five times in the eight chapters of the Song of Songs, a corpus of erotic love poetry. The importance of fruit trees is suggested by Deuteronomy 20:19–20, which prohibits the Israelite from cutting down fruit trees when laying siege to an enemy city. Deuteronomy 8:8 praises the Land of Israel for its plentiful grapes, figs, pomegranates, olives, and date syrup (*devash*).[81] Elsewhere the Hebrew Bible mentions the *tapu'ah* (usually identified as an apple), the sycamore fig, the mandrake, and the watermelon—which is mentioned only in the context of Egypt.[82] Dates, grapes, and figs could be eaten fresh but also dried and pressed into cakes. Grapevines and fig trees are paired to convey stereotypical Israelite holdings: "All the days of Solomon, Judah and Israel from Dan to Beersheba dwelt in safety, everyone under his own vine and under his own fig tree."[83] Leviticus 23:40 commands the Israelite to utilize the fruit of the *hadar* tree in the ritual for the festival of Tabernacles, and later Jewish tradition identified it as an *'etrog* or citron.[84] Only two kinds of nuts, pistachios and almonds, appear in the Hebrew Bible as specialty items, so these were probably not significant for the average Israelite.[85]

Salt was important for flavoring and preserving food. The book of Job asks, "Can what is tasteless be eaten without salt?"[86] It was an additive to the grain sacrifice (Leviticus 2:13), and because salt was a preservative, it symbolized permanence in the Hebrew Bible; God's covenant with the priesthood is called a "covenant of salt" (Numbers 18:19). Salt was obtained either through mining or via the evaporation of salt water from the Dead Sea or the Mediterranean. Coriander, cumin, and saffron are mentioned in the Hebrew Bible.[87] Numbers 11:5 records that Israelites pined for Egyptian onion and garlic, two vegetables that enhance the flavor of other foods, but these are never mentioned as readily available. Otherwise, the Hebrew Bible enumerates several other spices, but these were expensive and exotic ingredients for cosmetics, incense, and perfumed ointments rather than food condiments.

Food Scarcity and Charity

As noted earlier, disparities must have existed between the nutritional resources of various groups in ancient Israel depending on geography and social class.[88] Those who lived along trade routes enjoyed fish or nuts or spices more often than those more distant. Those who raised livestock consumed a greater quantity of milk products than grain farmers. The wealthy and families of the priestly and royal classes would have had greater access to meat.

Food scarcity in ancient Israel may be clarified by the distinctions made by Peter Garnsey, who distinguishes between *famine*, a critical shortage of essential foods leading to increased mortality; *food shortage*, a short-term reduction of available food supplies leading to rising prices, hunger, and increased mortality; and *chronic malnutrition*, which is long-term food deprivation.[89] Inhabitants of ancient Israel probably experienced famine once or twice over a lifetime and food shortages more frequently. The poor or landless may have experienced chronic malnutrition for much of their lives, weakening their resistance to disease and bringing early death. MacDonald extends the prevalence of chronic malnutrition to the Iron Age population of Israel in general and suggests that most suffered from "an inadequate diet, poor health, and low life expectancy."[90] Drought and siege would have only increased the desperation of the poor. Israel, reliant upon rainfall, was subject to years with little or no rain, and a common motif in the Hebrew Bible is departure from the land of Israel in search of food.[91] Passages concerning prolonged siege or drought mention cannibalism; however, such reports should be treated with skepticism.[92]

The Torah offers legislation intended to ameliorate the precarious food situation of the poor. For example, Leviticus 19:9–10 and Deuteronomy 24:19–21 command the Israelite landowner to leave behind various portions of his field and vineyard for the poor, and this practice is mentioned in the case of Ruth, a widow who enters the field of a wealthy landowner to pick up the grain stalks left behind.[93] The Torah also commands that the necessary tools for processing grain, the millstones, should not be taken as collateral for a loan and that employers pay day laborers before sundown and not delay payment at the employer's convenience.[94] Admittedly, in a time of famine or food shortages, these measures may not have helped the poor and landless. It is impossible to know if these laws were widely implemented, but they were carried into later Jewish religious law.

Food Laws and Social Boundaries

Food taboos create social boundaries. The function of dietary laws to separate Israelites/Jews from gentiles is apparent only in the later biblical era. In Exodus 34:15, Israel as a nation is warned against making covenants with the inhabitants of the Land of Canaan and the eating of their sacrifices, with the result that Israelite sons will marry Canaanite daughters and worship their gods. Here the problem is not the substance of the food itself but the socializing associated with festive meals. Numbers 25:1–3 tells of an incident in which eating sacrifices and social intercourse induced Israelites to worship other gods. The food prohibitions described earlier in this chapter are associated with Israel's sanctification and the avoidance of impurity. The goal of separating Israel from other nations is mentioned, but it is secondary to the objective of maintaining Israel's status as a "holy people."[95] David Kraemer notes that on a daily basis, the food prohibitions would have barely distinguished the Israelites from other ethnic groups because the staples common to all groups consisted of foods not restricted in any way: grains, legumes, vegetables, fruit, dairy products, and honey.[96] Only regarding meat eating would barriers exist, but as noted earlier, it does not appear that for most people, meat was eaten often. In the first half of the biblical period, Israelites constituted the dominant majority of the inhabitants of the Land of Israel, making it unlikely that social separation was the chief rationale for the dietary laws. Although the Hebrew Bible mentions foreigners and strangers residing in the Land of Israel, neither posed a significant threat to Israelite national identity.

The role of food restrictions as a bulwark between people grew in importance over time. After the destruction of Jerusalem in 586 BCE and the exile of its elite, Jews living in Babylonia become a small minority population. In the Land of Israel during the Hellenistic era, Jewish self-identification as a distinct, "holy" nation is threatened by new populations residing in the land or by Jews who wish to join the rival Greek culture. In both cases, food taboos assumed a heightened urgency for Jewish self-preservation. This is reflected in the book of Daniel, which scholars have dated to the Persian and Hellenistic periods. Daniel 1 tells of four learned and wise young men who were taken from Jerusalem to enter into service in the Babylonian court of King Nebuchadnezzar.

With Daniel as their spokesman, the men refuse to eat the food and wine provided by the court lest they are "defiled," and so they subsist only on legumes and water. Despite the fear expressed in the story that their health would deteriorate, "when the ten days [of testing] were over, they looked better and healthier than all the youths who were eating of the king's food" (v. 15). Endowed with superior wisdom, they then became the king's most trusted advisors, "ten times better than all the magicians and exorcists throughout his realm" (v. 20). Scholars differ over the reason behind the refusal of Daniel and his friends, but the most likely explanation is that in the Babylonian court, the choice of animals, the issue of blood disposal, and the eating of sacrifices made to other gods would not have conformed to Jewish practices.

Additional references to food laws serving as strong social boundaries are found in the Apocrypha and Pseudepigrapha, collections of ancient Jewish books dated to the last two centuries BCE and excluded from the Hebrew Bible. The book of Jubilees presents the patriarch Abraham's last words to his grandson Jacob as an admonition to separate himself from the nations and to "eat not with them," because "all their ways are a pollution and an abomination and uncleanness" (22:16). The books of Tobit and Judith also depict their heroes as scrupulously avoiding the food of non-Jews.[97] In 1 and 2 Maccabees, which tell of persecution under Antiochus IV Epiphanes, it is recorded that many pious Jews chose martyrdom rather than eat unclean food.[98]

Conclusion

Food is not merely a source for sustenance. In the often-challenging environment of ancient Israel, with its rocky soil and minimal water, ample harvests and fertile cattle were evidence of God's love and blessing. The Hebrew Bible emphasizes that Israel's God is deeply concerned with what Israelites, and indeed *all* people, eat. The ancient system of sacrificial offerings and food rituals was designed to reciprocate and request God's benevolence. Because Israelites believed their God was concerned not only with food but also with ethical behavior, sensitivity to life is embedded in the Torah's food laws, albeit in ways not always obvious to the reader. Later Jews, including those in our own era, interpreted biblical food-centered texts for their understanding of how best to relate to the environment, animals, and other people. Because the textual and physical evidence is limited and ambiguous, unanswered questions remain about food in this thousand-year period. We do not know the extent to which the food-centered laws were widely known and practiced in ancient Israel, although we do know that the belief that God cares about Jews' eating practices gets stronger in the Hellenistic era and becomes enshrined in postbiblical rabbinic literature. From the earliest era of Jewish history, dietary discipline and enjoyment of food were intrinsic to the ideal good life and to earning the distinction of being a nation holy to God.

NOTES

1. For a survey of the kinds of sources available regarding diet in ancient Israel, see MacDonald, *What Did the Ancient Israelites Eat?*, 10–15.
2. Deuteronomy 11:10–11 refers to this distinction.
3. Deuteronomy 11:13–15 (emphasis added).
4. See Deuteronomy 7:13, 11:14, 12:17; Jeremiah 31:11–12; Hosea 2:10, 24; Joel 2:19; Haggai 1:11; Nehemiah 5:11, 10:40; 2 Chronicles 31:5, 32:28.
5. 2 Kings 7:1, 16.
6. On the showbread, see Leviticus 24:5–9. Grain sacrifices are described in Leviticus 2.
7. See Meyers, "Having Their Bread," 21–22.
8. Leviticus 2:11.
9. See Genesis 40:1; Leviticus 24:5; 1 Samuel 28:24; Job 31:10; Ecclesiastes 12:3; Isaiah 47:2; Jeremiah 37:21; and Hosea 7:4.
10. See Leviticus 26:26 and Matthew 24:41. Also see Meyers, "Having Their Bread," 14–44; Meyers, "In the Household and Beyond," 24–25; Meyers, "From Field Crops to Food," 70–78.
11. Leviticus 24:1–4.
12. For example, see Exodus 25:6, 29:7, 29:21, 31:11, 35:8; Leviticus 8:2, 8:10, 21:10; 1 Samuel 10, 16; and 1 Kings 1.
13. See Ecclesiastes 9:8; Ezekiel 16:4, 9.
14. Walsh, *The Fruit of the Vine*, 29–40.
15. See Exodus 17; Numbers 20; 1 Samuel 30:12.
16. Numbers 13:23.
17. Lamentations 2:12.
18. Lichtheim, "Sinuhe," 1:79. Also see Jaggard, "Huge Wine Cellar Unearthed."
19. See Exodus 29:40; Leviticus 23:13; Numbers 15:5, 15:7; Deuteronomy 14:26.
20. See Judges 9:13; Psalms 104:15; Ecclesiastes 9:7, 10:19.
21. See Genesis 9:20–27, 19:30–38; Leviticus 10:9; Numbers 6:3–4; Isaiah 28:7–8.

22. *Devash* refers to bees' honey in at least two passages (Judges 14:8 and 1 Samuel 14:25), but elsewhere date syrup is assumed; see MacDonald, *What Did the Ancient Israelites Eat?*, 39–40; Milgrom, *Leviticus 1–16*, 189–90; Borowski, *Every Living Thing*, 161–63.

23. See Job 10:10; 2 Samuel 17:29.

24. Deuteronomy 8:7–9.

25. Anderson, "Sacrifice and Sacrificial Offerings," 5:872. He calls sacrifice a multivalent entity, as "various explanations of its function could coexist." Milgrom reviews different interpretations (Milgrom, *Leviticus 1–16*, 440–43).

26. Leviticus 7:28–34 dictates the portions given to the priesthood. See also Leviticus 17:4, which asserts that killing an animal for food without the necessary rituals is bloodshed, akin to homicide.

27. Numbers 15:1–5.

28. See Leviticus 27:26, 27:30–32; Numbers 18:13–24; Deuteronomy 14:22–29, 18:4, 26:2.

29. Deuteronomy 26:1–11.

30. See Deuteronomy 12:7, 12:11–12, 16:11, 16:14, 16:15; Samuel 20:5, 20:24.

31. The three pilgrimage festivals are discussed in Exodus 23:14–17, 34:18–23; Leviticus 23; and Deuteronomy 16. Baruch Levine notes that "in earlier times, the pilgrimage might have brought a family to a nearby altar," but Deuteronomy ordains that all sacrificial offerings be brought to one, central Sanctuary (*Leviticus*, 156).

32. Biblical references for Passover are Exodus 12:34, 12:39; Deuteronomy 16:3–4. For Shavuot, see Leviticus 23:14. For Sukkot, see Exodus 23:16, 34:22; Leviticus 23:33–36; Nehemiah 8:13–18; and Zechariah 14:18–19.

33. Genesis 1:24–26, 2:7, 2:19.

34. Genesis 8:8–17.

35. See Genesis 9:5–6; Exodus 21:28; Leviticus 20:15–16.

36. Leviticus 17:4. See Milgrom, *Leviticus 17–22*, 1457. He writes, "Elsewhere this phrase ['he has shed blood'] connotes the intentional murder of a human being."

37. The prohibition of consuming blood is stated five times in the Torah: Genesis 9:4; Leviticus 3:17, 7:26–27, 17:12–15; Deuteronomy 12:16. This prohibition is assumed in an early narrative, 1 Samuel 14:33. Sperling writes that the covering of blood reflects the idea that "what offends God should be hidden from his sight" as in Deuteronomy 23:14–15; Ezekiel 24:7–8 (Sperling, "Blood," 1:761–64). See also Milgrom, *Leviticus 1–16*, 704–6.

38. For humankind's evil nature, see Genesis 8:21. Gary Rendsburg terms Genesis 9:4's permission to eat meat "a divine acceptance of human inability to adhere to the utopia established at creation"; Rendsburg, "Vegetarian Ideal in the Bible," 322.

39. Milgrom, *Leviticus 1–16*, 733. See also Kraemer, *Jewish Eating*, 15–16; MacDonald, *What Did the Ancient Israelites Eat?*, 73–75, who cites others; Cooper, *Eat and Be Satisfied*, 3.

40. Leviticus 19:5–7.
41. 1 Kings 5:2–3.
42. Laws regarding plant life are found in Leviticus 19:9–10, 19:23–25, 23:22, 25:1–12; Deuteronomy 20:19–20, 23:25–26, 24:19–21.
43. Leviticus 11:3; Deuteronomy 14:6.
44. See Milgrom, *Leviticus 1–16*, 718–19; Rabinowicz, "Dietary Laws," 6:43.
45. Philo Judaeus, "Special Laws," book 4, 18–20.
46. Kraemer, *Jewish Eating*, 21–22. Kraemer bases his ideas on Howard Eilberg-Schwartz, "Animal Metaphors," 2–22.
47. For discussion, see Milgrom, *Leviticus 1–16*, 725–33.
48. Kraemer, *Jewish Eating*, 18. See also MacDonald, *What Did the Ancient Israelites Eat?*, 64.
49. For discussion, see Levine, *Leviticus*, 243–48.
50. Milgrom, *Leviticus 1–16*, 716.
51. See Leviticus 1:6, 17:13; Deuteronomy 12:16, 12:22–23.
52. Leviticus 7:26.
53. See Firmage, "Zoology," 6:1112–13. The Torah associates hunting with generally negative characters (Genesis 10:8–10 for Nimrod, Genesis 21:20 for Ishmael, and Genesis 25:19–34, 25:27 for Esau).
54. Pits, nets, and traps are mentioned in Isaiah 24:17; Jeremiah 16:15; Ezekiel 19:8 (for lions); Psalms 7:16, 35:7, 140:6; Proverbs 22:14, 26:27.
55. David mentions attacks by lions and bears on his flock animals (1 Samuel 17:34–37). Lion attacks are mentioned also in Judges 14:5; 1 Kings 13:24; 2 Kings 17:25–26; and elsewhere.
56. Leviticus 3:16–17, 7:22–25. Deuteronomy 12 does not mention *helev* in its law permitting nonsacrificial meat eating, thus it permits it outside of a sacrificial context.
57. Exodus 23:19, 34:26; Deuteronomy 14:21.
58. Tigay, *Deuteronomy*, 140.
59. Propp, *Exodus 19–40*, 286.
60. For discussion, see Hesse, "Animal Husbandry and Human Diet," 1:215; Firmage, "Zoology," 6:1131, 1134–35.
61. "Pig bones typically constitute only a fraction of 1% or are entirely absent," writes Dever, *Who Were the Early Israelites?*, 108.
62. See Judges 13:7; Ezekiel 4:14; Daniel 1.
63. Miller, "Hogs and Hygiene," 125–40.
64. See Owen, "Pigs and Pig By-Products at Garsana," 75–87.
65. For this idea, see Firmage, "Zoology," 6:1133–34.
66. Leviticus 11:10; Deuteronomy 14:9–10.
67. Genesis 9:2; Numbers 11:5; Nehemiah 13:16.
68. Job 40:31 speaks of spears for fishing, Ecclesiastes 9:12 portrays humankind as "fish enmeshed in a fatal net," while Habakkuk 1:14–16 mentions hooks and nets. See also Isaiah 19:8; Ezekiel 29:4, 47:10; Job 40:25–26; Ecclesiastes 7:26.

69. Borowski, *Every Living Thing*, 168–75; MacDonald, *What Did the Ancient Israelites Eat?*, 37–38.

70. Borowski, *Every Living Thing*, 176; MacDonald, *What Did the Ancient Israelites Eat?*, 38.

71. Milgrom, *Leviticus 1–16*, 661–64.

72. Amos 3:5; Hosea 7:12; Psalm 124:7; Proverbs 6:5, 7:23; Lamentations 3:52.

73. Isaiah 60:8 and Jeremiah 5:27–28 both speak of birds kept in cages. The law of Deuteronomy 22:6 mentions the collection of the eggs of wild birds.

74. Leviticus 1:14, 5:7; Milgrom, *Leviticus 1–16*, 166–68.

75. Art from Iron Age Israel depicts roosters in a fighting stance; therefore, it is possible that they were used for cock fighting and only later used for eating. See MacDonald, *What Did the Ancient Israelites Eat?*, 36–37; Borowski, *Every Living Thing*, 176–78.

76. Mark 1:6; Matthew 3:4. Also see Borowski, *Every Living Thing*, 159.

77. Milgrom, *Leviticus 1–16*, 734. See also Kelhoffer, "Did John the Baptist?," 302.

78. Flint-Hamilton, "Legumes in Ancient Greece and Rome," 371–85.

79. 2 Kings 4 mentions the consumption of wild plants, a vine and gourds, during a famine. In this instance, they prove to be poisonous.

80. The link between meat eating and joy is most obvious in Deuteronomy and in its use of the verb *samah* (Deuteronomy 12:7, 12:12, 12:18, 14:23–27, 16:11–14, 26:11, 27:7). See also Tigay, *Deuteronomy*, 122; Anderson, *Time to Mourn*, 19–26.

81. Numbers 13:23 says that the spies sent by Moses brought back fruit (pomegranates, grapes, and dates) as samples of the produce of the land.

82. A fruit called *dudaim* is mentioned in Genesis 30:14 and Song of Songs 7:14 and is usually identified as a mandrake, which was believed to enhance sexual arousal and fertility. The *tapuah* is mentioned in Joel 1:12; Proverbs 25:11; and Song of Songs 2:3, 5:5, 7:9, and 8:5. For the identification of *tapuah* as apple, see MacDonald, *What Did the Ancient Israelites Eat?*, 30. The ubiquity of the sycamore is suggested by 1 Kings 10:27. Watermelon is mentioned in Numbers 11:5.

83. 1 Kings 5:5.

84. The fruit of an *etrog* or citron is inedible, although its peel or rind can be candied or used for flavoring. Milgrom concludes, "In sum, the midrashic interpretations of the rabbis notwithstanding, the identification of this 'fruit' with the citron in doubtful" (Milgrom, *Leviticus 23–27*, 2041).

85. The term *'egoz* (Song of Songs 6:11) refers to nuts in general, not a specific kind of nut. Pistachios and almonds are mentioned in Genesis 43:11. Almond trees or branches are mentioned in Numbers 17:23; Jeremiah 1:11; and Ecclesiastes 12:5.

86. Job 6:6.

87. Coriander is mentioned to describe the appearance of manna (Exodus 16:31; Numbers 11:7), while Isaiah 28:25, 28:27 mentions cumin and black cumin, *kamon* and *qezah*. Song of Songs 4:14 refers to saffron.

88. MacDonald, *What Did the Ancient Israelites Eat?*, 91–93.

89. Garnsey, "Famine in History," 145–50.

90. MacDonald, *What Did the Ancient Israelites Eat?*, 87.
91. Genesis 12, 20, 26, 41–42; Ruth 1; 1 Kings 17.
92. Leviticus 26:29; Deuteronomy 28:57; 2 Kings 6:24–30; Lamentations 2:20, 4:10; Ezekiel 5:10. See MacDonald, *What Did the Ancient Israelites Eat?*, 60.
93. Ruth 2.
94. Leviticus 19:13; Deuteronomy 24:6, 24:15.
95. Leviticus 11:43–45 speaks of sanctification, but the goal of separating Israel from the nations doesn't appear until the summary passage in Leviticus 20:24, 20:26. Other passages that emphasize holiness are Exodus 22:30 and Deuteronomy 14:21, both of which concern the taboo of consuming blood. Ethnic distinction as a basis for dietary laws is evident in Deuteronomy 14, as the food prohibitions are preceded and followed by mention of Israel as a "holy people" (vv. 1–2 and v. 21).
96. Kraemer, *Jewish Eating*, 19–23.
97. Tobit 1:10–13; Judith 12:1–2.
98. 1 Maccabees 1:47, 1:62; 2 Maccabees 6:18–7:42.

BIBLIOGRAPHY

Anderson, Gary A. "Sacrifice and Sacrificial Offerings (Old Testament)." In *Anchor Bible Dictionary*, vol. 5, edited by David Noel Freedman. New York: Doubleday, 1992.

———. *A Time to Mourn, a Time to Dance*. University Park: Pennsylvania State University, 1991.

Borowski, Oded. *Every Living Thing: Daily Use of Animals in Ancient Israel*. Walnut Creek, CA: AltaMira, 1998.

Cassuto, M. D. *Commentary on Genesis*. [In Hebrew.] Jerusalem: Magnes, 1978.

Coogan, Michael. "In the Beginning: The Earliest History." In *The Oxford History of the Biblical World*, edited by Michael D. Coogan, 3–24. New York: Oxford University Press, 1998.

Cooper, John. *Eat and Be Satisfied: A Social History of Jewish Food*. Northvale, NJ: Jason Aronson, 1993.

Dever, William. *Who Were the Israelites and Where Did They Come From?* Grand Rapids, MI: William B. Eerdmans, 2003.

Eilberg-Schwartz, Howard. "Animal Metaphors in the Ritual and Narratives of Ancient Israel." *Journal of Ritual Studies* 2 (1988): 2–22.

Firmage, Edward. "Zoology." In *Anchor Bible Dictionary*, edited by David Noel Freedman. New York: Doubleday, 1992.

Flint-Hamilton, Kimberly B. "Legumes in Ancient Greece and Rome: Food, Medicine, or Poison?" *Hesperia* 68 (1999): 371–85.

Garnsey, Peter. "Famine in History." In *Understanding Catastrophe*, edited by J. Bourriau, 145–78. Cambridge: Cambridge University Press, 1990.

Goodfriend, Elaine. "Leviticus 22:24: A Prohibition of Gelding for the Land of Israel?" In *Current Issues in Priestly and Related Literature: The Legacy of Jacob Milgrom and Beyond*, edited by Roy E. Gane and Ada Taggar Cohen, 67–92. Atlanta: SBL, 2015.

Hesse, Brian. "Animal Husbandry and Human Diet in the Ancient Near East." In *Civilizations of the Ancient Near East*, vol. 1, edited by Jack M. Sasson, 203–22. Peabody, MA: Hendrickson, 2000.

Houston, Walter. *Purity and Monotheism: Clean and Unclean Animals in Biblical Law*. Sheffield, England: Sheffield, 1993.

Jaggard, Victoria. "Huge Wine Cellar Unearthed at a Biblical Era Palace in Israel." *Smithsonian*, August 27, 2014. www.smithsonianmag.com.

Kelhoffer, James A. "Did John the Baptist Eat Like a Former Essene? Locust-Eating in the Ancient Near East and at Qumran." *Dead Sea Discoveries* 11 (2003): 293–314.

Kraemer, David. *Jewish Eating and Identity through the Ages*. New York: Routledge, 2007.

Levine, Baruch. *Leviticus*. Philadelphia: Jewish Publication Society, 1989.

Lichtheim, Miriam. "Sinuhe." In *The Context of Scripture*, 77–82. Vol. 1 of *Canonical Compositions from the Biblical World*, edited by William W. Hallo and K. Lawson Younger Jr. Leiden: E. J. Brill, 2003.

MacDonald, Nathan. *What Did the Ancient Israelites Eat? Diet in Biblical Times*. Grand Rapids, MI: William B. Eerdmans, 2008.

Matthews, Victor H. "Treading the Winepress: Real and Metaphorical Viticulture in the Ancient Near East." *Semeia* 86 (1999): 19–32.

Meyers, Carol. "From Field Crops to Food: Attributing Gender and Meaning to Bread Production in Iron Age Israel." In *The Archeology of Difference: Gender, Ethnicity, Class, and the "Other" in Antiquity: Studies in Honor of Eric M. Meyers*, edited by Douglas R. Edwards and C. Thomas McCollough, 67–84. Annual of the American Schools of Oriental Research 60/61. Boston: American Schools of Oriental Research, 2007.

———. "Having Their Bread and Eating There Too: Bread Production and Female Power in Ancient Israelite Households." *Nashim* 5 (2002): 14–44.

———. "In the Household and Beyond: The Social World of Israelite Women." *Nordic Journal of Theology* 63 (2009): 19–41.

Milgrom, Jacob. *Leviticus 1–16: A New Translation with Introduction and Commentary*. Anchor Bible Series 3. New York: Doubleday, 1991.

———. *Leviticus 17–22: A New Translation with Introduction and Commentary*. Anchor Bible Series 3. New York: Doubleday, 2000.

———. *Leviticus 23–27: A New Translation with Introduction and Commentary*. Anchor Bible Series 3. New York: Doubleday, 2001.

Miller, Robert L. "Hogs and Hygiene." *Journal of Egyptian Archaeology* 76 (1990): 125–40.

Owen, David. "Pigs and Pig By-Products at Garsana in the Ur III Period." In *De la domestication au taboo: Le cas des suides dans le Proche-Orient ancient*, edited by Brigitte Lion, 75–87. France: de Boccard, 2006.

Philo Judaeus. "The Special Laws." Early Jewish Writings. www.earlyjewishwritings.com.

Propp, William H. C. *Exodus 19–40*. The Anchor Bible 2a. New York: Doubleday, 2006.

Rabinowicz, Harry. "Dietary Laws." In *Encyclopedia Judaica*. New York: Macmillan, 1972.

Rendsburg, Gary. "The Vegetarian Ideal in the Bible." In *Food and Judaism*, edited by L. J. Greenspoon, R. A. Simkins, and G. Shapiro, 319–34. Omaha: Creighton University Press, 2005.

Sarna, Nahum. *Genesis*. Philadelphia: Jewish Publication Society, 1989.

Sperling, C. David. "Blood." In *Anchor Bible Dictionary*, vol. 1, edited by David Noel Freedman. New York: Doubleday, 1992.

Tigay, Jeffrey. *Deuteronomy*. Philadelphia: Jewish Publication Society, 1989.

Walsh, Carey. *The Fruit of the Vine: Viticulture in Ancient Israel*. Harvard Semitic Museum Publications. Winona Lake, IN: Eisenbrauns, 2000.

2

Food in the Rabbinic Era

DAVID C. KRAEMER

The Roman destruction of the Jerusalem Temple in 70 CE created a hole at the center of Judaism to which all Jews would have to respond. The sacrificial offerings prescribed by the Torah could no longer be offered at the altar, leaving Jews bereft of a recognized means to repair their relationship with God. Laypeople could continue to offer required gifts of grain and produce to the priests, but those priests no longer had an arena in which their special functions and ceremonies could be enacted. Many of the long-standing structures of Jewish practice had been erased, and what would replace them was obvious to no one. Of all the groups competing for the authority to define a way forward, "the rabbis" were the most successful in forging a new path. Their vision and the new forms they created would take centuries to develop and triumph; this "Rabbinic Judaism" is the progenitor of almost all contemporary Jewish traditions, with the exceptions being the remaining populations of Karaite and Ethiopian Jews. As we will see, food played a pivotal role in the radical transformation of Jewish life between the birth of Rabbinic Judaism in the first century and the dawn of the High Middle Ages in the tenth, the thousand-year period that might be called the "long" rabbinic era.

A significant change in the lives of Jews, which affected eating as all other things, began centuries earlier (in the sixth century BCE) with the exile of biblical Judeans from their land to Babylonia and elsewhere. When they lived in these foreign lands—Babylonia, Syria, Egypt, and Asia Minor—their foodways changed with the locale. Judea itself, especially after the Greek conquest in the fourth century BCE, acquired many non-Jewish residents. As this book's previous chapter shows, when gentiles became regular neighbors, posing a perceived risk to the preservation of Jewish culture, the rabbis strengthened biblical food taboos and limited the sharing of meals and foods with others. The intermixing of the population in Judea increased when the Romans conquered the region in the first century BCE. Jewish emigration to other parts of the Roman Empire increased, sometimes due to the transfer of Jewish prisoners of war after revolts against Rome. The third Jewish uprising (132–35 CE) was cruelly suppressed, and the Romans renamed Judea *Palestina*; because of the hardships, large numbers of Jews left. Centuries later, the Diaspora (the dispersion of Jews outside of Israel) expanded geographically with the spread of Islam (seventh century CE) to northern Africa and Spain, and by the end of this thousand-year era, Jewish communities were established in Europe. Wherever Jews lived, their foods would be similar to their neighbors, although the diet of Jews who honored religious food restrictions would be noticeable in what they avoided.

Though we may speak of the thousand years from 70 to 1000 as "the rabbinic era," we must recall that, for large parts of this extended period, most Jews were not rabbinic. The rabbis began as a small group of male scholars in master-disciple circles in Palestine sometime in the first century. They came to believe that in addition to the revelation to Moses that was put into written form as the five books of the Torah, God revealed other teachings that were not recorded. In its fullest version, the rabbinic "myth" posits that these oral teachings included additional divine laws, details of the written laws, explanations, and esoteric matters. According to the mature rabbinic narrative, Moses transmitted the full Torah, written and oral, to the next generation's leaders, and they passed it down faithfully to the next generation's religious leaders, and they to the next. The rabbis regarded themselves as the latest recipients of the oral Torah. They sought to share their learning with each other and their disciples and win acceptance from the Jews at large. By the late second century, there were still no more than a few hundred rabbis. They served as authorities for only a small percentage of the local population and for almost no one beyond the Galilee itself.[1] However, they produced an abundant literature representing their traditions, opinions, and practices. Classic rabbinic literature includes the Mishnah (a code of rabbinic law), the Palestinian and Babylonian Talmuds (rabbinic discussions focused primarily on the Mishnah), and various compilations of *midrash* (biblical exegesis). From the second to the sixth century, these works were little more than sectarian documents.

In the period following the seventh-century CE Islamic conquest, this picture changed significantly. In these later centuries, the rabbis came more and more to be religious authorities for most Jews, and their practices—including eating practices—became widely accepted. Their authority was accompanied by the production of a new literature, that of the recognized heads of the rabbinic academies in Baghdad. These later rabbis, called *Geonim*, composed legal *responsa* (correspondences) and digests of *halakhah* (practical Jewish law) overwhelmingly based on the writings of the earlier, classical rabbis, incorporating abundant Talmudic commentary. Nonrabbinic Jews—some of whom were known as Karaites—remained scripturalists. They too left writings of importance, but nothing as abundant as did the rabbis. The diet and rules for food preparation prescribed by the Talmudic rabbis and Geonim became the basis for Jewish practice throughout the Diaspora.

Yet it must be said that there was no single, unified Jewish food culture that connected all these places over so long a period. In addition, the evidence for these different places and times is not equally abundant. The Mishnah and Talmuds provide a foundation for constructing a history of Jewish eating in Palestine and Babylonia. Geonic writings give a sense of the Jewish diet in the Near East in the last four centuries of the rabbinic era. For other places that lack a written record, we must rely on archaeology, but there is abundant archaeological evidence only for Jewish life in Palestine. Thus when we try to describe nonrabbinic Jewish diets or Jewish diets outside of Palestine and Babylonia (the geographical sites of classic rabbinic literature), we need to assume that they consisted of foods and ingredients that were produced locally and supplemented by food items that could be shipped and effectively stored over longer periods. In all places, wealthier classes could also acquire and consume rarer, luxury items. But within classes, the market was relatively uniform, meaning that any given population, including Jews, ate what was available on the local market.

Foods

During the rabbinic millennium, the Jewish diet privileged the "Mediterranean triad" of bread, wine, and olive oil, just as it had in the biblical era. The simple fact is that the diet of the region was relatively uniform and remained consistent from the ancient era forward. The Greek historian Herodotus, writing in the fifth century BCE, speaks of the Persian (Jews called this region Babylonia) diet as a model of *Mediterranean* culinary civilization.[2] From Palestine to Iraq to Egypt and North Africa, the hot, dry environment on lands near the sea or large rivers yielded similar foods for Jews and others to consume. Specific recipes differed—some regions had more fruits, vegetables, and spices and some had fewer—but the basic ingredients and overall balance of the diet were far more similar than different. The only significant changes in the Jewish diet over the course of this millennium were those restrictions necessitated by the prohibitions created by the rabbis, which appear to have been widely accepted by the end of this lengthy period.

The rabbis acknowledged the privileged status of bread and wine in the Mediterranean triad in their blessing system (discussed later) by requiring unique blessings for these two foods. Bread and wine served specialized ritual functions in both the early Christian-Jewish and rabbinic communities. In the early church, this took the form of the Eucharist. In rabbinic ritual, it found expression in the blessing that sanctified Sabbath and festival meals (*kiddush*) followed by the bread blessing (*ha-motzi*). Legal, narrative, and casual references to bread and wine are also widespread in rabbinic literature.

Not all breads were alike in the eyes of Palestinian Jews, as was obvious in the rabbinic literature from that region. The rabbinic blessing system considers a variety of criteria in determining which bread takes priority for recitation of a blessing, giving preference to the "superior" product: whole loaves are superior to partial loaves, fine (white) flour is superior to coarse flour, and wheat is superior to spelt, which is superior to barley. Such privileging relates to wealth and class differences and may also reflect an adoption of Roman cultural preferences.[3]

Similar distinctions of quality, correlated with wealth and status, are evident in wines. Aged wine was considered superior to new wine, and Italian wine was recognized as superior to other wine. Moreover, it was not merely the quality of the wine that gave expression to the social position of those partaking but the way the wine was used. Ritual use of the wine, in the manner of the Roman symposium, was considered by rabbis to be an elevated cultural act; in fact, in the opinion of one rabbi, if the wine was not mixed in a bowl, as at a symposium, it was not fit for the recitation of the specific blessing for wine. In the opinion of some rabbis, the drinking of wine was a mark of adult male status. In their description of the formal Passover Seder meal, during which the participants discuss the Exodus from Egypt, the rabbis required the drinking of four cups of wine—however, a prevailing rabbinic authority of the time is reported to have objected that women and children should not drink wine but "that which is fitting for them" instead.[4]

The following excerpt from the Mishnah is a good source for listing foods that were commonly eaten but whose importance made them subject to rabbinic rules:

2:3. These things belonging to gentiles are prohibited, and their prohibition extends to deriving any benefit: *Wine*, and *vinegar* of gentiles that was originally wine. . . . *Meat* on its way in to idolatrous worship is permitted, but that which comes out [from idolatrous worship] is prohibited . . . these are the words of R. Aqiba.

2:4. [A case where there are] wine-skins belonging to gentiles, or their bottles, and the wine of a Jew is stored in them, the wine is prohibited. . . .

The skins and grape seeds [left after pressing] belonging to gentiles are prohibited, and their prohibition extends to deriving any benefit—these are the words of R. Meir. . . .

Fish-hash [into which wine has been mixed] and cheese . . . belonging to gentiles, are prohibited. . . .

2:6. These things belonging to gentiles are prohibited, but their prohibition does not extend to deriving benefit: *Milk* milked by a gentile without a Jew overseeing him, and *bread*, and their *oil* (Rabbi [Judah] and his court permitted oil), and boiled foods, and crushed foods into which they put wine or vinegar, and hashed fish . . . these are prohibited, but their prohibition does not extend to deriving any benefit.[5]

The primary purpose of this Mishnah text is to limit Jews to eating only their own wine, meat, oil (although there is disagreement here), bread, and dairy products. In the experience of the authorities behind this Mishnah, wine and wine products are clearly very important parts of the diet, given the number of regulations pertaining to them. Meat is obviously a significant food. Dairy—meaning cheese and, less frequently, milk—is a staple, a product of the part played in the local economy by goats, sheep, and (in lower numbers) cattle. Fish is mostly consumed in a preserved state, given the difficulty of keeping fresh fish and the distance of much of the Jewish population from the sources of such fish. Evidence for this is found in the common mention of "fish-hash" in this and other rabbinic documents. Surviving physical evidence includes a small number of species: sea bream, tuna, mackerel, groupers, and mullets. The facts that these are all Mediterranean—as opposed to freshwater—species and that they are all found even at inland sites suggest a well-organized fishing industry, responding to a considerable demand for fish in the local diet.[6]

Based on other sources, we may round out this picture with legumes (beans, lentils, chickpeas, and vetch) and vegetables, along with a variety of local fruits, including figs, dates, carobs, pomegranates, melons, and plums. Water, collected during the rainy season and stored in cisterns, was drunk, but as noted earlier, wine mixed with water was the most important drink, and certainly one that was consumed even by common folk.[7] Despite this variety, the rabbis taught that only the seven fruits of the Land of Israel listed in Deuteronomy 8:7—wheat, barley, grapes, figs, pomegranate, olives, and dates—had been brought to the Jerusalem Temple as "first fruits" offerings.[8] These seven species served as important symbols in Jewish ceremonies and art and still do.

Meat also constituted a part of the Palestinian Jewish diet, but to what extent and on what occasions is not at all clear. Sheep and goats were the most widely consumed meats in Palestine, while beef was restricted primarily to the northern Carmel region. Common wisdom, repeated by most who have written on the Palestinian diet of the rabbinic period, suggests that, for all but the wealthy, meat was consumed primarily on significant occasions. This conclusion is supported by economic logic: if live animals were productive resources, useful for their labor and for renewable products such as dairy and wool, their owners would have been reluctant to slaughter them for food before the end of their productive lives. Only the wealthy, who had larger flocks and herds or could afford to purchase meat on the market, would regularly have eaten the meat of larger animals. The same considerations would not apply to fowl, whose flesh was more common in the diet.

The rabbis regularly associate meat with special occasions. They encourage the consumption of "small" meat—that of fowl and fish (which for them is not technically meat)—on the more common holy day, the Sabbath, and the flesh of larger animals on the annual festivals. About festival meals, they comment, for example, that "there is no joy without meat."[9] If meat is marked "special," then its consumption must have been sufficiently rare to convey that connotation. Literary testimonies also seem to support this picture. For example, a second-to third-century CE text, speaking of the rabbinic requirement to support formerly wealthy individuals who have fallen on hard times at the level of their former comforts, reports a case in which a far larger than average amount of meat is supplied. Commenting on this story several centuries later, the writers of the Palestinian Talmud declare, "Is it possible?!" Evidently, in Palestine, meat was sufficiently rare and expensive that regular consumption merited surprise; these sources imply that even the wealthy in Palestine consumed relatively small quantities of meat, while common persons consumed truly modest amounts.[10] A number of archaeologists argue on the basis of bone remains that meat consumption in the region was higher.[11] Yet firm conclusions cannot be drawn by weighing the evidence from specific sites and projecting it onto the region as a whole or for the entire era. Furthermore, it is difficult to know whether a particular location was representative of Jewish society as a whole or only of particular groups within it. Bone remains are essential for drawing conclusions, but remaining questions are many and conclusions, therefore, tentative. Considering these uncertainties and the weight of contemporary testimony, we conclude that meat consumption was more common than has been understood but still sufficiently infrequent to mark occasions when it was consumed as out of the ordinary and therefore special.

Stepping back from specifics, what can we say about dietary staples and the relative balance of foods in the Palestinian Jewish diet? One rabbinic text, in particular, has been taken as evidence of the overall diet. It lists a husband's obligations to his wife with respect to food, declaring that "one who provides his wife through an agent should not provide her with less than two *kabs* of wheat or [and?] four *kabs* of barley [for the six days of the week, the Sabbath being considered separately]. . . . He gives her half a *kab* of legumes and half a log of [olive] oil and a *kab* of dried figs or a *maneh* of pressed figs, but if he does not have these, he assigns her other fruits in their place."[12] Helping to put this list into perspective is another roughly contemporaneous text that describes what is to be supplied to a poor person to fulfill one's religious duty: "They do not give to a poor person going from place to place less than a loaf worth a *dupondius* [made from wheat costing at least] one *sela* for four *seahs*. If he stays overnight, we provide him with support for lodging, [namely] oil and legumes. If he spends the Sabbath, we give him food for three meals, [namely] oil, legumes, fish, and a vegetable."[13]

Unfortunately, there are many unanswerable questions that make it difficult to know what to do with these lists. For example, are the quantities suggested in these texts meant to be generous or basic? Are they meant to suffice for all the nutritional needs of the concerned party or only some of them? Do they reflect the conditions of years of plenty or years of deprivation? What is most striking about the lists of food offered in these two texts is how similar they are. The basic diet, at least, was composed of bread (wheat and barley), olive oil, legumes, vegetables, and fish for the Sabbath.[14]

Literary references to foods eaten by Babylonian Jews show few differences from the Palestinian diet. In the Babylonian Talmud, breads, wine, olive oil, and the like are discussed in similar fashion. The fourth-century Babylonian sage Rava mentions "preserved ginger from India," but such an imported delicacy might be found in Palestine as well. We also find reference to local preparations, including *habis* (pulp of flour, honey, and oil) boiled in a pot, sometimes containing chunks of bread, and *rihata* (a flour dish).[15] In the writings of the Geonim in the eighth to the eleventh century in Babylonia, there is little to suggest a significant shift in the diet, although beer and other fermented beverages replaced wine at the daily table (wine remained the beverage of choice for Kiddush). Because the Geonim lived in the Islamic orbit—many of the most prominent lived at the center of the empire, Baghdad—a summary of the "Islamic" diet in this region will tell much about what Jews ate. Historians have found that meat was eaten by the upper classes, and the meat of sheep was preferred to beef. Fowl was commonly consumed, as chicken was raised in cities and inexpensive. Legumes and vegetables were an important part of the diet and included beans, lentils, chick peas, eggplant, spinach, carrots, onions, and others. Fruits and nuts were very popular. Flatbreads were a staple, made from different qualities of wheat, depending on setting and affluence. Rice was also commonly consumed. Fish was eaten where available, but it was not highly valued by most. Nothing in the Geonic record stands in stark contrast to what this survey yields, and again, what defines a diet as Jewish is overwhelmingly its avoidances.[16]

Also offering a lens into the Jewish diet in the latter part of this period is the earliest evidence preserved in the Cairo Genizah, that massive storehouse of discarded written material preserving evidence of everyday life from the tenth century onward. If we assume that nothing significant changed in the conditions for food production in Egypt from the tenth through the twelfth centuries, when most of the Egyptian documents were recorded, the inventory of foods remained the same. According to S. D. Goitein's evaluation, "The local [Egyptian] diet was predominantly vegetarian." A surviving list for midweek shopping includes spices (coriander, garlic, pepper), fruits and vegetables (dates, bitter oranges, radishes), chickpeas, bread and water, and a small quantity of meat. Chickens are common in the surviving lists, along with other meats for Sabbaths and holidays and large quantities of dried fruits and nuts.[17]

One important question concerning the Jewish diet in the rabbinic era in Palestine and elsewhere relates to pig, prohibited to them by biblical law. As we have already written, we may assume that foods available to Jews were the same as those available to their neighbors, so if there was a distinct Jewish diet at all, it must have been because of the absence of foods that gentiles ate but Jews did not. The question we need to ask, then, is whether non-Jews commonly consumed pork, and did Jews actually avoid pork, such that pork-abstaining Jews would have been distinguished by their abstention?

Before the rise of Islam, a pork-rich diet was typical in Rome and environs, as well as in Roman colonies, but not elsewhere. In his review of animal remains from the Roman Empire, Anthony King notes that with respect to the east (including Palestine), pig consumption "was very low, with less than fifteen percent of the bone remains being from pigs." This would mean that if Jews did abstain from pork, they might have been distinguished thereby from their neighbors, but only barely. According to Justin Lev-Tov, however, "Dietary customs within the Jewish population of Palestine were probably more complex than has so far been acknowledged." He argues that "pigs and other forbidden species dot the Jewish communities of Palestine." Rather than assume that such forbidden foods indicate a gentile population in majority Jewish cities, Lev-Tov suggests that some Jews—those who were culturally more Romanized—may have consumed pork. Avoiding circular arguments, we must admit that the diet of Jews may have been less marked by the absence of pig than has been assumed. At the same time, other testimony suggests that some Jews avoided pork because they were Jews and that their avoidance of pork marked them as Jews in the eyes of their neighbors.[18] Jews who ate pork and other forbidden substances would not have been noticed by others for their abstention, so such testimonies cannot be used as evidence that all Jews avoided pork—only a sufficient number that they would have been noticed.[19] After the Islamic conquest of the lands in which Jews lived, the situation would have differed. Muslims, like Jews, eschew pork, so when Jews lived among Muslims who respected this taboo, nothing in their avoidance of swine flesh would have distinguished them from their neighbors. It is safe to assume that in Muslim lands, Jews did shun pork, but this would not have marked them as Jews.

Rabbinic Innovations

Our exploration of the impact of the rabbis on Jewish eating begins with an original rabbinic ritual: blessings before and after partaking of food. These start with the formula "Blessed are you, Lord, King of the universe," followed by mention of God's role as creator of the food that is consumed. The blessings generally applied to categories of food, so the blessing would continue with, for example, "who creates the fruit of the tree" or "who creates the fruit of the earth." The bread blessing ("who brings forth bread from the earth"), which is preceded by a ritual hand washing, commences every formal meal, as bread was understood to "make a meal." The rabbis also insisted on a blessing or blessings after eating, with an extended, compound blessing after a proper meal (i.e., one that included bread). When more than three men ate together, the blessing after the meal was accompanied by additional rituals.[20] Ideally, in a gathering of learned men such as themselves, the rabbis insisted that those present should discuss or hear words of Torah. According to Mishnah tractate Avot,

> Rabbi Shimon says: Three who ate at one table and did not say upon it words of Torah—it is as if they ate from the offerings of the dead, as it is said (Isaiah 28:8): "For all of the tables are full of vomit and feces without the Omnipresent." However, three who ate at one table and said upon it words of Torah—it is as if they ate from the table of the Omnipresent, blessed be He, as it is said (Ezekiel 41:22): "And he said to me, this is the table that is before the Lord."[21]

In this passage, Rabbi Shimon cites two biblical passages about sacrificial worship, the first expressing God's disgust for the rites conducted by drunken and corrupt priests and the second referring to the table in the Temple that held the showbread. In Rabbi Shimon's interpretation, Torah study takes the place of sacrificial offerings, and the rabbis take the place of the priests. Eating meals without uttering words of Torah is an offense against God, but the rabbis' sanctified eating brings God's presence into the world. His perspective was characteristic of his rabbinic cohort.[22]

Women did not participate in Torah study, although as domestic cooks, they were essential to this kind of table fellowship. This rabbinic teaching attests to their role: "The following are the kinds of work which a woman must perform for her husband: grinding corn, baking bread, washing clothes, cooking, suckling her child, making ready his bed and working in wool. If she brought him one bondwoman she need not do any grinding or baking or washing. If she brought two bondwomen, she need not even cook or suckle her child."[23] The Mishnah and Talmud assume that women spend much time in the home and expect them to behave modestly, but it is also clear that women were part of the traffic and commerce of the marketplace. Food was prepared domestically and in the market, and both domains were occupied by men and women.

Trade in food and goods infiltrated into semiprivate courtyards and even into the private domiciles.[24] Because classic rabbinic literature revolves around the concerns of the rabbinic elite, a group to which women did not belong, it is not certain whether wives (and children) routinely ate meals together with their husbands.[25]

There was an identifiable Jewish diet when Jews avoided the flesh of various animals eaten by others. But the Jewish diet was also increasingly distinguished over the course of this period by new rabbinic prohibitions. In fact, the Palestinian rabbis of the first and second centuries created a new eating regimen, later known as *kashrut*, which would ultimately come to define the diets of most Jews—male and female, young and old alike. They enumerated the foods that were kosher—permitted—and the rules for preparing them. The outstanding element of this new regimen was its prohibition of eating meat and dairy at the same meal. This was, the rabbis claimed, an expansion of the biblical law: "You shall not boil a kid in its mother's milk."[26]

The earliest expression of this rabbinic eating rule is found in the Mishnah. The fundamental rabbinic rule explicitly forbids the cooking of any dairy and any meat together, and it also clearly implies that eating them together is forbidden.[27] That this prohibition is original to Rabbinic Judaism is apparent in the words of the Jewish scholar Philo, who lived shortly before the time of the rabbis: "If anyone should desire to dress flesh with milk, let him do so without incurring the double reproach of inhumanity and impiety. . . . The man who seethes the flesh of [animals] in the milk of its own mother is exhibiting terrible perversity of disposition."[28] Cooking the animal's flesh in the milk of another animal's mother (prohibited by a simple reading of the biblical law) occasions no objection from Philo. The innovative quality of the rabbinic prohibition is also apparent when one reviews other Second Temple witnesses, none of whom—despite various references to Jewish eating and eating prohibitions—knew of this one. It is fair to say that the newness of the rabbinic prohibition is reflected in rabbinic discussions themselves, the confused state of which suggests that the practice was still in formation.

For example, the Babylonian Talmud asks how the Mishnah's obligation to separate meat and dairy is to be accomplished. Among the proposed steps for separating meat and dairy are rinsing one's mouth after eating one and before eating the other, wiping one's mouth, and waiting some time (until the next meal? until the next day?) before consuming the other category. The *Gemara* (the Talmudic discussion of the Mishnah) presents these methods one after the other, with no suggestion of how they relate to one another: Are they alternative methods, or must a person perform these separations in some combination? Some opinions, but not all, are stricter when meat is eaten first but not when dairy is the first food consumed. The meat of fowl seems to be treated more leniently than the meat of other kosher animals. More steps to assure the absence of mixing may be required at night, when the offending substance may not be seen, than during the day. Again, the *Gemara* offers no hint which of these principles is accepted in practice and which is not.[29]

Crucially, the detailed requirements for separation have no precedent in the Mishnah and thus offer evidence that, in the centuries following the rabbinic declaration that meat and dairy must be separated, the community of rabbis could not yet decide how this separation should be accomplished. In combination with the evidence of the absence of a prerabbinic prohibition, offered earlier, the confused and shifting state of the Talmudic record proclaims loudly that the rabbis had created a new set of prohibitions that distinguished them and their followers not only from gentiles but also from Jews who came before them. This being the case, it would also have separated rabbinic Jews—that is, Jews who accepted rabbinic authority—from Jews who had not yet adopted rabbinic practices. The fact that the opinions cited in the Talmud originated in both Palestine and Babylonia over the course of several centuries shows that this rabbinic practice had spread beyond the territory of Palestine.

To what degree did Jews beyond the circles of the rabbis observe this rabbinic eating prohibition? The Jewish dietary avoidances noticed by gentile observers are all biblical prohibitions. The fact that no witness reports on this rabbinic practice supports the conclusion that nonrabbinic Jews had not yet accepted it, at least in the Talmudic period itself (i.e., until at least the sixth century). The absence of any such notice should occasion no surprise, as in the opinion of current scholarship, rabbinic authority or influence was slow to spread beyond rabbinic circles, even in Palestine, let alone beyond.[30] Hence it is fair to say that there was no "rabbinic-Jewish diet" current in Jewish populations in the first half of the millennium beyond very small circles.

This picture would change considerably as the rabbis gained ascendency. By the eighth century, in the Islamic orbit, under the authority of the early Geonim, most Jews were certainly observing rabbinic strictures, in diet and otherwise.[31] The exception was the sizable minority of Jews who continued to remain faithful to the written Torah—hence their name Karaites, or scripturalists—and who repudiated rabbinic authority and practices as unauthorized innovation. Karaites rejected utterly the rabbinic practice of separating dairy and meat.[32] The Karaite diet was distinguished from the rabbinic diet in other ways too. For example, in the absence of clear scriptural standards concerning which birds are or are not permitted for consumption, Rabbinic Jews followed local customs, eating those birds that were deemed permissible by those before them. Karaite Jews, by contrast, avoided eating all birds but pigeons and turtledoves, whose acceptability was obvious in the Torah because they were permitted for sacrificial offerings. Finally, some Karaites refused to eat meat or drink wine as a sign of mourning for the destruction of the Jerusalem Temple; the rabbis had considered this practice during an early stage of their history but rejected it as being overly severe.[33]

Jews Dining Apart

In the end, what most distinguished Jewish eating in the Roman world and beyond was the refusal of Jews to dine with their neighbors. The statement of Tacitus (first–second century CE) that Jews "sit [*epulis*, dine] apart at meals" is frequently cited as evidence of this practice.[34] Even more explicit and extreme is Philostratus's report that Jews live "a life apart and irreconcilable that [they] cannot share with the rest of mankind in the pleasures of the table."[35] These observations can be said to reflect both the law and the practice of *some* Jews beginning in at least the second century BCE, who forbade themselves the consumption of "gentile foods"—that is, foods that were otherwise permitted but that had been prepared by gentiles. This included wine. However, we do not know whether separate Jewish eating and drinking was the norm.

The rabbis sought to make clear that the Torah mandated a high barrier between Jewish and gentile tables. The Mishnah lays the foundation of the laws seeking to accomplish this goal in tractate Avodah Zarah ("strange worship"). The tractate defines "idolatrous" worship—idols need not actually have been involved—and the distance a Jew must maintain from it. The tractate's second chapter elaborates practical regulations whose purpose is to establish such a distance. Among these laws are several (some are quoted earlier) prohibiting or limiting the consumption of gentile food. They preclude deriving any benefit from gentile wine and meat, as they may have been used for pagan worship. Jewish wine kept in skins that earlier contained gentile wine was similarly disallowed; other laws make explicit that the touch of a gentile renders the wine forbidden to a Jew. But the prohibitions extend to products that, unlike wine and meat, would not have been used in foreign worship. Products explicitly forbidden include "gentile" cheese and other dairy, bread, oil, and "boiled foods." The latter has commonly been understood to refer to any food cooked by a gentile.

The principle of Jewish control over preparation applied to the production of meat too. Biblical law mandated special care to be taken during animal slaughter to remove the blood, which was prohibited for consumption, but it is in rabbinic writings that the procedures are made explicit. *Shehitah*, kosher animal slaughter, is defined. The Mishnah specifies that land animals must be slaughtered cleanly at the neck, severing most of the trachea and esophagus, and bird slaughter varies slightly. The rabbis explained many other details—for example, which infirmities in the animal would render it prohibited and how to dispose of the blood. Most important for the matter of separate Jewish cuisine is that the rabbis insisted that meat slaughtered by a gentile, even one who followed proper procedures, was not permitted; kosher meat required a Jewish slaughterer. In short, Jews may have been eating the same kinds of meat as their gentile neighbors, but those faithful to rabbinic law would not purchase or eat their neighbors' meat. Again, the extent to which this rule was followed is unknown.[36]

There were other foods forbidden to Jews, not because of their ingredients but because they were prepared by non-Jews.[37] This category includes bread, wine, olive oil, and cooked legumes. In the Mishnah's late second-century Roman context, it is surely significant that, among other foods, the well-known "Mediterranean triad"—bread, wine, and olive oil—is subject to the prohibitions. That is, the most common and respected foods in the Roman world are forbidden for consumption by a Jew if they have been owned or prepared by a gentile. The consequences of these prohibitions, again both pragmatically and symbolically, are significant. The obvious result of their prohibition would be to make it very difficult to enjoy a meal with a gentile even in the home of a Jew—because of the consequences of gentile touch with respect to wine—and to do so in the home of a gentile would be nearly impossible. If meals are central to the establishing and maintaining of social connections, then neighborly relations between Jews and gentiles would be constrained. Indeed, the rabbis explicitly declare that this was their purpose in instituting the prohibitions. The most direct expression is a Talmudic statement explaining the legislation in the Mishnah as a causal chain: "Their bread and oil [were forbidden] on account of their wine, and their wine [was forbidden] *on account of their daughters*, and their daughters [were forbidden] on account of 'another thing.'"[38] That is to say, if a Jew shares bread and oil with a gentile, he is likely also to share wine; if he shares wine, he will become friendly with the gentile and perhaps come to know his daughter, with whom he might fall in love. She may then tempt him to cooperate in her idolatrous rites. In consideration of this fear, it is better not to eat together at all.

The length of this chain suggests that idolatry is not the only thing the rabbis were concerned about. In fact, elsewhere in this same deliberation, they admit as much, writing, "What did the sages see [that impelled them to prohibit gentile bread]? They were worried about marriage." The same concern motivated them to extend the prohibition of wine (which might be used in idolatrous worship) to any strong drink (which is not used for such worship).[39] Jews must be vigilant about maintaining their separation from gentile neighbors, the rabbis believed. This was why they strengthened such separation by forbidding commensality with gentiles.

This eating prohibition was designed to enforce separation on other levels as well. To begin with, to mark foods as taboo associated them, if only symbolically, with the forbidden foods of the Torah, saying that these foods, like those prohibited in Leviticus and Deuteronomy, are impure. The actual source of the judgment of "impurity" is not biblical but rabbinic.[40] From the rabbinic perspective, the immediate source of the impurity of the foods is the gentile who prepares or handles them. By extension, this marks the gentile as impure. To identify a class of people as impure is to mark them as taboo. These eating laws have a significant symbolic impact and should be regarded as part of a broad rabbinic project to create fear of the gentile and to mark him or her as "other." This manner of building boundaries was familiar to the rabbis from their historical-cultural context. According to the Roman culinary language, a person who ate the same foods as others but refused to share them at the same table was making a statement about who was civilized—a citizen—and who was not. Someone with whom one did not share these foods, who failed to uphold the dictates of the cultural code, was "other."[41] Ironically, therefore, a Jew who ate these same foods while refusing to share them with his neighbor was declaring, "As far as I am concerned, you are not civilized."

The rabbinic creation of a barrier between Jews and their neighbors could not be an absolute one; it was too demanding. An early rabbinic text called the Tosefta already provides evidence of disagreement with respect to the status of olive oil; according to its record, "Rabbi [Judah] and his court permitted oil." On this basis, it is reasonable to conclude that, after Rabbi Judah's governance of the rabbinic community—the mid-third century, shortly after the promulgation of the Mishnah—the prohibition against gentile oil was no longer in force. In addition, the Palestinian and Babylonian Talmuds both mention early compromises pertaining to bread and wine. For example, both conclude that, while gentile bread may be formally prohibited, this is so only if Jewish bread is available. If the only local baker is a gentile baker, his bread may be consumed without hesitation.[42] Further, the prohibition concerning wine handled by gentiles was qualified by some rabbis. Prominent sages of the same period suggested that Jewish wine, if mixed with water (as was customary), could not be contaminated. All agreed that "cooking" the wine would protect Jewish wine from the consequences of gentile contact.[43] In these ways, there might be few obstacles in the way of Jews and gentiles drinking together.

There appears to be a balancing act at play in the conflicting directions in rabbinic legislation pertaining to eating gentile food. The laws of gentile foods counsel separation, but compromises in those same laws yield, if only partially, to a lived reality characterized as much by mixing as by separation. In reality, Jews of this period mixed constantly with their neighbors, for reasons both commercial and social. In response, the rabbis sought to erect boundaries of attitude that permitted intercourse of one kind—social and commercial—but would assure that there is no intercourse of the other kind. Furthermore, Palestinian rabbis tended to rule more strictly than the Babylonian ones. When the center of rabbinic authority shifted to the east under the authority of the early Geonim, many Jews were certainly observing rabbinic strictures, in diet and otherwise. Under those conditions, while potential leniencies about separation from gentile foods were evident, the rabbis and those who followed them maintained their strictness about separating meat and dairy and avoiding pork and other forbidden animals. According to Karaite observers, who were uncomfortable with rabbinic leniencies and condemned social mixing, many Jews took advantage of the loopholes laid out by the rabbis.[44]

Special Meals

Another of the long-lasting contributions of the rabbis to Jewish foodways was their development of table practices for certain meals that involve symbolic foods, prayers, and ceremonies. For major life events such as a *brit milah* (circumcision), weddings, and feeding a mourner after the burial of a family member, the rabbis taught that there is a religious obligation to serve a meal. The poor had to be provided for at these times, either as guests at the meal or as recipients of charitable giving beforehand. The rabbis recommended appropriate foods, such as a feast (wine, bread, meat, delicacies) for weddings or round foods such as hard-boiled eggs and lentils for the meal of consolation. They maintained the practice of fasting on days connected to the destruction of the First and Second Temples, as well as for Yom Kippur, and discussed what should be eaten before and after these.

For the festivals of Sukkot, Passover, and Shavuot, the rabbis described what must be eaten for the days to be truly joyous. At these times too, Jews had to be especially careful to ensure that the poor had adequate food and could be joyous. The rabbis paid great attention to Passover eating. They devoted entire Mishnaic chapters, along with numerous pages of discussion in the Talmuds, to the dietary laws for the seven (for some regions, eight) days of Passover and the baking of unleavened bread. They shaped the Passover Seder meal into a prolonged ritualized event: it required certain foods, special ways of sitting or reclining at the table, rules governing who may be included at the event, and what topics of Torah and symbolic foods should be discussed. For all the festivals, the rabbis added elements to the blessings before and after the meal that reference the unique features of the day.

The rabbis' amplification of the biblical Sabbath observance resulted in significant changes in eating that would occur for this one day each week. To begin with, most labors required to prepare food were forbidden on the Sabbath, meaning that the abundant Sabbath dishes had to be prepared before the day began (this was probably already the case before the rabbis, as New Testament books refer to Friday as "Preparation Day").[45] To assure that hot food would be available during the Sabbath day (Saturday), the rabbis developed methods for preserving the heat of stew-like Sabbath dishes. They taught that the Sabbath should be pleasurable and include three full, formal meals, as opposed to the mundane two meals on a normal day. Again, they insisted that Jews not ignore the Sabbath food needs of the poor. Sabbath meals required significant advance preparation by women, of course, but also by men—as it was considered praiseworthy for men to prepare even if they had wives and servants who could do the work. Sabbath meals were to be the most lavish of the week. They must include two loaves of bread, wine, and ideally meat or fish and other delicacies. The rabbis described special rules of table comportment that included hearing words of Torah. The third meal of the Sabbath was to be a prolonged one that ended with a ceremony formally separating the Sabbath from the rest of the week.[46] Upon this rabbinic foundation, Jews of subsequent centuries constructed intricate, elaborate, and theologically rich mealtime ceremonies.

Conclusion

Jews and Judaism were radically different at the end of the tenth century than they were in the first. Mostly these changes did not affect the kinds of food Jews ate. The overwhelming majority of Jews remained in the Mediterranean basin and the Near East, where available foods and technology were similar to those in the distant past. Although a huge disruption in political and religious authority occurred in the few centuries before and after the turn of the millennium, once a modicum of Jewish religious unity was reestablished through the triumph of Rabbinic Judaism, fundamental beliefs found already in Israelite food culture remained: that God cares about the Jewish diet; that this diet should be distinctive, in certain ways, from that of the other nations of the world; and that food is a crucial instrument for worshiping God and celebrating life. At the same time, in a number of ways, Jewish eating was markedly different from the past. Most important, the locus of food-centered ritual now occurred in the home, not at the sacrificial altar. Eating itself came to be understood as potentially infused with holiness. Torah study became a way of expressing religious devotion. Jewish eating became more complicated, demanding more comprehensive separation from non-Jews and separation of meat and dairy. To a far greater extent than before, ways of preparing and eating food became tied to Jewish identity. Distinctive Jewish modes of eating became a way to preserve the Jewish nation for the future and ensure its continued holiness.

NOTES

1. On the various claims of this paragraph, see Schwartz, *Imperialism and Jewish Society*, 103–23.
2. Longo, "Food of Others," 156.
3. For the discussion of blessing bread, see Tosefta Berakhot 4:15. For a fuller discussion of the cultural privileging implied by the rabbinic blessings, see Kraemer, *Jewish Eating and Identity*, 77–86. On wheat versus barley, see Beer, *Taste or Taboo*, 19.
4. On wine quality, see Mishnah Avot 4:20 and Mishnah Sanhedrin 8:2. On blessing over mixed wine, see Tosefta Berakhot 4:3. On wine for women and children, see Tosefta Pesachim 10:4.
5. Mishnah Avodah Zarah 2:3–6 (emphasis added).
6. Also see Lev-Tov, "Upon What Meat?," 435–37.
7. Rosenblum, *Food and Identity*, 17–30; Broshi, *Bread, Wine, Walls and Scrolls*, 121–56 and 162; Dar, "Food and Archaeology," 327–32.
8. Exodus 23:19; Numbers 18:23; Deuteronomy 26:2; discussed in Mishnah Bikkurim.
9. Babylonian Talmud, Pesachim 109a.
10. See Tosefta Peah 4:10 and Palestinian Talmud, 109a. Another source who may support this is the Jewish scholar Philo, who suggests that animals were raised

for their renewable products, not for meat. He writes (in *On the Virtues* 144) of "innumerable herds of cattle in every direction" that are milked daily because "milk is the greatest source of profit to all breeders." Despite the great quantity of edible animals he sees around him in wealthy Alexandria, he fails even to mention that they might be used for their meat, suggesting the relative rarity of this practice.

11. King, "Diet in the Roman World," 185–87. Lev-Tov, "Upon What Meat?," 433, offers a more detailed examination of the archeological evidence from Palestine and suggests that "it is time to rethink and re-examine the 'meat as luxury food in the ancient world' hypothesis, given the growing amount of archaeological evidence which contradicts this long-held view." Yet while commenting on the "large numbers of broken and butchered animal bones," he admits that "we do not know how many meals, from how many people, over how much time, these piles of bones represent. . . . At the very least, these animals were slaughtered for meat once they no longer generated an adequate quantity of wool, milk, or labor."

12. Mishnah Ketubbot 5:8.

13. Tosefta Peah 4:8. According to Saul Lieberman's calculation, a *dupondius* would purchase half a *kab*, meaning that what is provided to a woman and to a poor person are not very different; see Lieberman, *Tosefta Ki-fshutah,* 1:183. For rabbinic responses to communal poverty and hunger, see Gardner, *Origin of Organized Charity.*

14. Also supporting this picture is Mishnah Baba Metziah, chap. 2, which addresses the question of one's responsibilities when one finds lost items. As this law speaks of the marketplace, and its focus on (possibly) lost food is only instrumental, its record is probably more "naïve" and therefore more accurate than the previous texts.

15. Babylonian Talmud, Berachot 36b, 37b.

16. For details, see Rosenberger, "Arab Cuisine and Its Contribution," 207–23.

17. Goitein, *Mediterranean Society,* 4:232–47.

18. For discussion, see Rosenblum, "Why Do You Refuse to Eat Pork?"

19. King, "Diet in the Roman World," 171–78, 185, writes with respect to the Eastern provinces, which include Palestine, that bone remains show that dietary meat was dominated by sheep and goat. Some sites, King remarks, have no pig remains at all, including Jerusalem and other identifiably Jewish sites. This is not, however, the case throughout Palestine, and there is evidence in Roman-dominated sites of high consumption of pork. See Lev-Tov, "Upon What Meat?," 432.

20. Kraemer, *Jewish Eating and Identity,* chap. 6.

21. Mishnah Avot 3:4.

22. For a similar sentiment, see Babylonian Talmud, Berakhot 64a: "Everyone who partakes of a meal at which a Torah scholar is seated is as if he enjoys the splendor of the Divine Presence. . . ."

23. Mishnah Ketubbot 5:5.

24. For a fine discussion of men, women, and the marketplace, see Baker, *Rebuilding the House of Israel*, chap. 3 and accompanying figures at the rear of the book. On the gender of professional bakers, see Rosenblum, *Food and Identity*, 24–25.

25. Rosenblum, *Food and Identity*, 123–32, surveys the scholarship on this subject for the era of the Mishnah.

26. Exodus 23:19; Exodus 34:26; Deuteronomy 14:21. See the previous chapter in this volume, Elaine Goodfriend, "Food in the Biblical Era."

27. Mishnah Hullin 8:1 and following.

28. Philo, *On Virtues*, sec. 144.

29. Babylonian Talmud, Hullin 104b–105a. There is no Palestinian Talmud on this Mishnah.

30. Schwartz, *Imperialism and Jewish Society*, 175–76. Shaye J. D. Cohen confirms this judgment in personal correspondence, dated March 18, 2015.

31. For an account of the triumph of rabbinic authority during this period, see Brody, *Geonim of Babylonia*.

32. Nemoy, *Karaite Anthology*, 266–67.

33. On Karaite permitted birds, see Nemoy, 16 and 33. On mourning customs, see 113; the latter may have been influenced by Muslim avoidance of alcoholic beverages. Rabbinic discussion of appropriate mourning for the Jerusalem Temple is found in Babylonian Talmud, Baba Batra 60b.

34. Tacitus, *Historiae* 5.5.2; Stern, *Greek and Latin Authors*, 2:26.

35. Philostratus, *Via Apollonii* 5.33; Stern, *Greek and Latin Authors*, 341.

36. Rosenblum, *Food and Identity*, 76–81. These rules are summarized in Mishnah Hullin.

37. In her discussion of these texts, Christine Hayes elides the difference between foods where kashrut is a real concern and cases where it is not, as in these cases. Her failure to make this distinction leads to problems in her readings of this Mishnah. See *Gentile Impurities and Jewish Identities*, 141.

38. Babylonian Talmud, Avodah Zarah 36b (emphasis added). For discussion, see Freidenreich, *Foreigners and Their Foods*, chaps. 3–5.

39. Babylonian Talmud, Avodah Zarah 35b and 31b.

40. Hayes, *Gentile Impurities and Jewish Identities*, 130, 134, 142, and passim. Hayes makes too much of the fact that gentile impurity is described by the rabbis as being of rabbinic as opposed to scriptural origin. In the rabbinic system, rabbinic laws are at least as hard or harder to bend or break than scriptural laws, and the rabbis' confession that these laws are "merely" rabbinic is found in elitist texts of the rabbis' own invention, communications of rabbis to rabbis and their disciples; it is doubtful that common people would have known this categorization.

41. Dupont, "Grammar of Roman Dining," 114.

42. Palestinian Talmud, Avodah Zarah 2:8, 41d; and Babylonian Talmud, Avodah Zarah 35b.

43. Palestinian Talmud, Avodah Zarah 2:3, 41a–b; and Babylonian Talmud, Avodah Zarah 29b–30a.

44. Nemoy, *Karaite Anthology*, 115–16.
45. See Mark 15:42; Luke 23:54; John 19:31.
46. For some rabbinic sources for Sabbath meals, see Babylonian Talmud, Shabbat 118a; Kiddushin 41a; Berachot 9b, 33a. On the third and concluding meal, see Babylonian Talmud, Pesachim 105a and Berachot 33a.

BIBLIOGRAPHY

Baker, Cynthia. *Rebuilding the House of Israel: Architectures of Gender in Jewish Antiquity*. Stanford: Stanford University Press, 2002.

Beer, Michael. *Taste or Taboo: Dietary Choices in Antiquity*. Totnes: Prospect Books, 2010.

Brody, Robert. *The Geonim of Babylonia and the Shaping of Medieval Culture*. New Haven: Yale University Press, 1998.

Broshi, Magen. *Bread, Wine, Walls and Scrolls*. New York: Sheffield Academic Press, 2001.

Dar, Shimon. "Food and Archaeology in Romano-Byzantine Palestine." In *Food in Antiquity*, edited by John Wilkins, F. D. Harvey, and Mike Dobson, 326–35. Exeter: University of Exeter Press, 1995.

Dupont, Florence. "The Grammar of Roman Dining." In *Food: A Culinary History*, edited by Jean-Louis Flandrin and Massimo Montanari, 113–27. New York: Columbia University Press, 1999.

Freidenreich, David M. *Foreigners and Their Foods: Constructing Otherness in Jewish, Christian, and Islamic Law*. Berkeley: University of California Press, 2011.

Gardner, Gregg E. *The Origin of Organized Charity in Rabbinic Judaism*. New York: Cambridge University Press, 2015.

Goitein, S. D. *A Mediterranean Society*. 6 vols. Berkeley: University of California Press, 1967–88.

Hayes, Christine. *Gentile Impurities and Jewish Identities*. Oxford: Oxford University Press, 2002.

King, Anthony. "Diet in the Roman World: A Regional Inter-site Comparison of the Mammal Bones." *Journal of Roman Archaeology* 12 (1999): 168–202.

Kraemer, David. *Jewish Eating and Jewish Identity through the Ages*. London: Routledge, 2007.

Lev-Tov, Justin. "'Upon What Meat Doth This Our Caesar Feed . . . ?' A Dietary Perspective on Hellenistic and Roman Influence in Palestine." In *Zeichen aus Text und Stein: Studien auf dem Weg zu einer Archäologie des Neuen Testaments*, edited by Stephan Alkier and Jürgen Zangenberg, 420–46. Tübingen: A. Francke, 2003.

Lieberman, Saul. *Tosefta Ki-fshutah*. 12 vols. New York: Jewish Theological Seminary of America, 1955.

Longo, Oddone. "The Food of Others." In *Food: A Culinary History*, edited by Jean-Louis Flandrin and Massimo Montanari, 153–64. New York: Columbia University Press, 1999.

Nemoy, Leon, ed. *Karaite Anthology*. New Haven: Yale University Press, 1955.

Rosenberger, Bernard. "Arab Cuisine and Its Contribution to European Culture." In *Food: A Culinary History*, edited by Jean-Louis Flandrin and Massimo Montanari, 207–23. New York: Columbia University Press, 1999.

Rosenblum, Jordan D. *Food and Identity in Early Rabbinic Judaism*. Cambridge: Cambridge University Press, 2010.

———. "'Why Do You Refuse to Eat Pork?': Jews, Food, and Identity in Roman Palestine." *Jewish Quarterly Review* 100 (2010): 95–110.

Schwartz, Seth. *Imperialism and Jewish Society, 200 B.C.E. to 640 C.E.* Princeton: Princeton University Press, 2001.

Stern, Menachem. *Greek and Latin Authors on Jews and Judaism*. 3 vols. Jerusalem: Israel Academy of Sciences and Humanities, 1976–80.

3

Food in the Medieval Era

JONATHAN BRUMBERG-KRAUS

It was told that the wealthy and learned Jews of medieval Provence took special care to feed many of the poor from their tables. When these generous benefactors died, their tables were made into the coffins in which they were buried. According to a rabbi who heard of and praised this custom, these pious Jews did this because they believed "the table in the house is like the altar in the Temple [and] just as an altar atones, so also a table [upon which one fed the poor] atones." By turning their tables into coffins, they taught by their example that even if one's power reaches to the clouds and one's wealth equals that of King Solomon, only the compassion and generosity bestowed upon the poor in this world, especially by feeding them, is what counts before the divine judge in the next world.[1]

As in the past, during the medieval era, Jewish eating and food behaviors were often expressed in terms of a relationship between Jews and God. In the eleventh to the sixteenth century—the period this chapter will cover—Jewish cuisine, rituals, and food laws became more complex, demanding, and variegated. Jewish settlements remained in Mediterranean lands, but Jews also established themselves in Spain and northern, central, and eastern Europe. In this era, the regional differentiation between Jewish practices became greater. Relative to the past, rabbinic authority over Jews' daily lives grew stronger. Muslim and Christian clerics insisted on Jews' theological inferiority and influenced rulers to support discriminatory policies toward their Jewish subjects. In response, the rabbis shaped foodways to affirm Judaism's superiority over other religions and emphasize Jews' unique and special relationship with God. Although rabbis legislated for all Jews regardless of class, they adopted behaviors and innovative theologies around eating that enhanced their own intra-Jewish standing by demonstrating their superior piety and authority. The title of the major law code composed in the sixteenth century, *Shulhan Aruch* ("Set Table"), and its accompanying commentary, *Mappah* ("Tablecloth"), signal the symbolic importance of the food-laden table in medieval Jewish life.

Food in Medieval Times

Medieval sources give ample evidence for historians to describe the daily meals of common people, and this depiction will help the reader understand the changes taking place. At the start of the medieval era, eating itself was technologically very simple. Dishes, tableware, cooking utensils, and tables themselves were minimal. Even in the homes of the wealthy, dinner tables typically consisted of boards set on trestles that were moved out of the way when meals ended. Linen tablecloths and napkins were widely used, but sometimes a tablecloth on the ground alone sufficed for outdoor dining. People did not eat their main meals on individual plates but on dried pieces of bread, so-called trenchers. Diners might be given spoons (and cooks certainly used larger spoons and ladles to cook and serve), but they were usually expected to bring their own knives. Forks were not in the picture yet; people ate primarily with their hands—hence the need for napkins and, among the more "refined" classes, hand-washing rituals.[2] People usually ate the main and largest meal of the day in the afternoon, typically stews or savory pies, and a lighter, plain supper in the evening. Many peasants and craftsmen ate some sort of breakfast at daybreak too, usually a porridge or gruel made from grains—although this was not recognized as a meal, and moralists disparaged it as being low class and appropriate only for children, the elderly, and the sick.

At the local level, food commerce, food preparation, and even some eating and drinking occurred in a context in which people collaborated, despite their different religious identities, and they bought their food from common local markets or grew it themselves. Jews by this time were generally no longer farmers, and they lived in villages, towns, and the few large cities of the Islamic and Christian empires. Although much of the populace lived on or near farmed lands, the number of towns and cities grew during the eleventh to the sixteenth century. Outside the large cities, people kept small livestock for milk, eggs, and occasionally meat on small plots of land. Bread was a staple food everywhere. Women would bring wheat grains to the communal mill and grind it into flour, although the very poor often supplemented the small amount they purchased with less costly barley, oats, beans, or chestnuts. In the villages and larger settlements, most people purchased their breads and pies from local bakers or baked their own foods in communal ovens, because only the very wealthy had ovens inside their homes.[3] Most common was an indoor hearth for heating and cooking food in a pot over a fire or warming it on heated stones. Communal butchers would slaughter larger animals for meat. Taverns made and served ale and wine and provided meals and beds for the night to travelers. While women were the primary cooks in homes, professional food preparers were usually men. Among the wealthy and nobility, male and female servants were in charge of or helped with domestic food preparation—the wealthier the householder, the more specialized the servants.[4] In Arab courts, chief cooks held very high status, and some composed learned treatises on banquet dishes in verse.[5]

In both the Muslim and Christian empires, medieval consumers had a reliable quantity of food. Except during periodic bad harvests, food staples were available. People knew how to preserve some foods for future use, such as salted or dried fish and meat and cheeses. The markets (*suq*s) and bazaars in the coastal cities of North Africa and the inland cities of the Islamic states in the Levant and Mesopotamia were places where food sellers sold their plentiful and varied foods such as already prepared meats, baked goods, snacks, drinks, spices, fruits, and vegetables. The extensive trade provided variety, although "New World" foods such as the potato, tomato, corn, cacao, and turkey were still unknown in the "old-world" lands. Arab and Jewish merchants acquired foods in the Mediterranean markets and sold them across distant lands. Jews played an important role in producing refined sugar and exporting it as well as spices and citrus fruits, and they of course ensured that foods required for Jewish rituals, such as *etrogim* (citrons) for the holiday of Sukkot, were available.[6] The wealthy living in the Christian West prized sugar and distilled flavorings produced through Arab technological innovations, spices imported from the East, and the elaborate sweet-and-sour stews and pies originating in the Muslim East. The pies and vermicelli eaten by Jewish communities in both Italy and Andalusia (southern Spain) were made according to recipes that originated in the Islamic East, and the *flodens* (fried flat cakes) and *kugels* (noodle puddings) of Central and Eastern European Jewish cuisine were introduced by traveling Jewish merchants.[7]

People drank a wide range of beverages. The most common was water and fermented or unfermented fruit juices. In Northern Europe, the typical drink was ale, cider, and mead (honey-based alcohol). Wine was the favored choice throughout the medieval world, even though Islamic law regarded it with it some disapproval.[8] It was often prepared in sweetened and spiced blends; infused with sage, roses, or cloves; or combined with ready-made mixtures of powdered spices and sugar. According to medical treatises from both Christian and Islamic lands, wine was beneficial to health.[9]

Regional agriculture, bad harvests, costs, and preservability shaped the diet, but religious factors also played a role. Christians were supposed to refrain from eating meat during the forty days of Lent and on Fridays year round, and there were numerous fast days in the religious calendar. Islam prohibited pork, alcohol, and blood, and the yearly month-long celebration of Ramadan required fasting during the day and feasting at night. Jewish law allowed only meat slaughtered by a Jew and prohibited a number of land animals, fish, and fowl. These were merely the larger principles; numerous religious customs and rules shaped everyone's eating practices.

Yet dietary religious distinction may have been a lot less pronounced than we might imagine, especially for the poor, whose less meaty and simpler diet was similar across the globe. Some religious food proscriptions, especially those that required separation from the foods of others, were probably not universally observed when religious groups lived in close proximity. Jews, Muslims, and Christians would share communal ovens. From the Muslim East to the Christian European West, they interacted with one another in the production, trade, and consumption of food and drink. We know of such intermingling because religious and sometimes political authorities decried and legislated against it. For example, Christian authorities legislated against Christians purchasing from Jewish butchers the parts of kosher animals unfit for kosher consumption, and Jewish, Christian, and Muslim clerics lamented that their coreligionists were socializing together over wine.

Because of the greater distance between Jewish population centers, a pronounced differentiation between Jewish cuisines appeared. The Jews of Spain, called Sephardim, as well as the Jews living in the lands to the east bordering the Mediterranean had what is now called a Mediterranean diet: primarily grains, wine, olive oil, vegetables and nuts, and small amounts of meat and fish. The Ashkenazim, or the Jews living in northern, central, and eastern Europe, relied on root vegetables, legumes, and fermented foods (including fish like herring) better suited to the shorter growing seasons and long winters. Significant differences in *kashrut*, the dietary laws, between Sephardic and Ashkenazic Jews began to appear at the end of the medieval era.

Political and Rabbinic Authority and Jewish Foodways

The political framework of medieval society affirmed both Jews' legitimacy as members of society and their corporate legal separatism—that is, their right to choose their communal leaders and live according to their own laws within the larger political-legal unit. Jews were not legally segregated but often lived clustered together in sections of towns and villages; it was only in the early sixteenth century that Christians and Muslim authorities imposed residential segregation upon Jews in some lands. Even where such residential segregation occurred, we have much evidence that Jews and gentiles had social contact with one another in each other's designated neighborhoods.

In the medieval period, the majority of Jews lived in Muslim lands in the eastern Mediterranean, North Africa, and other Arab lands. Muslims ruled Spain, which Jews called Sepharad, from the eighth to the twelfth century, and then it was gradually overtaken by Christian rulers. Muslims considered Jews and Christians "people of the Book" and therefore "protected peoples" (*dhimmi*) who held property rights, freedom of movement and occupation, and permission to practice their religion in peace. Nevertheless, the Pact of Umar—a political-religious document attributed to the second Muslim caliph—made them "second-class citizens" politically, socially, and theologically subordinate to Muslims. Jews in the multireligious Islamic lands tended to fare better than they did in Christian lands. In the former, they shared the language (Arabic—though Jews often wrote it in Hebrew letters), analogous religious legal traditions (*Shari'ah* and the oral Torah, respectively), literate intellectual traditions (Aristotelian and Neo-Platonic philosophy, Arabic poetry, and belles lettres), and even the common dietary prohibition of eating pork.[10] In some lands, Jewish rabbinic authorities rose to prominent positions in Islamic imperial courts.

Under the Abbasid Caliphate beginning in 750, Jewish self-governing rule became centralized under rabbinic leaders known as *Geonim* (discussed briefly in the previous chapter). Headquartered near the Islamic capital of Baghdad, they supplied the religious and social structures for the predominately urban Jewish communities in Spain, North Africa, and what the Jews called Babylonia (present-day Iraq and Persia). The Geonim were responsible for making the Babylonian Talmud the preferred basis for Jewish law (over the Palestinian Talmud) and for the standardization of Jewish prayer in the *siddur* ("order [of prayer]") that established the basic structure for subsequent Jewish liturgy. They disseminated their influence through their writings and by appointing rabbis who had been educated in geonic academies to distant communities. By the eleventh century, they had less control over Jewish communities at a distance. For example, influential rabbinic teachers in the Jewish communities of Egypt and Spain established independent local rule.[11]

In the eastern and especially western Christian lands, Jews lived under the protection and by the permission of local kings and lords, but they were treated as a subordinate group as a punishment for rejecting Christianity. They could not own land, and they were subject to professional restrictions and sometimes distinguishing dress requirements (special hats or badges). Jews' differences from their Christian neighbors and their sense of unity with one another were strengthened by their unique vernacular—for example, Judeo-Greek in Byzantine lands and Yiddish (Judeo-German) in the German and Slavic regions of Christian Europe. In addition, Jews had a higher level of literacy.

In Christian Europe, Jewish authority tended to be more decentralized than in the Islamic empire. Compared to the Islamic lands in northern Africa, the Middle East, and Muslim Spain, Ashkenazic Jewry tended to be more dispersed. As in the Islamic empire, Christian rulers delegated the direction of internal Jewish communal affairs to the Jews themselves. However, in Ashkenazic lands, Jewish governance typically operated at the local level under the most prominent—usually the wealthiest—members of the Jewish community, who then appointed specific rabbis as authorities of *halakhah* (Jewish law). Local Jewish communities had their own courts and administered their day-to-day affairs, such as arranging marriages and burials, appointing communal butchers and bakers, and so on. These separate communal institutions were not readily available in towns where there were only a few Jewish families. Even in Jewish communities that were big enough to support them, the rabbis' authority tended to be more limited in its geographic influence.[12]

As elsewhere, local rabbis directly engaged with the most mundane aspects of communal life, like the production, trade, preparation, and consumption of food, and adjudicated and even published written works addressing the questions and controversies that emerged from these activities. These dispersed rabbinic authorities communicated with each other and read each other's works (albeit in handwritten and copied manuscripts, since the printing press was invented in the fifteenth century). The rabbis of the Jewish communities in the Iberian Peninsula (Muslim Andalusia and Christian Castile, Aragon, and Catalonia) and Provence in southern France played a particularly important bridging role between Christian and Islamic cultures, since many were fluent both in Arabic and Hebrew and some in the vernaculars of their lands. Hebrew functioned as a lingua franca for the sharing of Jewish lore and law.

In the feudal system of Christian Europe, Jews were special subjects of the crown, but locally they were dependent upon the nobles on whose lands they lived. Christian rulers found it economically advantageous to protect the Jewish communities in their lands because of Jews' commercial contacts across the European continent and in the Muslim world and because Jews, unlike Christians, could lend them money. Jewish religious distinctiveness and economic roles could make them hated by their Christian neighbors, foster resentment among their Christian debtors, and subject Jews to the whims and political expedience of their Christian protectors who could expel or permit violence against them. Jews were expelled en masse from England, France, and the Germanic lands in the thirteenth through the sixteenth centuries, and their eastward migration brought them to Poland and Lithuania. Periodically the Catholic authorities mounted campaigns to convert the Jews—for example, in the campaigns of the Franciscan and Dominican orders in the thirteenth century and the humiliating disputations in which Christian clerics (some were Jewish converts to Christianity) "debated" Jewish leaders to prove the theological superiority of Christianity over Judaism. The Christian rulers of Spain sanctioned anti-Jewish riots and forced conversions from the late fourteenth century onward until they expelled all Jews in 1492.[13]

Rabbis believed that Jews' political and social denigration by gentiles was at odds with the elevated status Jews should have had. From their perspective, Jews were God's "chosen" people, morally superior and more educated than their non-Jewish neighbors. Medieval rabbis regarded it as their task to protect this status by studying, elaborating upon, and recording rules for the conduct of Jewish life. They were concerned to put all Jewish life under their understanding of Torah, and food practices were just one aspect of this larger goal. We do not know with certainty the extent to which these Jewish laws and practices developed in the medieval period were actually being followed and by whom, but we do know medieval Jewish rabbinic leaders possessed the authority to promulgate the food practices, and they were regarded by Jews and non-Jews as an elite in relation to other Jews.

There are a number of important figures whose writings contain key teachings on Jewish food and who will be referenced in this chapter. The Geonim from the eighth to the eleventh century laid the post-Talmudic foundation for Jewish practice. After them, Rabbi Moses ben Maimon (also known as Rambam or Maimonides, 1135–1204) in Islamic Spain (Andalusia) and Egypt wrote an influential code of law called *Mishneh Torah*. Rabbi Jacob ben Asher (1269–1340), who was born in the Christian lands of the Holy Roman Empire and then lived in Castile in Spain, produced a code called *Arba'ah Turim*. In northern France, Rabbi Shlomo Yitzhaki (also known as Rashi, 1040–1105) wrote commentaries on the Talmud. Subsequent scholars in France and Germany known as the Tosafists built upon Rashi's teachings, such as Rashi's grandson Rabbi Samuel ben Meir (also known as Rashbam, 1085–1158) and Rabbi Baruch ben Isaac of Worms (1140–1212). In Christian Spain, Rabbi Solomon ben Abraham ibn Adret (1235–1310) wrote *Torat Ha-Bayit* (Torah of the home), a legal treatise focused primarily on food and related subjects, and Rabbi Bahya ben Asher (1255–1340) assembled and systematized many disparate food traditions into a single work devoted to theory and practice of Jewish eating, titled *Shulhan Shel Arba* (Table of four). These and other rabbinic scholars commented upon, criticized, and supplemented with their particular local customs each other's teachings about food and food-related rituals, with an eye toward encouraging Jews in their communities to adopt the practices and the rationales they advocated.

Many of these medieval rabbinic traditions were eventually incorporated into what became the most authoritative code of Jewish law of the late medieval era, the *Shulhan Aruch*. Composed by Rabbi Joseph Karo (1488–1575), a Sephardic Jew who left Spain for the Ottoman Empire, the *Shulhan Aruch* represented Karo's own Sephardic Jewish customs. It was a complete summary of laws pertaining to all aspects of Jewish life, so only some sections of it were devoted specifically to food laws. Rabbi Moses Isserles of Krakow (1520–72) wrote a gloss that supplemented Karo's code with laws and customs drawn from his own Polish tradition; that is, the Sephardic and Polish traditions were preserved separately in the same work. Published in print form, the *Shulhan Aruch* was widely circulated, but it was not universally authoritative, especially for communities whose regional traditions differed. Eventually, however, the code's comprehensiveness made it the primary textual guide to *halakhah* (practical Jewish law) and codifying both "Sephardic" and "Ashkenazic" laws and customs.[14]

Jewish Food Practices within Medieval Society

The food rules and practices that medieval rabbinic authorities developed or encouraged and that had the greatest impact on subsequent Jewish foodways were in halakhah, theology, and liturgy. Although their innovations were based on earlier biblical and rabbinic traditions, their changes were clearly a response to the medieval reality. Jewish foodways under Torah as the rabbis envisioned them were to have three important effects. First, they would lessen the contact of Jews with gentiles. This had been an element in late biblical and classical rabbinic-era food practices, and the medieval rabbis were continuing and strengthening it. Second, rabbis suggested a stricter standard for themselves than what they could reasonably demand from the Jewish community at large. In doing so, they were demonstrating their superior piety and bolstering their credentials and class status upon which their Jewish authority was based. Third, rabbinic authorities sought to dignify and sanctify eating for all Jews—male and female, rich and poor—and counteract the social and theological humiliation intended by Islamic and Christian rulers. Rabbi Bahya ben Asher states this last point quite explicitly:

> We are distinguished by our regimen of pleasures from the nations who err, rebel, and sin. . . . In the desert . . . [God] set for us a table against the nations. . . . He gave us a marvelous portion of the bread in our law . . . [The] Torah of the Lord with us will save us. . . . The food on our table will help us recognize and remind ourselves to respect His greatness. Let us bless over the table of Him whose food we have eaten. It is not so with the wicked, whose sins have earned them an inextinguishable fire; their table lies before them like mire. Rising early in the morning they devour food and they do not call to the Lord; their hearts and eyes they raise to what delights them, but toward the One above not even the slightest look. Such is the sentence of the nations, that they are a vile and foolish nation filled with folk devoid of sense.[15]

It is important to remember the fundamental similarities, social interactions, and resources shared between Jews, Muslims, and Christians in the medieval era. Bahya's accentuation of differences between Jewish and gentile regimens of eating is more aspirational than it was reflective of the actual differences in what and how Jews and non-Jews ate and drank.

Indeed, medieval Islamic, Christian, and Jewish cuisines shared elements of what Rachel Laudan regards as a prevailing culinary philosophy. Christian and Muslim scholars clarified culinary principles in their learned tracts, and when Christian and Muslim rulers imposed these religions on their empires, they were also imposing a cuisine. By virtue of their inclusion in these empires and in broader cultural life, Jewish intellectuals accepted these principles and adapted them to Judaism.

One common notion, originating in ancient Greek medicine, was the belief that the human body contained four distinct humors (bodily fluids) that needed to be kept in balance. Medieval scholars advised which food and food combinations preserved or harmed the right balance of the humors. Furthermore, they believed that fire refined and purified the essence of the food and so enabled cooked food to be more healthful than fresh or raw food. Another common belief was that there was a hierarchy in modes of eating. That is, there was a distinction between the "high" cuisines for the court and humble cuisines for the urban and rural poor. The religious elite adapted this to elevate their own diet and thus their status over that of conventionally religious people.[16] Finally, Laudan argues that a third principle was a new understanding of sanctified eating: the medieval religious elite believed that ascetic or very regimented diets would bring salvation or enlightenment.[17] In the halakhic, ritual, and theological developments described in the rest of this chapter, these components of the medieval culinary philosophy find expression in new forms of Jewish eating.

Halakhic Innovations in Jewish Dietary Laws

Jewish communities throughout the medieval world eventually adopted three significant medieval expansions of food halakhah: enhanced prohibitions against mixing meat and milk, the prohibition of drinking the wine of gentiles, and Passover stringencies.

MEAT AND DAIRY

Medieval religious authorities broadened the thrice-repeated biblical commandment "You shall not boil a kid in its mother's milk" (Exodus 23:19, 34:26; Deuteronomy 14:21). As discussed in the preceding chapter, this precept was interpreted by the rabbis of the Mishnah and Talmud to prohibit mixing or cooking together all permitted milk products and land animals and to prohibit serving them together at the table—that is, during the same meal. Some rabbis adopted a stringent practice of waiting after eating meat before consuming milk and milk products, but the general rule was that it was sufficient to wipe one's mouth and hands or wash these with water to remove the residual tastes or particles of dairy and meat and maintain the separation between the foods.[18] The Geonim of the post-Talmudic era (eighth to eleventh century) generally followed these traditions.

During the following years, changes in the interpretation of the law are evident in certain regions. First, by the twelfth century, some rabbis specified the length of the temporal pause between eating meat and dairy. In *Mishneh Torah* and *Arba'ah Turim*, law codes composed in Sephardic Jewish societies, a six-hour wait after eating meat before eating milk products is required; this waiting time did not apply to eating meat after dairy. The rabbis of northern Ashkenazic Europe did not immediately adopt this Sephardic practice.[19] Second, in Ashkenazic lands, fowl was regarded in the category of meat (and therefore subject to the meat and dairy prohibitions), whereas Italian and Sephardic rabbis did not do so until some point in the sixteenth century. Third, in Ashkenazic lands, meticulously pious Jews began to insist upon maintaining separate dairy and meat pots and cooking utensils. For example, Rabbi Baruch ben Isaac (1140–1212) prohibits a spoon used for milk foods to stir a pot filled with a meat stew, and he notes that items used for milk foods should not be washed with items used to cook meat.[20] In the fourteenth century, the Sephardic *Arba'ah Turim* code requires that if metal pots are used to cook one category of food, they cannot be used to cook the other category of food unless they are first "koshered"; in contrast, ceramic pots used for one category could not be "koshered" and reused to cook food of another category. Rabbi Jacob ben Moses Moellin (ca. 1360–1427) of Germany affirms this in his summary of dietary laws, and he adds that the separate cooking utensils are in themselves considered dairy or meat, as opposed to just the foodstuffs cooked in them.[21]

It is important to consider what these new opinions can and cannot teach about actual common Jewish practice. We do not know whether the rules, most of which are performed in the privacy of the home, were generally obeyed. The consumption of meat increased in Europe during the late Middle Ages, and this would have increased the opportunity to honor the dairy-meat taboo.[22] While the rabbis were reluctant to add expensive restrictions, the requirement to wait a specific number of hours after eating meat did not add any costs. This was in contrast to the rabbinic rulings for physically separating meat and dairy pots and utensils. Given the meager set of cooking and serving utensils typical in the homes of the era, it seems unlikely that most Jews could afford separate cooking pots and utensils. Only those who aspired to the status of "holy" and who had the means would adopt this practice; scholars surmise that perhaps wealthier women, even more than men, were responsible for this stringency. Furthermore, at this time, no Jews in North Africa and Palestine were maintaining separate cooking pots and utensils.[23] Therefore, the Ashkenazic rabbinic authorities were fostering an intra-Jewish distinction between Ashkenazic and non-Ashkenazic Jews as well as between elite Jews who observed more stringent, more ascetic interpretations of rabbinic dietary rules and Jews who did not.[24]

WINE

As this chapter explained earlier, in lands where people of different religions lived side by side with each other, they also produced food alongside or with each other and bought food from and sold food to each other. Religious and sometimes political authorities discouraged some of these interactions, and the conclusion that these authorities were ignored is evident in their repeated complaints about and rulings against such mixing. The rabbis considered wine the most important food to keep separate. The previous chapter in this volume describes Talmudic rabbis' prohibitions and limitations on Jews' consumption of gentile-made wine and joint efforts in production, consumption, and drinking together of even Jewish-made wine. Yet we know that during the medieval era, some Jews worked with gentiles in wine production and trade. In Christian Europe, particularly in France, Spain, and Italy, Jews produced, traded in, and consumed wine. Jewish wine production frequently brought Jews into contact with Christians who worked in their vineyards and purchased their wine.[25] Rabbi Abraham ben Nathan Ha-Yarchi, writing in thirteenth-century Muslim Spain, reported that some Sephardic communities have no concern whatsoever that their wine might be produced and handled by Muslims. He wrote, "There are persons [Jews] who purchase their wine during the harvest season in villages in the house of Gentiles, and the Gentiles measure out the wine and give i[t] to the Jews in their skins. . . ."[26] Despite Islamic prohibitions on drinking alcohol, Muslims (especially those in the courtier classes) did imbibe. The rabbi expressed dismay that Jews drank wine with Muslims, echoing the Talmudic rabbis' fear of wine leading to intimate neighborly relations.

Medieval Jewish religious authorities had to interpret Talmudic wine prohibitions in light of the new realities. Did Talmudic proscriptions against drinking the wine of idol worshipers apply to the practitioners of Islam, who not only were monotheists but also rejected the use of icons? Was Christianity idolatry and was the use of wine in the Eucharist tantamount to offering libations to idols? To what extent should the economic realities, in which people of different religions worked and traded with each other, mitigate the inherited rabbinic prohibitions? Rabbinic decisions on wine provided parameters for the marking and crossing of social boundaries between Jews and gentiles and boundaries between a Jewish religious elite (who would follow rabbinic principles strictly) and ordinary Jews.

Medieval Jewish authorities proffered many nuanced opinions, but a glance at the rulings of three of them provides a range of some of the responses. Maimonides, who lived in Muslim lands, determined that Muslims are not idol worshippers, and so he permitted Jewish-made wine handled by Muslims for drink and trade. However, Maimonides considered Christians idol worshipers, and he regarded both their wine and Jewish-made wine touched by Christians to be off limits.[27] Second, Rabbi Samuel ben Meir, who lived in an Ashkenazic Christian cultural context, regarded the status of Christianity and Islam vis-à-vis idolatry as irrelevant, and he prohibited the wine of all gentiles and Jewish-made wine touched by them "because of their daughters"—that is, to preserve social segregation.[28] Third, Rabbi Solomon ben Abraham ibn Adret, who lived under Muslim and then Christian rule in thirteenth- and fourteenth-century Spain, recognized no drinking and financial prohibitions on certain fermented, intoxicating drinks made by Jews and handled by non-Jews, such as beer, boiled wine (*yayin mevushal*), or wine mixed with significant amounts of honey and pepper.[29]

Medieval rabbinic leniencies in the Islamic world on the grounds that Muslims are not idolaters may indicate a positive assessment of Islam or a more collegial relationship between Jews, Christians, and Muslims in Muslim Spain, or it could simply be an after-the-fact concession to the realities of Jewish-Muslim commercial and social interactions.[30] Rabbinic rulings were more restrictive in Christian lands. They had the effect of intensifying earlier prohibitions on drinking or deriving financial benefit from gentile wine and actually worked to the financial disadvantage of Jewish wine producers and dealers in northern France.[31] Wherever they lived, Jewish, Muslim, and Christian leaders were deeply invested in differentiating their religions and their congregations from each other. A different diet indicated a different identity. In Islamic lands, drinking wine was a sign distinguishing Jews from the Muslim majority (though not the elite courtier class) and associating them with Christian minorities. Pork abstention associated Jews with the Muslim majority and separated them from Christian minorities. Conversely, in Christian lands, Jews' avoidance of pork and blood differentiated them from the Christian majority, and it associated them with Muslim minorities.

PASSOVER STRINGENCIES

New halakhic demands also appeared for Passover foods. Biblical and rabbinic law prohibited the consumption of leavened forms of five grains (wheat, barley, rye, oats, and spelt). Beginning in the thirteenth century, European rabbis added a new restriction, a category of food they called *kitniyot* that includes legumes and rice. The underlying reason for this is unclear and was unclear even then. One medieval rabbinic authority from Provence explained that these foods "rise and become *hametz*" (leavened), noting that this was the accepted and "universal custom" among the rabbinic authorities in Ashkenaz. Another suggestion was that it is a stringency to avoid mistakenly eating hametz, because lentils and other beans could look like and be ground like wheat kernels. Perhaps the prohibition was the result of the European cultural belief that legumes were a "poor person's foods" and beneath the dignity of celebratory holiday food.[32] The practice did not extend outside of Ashkenaz. To this day, Sephardim and Jews with background in Muslim lands enjoy kitniyot on Passover, while Ashkenazic Jews continue to debate whether it is necessary to avoid them.[33]

Another Passover stringency originating in Ashkenazic lands was the mode of preparing matzah, the unleavened bread specially prepared for Passover. Matzah was a flatbread similar to what was typically eaten in the Mediterranean region, although no leavening would be added, and women of the household made it in a pan over a fire. At the Passover Seder meal, when participants recounted the story of the Exodus by use of food symbols arrayed on the table, they rolled this matzah around the *maror* (bitter herb) dipped in *haroset* (fruit relish) to make a type of sandwich.[34] Because such matzah would become stale quickly, women baked it frequently during the holiday. The change first occurred in fifteenth-century Germany, when rabbis ruled that in order to reduce the chance of natural leavening, enough matzah for the entire holiday should be prepared prior to the holiday by baking it at a high temperature in an oven; thus, matzah became a hard and dry cracker-like food. This demand removed matzah baking from women's domestic responsibilities and turned it over to communally designated men.

Although these examples of different Sephardic and Ashkenazic dietary practices during Passover seem to be influenced by what was most easily available seasonally in their respective regions, it is also clear that cultural factors were at work. Ashkenazic rabbinic authorities were choosing more stringent and more ascetic eating practices in these instances (Sephardic authorities chose more stringent standards in other aspects of kashrut[35]), exemplifying the "principle of hierarchy" typical of theocratic cuisines. Regional traditions were respected more than uniformity in worldwide Jewish practice. As in the case of the new meat and dairy demands, the rabbis were encouraging intra-Jewish distinctions between those who adopted their elite cuisines and those who did not.

New Liturgy and Theology: Eating with Books and Words of Torah

When Jews today read from wine-stained illustrated books at a modern Passover Seder or sing the Kiddush and grace after meals from a little booklet, they may feel that having books at the table during meals is normal and something that people (or at least Jewish people) have been doing from time immemorial.[36] However, only in the rabbinic era did the practice of speaking words of Torah at the table become part of Jewish practice, and having actual physical books started centuries later. Four ways of ritualizing eating and Torah study at the table appear in the medieval era. Medieval Christians recognized Jews as matzah eaters and pig abstainers, but through these table practices, Jews declared themselves "Torah eaters."

MEDIEVAL HAGGADOT

An important innovation from the medieval era was the development of the Passover *Haggadah*, the written text used to fulfill the commandment to recount the Exodus from Egypt during the evening meal on the first night of Passover, the Seder meal. Neither biblical nor Talmudic rabbinic writers mandated a script for the recounting of the Exodus, although the latter specified that certain topics must be included. Further, special foods are eaten in a set order—matzah, maror, haroset, and the matzah wrapped around the maror—and the participants are obligated to talk about these foods. According to the Mishnaic teaching, which became part of the Haggadah, "Rabban Gamliel used to say, 'Whoever does not mention these three things on Passover does not discharge his duty, and these are the Passover-offering, unleavened bread, and bitter herbs.'"[37] The Geonim first compiled separate scripts for the recounting in the seventh and eighth centuries, and thereafter many other versions appeared in which the basic elements of the service were augmented by commentaries, poetry, and *midrash*—that is, imaginative interpretations and applications of biblical passages. The purpose of the written Haggadot (plural) was to stimulate diners—men and women alike—to make dynamic associations between their ritual actions, their sense experiences of the food and drink, and their lives as followers of Torah.

Handmade illuminated versions of the Haggadah first appeared in the Christian lands in thirteenth-century Spain. These may have originally served to keep the children attentive to the Seder lessons or to stimulate discussion for children and adults by making visual associations of the Exodus story. Because of some of the details in the illuminations of the Haggadot, Katrin Kogman-Appel suggests they may have been composed in collaboration with popular preachers and rabbis.[38] Historians have noted that the phenomenon of illuminated Haggadot occurred during a time when the towns and cities were growing, and the greater security and wealth in such places enabled the establishment of book-making workshops. The small size of the Haggadah meant that the head of a Jewish family could afford to commission a simple illuminated version for the use in his home, and quite a few of these handwritten manuscripts from fourteenth- and fifteenth-century Germany have survived. The advent of printing changed matters even more dramatically, democratizing access to the books needed for the ritual practices of reading and eating.[39]

A class differentiation within the Haggadot is also evident. Illuminated Haggadot such as the Rylands, Sarajevo, and Golden Haggadot, with their fine calligraphy and lavish decorations, were obviously commissioned by very wealthy and educated Jews. They had both the financial means and the contacts to engage artists to produce Jewish books in accordance with their own tastes and religious needs of like high quality and in the contemporary style. Unlike the Christian books, however, the wine and food stains show that these Haggadot were actually used at the table. Furthermore, the images in the Jewish books asserted Jewish religious superiority. Michael Batterman suggests that depictions of the preparation and pictorial depiction of flat, round *matzot* (plural of matzah) in the illuminated Sephardic Haggadot, images characteristically painted in gold with elaborate geometric designs on them, may have been implicit, symbolic assertions of cultural equality or superiority to the dominant Christian Spanish culture. The matzah appears as a potent force and a badge of Jewish efficacy, empowering Jews culturally to respond to the Christian threat and to fortify their own position. The rituals, customary practices, and visual images of Passover functioned as polemical tools and lessons for the Jewish participants.[40]

EATING TORAH AS A JEWISH BOY'S INITIATION RITE
Another ritual connecting eating and learning is an initiation rite that first appeared in Jewish literature in twelfth-century Germany. Performed in the springtime between the holidays of Passover and Shavuot, it marked the beginning of formal Torah study for boys when they were five or six years old. The father wrapped the boy in a *tallit* (prayer shawl) and carried him to the home of his teacher. The child was placed on his teacher's lap and shown his writing slate, upon which honey was spread, and the boy was directed to lick the honey off the tablet. He was served peeled hard-boiled eggs and honey cake inscribed with Hebrew alphabet and some biblical phrases, and blessings and incantations against a demon of forgetfulness were recited.[41]

Although the ritual did not become widely practiced among Jewry as a whole, it demonstrates the association of eating and Torah study that emerged in the medieval era. At its simplest level, the ritual showed the young student that Torah study was pleasurable and desirable; it affirmed for his father and teacher the value of the boy's education and the importance of their own role in furthering it. The historian Ivan Marcus has shown that this ritual makes a deeper statement: when the child enters the stage in his life when he can study Torah, "the child enters the Torah (*nichnas la-torah*) by means of the Torah entering the child."[42] Through the consumption of Hebrew letters, Jews were asserting that they were people of Torah. They created this ritual to contrast with the primary religious ritual of the Christian majority, the Eucharist, which presented a holy wafer and wine as the body and blood of Christ to be eaten by the worshiper. The Jewish initiation ritual actually was inverting the symbolic meaning of the Eucharist. Scorned by Christians as deniers of Christ and, in extreme situations, as Christ killers and murderers of young Christian males in order to ritually use their blood, Jews "expressed elements of their Jewish religious cultural identity by internalizing and transforming various genres, motifs, terms, institutions, or rituals of the majority cultural in a polemical, parodic, or neutralized manner." Medieval Jews were giving the ingestion of Torah a symbolic power as a marker of distinctively Jewish identity, proclaiming themselves a people of the Torah.[43]

KABBALISTIC EATING

A new "theology of eating" emerged in twelfth- through fourteenth-century Provence and Christian Spain in Kabbalah, the collective term for writings and activities that are understood as "secret wisdom" transmitted over the generations by a rabbinic elite. These teachings include knowledge of God's inner workings, God's design of the universe, and the means to continually sustain and repair the world. The Zohar, the primary written document of Kabbalah, revived the metaphor of the biblical sacrifices for eating and deepened the rabbinic idea of the domestic table as a *mikdash me'at*, an altar or "mini-Temple." Medieval kabbalists taught that when enlightened Torah scholars eat with the proper intentions—this is fostered by discussing appropriate passages from the written and oral Torahs and reciting rabbinic table blessings—they are engaging in worship that is functionally equivalent to the service of the priests in the time of the Temple. Such a meal maintains the Divine Presence in the midst of the people of Israel and returns the divine energy in foods to its source.[44] The kabbalistic texts imagine these Torah scholars primarily as male, but there is nothing in principle that prohibits Jewish women from engaging in these or similar rites. Although the first practitioners of this kabbalistic eating were a small elite, their ideas spread to broader circles in many lands within decades.

A typical example of the kabbalistic interpretation of earlier ideas is the reworking of the biblical phrase "This is the torah [law] of beast and fowl" (Leviticus 11:46) as a theodicy justifying meat eating based on a theory of reincarnation.[45] They built upon an earlier Jewish tradition that, upon God's request, animals consented to be killed for food. According to kabbalistic teaching, an animal's soul may be reincarnated and raised to a higher level if the one consuming the animal is higher up in the great chain of being.[46] They explain this by comparing a Torah scholar's digestion to the sacrificial fires of the Temple in the *olah* sacrifice, the sacrifice that is totally consumed and ascends to its original source in God. The Hebrew Bible describes the offering being turned into *re'ah niho'ah*, "a pleasing aroma," before God. The intellect of the Torah scholar has the "fire" lit by the "light" of Torah—in contrast to the unlearned Jew—which enables him to "cook" denser, meatier substances into refined intellectual and spiritual "soul" or divine food. Foods that are considered more easily "raised," since they have souls that are less earthbound such as fowl or grain (birds fly in the air, plants grow "up"), may be eaten by the unlearned. Only Torah scholars should consume beasts that tread on the land with cloven hooves.[47] In fact, we know that medieval Jews ate red meat no matter their educational or spiritual status. However, this new theology of eating enacts the principle of hierarchy typical of theocratic cuisines: "if you are a holy man, eat like a holy man."

Another description of kabbalistic eating by Torah scholars defines it as a visionary, prophetic experience similar to that of the meal of the elders of Israel after the revelation at Sinai, referenced in Exodus 24:11: "And they *envisioned* (*va-yehezu*) God, and they ate and drank."[48] Further, such "real eating," as it was sometimes called, fuses together nourishment of the body and soul simultaneously and in a unified, mutually sustaining way. Kabbalists imagined this occurring both in this world and in the "world to come" after death and in the Messianic era.

RITUAL MANUALS AT NON-PASSOVER MEALS

Much of the kabbalistic theology of eating was disseminated in a new kind of book, a ritual manual, exemplified by Rabbi Bahya ben Asher's *Shulhan Shel Arba*. Bahya composed his eating manual to be used at the table in order that eating could be transformed into sanctified dining and so elevate participants to their highest potential. He understood the ritual enactment of eating as an act of receiving divine revelation.

Bahya divided his book into four "Gates" that provide reading and discussion material for the meal's duration. In the First Gate are the distinctive Jewish meal rituals of blessings and hand washing. In the Second Gate, he presents the kabbalistic interpretation of the "physiology" of eating as a sacred act that achieves the multiple effects described in the Zohar. Table manners fitting such lofty purposes are the subject of the Third Gate, and the Messianic Banquet reserved for the righteous at the end of time is described in the Fourth Gate. In each gate, Bahya provides interpretations of certain specific passages from the Torah.[49] While he did not organize his book as a script to be recited, he expects readers to glean talking points from the book to be discussed during meals. *Shulhan Shel Arba* functions like a running commentary, enumerating and providing extensive explanations of the specific blessings, washing, and other table rituals prescribed for Jewish meals. Bahya is prompting a chain of associations that transform a meal into a replication of the meal of manna in the desert wilderness, the experience of prophetic vision on Mount Sinai, divine service, and a foretaste of the Messianic world of the future. Here is Bahya's description of the effect of such a meal:

> And thus it is necessary that when one eats, he turn his thought (*mahshevato*) so that it rambles about (*meshotetet*) the Holy One Blessed Be He over each and every bite—according to the matter of "They envisioned God and they ate and drank" [Exodus 24:11].[50] This is like the way our sages interpreted "Let all that breathe (*kol ha-neshamah*) praise the Lord," over each and every breath (*kol neshimah ve-neshimah*) give praise to Him. . . . So you find yourself learning that *when a person stands over his table and eats with this thought in mind*, see! This eating is indeed physical and a natural activity, but see! It also revolves into a higher, intellectual

form of worship, and this is the reason why it is written, "In all your ways know Him," [Proverbs 3:6] as I discussed above. And if so, you see how one's eating is thought to be a perfect act of worship like one of the forms of divine service [i.e., the sacrifices], and the quintessential command- ment of all the commandments. And this is the point of having the right intention at a meal at the table—that the body be nourished by it and take its bodily portion from the bodily eating, and the soul by this act of thought is filled, fed, and satisfied as if from the choicest parts of "real eat- ing" of the ways of Ha-Shem [God] and His pleasantness, and regarding this it is said, "Your table is laid out with rich food" [Job 36:16].[51]

Furthermore, Bahya frequently employs demonstrative pronouns to make sure his readers make the explicit connection to the Temple altar—for example, the declaration "*This* is the table before the Lord!" (Ezekiel 41:22). He likens the physical gesture of ritually washing one's hands prior to eating and raising the ten fingers of one's hands upward to energy flowing up from the toes through the body and connecting back to the divine heavenly source. The words recited at the meal are like the smells and sights of aromatic oils and smoke wafting up to the heavens at the ancient Temple altar.

This high evaluation of eating in medieval Jewish thought not only enhanced the social status of the Jewish scholars who know the secrets of their ritualized eating in comparison to unlearned Jews; it also prom- ised an enhanced social status to even unlearned Jews over the non- Jews in power who legislated Jews' political and theological humiliation. By making Torah into a regimen over the appetites that distinguished Jews from gentiles, the Torah itself becomes the metonymic Jewish food—that is, it represents the Jews. When one attaches the words of Torah to the foods one eats while at the table, the food itself becomes a revelation of Torah, like the "real eating" that sustained Moses as he received the Torah from God. The multisensory, synesthetic experience of saying, hearing, seeing words of Torah with one's companions and touching "words of Torah" in books at the table becomes a way of "tast- ing" Torah at the table.

Bahya's *Shulhan Shel Arba* was popular. During the medieval era, it was copied relatively frequently in handy, table-sized formats.[52] In the fourteenth and fifteenth centuries, kabbalistic ideas and practices spread to all corners of medieval Jewish society, in Muslim as well as Christian lands, and Bahya's ritual manual played an important role. From 1500 to 1800, kabbalistic theology was accepted on the popular level in a simpler form and integrated into religious practices, legend, song, and ethics. Bahya's eating manual continued to be read and appeared in printed form, and it may be that it was an influential source for the other "theologies of eating" and liturgical compositions that appeared.[53] For example, in early eighteenth-century Ukraine, Sarah bas Tovim wrote a book of women's petitionary prayers, *The Tkhine of the Three Gates*, that equates the Jewish women's practice of separating a small piece of dough (*hallah*) and lighting the candles at the Shabbat table to the sacrificial worship of the high priest at the ancient Temple.[54] Later in that century and the next, Hasidic Jews likewise elevated all types of eating to the level of priestly worship. They used the term *avodah be-gashmiyut* (worship through material things) to refer to the process of "raising sparks" of divinity trapped in the material world and returning them to their source in the divine realm. This special worship can occur through all sorts of daily activities, but most frequently it occurs through eating in accordance with Jewish law.[55]

Conclusion

During the medieval era, the expansion of the Jewish Diaspora brought far more variety into religious life. Jewish communities became established in lands with far different climate and agriculture than before. Jewish cuisine expanded to include different foods and modes of food preparation than in the past. The authority of the rabbinic class increased, and rabbis produced a great number of halakhic and theological writings that touched all areas of Jewish life. Regional differentiation in food customs and laws became apparent, although the publication of law codes with wide appeal kept a measure of unity in religious practice. As before, rabbinic authorities sought to preserve Jewish cultural separateness despite interreligious collaboration in food preparation and trade. The rabbis were acutely aware of the pressures upon Jews—sometimes fierce, oftentimes friendly—to accept the religious views and practices of their non-Jewish neighbors and business associates. The developments in halakhah about separating meat and dairy, gentile wine and "mixed drinking," and Passover stringencies should be regarded partly as efforts to create a distinctive, sacred mode of Jewish eating in a challenging social and religious context. These and new Jewish food rituals enhanced the status of Jews as a whole in relation to the majority cultures and made a statement to Jews about the value of their religious practice. In the process, the rabbis found an outlet for their own pious expression and their sense of self-importance relative to ordinary Jews. For all Jews, eating played an important role in qualifying one to be among the righteous in this world and earning the banquet reward in heavenly world to come.

NOTES

1. Bahya, "Shulhan Shel Arba," 474.
2. Adamson, *Food in Medieval Times*, 156–58.
3. Adamson, 2.
4. Adamson, 55–57, 64, 102; Desportes, "Food Trades," 276, 278.
5. van Gelder, *God's Banquet*, 63–64.
6. Laudan, *Cuisine and Empire*, 143. Marks, *Encyclopedia*, s.v. "Sugar," 567; s.v. "Spice," 558–59; s.v. "Citrus," 134.
7. Cooper, *Eat and Be Satisfied*, 83–84.
8. Matthee, "Alcohol," 100–125.
9. Adamson, *Food in Medieval Times*, 50–51; Laudan, *Cuisine and Empire*, 137.
10. Efron, *Jews*, 151–55.
11. Efron, 156–61.
12. Efron, 178–87.
13. Efron, 184–86, 203–5.
14. Rabinowitz, *Encyclopaedia Judaica*, s.v. "Shulhan Arukh," 14:1475–77.
15. Bahya, *Shulhan*, 459.
16. Adamson, *Food in Medieval Times*, 42–44.
17. Laudan, *Cuisine and Empire*, 104.
18. Kraemer, *Jewish Eating*, 87–91.
19. Kraemer, 89–91.
20. He makes this point in his *Sefer Ha-Terumah*; also see Kraemer, *Jewish Eating*, 103.
21. This is in his *Sefer Maharil*; also see Kraemer, *Jewish Eating*, 105.
22. Kraemer, *Jewish Eating*, 93.
23. Kraemer, 102, 119–20.
24. Kraemer, 97, 106–7.
25. Soloveitchik, *Wine in Ashkenaz*, 37–39.
26. Kraemer, *Jewish Eating*, 131.
27. Freidenreich, *Foreigners*, 214.
28. Freidenreich, 219–20.

29. Ibn Adret, *Torat Ha-Bayit*, 512–13. Also see Freidenreich, 221–22.
30. Freidenreich, *Foreigners*, 220–23; Kraemer, *Jewish Eating*, 129–30.
31. Freidenreich, *Foreigners*, 216, citing the research of Haym Soloveitchik.
32. Marks, *Encyclopedia*, s.v. "Kitniyot," 316.
33. In 2016 the Conservative Movement of American Judaism overturned this prohibition; see Schoenfeid, "Conservative Movement."
34. See Marks, *Encyclopedia*, s.v. "Matza," 394; s.v. "Koraik (Wrap)," 325.
35. Marks, s.v. "Glatt," 226.
36. This section summarizes a more extensive discussion in my article "Mitzvot with the Mouth."
37. Mishnah Pesachim 10:5.
38. Kogman-Appel, *Illuminated Haggadot*, 222–23.
39. Narkiss, *Encyclopaedia Judaica*, s.v. "Haggadah, Passover: Illuminated Manuscripts."
40. Batterman, "Bread of Affliction," 61.
41. Marcus, *Rituals of Childhood*, 18–34.
42. Marcus, 77–78.
43. Marcus, 11–12. Also see Brumberg-Kraus, "Ritualization of Scripture."
44. Hecker, *Mystical Bodies*, 149–50.
45. Brumberg-Kraus, "Meat-Eating," 228–29.
46. Gikatilla, *Shaare Orah*, 11–12. See also Hecker, *Mystical Bodies*, 95–99.
47. Bahya, "Shulhan Shel Arba," 496. Also see Brumberg-Kraus, "Meat-Eating," 254.
48. Bahya, "Shulhan Shel Arba," 492–93.
49. Brumberg-Kraus, "Ritualization of Scripture," 17.
50. Bahya, "Shulhan Shel Arba," 492–93; Brumberg-Kraus, "Real Eating," 119–31.
51. Bahya, "Shulhan Shel Arba," 497.
52. Brumberg-Kraus, *Encyclopedia of the Bible*, s.v. "Communal Meals."
53. Gries, *Sifrut Ha-Hanhagot*, 82n137.
54. See Klirs, *Merit of Our Mothers*.
55. Jacobs, "Eating as an Act," 157–66. See also Hecker, "Eating," 81.

BIBLIOGRAPHY

Adamson, Melitta Weiss. *Food in Medieval Times*. Westport, CT: Greenwood, 2004.

Bahya ben Asher ben Hlava. "Shulhan Shel Arba." In *Kitve Rabenu Bahya*, edited by Charles Chavel, 453–514. Jerusalem: Mossad Ha-Rav Kuk, 1970.

———. "Shulhan Shel Arba | Jonathan Brumberg-Kraus' English Translation of Rabbenu Bahya Ben Asher's 14th Century Eating Manual." Translated by Jonathan Brumberg-Kraus. http://jkraus.webspace.wheatoncollege.edu.

Batterman, Michael. "Bread of Affliction, Emblem of Power: The Passover Matzah in Haggadah Manuscripts from Christian Spain." In *Imagining the Self, Imagining the Other: Visual Representation and Jewish-Christian Dynamics in the Middle Ages and Early Modern Period*, edited by Eva Frojmovic, 53–89. Leiden: Brill, 2002.

Brumberg-Kraus, Jonathan. "Communal Meals. IV. Judaism. C. Medieval and Modern Judaism." In *Encyclopedia of the Bible and Its Reception*. Berlin: Walter de Gruyter, 2009.

———. "Meat-Eating and Jewish Identity: Ritualization of the Priestly 'Torah of Beast and Fowl' (Lev 11:46) in Rabbinic Judaism and Medieval Kabbalah." *AJS Review* 24, no. 2 (1999): 227–62.

———. "'Mitzvot with the Mouth': Medieval and Early Modern Jewish Rituals of Eating, Reading, and Talking and Their Legacy." *Historia Religionum: An International Journal* 10 (2018): 65–78.

———. "Performing Myth, Performing Midrash at Rabbinic Meals." In *Meals in Early Judaism*, edited by Susan Marks and Hal Taussig, 99–114. New York: Palgrave Macmillan, 2014.

———. "'Real Eating': A Medieval Spanish Jewish View of Gastronomic Authenticity." In *Authenticity in the Kitchen: Proceedings of the Oxford Symposium on Food and Cookery*, 119–31. Totnes: Prospect Books, 2006.

———. "The Ritualization of Scripture in Rabbenu Bahya's Shulhan Shel Arba." *World Congress of Jewish Studies* 13 (2001): 1–17.

Brumberg-Kraus, Jonathan, Susan Marks, and Jordan D. Rosenblum. "Ten Theses Concerning Meals and Early Judaism." In *Meals in Early Judaism*, edited by Susan Marks and Hal Taussig, 13–39. New York: Palgrave Macmillan, 2014.

Cooper, John. *Eat and Be Satisfied: A Social History of Jewish Food*. Northvale, NJ: Jason Aronson, 1993.

Desportes, Françoise. "Food Trades." In *Food: A Culinary History from Antiquity to the Present*, edited by Jean Louis Flandrin and Massimo Montanari, 275–86. New York: Columbia University Press, 1999.

Efron, John, Steven Weitzman, and Matthias Lehmann. *The Jews: A History*. 2nd ed. London: Routledge, 2013.

Freidenreich, David. *Foreigners and Their Food: Constructing Otherness in Jewish, Christian, and Islamic Law*. Berkeley: University of California Press, 2011.

Gikatilla, Joseph ben Abraham. *Sha'are Orah*. Jerusalem: Mossad Bialik, 1970.

Gries, Ze'ev. *Sifrut Ha-Hanhagot: Toldoteha U-mekomah Be-Haye Haside R. Yisrael Ba'al Shem-Tov*. Jerusalem: Mossad Bialik, 1989.

Hecker, Joel. "Eating as a Spiritual Ecosystem." In *Jewish Mysticism and the Spiritual Life: Classical Texts, Contemporary Reflections*, edited by Lawrence Fine, Eitan P. Fishbane, and Or N. Rose, 78–85. Woodstock, VT: Jewish Lights Publishing, 2011.

———. *Mystical Bodies, Mystical Meals: Eating and Embodiment in Medieval Kabbalah*. Detroit: Wayne State University Press, 2005.

Ibn Adret, Solomon ben Abraham. *Torat Ha-Bayit Ha-Arokh Veha-Katsar*. 2 vols. Jerusalem: Mossad Ha-Rav Kuk, 2010.

Jacobs, Louis. "Eating as an Act of Worship in Hasidic Thought." In *Studies in Jewish Religious and Intellectual History, Presented to Alexander Altmann on the Occasion of His Seventieth Birthday*, edited by Siegfried Stein and Raphael Loewe, 157–66. Tuscaloosa, AL: University of Alabama Press, 1979.

Klirs, Tracy Guren. *The Merit of Our Mothers: A Bilingual Anthology of Jewish Women's Prayers*. Translated by Tracy Guren Klirs, Ida Cohen Selavan, and Gella Schweid Fishman. New York: Hebrew Union College Press, 1992.

Kogman-Appel, Katrin. *Illuminated Haggadot from Medieval Spain: Biblical Imagery and the Passover Holiday*. University Park: Pennsylvania State University Press, 2006.

Kraemer, David. *Jewish Eating and Jewish Identity through the Ages*. London: Routledge, 2007.

Laudan, Rachel. *Cuisine and Empire: Cooking in World History*. Berkeley: University of California, 2013.

Marcus, Ivan G. *Rituals of Childhood: Jewish Acculturation in Medieval Europe*. New Haven: Yale University Press, 1998.

Marks, Gil. *Encyclopedia of Jewish Food*. Hoboken, NJ: John Wiley, 2010.

Matthee, Rudi. "Alcohol in the Islamic Medieval Middle East: Ambivalence and Ambiguity." *Past and Present* 222 (2014): 100–125.

Narkiss, Bezalel. "Haggadah, Passover: Illuminated Manuscripts." In *Encyclopaedia Judaica*. Jerusalem: Keter, 1971–72.

Rabinowitz, Louis I. "Shulhan Arukh." In *Encyclopaedia Judaica*. Jerusalem: Keter, 1971–72.

Schoenfeid, Liza. "Conservative Movement Overturns 800-Year-Old Passover Ban on Rice and Legumes." *Forward*, April 14, 2016. http://forward.com.

Soloveitchik, Haym. *Wine in Ashkenaz in the Middle Ages*. Jerusalem: Zalman Shazar Center for Jewish History, 2008.

van Gelder, G. J. H. *God's Banquet: Food in Classical Arabic Literature*. New York: Columbia University Press, 2000.

4

Food in the Modern Era

JODY MYERS

A confusing variety of food vendors appear when a person wanders down the major street in a small Los Angeles Jewish neighborhood. Restaurant signs are in English, Hebrew, Farsi, Arabic, and Chinese; kosher-certified eateries have an official document hung in the window or on the door. Shanghai Diamond Garden Restaurant is an older establishment, and like the Chicken Chow takeout and café, it boasts its "Glatt Kosher" status. There are at least four sushi joints, and SushiKo is clearly kosher certified, while the one surrounded by crowds and food trucks, a trendy-looking gourmet "Asian fusion" café, is clearly not. Many restaurants bear Farsi names, such as Kabob by Faraj Restaurant and Sangak Grill. Factor's Famous Deli, "your home away from home since 1948," bears no kosher sign, although it certainly serves "Jewish food." An obviously kosher option is the friendly looking kosher pizzeria Nagilah Pizza, the *g* in its name filled with a "happy face" emoji, and its twin Nagilah Meating Place next door—kosher laws prohibit mixing dairy with meat, so these are separate but related eateries. Haifa Restaurant evidently serves Israeli food, as does Holy Grill Mediterranean Cuisine. There are two kosher French bakery-cafés and a kosher Viennese-sounding diner called Schnitzly. Surveying them all, one wonders what it means to eat like a Jew or to be a Jew today in this part of the world.

This chapter first considers the development of modern Jewish cuisines and what they teach about the integration and assimilation of Jews into their surrounding non-Jewish society. The six major Jewish migrations that occurred in the sixteenth through the twentieth centuries provide the framework for this overview. Second, this chapter focuses on the effects of modern industrialized and globalized food production on Jewish foodways.

At the start of the 1500s, Jews everywhere lived as a minority group under the authority of their local communal leaders, men who deferred to the decisions of rabbis about religious matters. By 1566, the breadth of *halakhah* (Jewish law) was summarized in the law code *Shulhan Aruch*, and with the exception of the Reform movement, it became fundamental to rabbinic decision-making thereafter. Historians agree that during the early modern era, Jews accepted the principles of kashrut, including the avoidance of food cooked by non-Jews, although there were differences in interpretation and strictness of practice. Jewish communal leaders enforced a great deal of Jewish custom and religious law. For example, if members of the Jewish community discovered that one of them was intentionally violating their legal norms, whether civil, criminal, or religious, they would bring the accused to be judged by the Jewish court. If found guilty, the violator would be socially shunned, be required to pay a fine, suffer a whipping, or temporarily lose specific communal privileges. Nevertheless, there was some collaboration in food production and trade with non-Jews, and well-to-do Jews likely employed non-Jewish servants in their homes.[1]

As in the medieval era, food preparation occurred primarily within individual homes in the hands of the women of the household. Villages and towns maintained a communal oven into which Jewish women would place, prior to the Sabbath, the stew dish (*cholent*) they would consume on midday Sabbath.[2] Bread was likely purchased from a communal—not necessarily Jewish—bakery. However, kosher slaughterers and butchers were men on the Jewish community's payroll, although in rural areas, nonprofessional women and men might do this work.[3] The religious calendar provided the framework for daily life and for Sabbath and holiday meals that required special foods and extensive preparation before the special day; the calendar likewise dictated fast days. Jewish custom mandated that a family's major life event, such as a circumcision or wedding, was to be celebrated by a meal to which the entire Jewish community was invited. Ideally, community funds and individual donations would help supply the food and other basic needs of the poorest members of the community.

Sixteenth-Century Sephardic Migrations

Jews were expelled from Spain in 1492 at the same time as Christopher Columbus's cross-Atlantic expedition, and in 1497, they were also expelled from Portugal. Over the next century, many of the Jews remaining in the Iberian Peninsula as converts who retained secret attachments to Judaism left for more tolerant lands where they could revert back to Jewish practices.[4] The Sephardic migrations occurred at the start of what food scholars call the "Columbian Exchange," the encounter of the biodiverse worlds of the "discovered" Americas with the "known" European, Asian, and African continents. Although the world had been for centuries connected by traders and migrants, the Columbian Exchange accelerated and extended global networks as never before.[5] Jews actively facilitated the Columbian Exchange because of their dispersion, migrations, and involvement in overland and sea trade.

Sephardic Jews moving to northwestern Europe or to the "New World" entered lands politically dominated by people of other religions. In France, where Jews were prohibited, they arrived as "New Christians," a designation referring to both their converted status and ethnic distinction. Many of them kept Jewish practices in secret, so this cohort would have at least publicly abandoned the dietary laws until they could openly practice Judaism in the eighteenth century, when France's laws changed. In contrast, sixteenth-century Holland welcomed the Iberian exiles as open Jews. The vibrant commercial center in Amsterdam was the hub of the new Atlantic trade network, and Sephardic Jews played a crucial role in the trade and production of foodstuffs grown in Dutch New World colonies. The autonomous and fully functioning Jewish communities of the Netherlands were governed by communal leaders who enforced Jewish religious law. Yet the Dutch gave primacy to commercial enterprise and instituted policies tolerant of Jews, heterodox Christians, and even freethinkers. The freedom within Amsterdam society was unprecedented, and Jewish community leaders confronted heresy and nonconformity among the Jewish population.

In all northwestern European lands, eventually Jews experienced greater contact and integration with non-Jewish society than before. Men and women were more likely to eat with non-Jews, establish business relations with them, and thus have to think differently about or violate halakhah relating to kosher food and prohibited commensality. Coffee, which had by this time had become a popular beverage in Ottoman lands, was in northwestern European cities typically imbibed in coffeehouses, where social mixing was the norm.[6] Historians regard this experience of integration and "boundary crossing" as fundamental to the later appearance of "enlightened" and rationalist thought among Jews in the West.

Most Sephardic Jews migrated eastward across the Mediterranean to the religiously tolerant Ottoman Empire, where they settled either in port cities or within easy distance from mercantile trade centers. Ottoman Jewry was urban and a mix of Jews from many lands who were instrumental in trading foods and goods across great distances. The Sephardim became dominant among the Jews, often overwhelming the "native" Jews by dint of their sheer number. Outside of the Ottoman Empire in North Africa (present-day Morocco), Jews were residentially segregated together in separate Jewish quarters, although they could visit the non-Jewish urban areas and markets by day. Wherever they lived in the Mediterranean region, Jewish religious authority remained relatively unchallenged by heretical and rationalist perspectives until the late nineteenth century.[7]

Unlike the situation of Sephardic Jews who settled in northwestern Europe or traversed the Atlantic, those who migrated to the eastern Mediterranean were moving to a similar geographical zone and could eat very similar foods to those in the lands of their origin. Wheat, olive oil, legumes, and a variety of vegetables that grew abundantly in the warm and sunny climate were the mainstays of the diet. Animal protein came from fish, sheep, and cheeses made from sheep or goat milk; cattle meat was less common. Spices and seasonings were abundant. Even during the prosperous years, there were many poor people, and Ottoman Jewish communities were known for levying taxes on the rich and middle classes to fund an extensive system of poverty relief that included generous "soup kitchens."[8]

Because Sephardic immigrants in Mediterranean lands settled among Jews who had inhabited the region for centuries, there were multiple categories of "Jewish food." For example, those who dwelled alongside Romaniyot Jews (so called because they traced their arrival from the time of the Roman Empire) were not accustomed to dishes featuring chicken because that fowl had not been widely raised in Spain.[9] The Sephardim were known for their love of meatballs made of ground veal or lamb mixed with spices and other ingredients, rolled into little balls and cooked; they called this dish *albóndigas*, a word derived from the Arabic word for hazelnut. The local meatballs, known by the Persian term *kofta*, meaning "ground up," were larger and oblong and had different spices, and the meat mixture did not contain vegetables. None of these "Jewish foods" held religious significance, although being meat- and labor-intensive, they were typically reserved for the Sabbath, holidays, and special occasions, and they were not eaten as often by the poor.[10] Yet aside from special foods like these, the cuisine of Jews and non-Jews in Muslim lands was virtually indistinguishable.

Fourteenth- through Seventeenth-Century Ashkenazi Migration

In contrast to the eastbound Sephardic migrations, the move of Ashkenazim from Germanic lands to Eastern Europe placed Jews into Christian societies with virtually no preexisting Jewish population and into a more rural environment. Compared to the Sephardim, they were more socially isolated and residing amid far fewer Jews. Jews served as agents of the Polish nobility by providing goods to the peasants, collecting taxes and tolls (e.g., on the use of mills) from the peasantry, and conveying crops and forest products to distant markets. In addition, Jews engaged in commerce and crafts in the towns and cities, and their importance in town and city commercial life grew in the eighteenth and nineteenth centuries, as did Jewish proprietorship of inns and taverns, where liquor—also largely produced by Jews—was sold.[11]

The harsher climate of Eastern Europe meant a shorter growing season, and the distance from long-distance overland caravan and sea trade routes meant that food was less varied even for those involved in the food trade. Spices were harder to come by, and seasonings differed: garlic, for example, was favored by Ashkenazim but not Sephardim.[12] Grains were the main food staple and supplied the bulk of the daily diet. Rye, barley, oats, millet, and buckwheat were more common than wheat, and plain sourdough dark rye bread was the principal daily food. Liquor made from grains (later, potato and other vegetables too) was a staple. Herring, which was fished in the Baltic and North Seas and preserved salted in barrels, was an everyday food along with local vegetables grown during the short summers and pickled to be eaten in the cold seasons. Since the chief source of meat in the region was the pig and the most common oil was lard, a sharp distinction developed between the diet of Jews and the dominant Christians. Jews' source of animal protein came primarily from fish, fowl (geese, primarily, and later chickens), and dairy. Meat from sheep or cattle was a luxury generally reserved for holidays and special occasions.

Except for meat, the Jewish cuisine differed little from that of the local population; for example, Ukrainian peasants flavored beet soup (borscht) with pork, while Jews substituted beef or made the soup as a dairy or *pareve* (neither meat nor dairy) item. Instead of lard, Jews used goose or chicken fat in meat dishes. Distinctive Jewish foods were the more labor-intensive Sabbath and holiday specialties. The Jews' stuffed (*gefilte* in Yiddish) pike that had been popular among upper-class Germans was, among Eastern European Jews, more likely to be made with whitefish or carp. Also adopted from German cuisine and unique to Jews in the region were the braided Sabbath bread loaves made with white (refined) wheat flour.[13] Wheat was an expensive import until the sixteenth century. Once it was locally produced, noodles (*lokshen*) became more popular, and the noodle pudding (*lokshen kugel*) became a regular Sabbath dish. Bakeries began to produce wheat or rye-wheat breads, and the bagel, which was produced by women in their home kitchens and hawked by their husbands and children in the towns, became a popular food.[14]

Modernization and Religious Transformations in Jewish Life

Before describing the subsequent mass migrations and their effect on Jewish foodways, I will describe the larger metamorphoses that are implied by the term *modernization*. In the premodern era, the authority and reach of the state was limited, and the ruler depended upon corporate entities such as the nobility, merchants, the clergy, and minority religious and ethnic communities to govern themselves and the "lower orders"; this is why Jews were permitted communal autonomy under the control of their leaders. Indeed, Jews' obedience to Jewish religious and custom law was ensured, although indirectly, by the non-Jewish state.

Political modernization, which began in eighteenth-century Europe, involves more efficient and direct centralized governments. Rulers diminished the power of religious authorities over the lives of groups and individuals and moved toward equalizing the obligations, privileges, and rights of their subjects. They eliminated or severely limited minority groups' autonomy.

In modernized political environments, the rulings of Jewish communal leaders applied to a much narrower sphere of activity; for example, Jewish communal leaders could govern religious institutions, but they could do little if Jews chose not to attend them. They could judge and excommunicate an errant Jew, but the punishment was merely a denial of religious privileges and a signal to the community to shun that person. A principal reason that many Jews in the modern period ceased to obey religious law is that they were no longer politically or socially required to do so. Furthermore, because the power and scope of Jewish community leadership diminished, as did communal funds that were now only the result of voluntary gifts, Jewish institutions weakened. Migrations also undermined traditional authority and institutions. From the late 1700s onward, an unprecedented degree of religious and ideological divisions appeared among Jews.

Economic changes had cultural effects. Economic modernization begins with a frame of mind that encourages saving and investment—as opposed to the practice of spending everything one earns—during a period when a surplus or credit is available. With the growth of technology and the state's encouragement, industrialized production of food, clothing, and other material goods rapidly increased. In rural areas, the number of jobs declined, and people moved to growing urban areas. Work became far more disconnected from muscle, and the workplace became separated from home. Long-standing gender roles were affected by the advances in women's health and longevity, and the applied technology and urbanization eased women's burden in acquiring and preparing food.

In the eighteenth and nineteenth centuries, the population increased at a rate never before seen, primarily because of improvements in public health; this accelerated population growth occurred worldwide, even in places with older economic patterns. At the start of the modern era, most Jews lived in villages and small towns, but by the end of the nineteenth century, Jews became increasingly urbanized. By 1925, about half of all Jews worldwide lived in cities of more than one hundred thousand inhabitants, and a quarter lived in cities of more than a million inhabitants. When they left behind smaller, more intimate communities, they were likely to leave behind their local cultural traditions; of course, they also formed new communities and traditions. A constant feature of urban life, however, is the proximity of people of different backgrounds who provide alternatives to one's received ways of thinking and living.[15] The extensive geographic mobility of the modern era was not only city centered; it also included the movement of Jews to frontier areas seeking economic opportunities—for example, as peddlers. There, too, they would come into closer contact with different kinds of Jews and non-Jews of different backgrounds.[16]

Halakhah governing food became stricter from the sixteenth century onward. This was partly caused by the use of individual dishes and eating implements in Western societies, where people began to accept that it was not "civilized" to eat with their fingers or eat directly out of a common serving vessel. This occurred first among Jews in German lands in the late medieval era, then in adjacent lands, and eventually to non-Ashkenazic Jews in Mediterranean lands and the Middle East. The proper Jewish home was minimally equipped with dairy, meat, and *pareve* utensils, pots, cutlery, and dishes; Jews who wanted to be exceptionally pious would add other forms of dairy and meat differentiation. The requirement for separate dairy and meat pots and utensils in food halakhah strengthened the preexisting rabbinic principle that Jews should avoid eating food in non-Jewish establishments.

The increasing strictness of food halakhah in the modern era contributed to the end of shared communal Jewish eating. One of the first instances of this occurred in eighteenth-century Eastern Europe with the emergence of Hasidism, a Jewish religious movement that emphasized ecstatic religiosity and asserted its independent religious authority. Hasidic rabbinic leaders insisted that their followers could eat only meat slaughtered with especially sharp honed knives. The higher Hasidic standard, at odds with halakhic precedent and the prevailing practice, resulted in the formation of separatist Hasidic communities and separate Hasidic kosher slaughtering.[17] The rift between Hasidim and non-Hasidim was perhaps the greatest—but certainly not the only—rift in commensality within religious Jewry. When rabbis realized that their authority was no longer respected by the whole of the local Jewish community, they no longer felt the need to issue moderate rulings that could be followed by all. They could impose stringent rules that only a portion of the Jewish community could follow. A spirit of compromise to ensure a regional norm—say, a shared Polish-Jewish tradition—became difficult to sustain. Competing standards of kashrut eventually became the norm in the modern era, being both a sign and a cause of widespread factionalism. These divisions are not only between Jews who faithfully practice Jewish law and those who do not; they also appear among Orthodox—including Hasidic—Jews. The term *Orthodox* is the modern term for Jews who strictly follow halakhah as defined by rabbis who believe they are faithfully following received traditions originating from God, and the law code *Shulhan Aruch* and its commentaries are the starting point for their rulings. Despite this commonality, Orthodox Jews are not organized as a single religious denomination and there is no single, accepted religious authority among them.

The predominant change in Jewish eating practices in the modern era, however, is a reduced commitment to or outright rejection of the dietary laws. This appeared in Jewish communities throughout the world at different times and in differing ways. This development is associated with European Jewish communities, however, which were the first to experience the type of modernization previously described, and the place where specific modern Jewish religious denominations were created. In Europe from the sixteenth century onward, rabbis increasingly noted the violation of food halakhah and denounced the practice of Jews eating in gentile food establishments and coffeehouses.[18] In nineteenth-century Western and Central Europe, not only were individual Jews ignoring commensal restrictions; rabbis too were calling for looser standards. Laymen and rabbis criticized halakhic requirements—including dietary laws—as arbitrary, antiquated, and interfering with normal social relations.

By midcentury, a cadre of rabbinic leaders who eventually formed the denomination known as Reform Judaism advocated far greater integration of Jews into larger society. They regarded the Torah's moral teachings and commandments as divine and religiously obligatory, whereas many of the rituals, ceremonies, and customs they regarded merely as means to serve moral and spiritual ends. The dietary laws fit into the latter category, and Reform rabbis considered it legitimate for individuals to decide how and if to observe these. Nevertheless, European Reform rabbis never officially rejected kashrut, and to this day, congregations that define themselves as Reform, Progressive, or Liberal will serve only kosher fish and meat at their gatherings.[19]

In contrast, Reform rabbis in America were more radical, and their rejection of the dietary laws played a formative role in the creation of separate Jewish religious denominations there. The key break occurred when traditional and reform-minded Jews in 1883 gathered to celebrate the founding of a seminary designed to train rabbis for the entire spectrum of American synagogues. To the horror of the traditionalist attendees, the menu for the meal included dairy and meat items and forbidden clams and frogs' legs. Later dubbed "the *treif* (unkosher) banquet," the event showed the impossibility of religious unity between American Jews. No longer needing to compromise, US Reform rabbis and lay leaders defined their shared principles in 1885 and declared the dietary laws no longer obligatory or even desirable for the modern Jew.[20] This negative stance was the norm within Reform Jewish synagogues and schools for the next hundred years.

Also advocating amelioration of strict halakhah were European and American rabbis who rejected Reform Judaism as too radical. They believed in the divine origin of the Torah and valued Jewish particularism and social cohesion, and they approved of the social separatism fostered by observance of the dietary laws. Yet they also accepted historic methodology and believed that Judaism had always evolved and should continue to do so, slowly and guardedly. This was essentially a conservative stance—hence the denomination was eventually named Conservative Judaism. It originated in Central Europe and found its largest following in twentieth-century America. The lay members affiliated with Conservative Judaism have not practiced halakhah, and certainly not the dietary laws, as strictly as their rabbis.[21] Conservative rabbis, in turn, today practice a form of kashrut more permissible than that of Orthodox Jews.

Late Nineteenth- through Early Twentieth-Century Ashkenazic Migration

The tremendously expanding Jewish population in Eastern Europe became impoverished in the nineteenth century because of the region's lagging economic development. The US beckoned, promising jobs, upward mobility, and an ample supply of a wide variety of food. More than two million European Jews relocated to the United States from 1881 to 1924, vastly outnumbering the "native" Jews. For Jews living in the Russian Empire at this time, potatoes provided much of the daily diet, but in America there were cheap and plentiful fish, fowl, and meat from cattle and sheep; dairy products; and a wide array of fresh fruits, vegetables, and nuts. Even those in the struggling labor class could afford to consume meat daily. In the crowded urban centers where the immigrants resided, food markets overflowed with eager customers.

Jews' determination to enjoy the American bounty after the years of privation in Europe influenced Jewish foodways.[22] First, immigrant families and the Jewish community in general became deeply conflicted over the extent to which the dietary laws should be honored, if at all. By this time, there were already religious divisions within American Jewry. Unlike in Europe, religion operated in its own type of "free market"; unlike in Europe, the state generally refused to regulate kashrut or get involved in the licensing of religious functionaries or in enforcing their decisions. Regulation of *shehitah* (kosher slaughter) was haphazard,[23] and people realized that meat purporting to be kosher might be no different from nonkosher meat except for its greater price—and consumers resented the higher price of even authenticated kosher meat.[24] Jews who lived in outlying towns or rural areas lacking kosher meat were generally unwilling to adopt a vegetarian diet or maintain older standards of kashrut. Some Jewish immigrants had already in Europe ceased to follow halakhah or to do so with any measure of strictness, and so the move to America did not radically change their religious observance. There were devout Jewish immigrants who successfully perpetuated the religious traditions they had followed in Europe, but they were a minority.[25] Within a few decades, many of the immigrants and their offspring practiced kashrut in a modified fashion: they ate kosher at home but not while eating in restaurants or the homes of others, they selectively honored prohibitions, and they would eat "kosher-style" familiar but not halakhically prepared foods.[26] The commensal prohibitions (against eating food prepared by non-Jews and eating with them in their homes) were generally not honored.

Another consequence of the contrast between American plenty and old-country deprivation was that immigrant Jews placed hearty eating at the center of Jewish social life. Judaism had always treated food preparation and eating as a means of serving God, and in America devout Jews could continue this with fuller platters. Immigrants who were no longer following halakhah retained and secularized Jewish food-centeredness. Religious and nonreligious alike held substantial family meals on the Sabbath, holidays, and special occasions; the programs of synagogues and benevolent societies featured dinners and banquets; and those with means gathered together in restaurants, clubs, and summer resorts. Consumption of street food and fast food became part of urban Jewish lives.

"Jewish food" was a recognizable and marketable commodity, although Jews regarded it with some ambivalence. On the one hand, the older generation (women, in particular) and businesses promoted and produced the "old-country" foods. The label was applied to a combined menu mixing European cuisines, such as Eastern European rye bread, bagels, gefilte fish, roast meats, borscht, and pickles, along with the sausages, cured meats, and pastries from Western and Central Europe. On the other hand, Jewish newcomers displayed an appetite for novel and foreign dishes. Younger women took advantage of the opportunities presented to them to learn American recipes and approaches to eating. The cookbooks written by Jewish women of this era demonstrate the diversity of the new palate. Alongside old-world Jewish favorites are recipes for Americanized Chinese, French, German, and Italian dishes.[27] Lack of loyalty to "Jewish food" did not necessarily indicate a lack of religious commitment or ethnic pride, for Jews who kept the laws of kashrut adapted their cuisine too. Over time, and especially in the mid-twentieth century, when immigration virtually ceased and the younger generation of American Jews grew increasingly similar to each other, so did their diets.

Late Nineteenth- through Early Twentieth-Century Sephardic Migration

Economic decline and political instability prompted migrations of Sephardic and other Jewish ethnic groups from the eastern Mediterranean (Levant) at the turn of the century. Ottoman lands that had been a haven for the Sephardim broke apart into new nation-states, and nationalist groups considered the Jews a foreign element. Although Jewish communal institutions weakened and secularization occurred, Levantine Jews were less riven by religious and ideological conflict compared to Central and Western European Jews. Rabbis did not form separatist congregations. The intra-Jewish factionalism described earlier featuring conflicts over foodways did not occur.[28]

The opening of the Suez Canal, a project of the French and British, prompted a migration of Jews from Asia Minor to Egypt. Wealthy Jews involved in commerce fostered elaborate foodways that combined French and Mediterranean features, and their dining culture was replicated by a similar class of Jews in the colonized urban centers across North Africa. Such families considered food a high art, and they took pride in having wives and servants prepare labor-intensive and complex delicacies. In contrast, the diet of poorer Jews in Egypt was far more limited. Simpler and less cosmopolitan, it revolved around the staples eaten by the laboring classes such as wheat bread, legumes, olives, vegetables, and eggs.[29]

Jewish immigrants from the Ottoman Empire and the Balkans who moved to the United States at this time were of course different from the Ashkenazic Jews arriving from Europe. To start with, they came in far fewer numbers; although the first Jewish immigrants to America in the colonial era were Sephardic, by this time the prevailing Jewish culture was Ashkenazic. The Syrian-Jewish immigrants in New York, whose vernacular was Arabic, did not generally mix even with other Sephardic Jews. Originating in a single country, they formed a more united group than the Ashkenazim, and the immigrant generation more easily established their own communal institutions and a greater measure of social cohesiveness and separatism.[30] Syrian-American Jews patronized kosher slaughterers and butchers approved by their rabbis, their own food markets supplied with their native foodstuffs, and their own communal eating establishments and caterers. They regarded their cuisine as far superior to all others available. The women continued to prepare the familiar labor-intensive recipes that involved intricate chopping, pounding, stuffing, and wrapping and new combinations of meats, fish, and vegetables. *Kibbeh* is just such a dish: it consists of a thin wheat shell formed from pureed bulgur, onion, and lamb filled with finely ground lamb or beef, onion, nuts, and spices; the carefully shaped item is then deep-fried.[31]

Ottoman Jews who migrated to America's West Coast were less insular and homogenous than the East Coast settlers but also organized themselves around food. In Seattle, for example, immigrants from Ottoman and Greek territories communicated easily with each other but not with English- or Yiddish-speaking residents of the city. An Ottoman Jew helped enter the fish trade by a non-Jewish Greek with whom he shared the Greek language was soon joined by other Jews from Ottoman and Greek territories who spoke Ladino, the old Spanish-Jewish language. Their food businesses and eateries in the seaside market were patronized by many Seattle residents; these same places served as a gathering place for Sephardic Jews originating from multiple Ottoman lands, unifying them socially and economically without the insularity and stricter religiosity of the East Coast Sephardic Syrians.[32]

Post–World War II Migrations of Jews to Israel

Approximately one million Jews immigrated to Israel in the dozen years after the 1948 establishment of the state. In the state's first four years, slightly more than three hundred thousand arrived from North Africa and Middle Eastern lands; slightly fewer came from Europe, and most of these were Holocaust survivors. Jewish political leaders in prestate Palestine and the young state were Ashkenazim with mixed attitudes toward the region's and the non-Ashkenazic Jews' historic foods: on the one hand, they regarded European culture and cuisine as superior to the local options; on the other hand, some regarded the Ashkenazic Jewish cuisine as inauthentic and unhealthful. All recognized that for practical reasons, the national diet needed to be produced locally by Jews' own efforts. Cultural and educational programs emanating from socialist and secular circles have celebrated Jewish agricultural efforts as Jews' noble return to their ancient role as farmers.[33] To this day, the fruits of the local harvest take center stage in public acknowledgments of the holidays of Sukkot and Shavuot.

By 1960, Israel became self-sustaining agriculturally through the communistic *kibbutz* and the less rigidly governed yet still communal *moshav* farms. The Israeli diet evolved into one similar to the historic Levantine and Middle Eastern Jewish diet: wheat bread, vegetables (the most common are cucumbers, tomatoes, and eggplants), legumes, olives and olive oil, and a wide array of herbs and spices. Orange orchards and vineyards, the former established primarily by Christians and Muslims and the latter by early Zionist pioneers, provide fruit and wine. The chief fowl is chicken, used for both its eggs and meat. Chicken is most typically prepared in the Viennese style as schnitzel: cut or pounded into thin pieces, breaded, and fried. Turkey and sheep are also sources of meat. Beef is likely to be imported, as cattle are raised primarily for the cheeses and fermented milk products that are daily staples. Two important Israeli street foods, shawarma and falafel, were previously common to the cuisine of multiple Middle Eastern peoples. Shawarma consists of thin slices of spiced lamb skewered on a vertical rotisserie and slowly roasted, and falafel is a dish of ground chickpeas and spices shaped into balls or flat disks and deep-fried. Both are stuffed along with salad and condiments into pita (round, hollow flatbread) or in folded single-layer wheat flatbread. A pastry stuffed with cheese or vegetables called *boreka*, an Ottoman Sephardic favorite, was also adopted in Israel as both a street snack and a domestic food.[34]

Israeli food is not the same as Jewish food, since at least 20 percent of the population in 2016 was not Jewish by religion or nationality.[35] The Jewish population comes from many distinctive immigrant groups, each possessing a cuisine that may or may not be associated with Jews in its origins. For example, Israeli Jews with roots in today's Uzbekistan are known for their varieties of pilaf, called *plov*, a dish common in Uzbekistan. In Israel, only the version unique to Uzbekistani Jews that was a Shabbat specialty—consisting of rice cooked together with chopped beef, calf or chicken liver, and coriander—could be considered "Jewish food."[36] Israeli food may be regarded as "Jewish" when it is expressed in the Jewish holiday and Sabbath foods because of Jews' cultural and demographic dominance in the state. On the other hand, from the perspective of non-Jewish Israelis, all foods eaten by the Jews and not by non-Jews might be considered "Jewish food."

Kashrut is not mandated by secular law in Israel, but since the state was founded, the ruling political parties placed public food (food served by government, army, and hospitals) under the supervision of Orthodox rabbis. Importing pork, even for private consumption, is prohibited by law; raising pigs for food has been permitted in some locales but is quite limited, and Jews involved in this enterprise face strenuous opposition from some religious circles.[37] Hotels, event halls, and supermarkets, which generally seek the widest of clienteles, are likely to be kosher. Although slightly less than half of the population in 2009 defined itself as secular (and either antireligious or simply nonreligious), at the same time a majority report that they are motivated by religious reasons to eat only kosher food at home and while dining out, and they also report that for religious reasons, they never eat pork.[38]

When the state reached its third decade and enjoyed greater prosperity, Israelis began to dine out at restaurants or fast food eateries offering regional and ethnic Jewish foods. The greater ease of travel abroad, and in particular the practice of young Israelis to trek through foreign lands after their years of army service, contributed to the establishment in Israel of South and East Asian restaurants and novel fusions of regional and international dishes. In the 1980s, Israel began to grant temporary visas to foreign workers, particularly Thais and Filipinos, leading to their foods becoming commercially available. While outdoor markets and the small neighborhood store remain places to shop, huge supermarket chains appeared throughout the country. People increasingly rely on packaged, prepared food. Kosher brands and regional specialties have found foreign markets for Jewish consumers, Israeli expatriates, and people who have toured the country.[39]

Late Twentieth-Century Migration from the Former Soviet Union to Israel

Between 1989 and 2000, slightly more than one million people from the Union of Soviet Socialist Republics and the newly independent lands formed from it (the USSR politically dissolved in 1991) migrated to Israel. In Israel they are known collectively as "Russians." Except for those from the Republic of Georgia, Russian immigrants were overwhelmingly secular in outlook and unfamiliar with Judaism. About three hundred thousand of these new Israeli citizens did not consider themselves Jewish, nor are they legally recognized as Jews. As a group the Russian immigrants are far more educated and accomplished than previous immigrants, and many among them regard their move to Israel as relocation to a place less culturally advanced and sophisticated than their native land. This judgment extends to the Israeli diet. Because the Russians came in such huge numbers and under flexible Israeli government policies that permit cultural preservation, they have created a strong subculture. Their migration is not as stark a break with their native land and culture as previously described migrations. Furthermore, no visa is required between Russia and Israel, enabling easy trips back and forth for those with the means.[40]

These immigrants were not the first to bring foods from the multifaceted Russian cuisine into Israel, since a large number of the Ashkenazim who arrived during the prestate era grew up in the same places. By this time, however, the economy was far stronger and included business interests eager to supply the new immigrants. Once again, foods like dark rye bread, borscht, stuffed cabbage, and pickled vegetables fill the dinner plates of old and young. Russian vodkas, beers, and liquors are now widely available. Most different than the past, however, is that the Russians' favorite meat appears to be pork, and quite a few of them see no reason to give it up. Their shops and restaurants offer cuts of nonkosher meat and prepared dishes that are anathema to religious Jews. Russians' food choices, though, are not merely rooted in Eastern Europe; these immigrants favor a broad range of elite European foods. A supermarket chain catering to their tastes has more than two dozen stores and produces its own line of foods.[41]

It is too soon to accurately assess the long-term effects of this migration's impact on Jewish foodways, although the short-term impact is obvious. While the Russians may not feel the need to adapt too much or become more religiously observant, their strong Israeli patriotism and the growing religiosity of the Israeli populace point them in that direction. As always, the immigrants and natives reciprocally influence each other.

The effect of these six mass migrations, especially the recent ones, is a highly diverse Jewish cuisine. Especially but not only in American and Israeli cities, which are Jewish immigration destinations, Jews are likely to eat foods from many different nations. This is not only a result of their origins in different lands; it is also a function of the food-centeredness of Jewish culture and the recent globalization of food production.

Industrialized Food Production and Government Regulation

Industrialized food production pertains to the large-scale growing and harvesting of plants; the raising and killing of land animals, fish, and fowl for food; and the processing and preservation of huge amounts of foods that, in their modified form, may be more easily transported elsewhere and will not quickly spoil. While there were instances of mass food production in the ancient and medieval eras, the difference in the modern era is in scale. Together, the use of slave or cheap labor, the assistance of government, and the application of scientific knowledge to production and distribution became more common and resulted in more food for more people. This both enabled and accelerated urbanization and the significantly higher population growth rate characteristic of the past two hundred years. Jews, a highly urbanized group in this era, were deeply affected.

The control and organization of labor are necessary for mass food production. Beginning in the fifteenth century, African slaves fueled the large European colonial plantations in the lands off the African coast, and by the seventeenth century, native peoples and imported African slaves constituted the work force in colonial plantations in the New World. Sugar was a key component of the Atlantic trade connecting the Americas, Africa, and Europe. Sephardic Jews established and owned sugar plantations in the Caribbean, built sugar mills and processing operations, and brokered export trade with Amsterdam.[42] They did much the same in the plantation-based production of the cacao bean. Cacao is native to the tropical areas of central and southern America, and it was transplanted into western Africa where it was then and still largely is produced by enslaved or severely exploited workers.[43] While Jewish law mandates that Jews liberate each other from servitude, and there is also the crime of *ona'at mammon* prohibiting monetary oppression as well as considerable legislation about workers' rights, rabbinic authorities have not ruled that food produced by Jewish—or any other—slaves or exploited workers is on that basis forbidden.[44]

Industrialized food production in the modern era is most obvious in processed food. By the mid-nineteenth century, technology was applied to food preservation and packaging to manufacture canned, ready-to-eat foods for national armies, and later these goods were produced for the expanding urban markets. By the early 1900s, the time that women needed to devote to acquiring and preparing food for the household had dramatically lessened. Their tasks became even easier midcentury with the availability of home refrigerators, freezers, and supermarkets. Women were not freed from being the primary family caretakers, but the advancements in food technology gave them more hours to work outside the home, pursue educational goals, and engage in community service and other interests, or within their homes, they had more time to focus on aspects of domestic life other than food.

Women who kept kosher realized that they might benefit from the new convenient nonmeat foods; the ingredients might be acceptable and the halakhic prohibition against eating certain foods prepared by non-Jews might not matter if the food were machine made. By the late 1800s, individual rabbis began to vouch for certain factory-produced foods (whether or not they were made by Jews), but assurance for the food's kosher status was more likely to come from the businesses' marketing departments rather than from a rabbinic voice or thorough investigation. Questions of kashrut became more complex in the early twentieth century, when manufacturers added ingredients—some of them new synthetic creations—in processed food such as stabilizers, emulsifiers, and preservatives. These were impervious to simple investigation, and even after US law mandated ingredient labels on processed food in 1938, it was not easy to determine whether a product contained prohibited substances. Housewives received conflicting information from rabbis and manufacturers, and so they often made decisions based less on rabbinic certification of food and more by their faith in certain brand names, studying the ingredient labels, reading publications geared toward the kosher consumer, and their own informal consultation with others.[45]

Only in the post–World War II era were significant advances made in kosher certification. Certification businesses under Orthodox rabbinic leadership began to inspect food-manufacturing processes, create trademark symbols indicating rabbinic approval, and offer consultative services to food companies interested in supplying the kosher market. Eventually, the multiple Orthodox certifiers managed to agree on many common standards. Because food processing became highly globalized—a manufacturer might obtain ingredients for a single cookie recipe, for example, from a half-dozen vendors all located in different countries—the kosher certifiers send inspectors to wherever ingredients originate. By the 1990s, the number of kosher-certified foods began to increase exponentially. Food manufacturers learned that kosher certification symbols on food labels reassure consumers of all backgrounds that food is safe; furthermore, the largest producers of industrialized food for various reasons agreed to the nonmeat ingredients favored by the kosher certifiers.[46]

Important cultural and economic developments have stemmed from the expansion of kosher certification. First, kosher certification has created a niche Jewish food economy for Orthodox Jews. Kosher certification requires partnerships between business owners (who may or may not be Jewish) and kashrut inspectors. The kashrut certification agencies or individual certifiers charge a fee for their services, which consist of guiding and checking the food business's purchases, regularly inspecting operations, and in some cases requiring that Jews actually begin the production process. In cities with a sizable Orthodox population, there are local certification agencies for restaurants, caterers, and other food venues that wish to advertise themselves as in compliance with halakhah. Restaurant owners must pay for kosher certification and permit the routine inspection of their accounts, inventory, cooking, and serving practices. Owners with a clientele that prefers kosher food but are not scrupulous about the rules may avoid the expense and simply declare their kosher status without rabbinic verification. The certifiers employ their own aggregate of male workers and inspectors among the Orthodox population. Typically, their profits are channeled into the educational, religious, and social welfare institutions of the Orthodox population, helping to sustain and strengthen that community.[47]

Second, industrialized food production and professional kosher certification play a role in fostering greater strictness in kashrut standards. In the immediate post–World War II years, Orthodox rabbinic supervisors began to prohibit inclusion of any trace of nonkosher animal ingredient in kosher food and demanded a greater degree of separation between kosher and nonkosher ingredients in food-manufacturing companies than ever before. One reason for this was that much of the authority and actual work of kashrut changed: whereas it used to be the province of women, kosher certification and industrialized food and the kosher certification that accompanied it moved kashrut outside the home into the hands of professional men. The involvement of paid experts tends to lead to stricter standards, and the community's economic dependence on kosher certification reinforces this perceived need. Second, the greater wealth of Orthodox society means that rabbis are less inhibited about requiring more expensive or time-consuming stringencies. By the postwar era, they were no longer legislating for Jewish society as a whole, which would be unlikely to follow such demands, but for subgroups who would. Finally, during the World War II and postwar era, refugee and Holocaust-survivor rabbis established insular, separatist Orthodox religious communities in America, and they did not favor leniencies or rulings that permit eating the foods made by non-Jews.[48]

However, it is not accurate to point only to the rabbis for instigating these postwar changes; pressure certainly has come from laypeople for a variety of spiritual, psychological, and social reasons. For example, Jews who embrace a modern outlook value precise measurements, scientifically verified research, and common-sense logic, even in kashrut. They regard the centuries-old precedents allowing some contact and mixing of permitted and prohibited foods as inconsistent and too permissive. Advanced technology, chemical cleaners, and household appliances permit an extremely high level of cleansing that has become the standard and becomes identified with ritual purification.

When industrialization is applied to the manufacture of food used for specific Jewish rituals, it can prompt concerns about authenticity. A case in point is matzah, the unleavened bread eaten on Passover. Halakhah requires that the matzah used for the ritual Seder meal not only must be especially guarded from fermentation; it also must be made with the intent to fulfill the religious commandment. These conditions apply to the selection of wheat kernels, their milling into flour, the hasty mixing of flour with water, and the shaping and baking of the dough in the communal oven. Consequently, the mid-nineteenth-century invention of a matzah-making machine was not simply accepted outright. Eventually, most rabbis recognized that mechanization enables greater exactness and standardization of preparation, and they accepted machine-made matzah used for the Seder when the process includes proper-minded individuals watching the process. Preference for entirely handmade matzah still persists for those who regard the handmade version to be necessary and worth the added cost.[49]

Kosher meat production during the industrialized food era has to meet requirements created in the preindustrialized past. To be kosher, permitted mammals and fowl must be slaughtered by a *shochet* (kosher slaughterer) who is a specially trained and devout Jew. The shochet uses a sharp knife to cut the major neck arteries on the intact and fully conscious animal placed into a specified position so that blood pours out. Another trained and similarly devout inspector then examines the cut and the animal's innards, for only meat slaughtered properly and from an animal free of forbidden blemishes may be kosher. The prohibited parts of the animal must be removed, and the blood on the remainder must be washed away. It is a slow and careful operation, and in the past, it was typically managed by the local Jewish community that also controlled the workers' wages and the meat's final price.[50]

In contrast to these religiously circumscribed practices, modern mass production is defined in secular, scientific terms, and there is a financial preference for quick, efficient procedures. Fostered by the relatively free market, business owners set wages, conditions of employment, and food prices in order to maximize their profits. Their freedom is limited by the state, which—unlike in the past—gets involved because of society's concerns for humane animal treatment, public health, and conditions of labor. While mass-produced meat is cheaper for most people, the production changes do not help kosher meat production to the same extent for two reasons: first, shehitah requires specially skilled employees that cannot be replaced by machinery; second, many aspects of industrialized agriculture result in animals with injuries and blemishes that disqualify the meat as kosher, thus reducing its value. Already in the 1960s, it was clear that the added expense of kosher meat and the need to purchase it in specialty butcher shops prompted Jewish housewives who are not Orthodox to prefer cheaper and more readily available non-kosher meat.[51]

In the modern era, a new issue emerged. Since the mid-nineteenth century, animal welfare advocates have advocated that large animals must be stunned unconscious prior to slaughter. However, kosher animal slaughter requires an intact and fully conscious animal at the time of slaughter, and the animal must be positioned to enable the shochet to cut the beast's major neck arteries properly. Many animal welfare advocates, politicians, or others claiming a concern for animals have regarded kosher requirements as primitive and cruel.[52] While some opposition to nonstunned slaughter, including kosher slaughter, does not appear driven by anti-Semitism, during the early twentieth century, antisemitic organizations used the concern for humane slaughter as an opportunity to gain respectability for their anti-Jewish campaigns. Shehitah was outlawed in some Central European states during the 1930s and 1940s as part of obviously antisemitic legislation.[53]

In less hostile settings, however, Jews sometimes need to publicly defend shehitah as humane and lobby for its continued legal standing. In the United States, Orthodox halakhic authorities, who currently hold a virtual monopoly on certifying kosher meat, have resisted changes in the immediate preslaughter handling and positioning of animals called for by some humane advocates, including those supportive of kosher slaughter as such.[54] The highly respected animal welfare expert Dr. Temple Grandin argues that shehitah can be considered humane when it involves proper handling of the animals; in an industrialized system, however, this requires the use of specialized equipment, extensive training, auditing, and the slowing of the production line, all of which add to the cost of the meat.[55] However, some kosher authorities require that animals be inverted before slaughter so that the shochet is standing above the animal, and this does not allow for the kosher slaughter methods Grandin considers most humane. Even when these improvements are used, there is still opposition to kosher slaughter in many European contexts, but this degree of opposition is rare or nonexistent in the United States.[56]

Wide publicity given to the problems of industrialized food production has brought "food ethics" to the attention of the Jewish community, especially liberal and progressive Jews. Innovative policies and pro-grams such as the Coalition on the Environment and Jewish Life, Mazon ("a Jewish response to hunger"), Jewish food banks, synagogue gardens, and Jewish community gardens were designed to counteract the destructive effects of economic modernization on the environment and the poor. The 2004 public exposure of cruel shehitah procedures—and later revelations of unethical treatment of workers and financial fraud—at Agriprocessors, then the largest American glatt kosher meat company, shook the Jewish community. The scandal widened the religious divide between Orthodox and liberal Jews. American non-Orthodox denominations issued proposals for a new definition of kashrut, one that gives priority to humane animal treatment, ethical treatment of workers in the food industry, and environmental sustainability.[57] To many non-Orthodox Jews, eating kosher meat, not mixing meat and dairy, and avoiding prohibited foods became even less pertinent than before. For many who embrace the ideal of ethical eating, kosher meat has been discredited.

Conclusion

At the start of the modern era, Jews everywhere honored the laws of kashrut in food production, commerce, and dining practices, but by the end, the situation would look quite different. Among Jews today who obey rabbinic law, there are many versions of the kosher laws that prevent shared meals. The vast majority of American Jews—who constitute 40 percent of world Jewry—do not practice kashrut at all. In the 1990s, American Reform rabbis began to reappraise the earlier denominational disdain for kashrut and suggest its practice, and many Reform institutions now honor it to some extent; still, their congregants, and secular Jews generally, find more meaning in the ideals of ethical eating irrespective of kashrut. While a majority of Jews in Israel—also 40 percent of world Jewry—honor the dietary laws, at this time, even they are raising serious concerns about the Orthodox rabbinate's control of kosher certification.

Judaism's construction of sacred time asks Jews to see themselves as living between the perfection of the mythical Eden and a hoped-for perfection of the Messianic age; for now, humanity is stuck in the imperfect middle era. Premodern food production was troubling for its slave-produced food. Today, slavery in food production continues, and there are also newer and often intertwined forms of exploitation of the environment, farmed animals, farm workers, and even farmers themselves. As in the past, many people are not concerned about the harm caused in getting food to their tables, preferring to focus on the benefits that modernity has conferred upon the human diet. Increasingly, though, there are articulate voices sounding the alarm about the damage caused by our hunger for cheap, quick, and plentiful food.

The six modern mass Jewish migrations led to new cuisines and combinations, creating great diversity within Jewish cuisine. Today's globalized food economy and culture is producing new fusions and erasing earlier distinctions altogether. Indeed, the multitude of eating options is for many Jewish "foodies" a feature of modern life to celebrate. This chapter has shown how we came to these different kinds of diversity, and it also points to the current challenges and future possibilities.

NOTES

1. Katz, *Tradition and Crisis*, describes the early modern era in Western and Eastern European lands. For Jews in Muslim lands, see Benbassa and Rodrigue, *Sephardi Jewry*; Stillman, *Jews of Arab Lands*.

2. For discussion, see Kraemer, *Jewish Eating*, 132–33. On the Sabbath stew, see the chapter in this volume by Katalin Rac.

3. On female slaughterers in Italy, see Bonfil, *Jewish Life in Renaissance Italy*, 132–33.

4. For discussion, see Efron, Weitzman, and Lehmann, *Jews*, 215–16.

5. Pilcher, *Food in World History*, 19–26.

6. Horowitz, "Coffee." On the cultural effect of the coffeehouses on European Jewish life, see Liberles, *Jews Welcome Coffee*.

7. Benbassa and Rodrigue, *Sephardi Jewry*, chaps. 1 and 2; Efron, Weitzman, and Lehmann, *Jews*, 217–20.

8. See Marcus, *Jew in the Medieval World*, 416, for a description of the extensive food charity of Dona Gracia Mendes in Constantinople. See also Efron, Weitzman, and Lehmann, *Jews*, 219–20.

9. On the history of raising chickens for food in Europe, see Cooper, *Eat and Be Satisfied*, 109–10; and Marks, *Encyclopedia*, s.v. "Chicken."

10. For discussion, see Cooper, *Eat and Be Satisfied*, 132–33; Roden, *Jewish Food*; Marks, *Encyclopedia*, s.v. "Álbondiga."

11. Dynner, *Yankel's Tavern*, focuses on the Jewish role in liquor production and trade in the nineteenth century.

12. See the chapter on garlic in this volume by Jordan Rosenblum. See also Horowitz, "Remembering the Fish," 73–77.

13. Cooper, *Eat and Be Satisfied*, 173–76, discusses ingredients added in later years to the simple bread recipe. Roden, *Jewish Food*, 549–50, references the absence of a specific kind of Sephardic Sabbath bread. The braided Sabbath bread was unknown at the time to Ottoman Jews.

14. Marks, *Encyclopedia*, s.v. "Bagels," "Lokshen," and "Wheat." On the Sabbath *lokshen kugel*, see Nadler, "Holy Kugel."

15. Morineau, "Growing without Knowing," 374–82. Information on Jews is found in Mendes-Flohr, "Demography," 705.

16. Diner, *Roads Taken*, 2–7.

17. Katz, *Tradition and Crisis*, 208n15.

18. Kraemer, *Jewish Eating*, 136.

19. In Europe, the term for "Reform" is *Liberal* or *Progressive*. Postings about the conferences of the European Union for Progressive Judaism indicate the food policies—for example, www.eupj.org, accessed July 3, 2016.

20. Sarna, *American Judaism*, 144–51.

21. Dorff, *Unfolding Tradition*, 51, 53.

22. The points in this section are drawn from the rich account of immigrant Jewish foodways in Hasia Diner, *Hungering for America*, 178–219.

23. New York State intermittently regulated the use of the term *kosher*.

24. Gastwirt, *Fraud, Corruption, and Holiness*; Hyman, "Immigrant Women and Consumer Protest."

25. Gurock, *Orthodox Jews in America*, 79ff.

26. Joselit, *Wonders of America*, 173–74.

27. Rubel, "'Jewish' Joy of Cooking?," 284–87.

28. This is a repeated theme in Goldberg, *Sephardi and Middle Eastern Jewries*, 28–29, 81–84, 89–98.

29. Roden, *Jewish Food*, 5–9, 212, 229.

30. Zenner, *Global Community*, 127ff.

31. Roden, *Jewish Food*, 412–14; Marks, *Encyclopedia*, s.v. "Kibbeh," notes that Jews whose origin is Aleppo claim sixty distinct recipes for the dish.

32. Micklin, "Seattle Sephardim"; Washington State Jewish Historical Society, *Yesterday's Mavens*, vii–viii.

33. Raviv, *Falafel Nation*.

34. Raviv, 1–26; Marks, *Encyclopedia*, s.v. "Israel," "Cheese," "Schnitzel," "Falafel," "Shawarma," "Boreka."

35. "Jewish" in Israeli state law is a designation of nationality, and yet an individual's religious status as a Jew has been in the hands of the Orthodox rabbinate with standards that result in a person declared Jewish by the state but not by the rabbinate. Israel's citizenry also includes people who follow Islam, Christianity, the Druze religion, and so on.

36. Marks, *Encyclopedia*, s.v. "Plov"; Roden, *Jewish Food*, 456.

37. Barak-Erez, *Outlawed Pigs.*
38. The survey of Israelis that produced these statistics does not query what respondents mean when they describe their food as kosher. The claim that 75 percent keep kosher at home is from Guttman Center, "Portrait of Israeli Jews," 13–14. The Pew Research Center, "Israel's Religiously Divided Society," indicates 63 percent.
39. On the marketing and more frequent eating of hummus beginning in the 1990s, see Marks, *Encyclopedia,* s.v. "Hummus."
40. Rubin, *Israel,* 140–43. At the time of this latest migration, Israeli law permitted the immediate granting of citizenship to the children of a Jewish parent (father or mother) or the spouse of a Jew. From 1971 to 1981, a sizable number of Jews from Georgia immigrated to Israel, and most of the remainder immigrated in the 1990s; see Zand, Neishtat, and Beizer, *Encyclopaedia Judaica,* s.v. "Georgia."
41. This is Tiv Ta'am, which had thirty-eight outlets in 2018; see www.tivtaam.co.il. See also Rubin, *Israel,* 142.
42. Cooper, *Eat and Be Satisfied,* 142–43.
43. See Prinz, *On the Chocolate Trail.*
44. See in this chapter for a discussion of this ethical problem.
45. The points in this section are drawn from Horowitz, *Kosher USA,* 75–104.
46. For discussion, see Horowitz, 116–25.
47. For example, the Orthodox Union, whose kosher division is the most widely used in the US, claimed on its website that "all revenues from OU Kosher are used to fund the OU's community activities"; see Orthodox Union, www.ou.org, accessed January 3, 2016. Also see Horowitz, *Kosher USA,* 101–2.
48. Sarna, *American Judaism,* 293–306. See also the chapter by Zev Eleff in this volume.
49. Sarna, "How Matzah Became Square."
50. Berman, *Shehitah,* 176–93, historically surveys the practice in Jewish communities around the world to tax shehitah and/or meat purchases to help defray a variety of communal expenses.
51. Horowitz, *Putting Meat on the American Table,* 18–42; for the kosher meat industry, Horowitz, *Kosher USA,* 163ff. In 1990, Orthodox kosher certifiers imposed far stricter standards known as glatt, which reduced the percentage of slaughtered mammals that would, upon inspection, be designated kosher.
52. They also find cruel some modes of handling in shehitah. Preshehitah handling has varied according to local custom and halakhic traditions. On the halakhic distinction between animal handling and shehitah itself, see Helfgot, *Community, Covenant, and Commitment,* 64.
53. See Judd, *Circumcision, Kosher Butchering.*
54. Gross, *Question of the Animal,* chap. 2.
55. Grandin, "Recommended Ritual Slaughter Practices," www.grandin.com.
56. Library of Congress, "Legal Restrictions on Religious Slaughter in Europe," https://loc.gov.
57. The Conservative Movement initiative known as Magen Tzedek was founded in response to Agriprocessors; see www.magentzedek.org/. *The Sacred Table:*

Creating a Jewish Food Ethic is an anthology published by the American Reform rabbinical organization with multiple articles that include this concern. "Tav HaYosher" is a certification program launched by Orthodox Rabbi Shmuly Yanklowitz that identifies kosher restaurants whose owners pledge to follow social justice principles regarding their workers; see http://utzedek.org. See the chapter in this volume by Moses Pava.

BIBLIOGRAPHY

Barak-Erez, Daphne. *Outlawed Pigs: Law, Religion, and Culture in Israel*. Madison: University of Wisconsin Press, 2007.

Benbassa, Esther, and Aron Rodrigue, eds. *Sephardi Jewry*. Berkeley: University of California Press, 2000.

Berman, Jeremiah Joseph. *Shehitah: A Study in the Cultural and Social Life of the Jewish People*. New York: Bloch, 1941.

Bonfil, Robert. *Jewish Life in Renaissance Italy*. Translated by Anthony Oldcorn. Berkeley: University of California Press, 1994.

Cooper, John. *Eat and Be Satisfied: A Social History of Jewish Food*. Northvale, NJ: Jason Aaronson, 1993.

Diner, Hasia R. *Hungering for America: Italian, Irish, and Jewish Foodways in the Age of Migration*. Cambridge, MA: Harvard University Press, 2001.

———. *Roads Taken: The Great Jewish Migrations to the New World and the Peddlers Who Forged the Way*. New Haven, CT: Yale University Press, 2015.

Dorff, Elliot N. *The Unfolding Tradition: Philosophies of Jewish Law*. New York: Rabbinical Assembly, 2011.

Dynner, Glenn. *Yankel's Tavern: Jews, Liquor, and Life in the Kingdom of Poland*. New York: Oxford University Press, 2014.

Efron, John, Steven Weitzman, and Matthias Lehmann. *The Jews: A History*. 2nd ed. London: Routledge, 2013.

Gastwirt, Harold P. *Fraud, Corruption, and Holiness: The Controversy over the Supervision of Jewish Dietary Practice in New York City, 1881–1940*. Port Washington, NY: Kennikat, 1974.

Goldberg, Harvey E., ed. *Sephardi and Middle Eastern Jewries: History and Culture in the Modern Era*. Bloomington: Indiana University Press, 1996.

Grandin, Temple. "Recommended Ritual Slaughter Practices." Dr. Temple Grandin's Website. www.grandin.com.

Gross, Aaron S. *The Question of the Animal and Religion: Theoretical Stakes, Practical Implications*. New York: Columbia University Press, 2015.

Gurock, Jeffrey S. *Orthodox Jews in America*. Bloomington: Indiana University Press, 2009.

Guttman Center for Surveys of the Israel Democracy Institute. "A Portrait of Israeli Jews: Beliefs, Observance, and Values of Israeli Jews, 2009." http://en.idi.org.

Helfgot, Nathaniel, ed. *Community, Covenant, and Commitment: Selected Letters and Communications of Rabbi Joseph B. Soloveitchik*. Jersey City, NJ: Ktav, 2005.

Horowitz, Elliot. "Coffee, Coffeehouses, and the Nocturnal Rituals of Early Modern Jewry." *AJS Review* 14 (1989): 17–46.

———. "Remembering the Fish and Making a Tsimmes: Jewish Food, Jewish Identity, and Jewish Memory." *Jewish Quarterly Review* 104 (2014): 57–59.

Horowitz, Roger. *Kosher USA: How Coke Became Kosher and Other Tales of Modern Food.* New York: Columbia University Press, 2016.

———. *Putting Meat on the American Table.* Baltimore: Johns Hopkins University Press, 2007.

Hyman, Paula. "Immigrant Women and Consumer Protest: The New York City Kosher Meat Boycott of 1902." *American Jewish History* 70, no. 1 (1980): 91–105.

Joselit, Jenna Weissman. *The Wonders of America: Reinventing Jewish Culture, 1880–1950.* New York: Henry Holt, 1994.

Judd, Robin. *Circumcision, Kosher Butchering and Jewish Political Life in Germany, 1843–1933.* Ithaca, NY: Cornell University Press, 2007.

Katz, Jacob. *Tradition and Crisis: Jewish Society at the End of the Middle Ages.* Rev. ed. Syracuse: Syracuse University Press, 2000.

Kirshenblatt-Gimblett, Barbara. "Food and Drink." YIVO Encyclopedia of Jews in Eastern Europe. 2010. www.yivoencyclopedia.org.

Kraemer, David C. *Jewish Eating and Identity through the Ages.* New York: Routledge, 2007.

Liberles, Robert. *Jews Welcome Coffee: Tradition and Innovation in Early Modern Germany.* Waltham: Brandeis University Press, 2012.

Library of Congress. "Legal Restrictions on Religious Slaughter in Europe." Accessed January 21, 2019. https://loc.gov.

Marcus, Jacob Rader, ed. *The Jew in the Medieval World: A Sourcebook.* Rev. ed. Cincinnati: Hebrew Union College Press, 1999.

Marks, Gil. *Encyclopedia of Jewish Food.* Hoboken, NJ: John Wiley, 2010.

McNeill, William H. "How the Potato Changed the World's History." *Social Research* 66 (1999): 67–83.

Mendes-Flohr, Paul, and Jehuda Reinharz, eds. "The Demography of Modern Jewish History." In *The Jew in the Modern World: A Documentary History*, 879–91. New York: Oxford University Press, 1980.

Micklin, Lee. "Seattle Sephardim: Early Beginnings." HistoryLink.org. www.historylink .org.

Morineau, Michel. "Growing without Knowing Why: Production, Demographics, and Diet." In *Food: A Culinary History from Antiquity to the Present*, edited by Jean-Louis Flandrin and Massimo Montanari, 374–82. New York: Columbia University Press, 1996.

Nadler, Allan. "Holy Kugel: The Sanctification of Ashkenazic Ethnic Foods in Hasidism." In *Food and Judaism*, edited by Leonard J. Greenspoon, Ronald A. Simkins, and Gerald Shapiro, 193–214. Omaha, NE: Creighton University Press, 2004.

Pew Research Center. "Israel's Religiously Divided Society, 2016." www.pewforum.org.

Pilcher, Jeffrey M. *Food in World History.* New York: Routledge, 2006.

Prinz, Deborah R. *On the Chocolate Trail: A Delicious Adventure Connecting Jews, Religions, History, Travel, Rituals and Recipes to the Magic of Cacao*. Woodstock, VT: Jewish Lights, 2012.

Raviv, Yael. *Falafel Nation: Cuisine and the Making of National Identity in Israel*. Lincoln: University of Nebraska Press, 2015.

Roden, Claudia. *The Book of Jewish Food: An Odyssey from Samarkand to New York*. New York: Alfred A. Knopf, 2003.

Rubel, Nora. "A 'Jewish' Joy of Cooking? How a 20th Century Cookbook Containing Frog's Legs, Snails, and Ham Became a Beloved Jewish Icon." In *The Value of the Particular: Lessons from Judaism and the Modern Jewish Experience*, edited by Michael Zank and Ingrid Anderson, 268–97. Leiden: Brill, 2015.

Rubin, Barry. *Israel: An Introduction*. New Haven, CT: Yale University Press, 2012.

Sarna, Jonathan D. *American Judaism: A History*. New Haven, CT: Yale University Press, 2006.

———. "How Matzah Became Square: Manischewitz and the Development of Machine-Made Matzah in the United States." In *Chosen Capital: The Jewish Encounter with American Capitalism*, edited by Rebecca Kobrin, 272–88. New Brunswick, NJ: Rutgers University Press, 2012.

Stillman, Norman. *The Jews of Arab Lands*. Philadelphia: Jewish Publication Society, 1979.

Washington State Jewish Historical Society. *Yesterday's Mavens, Today's Foodies: Traditions in Northwest Jewish Kitchens*. Seattle: Peanut Butter Publishing, 2011.

Zamore, Mary L., ed. *The Sacred Table: Creating a Jewish Food Ethic*. New York: Central Conference of American Rabbis, 2011.

Zand, Michael, Mordkhai Neishtat, and Michael Beizer. "Georgia." In *Encyclopaedia Judaica*, 7:495–501. Detroit: Macmillan, 2007.

Zenner, Walter. *A Global Community: The Jews from Aleppo, Syria*. Detroit: Wayne State University Press, 2000.

Food and Culture

Introduction to Part 2

JORDAN D. ROSENBLUM

There is no singular culinary category of "Jewish food." As discussed in the introduction to this volume, different Jewish communities in different times and places developed culinary preferences and styles, but these do not coalesce into a universal culinary category. In general, Jewish communities adopted local cuisines and tweaked them to accord with kosher laws. However, there are exceptions. For example, in New York City in the twentieth century, Jewish immigrants from various European countries swapped recipes and developed the menu of the "Jewish deli."[1] Many delis were "kosher style," meaning that they almost certainly did not serve pork, and they likely did not directly mix milk and meat, and yet perhaps the most famous "Jewish deli" sandwich, the Reuben, mixes meat and cheese—a violation of rabbinic food law.

Sometimes food is labeled "Jewish" because Jews are considered the group that introduced a foreign foodstuff to a new location (e.g., Polish bagels in America) or because others simply associate Jews with a particular food (e.g., the artichoke among early modern Italians).[2] For myriad reasons, Jews and different foods are connected. Sometimes, these connections last for a brief moment; other times, they endure for millennia. For those that last, the association rarely has a stable meaning. Like all things, it changes over time.

In this part, we consider several studies of food and culture that might be considered to constitute "Jewish food." The first chapter, by Jordan D. Rosenblum, surveys the three-thousand-year history of associating Jews with garlic. This chapter introduces the concept of food as a "metonym." When a food functions as a metonym, the food itself—and those who are and are not associated with that food—serve to define a person's or group's identity based on their connection/disconnection from that food. From the Hebrew Bible to "kosher dill pickles" in the modern Jewish deli, garlic has served as a metonym—a symbolic representation of

Jews and Jewishness. As we shall see, this metonymic function is sometimes positive and other times negative, sometimes self-imposed and other times externally applied. And the same food can have multiple meanings when we travel across space and time.

The next two chapters function as a subsection, in which the concept of "Jewish food" is expanded to consider both the food itself and the food practices surrounding it as well. This allows for examination of both culinary regulations (what one does and does not eat) and commensal regulations (how and with whom one eats).[3] David M. Freidenreich explores how discussions about food and food practices served as reflections on "Jewishness" in premodern Jewish, Christian, and Muslim communities. Using Jewish, Christian, and Muslim sources, Freidenreich argues that "these authorities agree both that the difference between Jews and non-Jews matters and that food is an ideal medium through which to emphasize this distinction—even though the distinction itself is not really about food." Food and food practices serve as a metonym for difference, even when the food and food practices themselves are a means to an end, with the ultimate goal being about communal distinction. Susan Marks then considers how ancient rabbis drew on Roman libation practices to develop their own wine-related grace after meals (Hebrew: *birkat ha-mazon*) ritual. While previous studies focus on the liturgical text of the blessing, Marks focuses on the ritual actions surrounding wine drinking in this context. Postmeal wine ritual, then, becomes a means for the ancient rabbis to signal their relationship to, and distinction from, their Greek and Roman neighbors.

With Rachel B. Gross's chapter, we return to food itself. Or rather, to the substances in which food is cooked. Gross investigates the fascinating history of Crisco, teaching us the backstory of the role that Jewish consumers played in the marketing of this cooking oil. While Crisco offered a nonmeat, nondairy (*parve*) alternative to schmaltz (rendered chicken fat), its success as a food product is bound up in the tale of modern marketing, the rise of the kosher certification industry, recent concerns regarding trans fats, and the modern foodie re-embracing of schmaltz.[4]

Zev Eleff slathers another fatty layer onto the story of Jews with a focus on cooking oils. Opening with the importance of schmaltz, Eleff introduces us to another new cooking product encountered by American Jews in the early twentieth century: peanut oil. While there are many overlaps with the Crisco story, there is an important difference that generates this chapter: the controversy over whether peanuts are allowable to be consumed by Ashkenazi Jews on Passover. At stake is the ability to use peanut oil. As this story unfolds, we learn of how the stringent interpretations of Hungarian Jewish immigrants influenced kosher policy in general and the kosher-for-Passover status of peanut oil in particular. Peanut oil then becomes a lens through which to view the general rightward shift within American Orthodox Judaism over the course of the twentieth-century America.

In the final chapter in this part, we turn from Hungarian Jews in America to Hungarian Jews in Hungary, when Katalin Franciscka Rac introduces us to the story of how a popular Sabbath dish became a secular Hungarian favorite. In the process, we learn about the long history of Sabbath cholent (and related dishes) and how a particular form of the dish, *sólet*, became popular among non-Jews in Hungary. In the process, Rac tells the story of Jewish integration into Hungary, as symbolized by the transition of this particular dish from a Sabbath meal to a canned product often featuring pork sausage. The story of cholent in Hungary, then, becomes a lens through which to view the establishment of Jews as Hungarian citizens, both from an internal and external perspective. While sólet appears on many Hungarian plates, the narrative of how it got there and what that journey means varies based on the perspective of the one viewing—and eating from—that plate.

Taken together, the chapters in this part begin a conversation about the ways that foods and food practices define Jews, Jewishness, and relationships between Jews and non-Jews. Though they do not cover the entirety of this rich and varied story, these chapters introduce key elements and offer important bibliographic references of where to continue to read beyond the boundaries of this volume. We have learned the long history of Jews and food, so now we turn to a few fascinating studies in food and culture.

NOTES

1. Merwin, *Pastrami on Rye*; Sax, *Save the Deli*.
2. Balinska, *Bagel*; Marks, *Encyclopedia of Jewish Food*, 24.
3. See Rosenblum, *Food and Identity*, 3.
4. On modern marketing and the rise of kosher certification agencies, see Horowitz, *Kosher USA*.

BIBLIOGRAPHY

Balinska, Maria. *The Bagel: The Surprising History of a Modest Bread*. New Haven: Yale University Press, 2008.

Horowitz, Roger. *Kosher USA: How Coke Became Kosher and Other Tales of Modern Food*. New York: Columbia University Press, 2016.

Marks, Gil. *Encyclopedia of Jewish Food*. Hoboken, NJ: John Wiley, 2009.

Merwin, Ted. *Pastrami on Rye: An Overstuffed History of the Jewish Deli*. New York: New York University Press, 2015.

Rosenblum, Jordan D. *Food and Identity in Early Rabbinic Judaism*. New York: Cambridge University Press, 2010.

Sax, David. *Save the Deli: In Search of Perfect Pastrami, Crusty Rye, and the Heart of Jewish Delicatessen*. New York: Houghton Mifflin Harcourt, 2009.

5

A Brief History of Jews and Garlic

JORDAN D. ROSENBLUM

After the Exodus from Egypt, when the Israelites wandered in the desert, they grew tired of eating only manna. Comparing the varied diet that they ate as slaves in Egypt to the unvaried diet that they now enjoyed as free women and men, a few troublemakers complained: "The riffraff in their midst felt a gluttonous craving; and then the Israelites wept and said, 'If only we had meat to eat! We remember the fish that we used to eat free in Egypt, the cucumbers, the melons, the leeks, the onions, and the garlic. Now our gullets are shriveled. There is nothing at all! Nothing but this manna to look to!'" (Numbers 11:4–6).[1] Among the list of their favorite foods is garlic (modern botanical classification: *Allium sativum*). Beginning with this reference, the only mention of garlic in the Hebrew Bible, we shall briefly explore the historical association between Jews and garlic that develops over the next three millennia.[2] In doing so, we shall see how garlic eventually functions both internally (by Jews) and externally (by non-Jews) as a symbol that represents Self and Other—or, in the terminology favored in anthropology and food studies, how garlic operates as a metonym for Jews.[3]

The first identification of Jews with garlic appears in the Mishnah and Talmud, rabbinic writings that date, respectively, to the third and the seventh centuries CE. The rabbis of the Mishnah understood Jewish garlic consumption to be so identifiable that they referred to Jews as "garlic eaters."[4] Centuries later, the Talmud attests that Jews enjoyed their favorite food on their favorite day of the week: the Sabbath.[5] Perhaps the association between garlic and the Sabbath is due to the well-attested ancient understanding—popular among both Jews and non-Jews—that garlic was a potent aphrodisiac.[6] Since the rabbis understood the Sabbath to be an optimal time for procreation, garlic was an obvious Sabbath spice, as "it causes love to enter and desire to go forth."[7] Elsewhere, garlic is called a Sabbath delight, with the same sexual implications of the word *delight* as in the sexually suggestive song "Afternoon Delight."[8] Further, according to the Babylonian Talmud,

> [Ezra ordained] "that garlic should be eaten on Friday evenings" because of marital relations [which are required to take place on the Sabbath], as it is written: "That brings forth its fruit in its season" [Psalm 1:3], and Rabbi Judah, and some say Rav Nahman, and some say Rav Kahana, and some say Rabbi Yohanan, said:[9] this refers to the one who performs his marital duty every Friday night.
>
> Our rabbis taught: Five things were said regarding garlic: (1) it satisfies [the appetite]; (2) it warms [the body]; (3) it brightens the face; (4) it increases virility; and (5) it kills parasites in the intestines. Some say it causes love to enter and desire to go forth.[10] (Babylonian Talmud, Bava Qamma 82a)

In ascribing this practice to the biblical figure Ezra, the rabbis backdate the Jewish tradition of eating garlic on the Sabbath by about one thousand years prior to the editing of the Babylonian Talmud. While this does not mean that non-Jews did not enjoy eating garlic, the rabbis presume an ancient and intimate connection between Jews and garlic. The veracity of this claim, however, is much less important than the rabbinic belief that the association between garlic, Jews, and the Sabbath is a long-standing tradition.

Another important datum we learn from this text relates to the five things taught regarding garlic. The first four (as well as the additional one appended on the end) clearly have sexual connotations, but the fifth statement makes a rather nonsexual claim—namely, that garlic has medicinal properties (after all, what is less sexy than intestinal parasites?).[11] In fact, many rabbinic texts laud the health benefits of garlic.[12] The connection between garlic and health continues into later eras. In the medieval period, it played a role in folk medicine;[13] and in the modern period, some went so far as to claim that garlic ingestion protected Jewish (and fellow garlic-loving Italian) immigrants to America from tuberculosis.[14]

While garlic had the potential to stimulate and heal one's body, the rabbis were aware of one major side effect of eating garlic: bad breath. "Shall one who ate garlic and his breath smells, return and eat garlic again, so that his breath should continue smelling?" (Babylonian Talmud, Berakhot 51a) was a rabbinic idiom for "two wrongs do not make a right." Yet even for a group who confessed a deep love for garlic, sometimes the odor bothered some, as was the case for Rabbi Judah the Patriarch, who asked a student smelling of garlic to leave his classroom.[15] There were also polemical accusations that Jews possessed a foul aroma,[16] though they appeared neither as often nor in direct association with garlic as occurred in later periods, as we see in regard to the *foetor judaicus*, or the "Jewish stench."

The *foetor judaicus* was a subject of antisemitic ridicule in medieval, early modern, and modern times. It is this prejudice that lurks in the background of Geoffrey Chaucer's *Canterbury Tales*, when the Summoner's love of garlic represents his "spiritual deformity. . . . This dietary preference makes the Summoner akin to 'the Jews.'"[17] The presumed odious aroma of Jews was a metonym for their presumed repugnant natures.[18]

A visual representation of this association is the sixteenth-century image of a Jew in Worms, Germany, who holds a moneybag in his left hand and a garlic clove in his right hand (figure 5.1).[19] There are multiple layers of interpretation for this image. First, it is from Worms, which, alongside Speyer and Mainz, was one of the three Rhineland communities with vibrant Jewish populations that were called by the acronym *Shum*,[20] which is the Hebrew word for "garlic." Second, notice what the Jewish man is holding.[21] The repugnant stereotypes of Jew as usurer and garlic eater are both represented. Further, given the common cultural prominence of the right hand, this could be taken to mean that, for the Jew, garlic is even dearer to his heart than money—quite the claim. Finally, note the gendering of this image: a male is holding a foodstuff, and home cooking is often gendered as female.[22] This serves both to emasculate the feminized Jewish man and metonymically to remind its viewer of his intrinsic Jewish stench.

Literature of the past several centuries abounds with negative references to Jews, garlic, and the *foetor judaicus*.[23] In the eighteenth century, Johann Jacob Schudt declared, "The palaces of the Jews may be most

Figure 5.1. Thesaurus picturarum by Marcus (also "Markus")
Lamm, ca. 1600

elegant and furnished with exquisite furniture and delicate decorations,
but when one enters one finds Jews smelling of garlic there."[24] In the
nineteenth century, August Graf von Platen gibed Heinreich Heine, a
convert from Judaism and his poetic competitor, that he "would not
want to be his lover, since his kisses exude garlic."[25] In the twentieth
century, the Kinks, a British band famous for numerous hits, including
"You Really Got Me," penned a catchy tune called "When I Turn Off the
Living Room Lights," which features the following lyrics:

Who cares if you're Jewish
and your breath smells of garlic,
and your nose is a shiny red light.
To me you are gorgeous,
and everything's right
when I turn off the living room light.[26]

In all these instances, garlic serves as a metonym, as a representation of the Jew as the odorous Other.

The association between Jews and garlic lurks in the shadows of another antisemitic polemic: vampire lore. While their appearance in recent popular culture like *Buffy the Vampire Slayer* or the *Twilight* trilogy might lead one to think that vampires are more about teenage angst, vampires have long served as a metaphor for the threatening Other, especially in regard to Jews.[27] The vampire, speaking in a (sometimes muted) foreign accent, seeks to suck their victim's blood, which either kills the victim or turns them into a vampire. Christian symbols scare the vampire off, which is why keeping a crucifix, a rosary, and/or holy water handy is a good idea. Since popular antisemitic polemics (especially the blood libel) inform much of the common vampire lore, an interesting question arises: if "the vampire" represents "the Jew," then why would garlic be such a well-known apotropaic—that is, a means of warding evil forces off? After all, Jews love garlic! Then why do vampires run away from garlic? One answer may be drawn from the insight that this common vampire lore is partly intended as an anti-immigration polemic in which the vampire/Jew tries to secretly assimilate into society and then terrorize it from within. Thus a vampire "flees garlic . . . [because] it reveals his true self, which must remain disguised if his parasitical quest is to succeed."[28] It is garlic's very association with Jews that reveals the hidden vampire/Jew.

There is evidence also that Jews internalized this metonymic association and used it themselves to signal their status as an outsider to dominant, non-Jewish culture. A complex and fascinating example of this phenomenon is the early modern Jewish tradition of Nittel Nacht, which consists of "a cluster of Jewish observances carried out on Christmas Eve. From the early modern period onwards, many European Jews marked the arrival of the Christmas holiday by putting aside their holy books, refraining from sexual relations, consuming garlic, staying up late, and holding rowdy gatherings (often centered on card playing)."[29] Eating garlic on Christmas Eve was one way to signal resistance to that day, both against their dominant Christian culture and as a means of spiritual/literal protection, since garlic was understood as an apotropaic that warded off demons and spirits.[30] Jews eating garlic on Christmas Eve was therefore a dietary practice that served both medical and metonymic purposes.

For more than three thousand years, sources by and about Jews testify to a particular fondness for garlic.[31] Exemplary of this phenomenon, and a fitting conclusion to this brief chapter about the historical function of garlic as a metonym for Jewish identity, is the case of the "kosher dill pickle." According to the late Gil Marks, a chef, rabbi, and Jewish food expert, "True 'kosher dills,' short for kosher-style or Jewish-style, never contain vinegar, but rather rely solely on lactic acid fermentation, which, like the fermentation of sauerkraut, produces a distinctive acidity and flavor. The addition of whole garlic also marks cucumbers as 'kosher dills.'"[32] While there are various technical reasons the absence of vinegar is advantageous from the perspective of certifying a foodstuff as kosher,[33] note Marks's language. The word *kosher* stands in for "kosher-style or Jewish-style," meaning that the word does not refer to the actual kosher status of the pickle (which may or may not be certified kosher). Rather, it is made in the style of a kosher food. Further, the word *kosher* more likely metonymically stands in here for "Jewish." And what makes these pickles "Jewish"? Garlic.

NOTES

Though any errors that remain are my own, I benefited greatly from the feedback of many of the contributors to this volume, especially David Freidenreich (and his students at Colby College, who read an early draft of this chapter in his class) and Jody Meyers.

1. Jewish Publication Society (JPS) translation. For early interpretations of the role of garlic in this passage, see, for example, Philo, *Who Is the Heir?*, 78–80 (allegory for corrupt food/people/Egypt); and Babylonian Talmud, Yoma 75a (that manna tasted like all foods, except the five fruits and vegetables mentioned in Numbers 11:5).

2. Although garlic is often mentioned alongside two other members of the onion genus *Allium* (leeks and especially onions), this chapter will focus on garlic. Perhaps one day I will write about the association between Jews and these other closely related vegetables. Further, space constraints prevent me from discussing

every relevant text; as such, this brief chapter will, by necessity, be a selective history.

3. For a brief discussion, see Ohnuki-Tierney, *Rice as Self*, 129–31. Garlic is not the only food that functions in this manner. For example, a roughly similar narrative can be constructed in regard to pork (a history that I intend to explain in a future project).

4. Mishnah, Nedarim 3.10. See Rosenblum, *Food and Identity*, 47.

5. See, for example, Mishnah, Nedarim 8.6; Jerusalem Talmud, Nedarim 8.7, 40c; Tanhuma Beshallah 4.3. Of course, Jews also enjoyed garlic every day of the week (see Rosenblum, *Food and Identity*, 47n42).

6. For rabbinic references to garlic as an aphrodisiac, see, for example, Babylonian Talmud, Yoma 18a–b; Avot d'Rabbi Natan B:48; and the following sources. For this understanding in non-Jewish sources, see, for example, Pliny, *Natural History*, 20:23. Some Buddhists forbid garlic based on the understanding that garlic stimulates sexual desire.

7. Jerusalem Talmud, Megillah 4.1, 75a. See Satlow, *Tasting the Dish*, 279 (and on the general rabbinic association between Sabbath and procreation, see pp. 278–80).

8. Babylonian Talmud, Shabbat 118b. Similarly, see Diemling, "'As the Jews Like to Eat Garlick,'" 218. "Afternoon Delight" was released by Starland Vocal Band in 1976, who won a Grammy for the album on which it appeared. Lyrics can be found at https://play.google.com (accessed July 17, 2018).

9. The exact rabbi who uttered this statement is disputed; therefore, the text notes all its possible attributions.

10. The standard printed edition reads ". . . and jealousy goes forth." I have emended the text for three reasons: (1) there is manuscript evidence for doing so; (2) the wording of this last line mirrors Jerusalem Talmud, Megillah 4.1, 75a, discussed earlier in the chapter; and (3) "desire" makes more sense in this context.

11. The first century CE non-Jewish physician Dioscorides (*De Materia Medica*, 2:181) also believed that garlic could kill intestinal parasites.

12. For example, see Babylonian Talmud, Gittin 69a (toothache remedy); and Babylonian Talmud, Eruvin 55b–56a. On some other potential issues with handling garlic, see, for example, Babylonian Talmud, Niddah 17a (on evil spirits resting on peeled garlic bulbs); Babylonian Talmud, Betzah 7b, 25b (on snake venom and uncovered, pulverized garlic and on proper etiquette for garlic eating, respectively). Jews were not the only ancient Mediterranean group that lauded the medicinal properties of garlic. No less an authority than the famous Greek physician Galen extolled the healing properties of garlic—even commenting that it had the added side effect of reducing flatulence. See Galen, *Method of Medicine*, 12.8 (865–66).

13. See, for example, Zohar 2:80a; in general, Hecker, *Mystical Bodies, Mystical Meals*, 110–11. Though it should be noted that Maimonides, a physician and famous medieval rabbinic authority, declared consumption of garlic to be harmful (Mishneh Torah, Hilkhot De'ot, 4:9).

14. See Hart, *Healthy Jew*, 166.
15. See Babylonian Talmud, Sanhedrin 11a.
16. For example, Ammianus Marcellinus, *Rerum Gestarum*, 22.5:5, in which he accuses Jews of possessing a foul odor (*Iudaeorum fetentium*), though the explicit connection between this Jewish odor and garlic is by no means explicit, contra Feliks, "Garlic," 7:329.
17. Litvak, *Jewish Persona*, 96.
18. For additional references, see Diemling, "'As the Jews Like to Eat Garlick'"; Litvak, *Jewish Persona*, 93–97, 233–78.
19. Thesaurus picturarum by Marcus (also "Markus") Lamm ca. 1600 (accessed February 4, 2019). I would like to thank Amos Bitzan for helping me locate this image.
20. *Sh* = Speyer; *u* = Worms (the Hebrew letter *vav* can represent both a *u* and *v* sound); and *m* = Mainz.
21. There is an accompanying image of a Jewish woman holding a goose, a fowl associated with the Jewish kitchen. For discussion, see Diemling, "'As the Jews Like to Eat Garlick,'" 218.
22. Here I am building on the interpretations of Litvak, *Jewish Persona*, 94.
23. See note 18.
24. For references and discussion, see Diemling, "'As the Jews Like to Eat Garlick,'" 226–27; Litvak, *Jewish Persona*, 96.
25. See Diemling, "'As the Jews Like to Eat Garlick,'" 215. On claims that baptism can/cannot cleanse Jews of the *foetor judaicus*, see Trachtenberg, *Devil and the Jews*, 48–50.
26. To listen to this song, see https://www.youtube.com/watch?v=jpwGGJYCCJo (accessed July 17, 2018). An explanation of the lyrics by Ray Davies, lead singer and songwriter for the Kinks, was posted online, though the link no longer works; see http://swampdpopculture.blogspot.com (accessed August 24, 2016).
27. See Robinson, *Blood Will Tell*, though an important lacuna is its absence of garlic-related discussion.
28. Litvak, *Jewish Persona*, 245–46.
29. Scharbach, "Ghosts in the Privy," 340.
30. In general, see Scharbach, "Ghosts in the Privy." Scharbach (362–63) notes that some Christians also used garlic as an apotropaic, and even on Christmas; however, this practice was particularly associated with Jews, and significant metonymic meaning was attached to the garlic when Jews did so versus when some Christians did.
31. For additional historical references to Jews and cooking with garlic, see, for example, Cooper, *Eat and Be Satisfied*, 85, 124–25, 127–28; Diner, *Hungering for America*, 160, 162–63, 169; Horowitz, "Remember the Fish and Making Tsimmes," 73–77; Kugelmass, "Green Bagels," 65 passim; and Marks, *Encyclopedia of Jewish Food*, 217–18.
32. Marks, *Encyclopedia of Jewish Food*, 458–59.

33. For brief discussion and references in regard to classical rabbinic sources, see Freidenreich, *Foreigners and Their Food*, 52–54, 57–58, 61.

BIBLIOGRAPHY

Ammianus Marcellinus. *Rerum Gestarum*. Translation by J. C. Rolfe. *Ammianus Marcellinus, History, Books 20–26*. Loeb Classical Library 315. Cambridge: Harvard University Press, 1940.

Cooper, John. *Eat and Be Satisfied: A Social History of Jewish Food*. Northvale, NJ: Jason Aronson, 1993.

Diemling, Maria. "'As the Jews Like to Eat Garlick': Garlic in Christian-Jewish Polemical Discourse in Early Modern Germany." In *Food and Judaism*, edited by Leonard J. Greenspoon, Ronald A. Simkins, and Gerald Shapiro. Studies in Jewish Civilization 15. Omaha: Creighton University Press, 2005.

Diner, Hasia. *Hungering for America: Italian, Irish, and Jewish Foodways on the Age of Immigration*. Cambridge, MA: Harvard University Press, 2001.

Dioscorides. *De Materia Medica*. Translation by Lily Y. Beck. *De Materia Medica*. Altertumswissenschaftliche Texte und Studien 38. New York: Georg Olms Verlag, 2017.

Feliks, Jehuda. "Garlic." In *Encyclopaedia Judaica*, 2nd ed., 7:328–29. Jerusalem: Keter Publishing House, 1973.

Freidenreich, David M. *Foreigners and Their Food: Constructing Otherness in Jewish, Christian, and Islamic Law*. Berkeley: University of California Press, 2011.

Galen. *Method of Medicine*. Translation by Ian Johnston and G. H. R. Horsley. *Galen, Method of Medicine, Books 10–14*. Loeb Classical Library 518. Cambridge: Harvard University Press, 2011.

Hart, Mitchell B. *The Healthy Jew: The Symbiosis of Judaism and Modern Medicine*. New York: Cambridge University Press, 2007.

Hecker, Joel. *Mystical Bodies, Mystical Meals: Eating and Embodiment in Medieval Kabbalah*. Detroit: Wayne State University Press, 2005.

Horowitz, Elliott. "Remember the Fish and Making Tsimmes: Jewish Food, Jewish Identity, and Jewish Memory." *Jewish Quarterly Review* 104, no. 1 (2014): 57–79.

Kugelmass, Jack. "Green Bagels: An Essay on Food, Nostalgia, and the Carnivalesque." *Yivo Annual* 19 (1990): 57–80.

Litvak, Leonid. *The Jewish Persona in the European Imagination: A Case of Russian Literature*. Stanford Studies in Jewish History and Culture. Stanford: Stanford University Press, 2010.

Marks, Gil. *Encyclopedia of Jewish Food*. Hoboken, NJ: John Wiley, 2010.

Ohnuki-Tierney, Emiko. *Rice as Self: Japanese Identities through Time*. Princeton: Princeton University Press, 1993.

Philo. *Who Is the Heir of Divine Things?* Translation by F. H. Colsom and G. H. Whitaker. *Philo, Volume IV*. Loeb Classical Library 261. Cambridge: Harvard University Press, 1932.

Pliny. *Natural History*. Translation by W. H. S. Jones. *Pliny, Natural History, Books 20–23*. Loeb Classical Library 392. Cambridge: Harvard University Press, 1951.

Robinson, Sara Libby. *Blood Will Tell: Vampires as Political Metaphors before World War I*. Boston: Academic Studies, 2011.

Rosenblum, Jordan D. *Food and Identity in Early Rabbinic Judaism*. New York: Cambridge University Press, 2010.

Satlow, Michael L. *Tasting the Dish: Rabbinic Rhetorics of Sexuality*. Brown Judaic Studies 303. Providence: Brown Judaic Studies, 1995.

Scharbach, Rebecca. "The Ghosts in the Privy: On the Origins of Nittel Nacht and Modes of Cultural Exchange." *Jewish Studies Quarterly* 20, no. 4 (2013): 340–73.

Trachtenberg, Joshua. *The Devil and the Jews: The Medieval Conception of the Jew and Its Relation to Modern Anti-Semitism*. Philadelphia: Jewish Publication Society of America, 1983.

6

Jewish, Christian, and Islamic Perspectives on Food and Jewishness

DAVID M. FREIDENREICH

Why should one eat—or avoid—Jewish food? What makes food "Jewish" in the first place? These questions feature prominently not only in rabbinic and other Jewish texts but also in the classical sources of Christianity and Islam. The authors of these influential works disagree over what food to eat and, more fundamentally, over what Jewishness is, but they all agree that the difference between Jews and non-Jews matters. They also agree that food is an ideal medium through which to emphasize this distinction, even though the distinction itself is not really about food.[1]

Jewish, Christian, and Islamic sources from antiquity through the Middle Ages contain rules about not only the ingredients in one's food—pork, for example—but also the person who makes it and the people with whom one eats it. Laws that focus on food preparation and commensality (sharing meals) are especially important for understanding how religious authorities use food to distinguish Jews from non-Jews. For example, we have all experienced the power of informal norms about who you can or cannot eat with in cafeterias; these norms reinforce group identities and social hierarchies in powerful ways. Not long ago, Southern states had laws mandating racial segregation at lunch counters as a means of ensuring that no one would publicly violate color-based social norms.

Prohibitions against shared meals and restrictions on whose food one may eat powerfully convey the message that the divide between "Us" and "Them" ought not to be bridged. Not only that, antisocial behavior of this nature reinforces stereotyped ideas about who They are and, more important, who We are. Some American supporters of the 2003

Iraq War, for example, refused to eat food associated with the French because France opposed the war. The Republican-controlled House of Representatives even barred french fries from congressional cafeterias, replacing them with "freedom fries." The calorie count of the fries stayed the same, but those who insisted on avoiding "French" food recognized that rhetoric matters: only "freedom fries" bolster the kind of American identity that lends itself to support of regime change through military intervention.

The premodern legal traditions of Judaism, Christianity, and Islam contain a variety of norms that promote self-segregation or abstention from food associated with adherents of foreign religions, although it is important to emphasize that adherence to these laws was inconsistent at best. If a rabbi, a priest, and a pair of imams walked into a cafeteria but insisted on following all these traditional restrictions, the result would be a very bad joke. The rabbi would order a salad, worrying not only about the ingredients in other menu items but also about the likelihood that the cooks are not Jewish. The priest, in contrast, would refuse the food if the cooks *are* Jewish and would refuse to eat with the rabbi in any case. The Shi'i imam would order a salad and sit at his own table, concerned about the Jewish (or Christian) identity both of the cooks and of his dining companions. Only the Sunni imam could make the case for eating almost anything Jewish or Christian cooks prepared in accordance with their own traditions' norms, and he and the rabbi could at least share a table. Beyond the tragicomic outcome of this doomed effort to go out for lunch together, what is "funny" about this scenario is that all four of these clergy members are motivated in part by concerns regarding the Jewishness of their meal.

The rabbi in our imaginary cafeteria would order a salad in part because other foods on the menu might contain biblically prohibited ingredients (see chapter 1 for further details). Keeping kosher, in other words, is a way to express one's Jewishness, defined in this respect as adherence to the Torah's instructions. Biblical dietary laws, however, were not designed to segregate ancient Israelites, the ancestors of the Jewish people, from their Canaanite neighbors: archeological evidence indicates that the Torah permits the vast majority of food consumed in the region.

The Torah does not aspire for Israelites to eat differently from their neighbors but rather, you might say, to eat similarly to God. Because kosher animals resemble animals fit for sacrifice in the Temple, those who keep kosher affirm their membership in what the Bible describes as "a kingdom of priests and a holy nation" (Exodus 9:6) that seeks to emulate and be close with God. More fundamentally, the Torah portrays the Israelite's act of distinguishing between permitted animals and other species as being similar in nature to the divine act of distinguishing between Israelites and other peoples (Leviticus 20:24–26). Bible scholar Jacob Milgrom put it this way: "As God has restricted his choice of the nations to Israel, so must Israel restrict its choice of edible animals to the few sanctioned by God."[2]

The practice of selecting and preparing one's meat in accordance with God's laws reinforces in Israelites a sense of distinctiveness, even if the choices Israelites make are not in fact different from those of their neighbors. Like Americans who insisted on eating freedom fries instead of french fries, Israelites ingested the same meat as their Canaanite neighbors but also internalized a particular way of viewing themselves and their world. By adhering to biblical dietary laws, Israelites affirmed their self-understanding as holy—that is, distinctive, set apart by God from all other peoples to live in a God-like manner.

Of course, Judaism of the Middle Ages and today is not the religion of the Bible, and that was already true more than two thousand years ago. Jewish practices, Jewish values, and the definition of Jewishness itself evolved as Jews absorbed new ideas from their ever-changing surroundings. A number of particularly significant changes occurred during the Hellenistic period, when Greeks ruled the Eastern Mediterranean.

Following the conquests of Alexander the Great in 332 BCE, the Land of Israel became home to a large number of pork-loving Greeks. In this era, adherence to biblical dietary laws clearly marked Jews as different from the surrounding society. Even Jews who resisted assimilation, however, internalized many aspects of Hellenistic (i.e., Greek) thought and culture. So, for example, Jews in the Greek city of Alexandria interpreted biblical dietary laws in light of virtues promoted by Greek philosophers. Keeping kosher, these philosophically inclined Jews declared, keeps Jews morally upright by promoting virtues such as cleanliness and righteousness while discouraging vices like violence and promiscuity. To paraphrase, by forbidding pork, the Torah prevents its adherents from acting like pigs. No rationale of this sort appears within biblical accounts of the dietary laws, which explain these rules in terms of holiness, not morality.

Another Hellenistic concept embraced by these Jews relates to the distinction between Us and Them. Greek thinkers divided the world into two groups—namely, Greeks and barbarians—and they largely ignored distinctions among foreigners. Jewish thinkers of this era also began to see the world in binary terms and to classify all non-Jews as "gentiles," plain and simple. Specifically Jewish food practices began to function as a means of distinguishing Jews from gentiles.

Hellenistic Jews used stories about food to express their ideas regarding the ideal relationship between being Jewish and interacting with the dominant Greek society. Biblical heroes from Abraham to Esther share meals with foreigners in a completely nonchalant fashion: the identity of the dining partners is simply irrelevant to the plot. In Alexandria, however, Jews told stories of heroes who insist on keeping kosher but nevertheless earn the respect of gentile kings. In the Letter of Aristeas and similar works, the act of sharing a kosher meal with the Greek king symbolizes both the storytellers' commitment to preserving their Jewish distinctiveness and the acceptance within Hellenistic society to which these storytellers nonetheless aspire. At the same time, Jews in Jerusalem and the surrounding region of Judea began telling stories about heroes who not only keep kosher but also abstain from all food prepared by non-Jews. The prophet Daniel, for example, refuses to eat food provided to him by a gentile king, even though earlier biblical figures ate such food. In another tale, Judith's refusal to eat food prepared by gentiles enables her to save the Jewish people from certain destruction. "Separate from the gentiles, and do not eat with them," Abraham warns Jacob in Jubilees 22:16, expressing a norm that would have been unrecognizable to the authors of Genesis. Jewishness, according to these Judean authors, entails self-segregation from gentiles.

For Jews in the Hellenistic world, keeping kosher was not just about the ingredients of one's food but also about who prepares it and who shares it. These food practices preserve a distinctive Jewish identity by marking the difference between Jews and their gentile neighbors. It is no coincidence that this development in the function of Jewish food norms occurs during the Hellenistic era, when members of minority groups could literally become Greeks through a process of enculturation that included the adoption of Hellenistic food practices.

Rabbinic Judaism, the variety of Judaism that has been dominant for roughly the past fifteen hundred years, emerged in Judea during the first centuries of the Common Era; it revolves around the related texts of the Mishnah, compiled circa 200 CE, and the Talmud, whose Babylonian version was more or less complete by the year 600. As Judean (rather than Alexandrian) Jews, the rabbis who contributed to the Mishnah took for granted their community's norms forbidding food prepared by gentiles. As scholars obsessed with categories and principles, rabbis of the second through the sixth centuries transformed these norms into a laundry list of specific rules, all grounded in notions of what it means to be Jewish (see chapter 2 for further details). Some of these rules, like the prohibition against eating finely minced fish prepared by gentiles, address the fact that gentiles might use nonkosher ingredients: We, as Jews, follow the Torah's commandments; They, the gentiles, do not. Other rules, like the prohibition against drinking wine made or even touched by gentiles, reflect concern that gentiles regularly offer idolatrous wine libations: We worship the one true God while They are all polytheists.

In addition, rabbinic law prohibits eating bread baked by gentiles, cheese made by gentiles, the meat of animals slaughtered by gentiles, and foods cooked by gentiles. The common denominator in rules of this nature is that these foods are all transformed during their preparation process. Bread, after all, does not grow on trees; similarly, it takes a butcher to turn a cow into beef. The anthropologist Claude Lévi-Strauss famously linked the oppositional terms "raw" and "cooked" with "natural" and "cultural."[3] The rabbis did the same thing when discussing gentile chefs: foods cooked by non-Jews bear indelible traces of non-Jewish culture. By insisting that only Jews may properly perform butchery, baking, cooking, and similar acts of food preparation, the Mishnah and the Talmud teach that Jewishness constitutes the ideal human culture and that Jews should remain aloof from gentile cultures. This is why the rabbi we left in our imaginary cafeteria would be ordering a salad for lunch rather than a cooked vegetarian entrée.

Some Talmudic rabbis clearly believed that following these rules about gentile food would prevent Jews from socializing with or, even worse, marrying their gentile neighbors. Other rabbis, however, were perfectly comfortable with the prospect of food-related interaction between Jews and gentiles within the constraints previously described. These rabbis, unlike their segregationist colleagues, seem to feel that the very act of taking precautions when eating with gentiles is sufficient to reinforce a distinctive Jewish identity and prevent undue intimacy. Just as Israelites who choose kosher meat are reminded that God has chosen them, rabbinic Jews who are careful with the food of gentiles remember that God has distinguished Israel from the nations. The difference between Jews and non-Jews matters regardless of how these rabbis define Jewishness, and in one way or another, food reinforces that distinction.

In some respects, the rabbinic approach to conceptualizing Jewishness is commonplace. Humans often divide the world into Us and Them and regard their own community as special. While the rabbis employed a simple binary distinction, however, Christian and Islamic authorities developed more complex ways of classifying foreigners. These added complexities, often expressed through rules about food, reflect the importance that Christians and Muslims continued to ascribe to Jewishness even as they distinguished themselves from the Jews.

In sharp contrast with later Christians, Jesus and his first followers observed Judean norms about food. Not only did Jesus keep kosher; he refused to eat with gentiles and, in one incident, compares gentiles to dogs unfit to sit at the table of God's Jewish children (Mark 7:27–28; cf. Matthew 15:26–27). Many of his followers, however, believed that Jesus's death and resurrection signaled the beginning of a new era in which Jews and gentiles alike could attain salvation through faith in Christ. Paul, among others, declared that Greeks could join the church without first committing themselves to Jewish practices like circumcision and keeping kosher. In his Letter to the Galatians, Paul also insisted that Jews and Greeks should participate as equals in the shared meals that defined the early Christian community (2:11–14). In fact, the very act of eating together established Christianity as a religion that supersedes the particular identities of Jews and Greeks. By eating with all fellow believers, Christians affirmed the notion that Jewishness is no longer an especially significant characteristic. Over time, however, Jewishness became quite significant to Christian identity—as a negative foil.

For several centuries after Jesus's death, Christian food practices served not only to bridge the gap between believers of different ethnic backgrounds but also to distinguish those Christians from both Jews and Greeks. Unlike Jews, Christians rejected biblical food restrictions: They, the Jews, follow the Old Testament literally by abstaining from the meat of certain animals, while We, the Christians, understand the text in its spiritual sense and therefore eat meat without distinction. Christians interpreted the Torah's laws as allegorical lessons in morality, insisting that God never wanted anyone to actually abstain from pork—God's true message is simply that humans should not act like pigs. (Alexandrian Jews, in contrast, believed that God forbade not only acting like pigs but eating them too.) Christians did not, however, eat all kinds of meat: unlike Greeks, Christians refused to eat food offered to idols. Abstention from such food and, with it, the affirmation of monotheism were such important parts of early Christian identity that when Roman emperors required their subjects to offer sacrifices, many Christians chose to become martyrs rather than comply. With the Christianization of Rome, however, the distinction between Christians and Greeks quickly disappeared.

The distinction between Christianity and Judaism persisted. After all, both Jews and Christians laid claim to the same God and the same biblical texts, yet Jews understood God and the Bible very differently from Christians. Not only that, Jews and Christians alike claimed to be the spiritual heirs of the biblical People of Israel, the uniquely holy nation. When holiness is defined in zero-sum terms, Judaism must be wrong for Christianity to be right. By ascribing negative characteristics to Jewishness, Christian authorities were able to reinforce the message that contemporary Jews had forfeited to Christians the unique relationship with God established in the Bible.

Leaders of the church defined Jews not merely as non-Christians but as anti-Christians, the polar opposite and eternal enemies of the truly holy people. Early medieval canon law (the law of the Church) expresses the notion that Jews not only fail to act in accord with Christian charity but actively seek to harm Christians. It suggests that Jews do not merely engage in sex, ignoring the Christian ideal of celibacy; they seek illicit sex with unwitting nuns. Pagans simply lack knowledge of Christ, but Jews stubbornly spurn such knowledge even after their nominal conversion to Christianity.[4]

On the flip side of the same coin, Christian authorities defined themselves as anti-Jews, and they used rules about food to express this self-definition. Even though Christians may eat all food regardless of the prohibitions found in the Torah, from the fourth century into modern times, they were not allowed to eat food prepared by Jews or to share meals with Jews. One finds, for example, the following pair of late antique laws in Gratian's highly influential twelfth-century compilation: "No one of priestly rank, nor any layperson, may eat the unleavened bread of the Jews" and "All clerics and laity should henceforth avoid the meals of Jews, nor should anyone receive them at a meal" (Decretum C. 28 q. 1 cc. 14–15). These laws remained on the books until the early twentieth century, and several modern popes reiterated them. An oft-cited edict by Pope Pius VI (1775), for example, declares that "the Jews may not eat, nor drink, or have any other familiarity or conversation with Christians, nor Christians with Jews."[5]

Prohibitions against shared meals reflect concern that Jews, like Christian heretics, will lead the faithful astray through their false interpretations of the Bible and God's will. Prohibitions of food prepared by Jews, meanwhile, compare that food unfavorably to meat offered to idols. Church leaders offered especially harsh polemics against Passover matzah, which they portrayed as the diabolical inverse of the communion wafer consecrated during Mass.

The rhetoric associated with Jewish food paints a picture of Jews as both pagans and heretics: the ultimate outsiders and insiders gone horribly bad, all rolled into one terrifying image of everything Christianity condemns. By forbidding foods tainted by Jewishness, Christian authorities sought to protect their followers from succumbing to "Jewish" characteristics: just as humans should not act like pigs, Christians should not act like Jews and, as a precautionary measure, should not eat "Jewish" foods either. This is why the priest in our imaginary cafeteria would refuse food prepared by Jewish cooks and insist on eating at a separate table from the rabbi.

The Sunni imam, in contrast, would happily eat with the rabbi (or the priest), sharing any food prepared in accordance with Jewish norms (although Christian norms are more problematic). After all, the Qurʾan declares with reference to Jews and Christians that "the food of those who were given the Book is permitted to you" (5:5). The Qurʾan portrays the Bible as an authentic divine revelation and recognizes Judaism and Christianity as legitimate even as it describes Islam itself as the latest and greatest of the three Abrahamic religions. Islamic law makes manifest the inferiority of non-Muslims by imposing special taxes and a variety of discriminatory regulations. (Medieval Christian rulers imposed the same kinds of regulations on their own religious minorities as well.) Sunni authorities, however, symbolically elevate Judaism and Christianity over other non-Islamic religions by declaring that Muslims may eat meat prepared by Jews and Christians.

Sunni Islam has always been the numerically and politically dominant of Islam's two major branches. Medieval Sunni authorities highlight the permissibility of Jewish and Christian food as a means of emphasizing the fact that all recipients of God's revelations are alike in fundamental respects. Sunni Islam teaches that popular consensus is a source of authoritative information about God's will, and the legitimacy granted to Judaism and Christianity serves to enlarge the circle of those who agree on certain core principles of Islam. By asserting that even Jews and Christians have access to knowledge of God's will, Sunnis also bolster their claim that all Muslims have access to such knowledge. This claim is key to Sunni arguments against proponents of Shiʿi Islam: because most Muslims are Sunnis, their consensus opinion demonstrates that Sunni Islam must be right. Notice that Sunnis use rhetoric about Jewishness and Jewish food to advance Sunni claims in an internal Islamic dispute to which Jews themselves are mere bystanders.

Shiʿi authorities also used food practices and rhetoric about Jews (and Christians) in order to advance a particular way of viewing Islam. Unlike their Sunni counterparts, whose permission of Jewish food affirms the similarities between Judaism and Islam, medieval Shiʿis stressed the differences between Islam and its predecessors. Attacking the symbolically significant permission of Jewish and Christian food, Shiʿi authorities declare that Jewish and Christian butchers are incapable of properly invoking God when slaughtering animals because of their incorrect theologies. Shi'is also assert that all non-Muslims are impure and transmit impurity through contact. That is why the Shi'i in our imaginary cafeteria would insist on an undressed salad—raw, dry vegetables cannot become impure—and would avoid sitting next to non-Muslims.

Shi'is criticized Sunnis for their willingness to eat the food of Jews and Christians, pointing to this practice as proof that Sunnis fail to understand God's will and are not in fact good Muslims. This critique reflects the Shi'i belief that true knowledge of God is not accessible to all Muslims, let alone to non-Muslims like the Jews. Rather, such knowledge comes only through the teachings of Muhammad's descendants, the Shi'i imams. Shi'is used rhetoric about Jews to disparage Sunnis much as House Republicans used rhetoric about the French to disparage Democrats who, like the French government, were reluctant to support the Iraq War. By implication, french-fry-eating Democrats do not value freedom and are not truly American. French citizens were not the primary target of Republican opposition to french fries, and similarly the Jews were not the primary target of Shi'i condemnations of Jewish food. Jews and their food were simply caught in the cross fire of an internal Islamic dispute over whether Muslims ought to respect or disparage Jewishness.

Why did Shi'is, Sunnis, and Christians alike devote so much attention to the Jewishness of their food, whether to avoid it or, in the case of the Sunnis, to embrace it? Because, to draw on another famous notion of Claude Lévi-Strauss, Jewish food—and, more broadly, Jewishness itself—is "good to think with" regardless of whether it is also good to eat.[6] On this, the rabbis who contributed to the Mishnah and the Talmud would wholeheartedly agree. Rules about food defined as "Jewish" offer a concrete means of addressing the abstract distinction between Jews and non-Jews. This distinction contributed to the self-identity espoused by those who spoke not only for Judaism but also for Christianity and Islam, albeit in very different ways.

The importance of rules about food as a means of distinguishing Jews from non-Jews is especially apparent in medieval rabbinic discussions about wine associated with gentiles. The Mishnah and Talmuds forbid Jews from drinking or even selling wine that non-Jews have touched out of concern that gentiles might have offered a portion of that wine as a sacrifice to their gods: Jews, after all, may not participate even indirectly in idolatrous worship. Medieval rabbis, however, were well aware that their Muslim and Christian neighbors did not offer wine libations. Even those Muslims who violated Islamic prohibitions against alcohol did not use it in their worship, and within Christianity, only ordained priests consecrated wine through performance of the Eucharist. Some medieval rabbis also recognized Islam—and, less frequently, Christianity—as a monotheistic religion. These authorities nevertheless bent over backward to preserve traditional prohibitions regarding gentile wine, even when doing so entailed significant economic and social costs. The newfound rationale that proved most enduring was that the prohibition of gentile wine, like that of various other foods prepared by non-Jews, is meant to prevent Jews from marrying gentiles. What mattered most to medieval rabbis, however, was not the rationale behind these prohibitions but rather their function as a marker of gentile otherness and Jewish distinctiveness. Monotheism may no longer set Jews apart from their neighbors, but food practices still do the trick.

Christian and Islamic authorities also defined their respective communities in part by means of reference to—and rejection of—Jewish food practices. Because God favors Us over Them, Christians and Muslims asserted, we are free to eat meat, which Jews refuse to consume. But how does this principle apply to "Jewish" meat that Jews regard as nonkosher? The process of creating kosher meat, after all, involves the creation of nonkosher meat as well: Jewish butchers might discover after properly slaughtering a permitted animal that its meat is in fact not kosher according to rabbinic law due to an internal defect, and the Torah itself forbids eating certain portions of the animal. May Christians or Muslims consume this perfectly edible meat? This question proved especially good to think with, and the heated debates that it provoked among medieval Christian and Sunni scholars offer valuable insights into how these authorities thought about the relationship between food and Jewishness.

The most striking aspect of these internal debates among Muslims on the one hand and Christians on the other is that the participants all define Jewishness in terms of Islamic or Christian—rather than Jewish—sources. Sunnis uniformly hold Jewish meat to standards derived from the Qur'an rather than the Torah or rabbinic tradition.

They merely disagree over whether the Qur'an authorizes Jews to obey pre-Islamic dietary laws, whether it imposes on contemporary Jews only Islam's more lenient norms, or whether it assigns harsher food restrictions to Jews in punishment for the Jews' refusal to embrace Islam. Similarly, Christians who engage this question draw entirely on Roman law and canon law to determine the Jewishness of meat from animals that Jewish butchers slaughter, taking for granted that Christians must avoid everything "Jewish." None of the participants in these debates bothered to ask the opinion of Jewish butchers or rabbis: they regarded the definition of Jewish food, and of Jewishness itself, as being too important to be left to Jews. This definition, after all, relates directly to the ways in which these authorities understood their own religious identity: Christianity is anti-Jewish, while (according to Sunnis) Islam is similar to Judaism but only to a limited degree.

House Republicans likewise did not bother to ask the opinions of Democrats or the French regarding the nature of "french fries" before changing the labels in the congressional cafeteria. The relationship of fries to freedom, after all, rested on rhetoric, not on anything intrinsic to either the potatoes or the principle of liberty. The same is true with respect to the Jewishness of food. Jews, Christians, and Muslims defined a wide variety of foods as "Jewish" or "not Jewish" for a wide variety of reasons, including some rationales that evolved over time. The act of ascribing Jewishness to food serves to define both the food and the meaning of Jewishness. Perhaps more important, that act also serves to differentiate Jews from non-Jews, much as the insistence on eating "freedom fries" marked supporters of the Iraq War as distinct from other Americans. Food is merely a useful medium for conveying the distinction between Us and Them.

Today, it is not unusual for rabbis, priests, and imams to share meals together. They may all make a point of eating food that is both kosher and halal, or they may ignore traditional dietary laws entirely, or they may order different items on the menu. Christian attitudes toward Jewishness have changed radically: most denominations now firmly reject the notion that Judaism is anti-Christian and that Christians must therefore be anti-Jewish. Islamic attitudes toward Jewishness have evolved as well. As for contemporary Jewish attitudes toward Jewishness, the chapters in this volume provide a small taste of their diversity. Food practices, after all, continue to mark Jews as Jewish, whatever "Jewish-ness" may mean.

NOTES

1. This chapter summarizes, albeit with a somewhat different emphasis, argu-ments made in Freidenreich, *Foreigners and Their Food*. I have therefore kept citations to a bare minimum. The chapter originated as a lecture that I delivered over several years at various universities and synagogues, and I am grateful for the feedback that I received in these venues. Several Colby College students—Kristin Esdale, Skylar Labbe, Sarah Jeanne Shimer, Sarah Shoer, and Anna Spencer—offered valuable comments on preliminary drafts of this work.
2. Milgrom, *Leviticus 1–16*, 724.
3. Lévi-Strauss, *Raw and the Cooked*.
4. See further Freidenreich, "Jews, Pagans, and Heretics." On the use of negative ideas about Jews as a means of self-definition more broadly, see Nirenberg, *Anti-Judaism*.
5. Translated in Kertzer, *Popes and the Jews*, 29.
6. Lévi-Strauss, *Totemism*.

BIBLIOGRAPHY

Freidenreich, David M. *Foreigners and Their Food: Constructing Otherness in Jewish, Christian, and Islamic Law*. Berkeley: University of California Press, 2011.

———. "Jews, Pagans, and Heretics in Early Medieval Canon Law." In *Jews in Early Christian Law: Byzantium and the Latin West, 6th–11th Centuries*, edited by John Tolan, Nicolas de Lange, Capuchine Nemo-Pekelman, and Laurence Foschia, 73–91. Turnhout: Brepols, 2013.

Kertzer, David I. *The Popes and the Jews: The Vatican's Role in the Rise of Modern Anti-Semitism*. New York: Knopf, 2001.

Lévi-Strauss, Claude. *The Raw and the Cooked*. Translated by John and Doreen Weightman. New York: Harper & Row, 1969.

———. *Totemism*. Translated by Rodney Needham. Boston: Beacon, 1963.

Milgrom, Jacob. *Leviticus 1–16: A New Translation with Introduction and Commentary*. Anchor Bible Series 3. New York: Doubleday, 1991.

Nirenberg, David. *Anti-Judaism: The Western Tradition*. New York: Norton, 2013.

7

How Ancient Greeks, Romans, Jews, and Christians Drank Their Wine

SUSAN MARKS

When I was seven years old, my mother and stepfather married in an intimate service with a rabbi, a handful of grown-ups, my two younger brothers, and me. That night my grandparents hosted a dinner for them downtown with lots and lots of people. Mostly I remember the toasts. After dinner, everyone raised glasses of champagne, and one person after another offered good wishes. I was fascinated. Little did I realize that there had been a long history of blessings at the end of the meal in Jewish tradition and in other cultures as well. The glass of wine for the rabbinically proscribed grace after meals, hereafter *birkat ha-mazon*, stands as such a critical part of the rabbinic practice that, halakhically, "if there is only one cup of wine, it is reserved for the purpose of birkat ha-mazon."[1] Similarly, Hellenistic and Roman diners offered libations to their own deities when dining concluded, beginning the after-dinner festivities.

This chapter asks about the actions of those who enacted birkat ha-mazon and thus differs from studies that primarily consider the *text* of this blessing. Rabbinic texts describe the act of blessing at mealtimes as bookends to dining. In the Mishnah, written in the third century CE, and the Babylonian Talmud, written in the fourth to the fifth century CE, an opening blessing depends on what sort of food awaits—whether it is "fruit of the earth," "fruit of the tree," and so on or bread.[2] If there is a blessing over bread, constituting the eating of a "meal," then this meal requires a birkat ha-mazon over a cup of wine, and additional blessings can be added to celebrate a wedding or to observe other occasions.[3] Unfortunately, however, what text there is of birkat ha-mazon in Talmud does not prove altogether helpful, as apparently those who led the blessing were expected to improvise, and the text of this blessing remained in a state of flux for hundreds of years.[4] Texts of birkat ha-mazon found in the Cairo Geniza (tenth to thirteenth century) "served as complete alternatives," supplanting rather than supplementing earlier talmudic versions.[5] It appears that while we might have thought sixth-century rabbinic debates signal a push to regularize textual aspects of this practice, the competing evidence reminds us that more likely the ones leading birkat ha-mazon based their blessing upon a slightly more fixed core of requirements.[6] Recognition that the text of blessings remained ephemeral for several more centuries suggests the need to instead turn our attention to the ways that rabbinic narratives describe the practices, actors, and context that make up birkat ha-mazon.

Other writers have explicitly avoided considering similarities between birkat ha-mazon and Roman libations, focusing instead on the rabbis' distrust of how the libations of others could affect the purity of wine that might be safely used: "These things that belong to gentiles are forbidden, and it is forbidden to have any benefit at all from them: wine, or the vinegar of gentiles that at first was wine."[7] This avoidance assumes that gentile wine has been devoted to other gods. In this way, rabbinic literature consistently caricatures the practice of their neighbors, describing them performing exaggerated actions that differ from well-attested evidence of the nature of these contemporaneous Roman practices.[8] This distancing within rabbinic literature has concealed shared practices.

By overcoming this reluctance to reflect on libation practices and by considering especially Roman and talmudic practices concerning the ways the host assigns leadership of the wine offering, prepares for the offering by arranging for handwashing, and designates one to invite the rest of the group, this chapter argues that the rabbis used the customs of their day to celebrate their gratitude for divine beneficence, and their shared practice can also suggest new insights into the ways social status played out among rabbis as they dined. A final evaluation of the rabbinic choice of wine for blessing reveals one difference—the rabbis offered mixed wine to their God rather than unmixed wine as is generally understood to figure in Roman libation practice. Ultimately it appears more probable that this reflects a need to revise our default understanding of ways that later Roman libation practices had evolved rather than a rabbinic difference, but the establishment of a subtle Jewish difference is also possible.

Libations and the Hellenistic and Roman Banquet

There are two particularly striking structural features of birkat ha-mazon. First, it follows rather than precedes that which it blesses. More often, blessing comes prior to action, as in the case of blessings over various kinds of food, the blowing the Shofar, or the lighting of the Hanukah or Shabbat lights. In contrast, diners recite birkat ha-mazon at the end of the meal, recalling the food eaten in retrospect. Birkat ha-mazon answers the following questions: Was this a meal? Did this occasion include enough bread to qualify as a meal (as opposed to sharing only a taste or two of side dishes)? Did they actually dine—that is, did they engage in at least some of the many interactions of guest and host that come of eating together? The very act of inviting others to bless constitutes an affirmative answer to these questions.

The second structural feature, or set of features, of birkat ha-mazon involves the actions related to leading the blessing. Various rabbinic narratives describe (1) the host of the meal assigning the role of leading birkat ha-mazon; (2) the host or designate overseeing preparations for the blessing, including handwashing and mixing the wine; and finally, (3) the one designated to do the "inviting" uses an invitation, hereafter *zimun*, to invite all those present to join in blessing. The current twenty-first-century form of this zimun amounts to a call and response. We do not know exactly how formalized such a back-and-forth practice was in this earlier era, but as we shall see, there is an insistence that a leader be designated, since birkat ha-mazon includes a zimun by a leader rather than just the group recitation. The argument, concerning where the zimun stops and the rest of the blessing begins, reveals a text that has not yet been fixed: "The one who says that two or three [benedictions make up birkat ha-mazon] holds that [the benediction of the zimun] extends up to 'Who sustains,' while the one who says three or four [benedictions make up birkat ha-mazon] holds that it extends up to 'Let us bless.'"[9] Whether fixed or not, this evidence attests to the importance of the zimun as part of the blessing. The role of the host, the preparations, and this important invitation recall practices that constitute Roman libations.

Recent scholarship has converged to argue for a typology of Greek, Roman, Jewish, and Christian meals that better articulates shared themes and practices than had the piecemeal approaches that preceded it.[10] Instead of differentiating between symposia, funerary banquets, sacrificial meals, meals of associations, mystery meals, everyday meals, and so forth, this line of research successfully presents a "common banquet tradition."[11] A summary of these typological elements include the following:

- the reclining of (more or less) all participants while eating and drinking together for several hours in the evening
- the order of a supper (*deipnon*) of eating, followed by an extended time (*symposion*) of drinking, conversation, and performance
- marking the transition from *deipnon* to *symposion* with a ceremonial libation, almost always wine
- leadership by a "president" (*symposiarch*) of the meal—a person not always the same as the host, and sometimes a role that was contingent or disputed[12]

This focus on shared early meal traditions has helped reveal the centrality of the meal to the social formation of these cultural neighbors. Of course, traditions that span geographical locations and several centuries from Plato (fifth to fourth century BCE) to the third and fourth centuries CE must give pause to any historian who recognizes the demands of local and temporal issues, but an ongoing literary tradition bridges distance between these real meals.

Whether aspirational, satirical, or critical, meals figured largely in texts from Plato to Philo to New Testament Gospels to Plutarch. Diners in the ancient world serve simultaneously as models for this literary outpouring and as actors enacting practices influenced by literary allusions. Actual meals existed in dialogue with literary visions of meals, each mirroring the other and each differently reflecting wealth, wisdom, colonial relations, gender, class, religion, and ethnicity.[13] In addition, from the point of view of one trying to reconstruct or imagine ancient traditions, all the evidence that does not come from art and archaeology must rely on literary accounts. In other words, as we study various meals based primarily on literary sources, we become aware that these presentations often know of each other. The meal described may well be part of a larger current as well as of a particular time and place. Thus a Passover Seder can employ the rhythms of a symposium while articulating the particulars laid out in Exodus, in the fraught era after the destruction of the Temple.[14] In the example of the Seder, as elsewhere, a focus on shared traditions allows the particulars of a given meal to take on a special significance and reveals clues about temporal and historical factors missed if one treated each meal custom in isolation.

Wine and libation hold pride of place in this typology. Wine marks the end of eating and the beginning of drink and discussion. Other Roman libation and sacrificial practices existed, and "evidence, which includes valuable data from domestic shrines, suggests that *libationes* of liquids, incense, fruits, or cakes were often seen as more practicable and economically more feasible, and hence much more common, than animal sacrifice," but wine was most common.[15] Ancient wine was thick and syrupy and needed to be mixed with water before it was consumed. Greek custom had been to mix wine for libation as well as for drinking, but as an example of a cultural difference, by the time Hellenistic and Roman meals took over these traditions, more emphasis was placed on the meal than the drinking party, and the earlier Greek large *krater* for mixing wine, libating, and drinking had disappeared, replaced by smaller personal vessels.[16] Roman wine poured to the gods was unmixed, as "only gods and barbarians drink their wine neat."[17]

In the typical practice of Greek symposia, the host may retain the honor or designate the guest with the most status to serve as *symposiarch* to lead the wine libation. This practice continues into the Roman period, since "whenever Plutarch was chosen to be symposiarch at one of the banquets he attended, the custom was called an 'ancient' one that was in danger of being abandoned. This suggests that it had become a less common practice, but that it was still well known."[18] Before such an offering, the dinner had to be cleared, and all made ready for the libation, including diners washing their hands. In the words of Athenaeus, "Now at last, the floor is swept, and clean are the hands of all the guests, and their cups as well. . . . The mixing-bowl stands full of good cheer; and another wine is ready."[19] Then finally, the symposiarch led the offering, and "some introductions also were made by the symposiarch throughout the evening. Since many meals included rowdy behavior, an enforcer of civility was often necessary. This role, as well as the leading of discussion, was sometimes performed by the *symposiarch*."[20] The symposiarch's leadership role is limited to the one particular meal but requires exercise of social skills nevertheless.

Rabbinic Birkat Ha-Mazon and Libation Practice

Having considered the assigned roles and practices of libation as outlined in Greek and Roman texts, the parallels in birkat ha-mazon as it appears in rabbinic narratives become apparent. I consider these in the order of the meal (the designation of a leadership role, handwashing as preparation, and the demonstration of leadership ability in the performance of the role) rather than in chronological order or by source. Temporal historical questions will be taken up later in examining why the rabbis mixed wine when it has been our understanding that other Romans did not.

The first narrative emphasizes what it means to be chosen to lead birkat ha-mazon. It shows the power that rests in the hand of the host and of the one designated to bless. While it offers an unusual case, it seems to also hint at well-recognized tensions between those in these positions of ritual leadership, even if these are temporary positions, ending with the meal. In this narrative, King Yannai brings Shimon into the dining room at the end of a meal in order to accuse him of fraud. As an additional surprise, Yannai assigns Shimon the role of leading birkat ha-mazon, even though he has not shared their meal. Shimon, in turn, uses his leadership to disrupt. Yannai signals the arrival of birkat ha-mazon by mixing wine: "He mixed wine for him in order that he might bless, whereupon [Shimon] said: 'Let us say Grace for the food which Yannai and his companions have eaten.' [Yannai] responded: 'I have never heard "Yannai" in this blessing!' [Shimon] exclaimed: 'What do you want me to say? "Let us bless the food which we have eaten," when I have not eaten anything?!'"[21] The two spar over the appropriate form for a blessing led by one who had not partaken of the meal. Meanwhile, both understand that mixed wine indicates the readiness to bless birkat ha-mazon. This agreement looms large in the context of other disagreements, allowing a glimpse of the tension in leadership roles typical of ancient meals as well as the practice of mixing that differs from understood Roman libation practice.

The next story reveals a different sort of tension between host and the one who will lead the blessing. The host in this narrative appears less confrontational, but the one assigned to lead nevertheless fears the obligation placed upon him. Additionally, this story shows handwashing as preparation for the blessing. In Greek and Roman banquets, the assembled washed after the meal before performing the libation. Here, the one responsible for saying the zimun washes first in preparation for leading birkat ha-mazon. The leader uses this fact to try to signal subtly to the one he had selected, but the subtlety fails: "The one who first washes his hands after a meal says the blessing. Rav and Rabbi Hiyya were once sitting before Rabbi at dinner. Rabbi said to Rav: 'Get up and wash your hands.' He saw him trembling [perhaps with fear that Rabbi might have found his hands dirty]. Rabbi Hiyya said to him: 'Son of princes! He is telling you to think over birkat ha-mazon.'"[22] This narrative leaves the reason for Rav's lack of understanding ambiguous. Does he misunderstand because this practice is relatively new to him or to rabbinic meals or because it remained in flux? Or is he anxious or distracted? The latter may be possible given the teasing response of his colleague, Rabbi Hiyya, who gratuitously calls him "Son of princes!" This text shares with the story of Shimon and King Yannai anxiety about this ritual obligation and being designated to lead. One might expect that the one designated to recite the zimun and lead birkat ha-mazon would treat it as an honor, but the honor comes with added pressure.

Apparently birkat ha-mazon, with whatever improvisational challenge the leader faced in leading the zimun and blessing, constituted a means of establishing one's fitness for the status one had achieved in this status-conscious world. Recall that the Roman host either kept the role of the symposiarch, leading the libation himself, or assigned it as an honor. This play of status and honor remains central to birkat ha-mazon. The one chosen to lead demonstrates his ability to discharge the duties pertaining to this meal—and beyond the meal as well—by implication. These narratives entertain questions about the risks of leading and the qualities needed to assume a leadership role, but they also affirm a hierarchy. Tellingly, we learn most about the hierarchical structure of birkat ha-mazon when those involved push back against it.

The following story concerns younger disciples who challenge the importance of negotiating status in this blessing by exploring an egalitarian alternative: "Judah son of Meremar and Mar son of Rabbi Ashi and Rabbi Aha from Difti took a meal with one another. Not one of their group was more deserving to bless than the other. They interpreted the Mishnah, that 'if three persons have eaten together it is their duty to invite [with a zimun],' as applying only where one is superior. . . . Thus each said [the blessing] for himself. Thereupon they came before Meremar and he said to them: you have performed the obligation of blessing, but you have not performed the obligation of invitation."[23] In his pronouncement, Judah's father emphasizes that without reenacting their hierarchical relationships, they have not fulfilled their obligations. As was the case with Yannai and Shimon or the hesitant Rav, this narrative also reveals tensions between the young diners and the one diner's father. Each text that transmits the practice of birkat ha-mazon reveals a different concern and a different vision of ideal social interaction. Thus the practice of birkat ha-mazon resembles other Greek and Roman meal practices in its occasional ambivalence as well as in its execution.[24] One recent understanding concludes that "meal practices are not incidental to the social dynamics of the Hellenistic era but rather a key dynamic in negotiating certain key social issues of Mediterranean society."[25] The wine offering and blessing not only honored the relevant god; it simultaneously served as a way for the group to structure and restructure itself.

The Mixing of Wine

The comparison of birkat ha-mazon to Roman libations not only demonstrates distinct similarities between the two offerings but also reveals a puzzling difference: the rabbis used mixed wine for their blessing in contrast to the Romans, who used unmixed wine. It seems possible that Jews may have intentionally made a distinction between their blessing and Roman libations as we see elsewhere within Jewish meal practices, specifically in Jewish dietary laws.[26] Nevertheless, it begins to become apparent that later Roman meals—including Jewish and Christian meals—exhibit important differences from the "typical" Roman meals that inform earlier studies. If this is the case, the pursuit of understanding rabbinic use of unmixed wine may facilitate an understanding of these significant changes while also suggesting that the rabbis, serving their own God with their own wine, found no need to further distinguish their libation practices from those of their neighbors.

Does Sanctifying Mixed Wine Represent a Jewish Tradition of Difference?

The land of Israel, like other Mediterranean lands, developed a wine industry. Biblical literature attests to the cultivation of several different varieties of wine,[27] with the book of Ezekiel alluding to Lebanon trading with Israel for a particular kind of wine.[28] Israelite libations may have predated the Temple, while certainly biblical literature reveals the formal inclusion of wine as part of official Temple practice: "the primary offering of public worship" was "embellished by the addition of accompanying offering on a regular basis. . . . The two major sacrifices, the *olah* 'burnt offering' and the *zebah* 'sacred feast' . . . were regularly accompanied, in many rites, by a grain offering (*minhah*) and a libation (*nesek*), consisting of wine."[29] This regular vision of wine's place at the Temple establishes wine libations as a recognized part of Israelite religion. The book of Ezekiel then develops it as "part of the regiment projected for a restored Temple."[30] In these clues to early Israelite use of wine, the only mention of mixing wine comes in the warning by the prophet Isaiah against those who "fill a mixing bowl for heathen gods."[31] This sounds a cry against those who follow other gods, but whether it also raises concerns about the practices of mixing an offering is harder to judge.

Centuries later (third to second century BCE), Sirach described in some detail what seems to be the ongoing rite of his time, the pouring of wine at the foot of the altar: "[The priest], finishing the service at the altars, and arranging the offering to the Most High, the Almighty, reached out his hand to the cup and poured a libation of the blood of the grape he poured it out at the foot of the altar, a pleasing odor to the Most High, the King of all."[32] Despite this greater precision, he too makes no mention of mixing or not mixing. Only in rabbinic literature, as it offers its own learned or imagined interpretation of a long ago Temple service (many decades after the Temple had been destroyed), does a description of Temple libations include a reference to mixing. This particular mixing does not occur in advance of the libation but as the wine and water flow around the altar at Sukkot: "Water was drawn from the Siloam Pool, carried with great fanfare in a formal procession to the Temple, and placed in a bowl set on the south-western corner of the altar. The priest poured a libation of wine into a second bowl in such a way that the two libations flowed onto the altar simultaneously."[33] The rabbinic accounts of this elaborate event describe a Temple rite not reported in earlier texts.[34] It has been suggested that this description concerns a seasonal wine feast associated with the first new wine of the season.[35]

A contemporaneous witness substantiates the importance of wine for the festival of Sukkot, if not the mixing of wine and water. Plutarch (first to second century CE), an outside observer, connected this festival with both Dionysus and Bacchus, the Greek and Roman gods of wine.[36] Plutarch appears to conflate the fasting of Yom Kippur with the practices of Sukkot, but many aspects remain familiar to the later reader, and one can certainly imagine how the greenery of Sukkot would look to one who saw ivy/branches/greenery as symbolic of Dionysus:

> First . . . the time and character of the greatest, most sacred holiday of the Jews clearly befit Dionysus. When they celebrate their so-called Fast, at the height of the vintage, they set out tables of all sorts of fruit under tents and huts plaited for the most part of vines and ivy. They call the first of the days of the feast of Tabernacles. A few days later they celebrate another festival, this time identified with Bacchus, not through obscure hints but plainly called by his name, a festival that is a sort of "procession of Branches" or "Thyrsus Procession" in which they enter the temple each carrying a thyrsus.[37]

Plutarch writes of the booths (known in Hebrew as *sukkot*) so central to the festival and the procession of branches (Hebrew: *lulav*) also described in biblical description of the festival[38] from his point of view. He sees them as connected to wine. These texts indicate that, at the occasion of this festival, wine flowed generously enough so that Plutarch had heard of it, and the rabbis also thought of wine when they thought of this festival and describe water and wine mixing at the Temple altar.

If we are looking for evidence that the Jews blessed mixed wine in contrast to the Roman practice of offering unmixed wine as a way to differentiate their practice, this contemporaneous evidence for some wine-related practice might support such an argument. Rabbinic descriptions of mixed wine and water at the altar at Sukkot suggest that, in their eyes, God accepted mixed wine libation at the time of the Temple. This might be used to argue for such a practice in the face of a differing Roman practice, although no contemporaneous witness makes this argument. We may think of allusions to the Temple and mixed wine as pointing to a significant identification of their tradition with earlier Jewish practice, as if the rabbis are backdating their own practice, but the evidence is too slender to prove definitive.

Does Mixed Wine Represent a Change in Roman Practice?

Jews were not alone in mixing wine. Early Christian leaders wrote of the need to mix wine for blessing. These authors stressed the need to mix water and wine and not recite blessings over plain water only, as some ascetics urged: "Polemics against the eucharistic use of water were widespread, including writings by Clement of Alexandria, Irenaeus, and Cyprian of Carthage, who underscored the necessity of mixing water and wine at the eucharist, and there is rather odd reference to 'water and wine mixed with water' in Justin Martyr's description of the Eucharistic liturgy in his *First Apology* 65."[39] Research into Eucharistic traditions argues for a variety of early practices, all situated at meals that fit the same patterns of Roman meals discussed here.[40]

Of particular interest to our discussion of birkat ha-mazon, in Luke's gospel, there is a Eucharist tradition with two cups of wine: "Then he took a cup, and after giving thanks he said, 'Take this and divide it among yourselves. . . .'. . . Then he took a loaf of bread, and when he had given thanks, he broke it and gave it to them. . . . And he did the same with the cup after supper. . . ."[41] This tradition emerges as scholars recognize evidence for varied proto-Eucharistic practice, thus revisiting material that some had earlier dismissed instead by accepting a shorter version of Luke (one that omits verses 19b–20).[42] Meanwhile, this allusion to a second cup of wine after the food appears very similar to the wine of birkat ha-mazon following the meal. This glimpse of similar practices, as well as ongoing Christian debates about the mixing of water and wine, discloses a context in which the rabbis would not have been the only ones mixing wine for blessings. If rabbinic Jews intended to distinguish themselves from Roman practice by mixing wine, they had company.

It also appears possible that this practice shared by Jews and Christians was shared by other Romans. Recent archaeological evidence suggests a possible change from elite Roman dining practice to a more convivial, subelite, group practice in the late third and fourth centuries and thereafter. An evaluation of the vessels found in ancient Eastern Roman archaeological sites uncovers a noticeable shift to larger vessels that would have been shared by diners and away from smaller, individual sizes.[43] This vision finds support in Plutarch and Pliny, who reflect the wish for conviviality. For instance, Plutarch reports that his dinner companion argues for the benefits of shared portions: "Where each guest has his own private portion, companionship perishes."[44] While we again recall that literary sources cannot be read as actual practice, when literary support coincides with archaeological evidence, the sources do suggest a change in dining practices. Perhaps the late Roman practice hearkened back to earlier ideas: "Plutarch maintains that while the common practice at private affairs during the second century was to service each guest individually, so that each controlled his own portions, there also existed at least as a cultural memory a tradition of serving shared portions among assembled guests."[45] Altogether, this suggests fourth-century Roman practice might differ from generalizations based on elite Roman banquets in the first century.

Moreover, some of these rabbinic narratives appear in the Babylonian Talmud, beyond the edge of the Roman Empire. Practices considered by the Babylonian Talmud must travel in the memory of early residents or other contemporaneous travelers or in the imaginations of both. This is not the place to deal with the complexities of the relationship between Palestine and Babylonia, except to note that archaeological evidence suggests that these changes in dining practices also seem to have affected the very edge of the Roman influence. Found initially in the Eastern part of the Roman Empire, recent research confirms these changing patterns for Roman Britain as well.[46]

If this new line of research focuses mostly on food and conviviality, it also allows for us to extrapolate concerning wine service. As this research is at an early stage, one can only speculate as to causes. Perhaps the growth of Christianity had an influence, or alternately, Jewish and Christian practices shared in late Roman subelite "community-building efforts" may have influenced the practice.[47] Either way, this research into later Roman vessels suggests a need to revisit accepted understandings of "normal" Roman practice. Whatever the cause of such shifts, a sea change in Roman dining practices might indeed have affected practices surrounding mixing wine for libations. Jewish practice might therefore reflect such a change in Roman practice and a new emphasis on conviviality as well as hierarchy rather than witness an attempt to distance itself.

Conclusion

Having examined birkat ha-mazon in light of Roman wine libations, similarities prove easier to pin down than differences. The ritual actions performed belong to a typical symposiastic meal: the host appointing the one who will lead the blessing, the one chosen then washing in preparation, and finally this leader inviting all to bless. A look at instances of these similarities reveals rabbis engaging the particulars of these Greek and Roman practices and considering the implications of hierarchal order, including the need to push back. Understanding birkat ha-mazon in this context helps situate these rabbinic questions in the context of Roman explorations and reveals interactions around status as they play out at meals.

This connection between rabbinic and Roman context for meals becomes particularly interesting when we begin to observe ongoing changes in Roman practice. In contrast to so many similarities, rabbinic practices differed from typical Roman libation practice, which used unmixed wine, while the rabbis mixed wine for birkat ha-mazon. Further examination reveals, however, that this difference may or may not prove significant. A possible precedent exists in Sukkot Temple libations, as described by the rabbis, with the occasion confirmed by Plutarch, if not the mixing of wine and water. So one might imagine rabbinic intent to differentiate themselves from other Romans for the sake of difference and in remembrance of the Temple, although the evidence is slim. In either case, it reveals key changes toward the end of the Roman period, crucial for understanding the rabbis.

Meanwhile, recent research has begun to suggest that Roman meal practices might have changed by the time of the fourth century, with a move toward communal, convivial practices. Whether these changes include larger vessels for wine as well as food is not addressed as explicitly in this scholarship but seems quite possible. In any case, Christian practice appears to resemble Jewish practice when it comes to mixing wine. The possibility of such a shift in practice certainly argues for continued research in this area as well as the need to examine other aspects of Jewish meal practice that might relate to changing Roman practice. Rabbinic accounts of birkat ha-mazon suggest that the practice of who blesses and how to bless meant something to rabbinic leaders and may turn out to be something they shared with a changing Roman empire.

NOTES

1. Mishnah Berakhot 8.8. I offer many thanks to Sarah Schwarz and Debra Bucher for their thoughtful responses to earlier drafts of this chapter as well as my gratitude to David Freidenreich and his class at Colby for their reflections on a later draft.

2. Mishnah Berakhot lays out these and other categories and explores protocols for blessing. See Kraemer, *Jewish Eating and Identity*, 73–86; Zahavy, *Mishnaic Law*, 77–97.

3. See Babylonian Talmud, Berakhot 41b, which explains that "a blessing over bread suffices for other foods integral to the meal."

4. Zahavy, *Mishnaic Law*. Weinfeld finds that scroll fragment 4Q434 "adduces clear evidence about the existence of the grace after meals at Qumran, not only in general cases but even in the specific case at the house of the mourner" ("Grace after Meals in Qumran," 429). Rosenblum disagrees (*Food and Identity*, 99n229).

5. Shmidman, "Developments within the Statutory Text," 110. Additionally, Shmidman counters Weinfeld's suggestion, suggesting that fragment 4Q434 "might have been intended for the Sabbath rather than for the house of mourning" (123n46). Shmidman argues based on other manuscripts that contain this verse (110).

6. For this general argument, see Heinemann, who explains that "we shall observe a variety of stylistic phenomena which do not conform to the accepted halakhic rules for the formation of benedictions" (*Prayer in the Talmud*, 7; see also 156–92). Many prayer texts preserve a collection of archaic forms and not

necessarily a single "original" prayer (*Prayer in the Talmud*, 67–69, 74, and 290). Meanwhile, earlier Heinemann had argued that *birkat ha-mazon* might have been fixed early on, since the blessing precedes the standardization of the blessing formulas ("Birkath Ha-Zimun and Havurah-Meals," 26).

7. Mishnah Avodah Zarah 2.3. Fishbane suggests that biblical foundation of this prohibition (Deuteronomy 32:28) indicates that concern with libation practices likely predates awareness of Greek and practices; nevertheless, the rabbis work out the halakhic details of what it means to benefit from this wine (*Deviancy in Early Rabbinic Literature*, 153).

8. Stern, "Compulsive Libationers," 39. See also Freidenreich, *Foreigners and Their Food*, and in the present volume concerning wine and neighbors.

9. Babylonian Talmud, Berakhot 46a.

10. Working on different continents, Klinghardt, *Gemeinschaftsmahl und Mahlgemeinschaft*, and Smith, *From Symposium to Eucharist*, each developed a similar emphasis on shared meal traditions.

11. Smith, *From Symposium to Eucharist*, 3.

12. Taussig, *In the Beginning*, 26, summarizing and referencing Klinghardt, *Gemeinschaftsmahl und Mahlgemeinschaft*, 45–152 and Smith, *From Symposium to Eucharist*, 13–46.

13. Brumberg-Kraus, "Contrasting Banquets"; Konig, *Saints and Symposiasts*.

14. Stein argued that the Passover Seder is best understood as a symposium, found in Plato and other literary sources. This argument emphasized that diners recline, adopting the posture of free elite symposiasts. At the Seder, they dine, drink, and discuss the philosophic importance of freedom ("Influence of Symposia," 30–31). Seen in the cultural milieu of its time, this meal appears like one described in neighboring literary sources and witnessed also by frescos, mosaics, and dining rooms (Dunbabin, *Roman Banquet*; Osiek, "What Kinds of Meals?"). Bokser pushed back against this argument, emphasizing biblical roots (*Origins of the Seder*, esp. 89–93). Considering both Stein and Bokser, Smith (*From Symposium to Eucharist*) understands Jewish meals as part of this overarching typology, and Hauptman ("How Old Is the Haggadah?") argues that an early Tosefta, or Ur-Mishnah, describes a symposium and that the Mishnah revised the order and moved the discussion from after the meal to during the meal. Now few who study meals would deny a relationship between the Seder, as it develops in the second and third centuries, with meals (both literary and real) that go back several centuries. While most have accepted this argument, scholars have only recently begun examining other aspects of Jewish meals in light of these shared traditions (Brumberg-Kraus, "Meals as Midrash"; Rosenblum, *Food and Identity*; Brumberg-Kraus, Marks, and Rosenblum, "Ten Theses"; Hauptman, "Thinking about the Ten Theses"; and other essays in Marks and Taussig, *Meals in Early Judaism*). See also Klein, "Torah in Triclinia," who considers the implications for rabbinic literature of the archaeology of Jewish dining spaces.

15. Bendlin, "Libations, Roman," 4052–53.

16. Dunbabin, *Roman Banquet*, 24.

17. Dunbabin, 20.

18. Smith, *From Symposium to Eucharist*, 34, referencing Plutarch, *Quaestiones Conviviales* 620a (translation in Clement and Hoffleit, *Plutarch, Moralia*, 363).

19. Athenaeus 11.462c–d, quoting Xenophanes of Colophon, sixth century CE, discussed in Smith, *From Symposium to Eucharist*, 28.

20. Taussig, *In the Beginning*, 79.

21. Genesis Rabbah 91.3.

22. Babylonian Talmud, Berakhot 43a.

23. Babylonian Talmud, Berakhot 45b.

24. Smith discusses ways of enacting status at Greco-Roman meals as well as voices such as Martial and Pliny that "argue against prevailing customs" (*From Symposium to Eucharist*, 44–45).

25. Taussig, *In the Beginning*, 85.

26. See Rosenblum, *Food and Identity*.

27. Paul "Classifications of Wine."

28. Paul discusses this special "wine of Helbon" ("Classifications of Wine," 44). For an overview of factors differentiating one ancient wine from another, including type of grape, time allowed to ferment, age, spices, and color, see Yievin, "Food," 117.

29. Levine, *Numbers 1–20*, 385.

30. Levine, 385, regarding Ezekiel 45:17.

31. Isaiah 65:11. New Jewish Publication Society translates this as "fill a mixing bowl for Destiny" but notes this as "names of heathen deities."

32. Sirach 50.14–15; see discussion in Rubenstein, "Sukkot Wine Libation," 576n5.

33. Rubenstein, "Sukkot Wine Libation," 575, describing Mishnah Sukkah 4.9–10.

34. Rubenstein also describes hints found in Qumran scrolls, Jubilees, the Testament of Levi, and the Genesis Apocryphon, as well as rabbinic texts ("Sukkot Wine Libation," 588).

35. Rubenstein, 590.

36. Schäfer discusses Plutarch's presentation as a "positive and sympathetic" example of theocrasy, the blending of various gods in one highest God (*Judeophobia*, 50, 53–54).

37. Plutarch, *Quaestiones Conviviales* 4.6.2 (671).

38. Leviticus 23:39–43.

39. Johnson, "Apostolic Tradition," 48.

40. McGowan, "'First Regarding the Cup'"; Smith, *From Symposium to Eucharist*.

41. Luke 22:15–20, NRSV.

42. McGowan examines this two-cup tradition as part of a larger exploration of varied Eucharist practice ("'First Regarding the Cup,'" 551).

43. My thanks to Jason Lundock for bringing this new research to my attention, including Hudson, "Changing Places," and Lundock, "Study of the Deposition."

44. Plutarch, *Quaestiones Conviviales* 2.10.2, cited by Hudson, "Changing Places," 664, who also discusses Pliny, *Epistulae* 2.6.

45. Hudson, "Changing Places," 666.
46. Lundock "Study of the Deposition," 262–64.
47. Hudson, "Changing Places," 692.

BIBLIOGRAPHY

Bendlin, Andreas. "Libations, Roman." In *The Encyclopedia of Ancient History*, 1st ed., edited by Roger S. Bagnall, Kai Brodersen, Craig B. Champion, Andrew Erskine, and Sabine R. Huebner, 4052–53. Oxford: Blackwell Publishing, 2013.

Bokser, Baruch M. *The Origins of the Seder: The Passover Rite and Early Rabbinic Judaism*. Berkeley: University of California Press, 1984.

Brumberg-Kraus, Jonathan. "Contrasting Banquets: A Literary Commonplace in Philo's *On the Contemplative Life* and Other Greek and Roman Symposia." In *Meals in the Early Judaism: Social Formation at the Table*, edited by Susan Marks and Hal Taussig, 163–73. New York: Palgrave Macmillan, 2014.

———. "Meals as Midrash: A Survey of Ancient Meals in Jewish Studies Scholarship." In *Food and Judaism*, vol. 15, edited by L. J. Greenspoon, R. A. Simkins, and G. Shapiro, 297–317. Omaha, NE: Creighton University Press, 2004.

Brumberg-Kraus, Jonathan, Susan Marks, and Jordan Rosenblum. "Ten Theses Concerning Meals and Early Judaism." In *Meals in the Early Judaism: Social Formation at the Table*, edited by Susan Marks and Hal Taussig, 13–39. New York: Palgrave Macmillan, 2014.

Clement, Paul A., and Herbert B. Hoffleit, trans. *Plutarch, Moralia*. Vol. 8. Loeb Classical Library 424. Cambridge: Harvard University Press, 1969.

Dunbabin, Katherine M. D. *The Roman Banquet: Images of Conviviality*. Cambridge: Cambridge University Press, 2010.

Fishbane, Simcha. *Deviancy in Early Rabbinic Literature*. Leiden: Brill, 2007.

Freidenreich, David M. *Foreigners and Their Food: Constructing Otherness in Jewish, Christian, and Islamic Law*. Berkeley: University of California Press, 2011.

Hauptman, Judith. "How Old is the Haggadah?" *Judaism* 51, no. 1 (2002): 5–18.

———. "Thinking about the Ten Theses in Relation to the Passover Seder and Women's Participation." In *Meals in the Early Judaism: Social Formation at the Table*, edited by Susan Marks and Hal Taussig, 43–57. New York: Palgrave Macmillan, 2014.

Heinemann, Joseph. "Birkath Ha-Zimun and Havurah-Meals." *Journal of Jewish Studies* 13 (1962): 23–29.

———. *Prayer in the Talmud: Forms and Patterns*. New York: de Gruyter, 1977.

Hudson, N. "Changing Places: The Archaeology of the Roman *Convivium*." *American Journal of Archaeology* 114 (2010): 663–95.

Johnson, Maxwell E. "The Apostolic Tradition." In *The Oxford History of Christian Worship*, edited by G. Wainwright and K. B. Westerfield Tucker, 32–75. New York: Oxford University Press, 2006.

Klein, Gil. "Torah in Triclinia: The Rabbinic Banquet and the Significance of Architecture." *Jewish Quarterly Review* 102, no. 3 (2012): 325–70.

Klinghardt, Matthias. *Gemeinschaftsmahl und Mahlgemeinschaft: Soziologie und Liturgie frühchristlicher Mahlfeiern.* Texte und Arbeiten zum neutestamentlichen Zeitalter 13. Tübingen: Francke Verlag, 1996.

König, Jason. *Saints and Symposiasts: The Literature of Food and the Symposium in Greco-Roman and Early Christian Culture.* Cambridge: Cambridge University Press, 2012.

Kraemer, David C. *Jewish Eating and Identity through the Ages.* New York: Routledge, 2007.

Levine, Baruch. *Numbers 1–20: A New Translation with Introduction and Commentary.* New York: Doubleday, 1993.

Lundock, Jason. "A Study of the Deposition and Distribution of Copper Alloy Vessels in Roman Britain." Doctoral thesis, King's College London, 2014.

Marks, Susan, and Hal Taussig. *Meals in the Early Judaism: Social Formation at the Table.* New York: Palgrave Macmillan, 2014.

McGowan, Andrew. "'First Regarding the Cup . . .': Papias and the Diversity of Early Eucharistic Practice." *Journal of Theological Studies* 46, no. 2 (1995): 551–55.

Osiek, Carolyn. "What Kinds of Meals Did Julia Felix Have? A Case Study of the Archaeology of the Banquet." In *Meals in the Early Christian World: Social Formation, Experimentation, and Conflict at the Table,* edited by D. E. Smith and H. Taussig, 37–56. New York: Palgrave Macmillan, 2012.

Paul, Shalom M. "Classifications of Wine in Mesopotamian and Rabbinic Sources." *Israel Exploration Journal* 25, no. 1 (1975): 42–44. Reprinted in *Divrei Shalom: Collected Studies of Shalom M. Paul on the Bible and the Ancient Near East, 1967–2005.* Leiden: Brill, 2005.

Rosenblum, Jordan D. *Food and Identity in Early Rabbinic Judaism.* Cambridge: Cambridge University Press, 2010.

Rubenstein, Jeffrey L. "The Sukkot Wine Libation." In *Ki Baruch Hu; Ancient Near Eastern, Biblical, and Judaic Studies in Honor of Baruch A. Levine,* edited by R. Chazan, William W. Halo, and L. H. Schiffman, 575–91. Winona Lake, IN: Eisenbrauns, 1999.

Schäfer, Peter. *Judeophobia: Attitudes towards the Jews in the Ancient World.* Cambridge, MA: Harvard University Press, 1997.

Shmidman, Avi. "Developments within the Statutory Text of the *Birkat Ha-Mazon* in Light of Its Poetic Counterparts." In *Jewish and Christian Liturgy and Worship: New Insights into Its History and Interaction,* edited by Albert Gerhards and Clemens Leonhard, 109–26. Leiden: Brill, 2007.

Smith, Dennis E. *From Symposium to Eucharist: The Banquet in the Early Christian World.* Minneapolis, MN: Fortress, 2003.

Smith, Dennis E., and Hal Taussig, eds. *Meals in the Early Christian World: Social Formation, Experimentation, and Conflict at the Table.* New York: Palgrave Macmillan, 2012.

Stein, Siegfried. "The Influence of Symposia." *Journal of Jewish Studies* 8 (1957): 13–44. Reprinted in *Essays in Greco-Roman and Related Talmudic Literature.* New York: Ktav, 1977.

Stern, Sacha. "Compulsive Libationers: Non-Jews and Wine in Early Rabbinic Sources." *Journal of Jewish Studies* 64, no. 1 (2013): 19–44.

Taussig, Hal. *In the Beginning Was the Meal: Social Experimentation and Early Christian Identity*. Minneapolis, MN: Fortress, 2009.

Weinfeld, Moshe. "Grace after Meals in Qumran." *Journal of Biblical Literature* 111 (1992): 427–40.

Yievin, Ze'ev. "Food." In *Encyclopedia Judaica*. 2nd ed. Vol. 7. Detroit: Macmillan Reference USA in association with Keter Publishing House, 2007.

Zahavy, Tzvee. *The Mishnaic Law of Blessings and Prayers: Tractate Berakhot*. Atlanta, GA: Scholars, 1987.

8

Jews, Schmaltz, and Crisco in the Age of Industrial Food

RACHEL B. GROSS

Crisco is Kosher. Rabbi Margolies of New York, said that the
Hebrew Race had been waiting 4,000 years for Crisco.
—Marion Harris Neil, *The Story of Crisco*[1]

In 1933, the consumer goods company Procter & Gamble (P&G)
published an eighty-two-page recipe book written in English and Yiddish, a language commonly spoken by Central and Eastern European
Jews, titled *Crisco Recipes for the Jewish Housewife*.[2] As strange as this
corporate coupling of Jewish women and Crisco may seem on first
acquaintance, it was no anomaly. Rather, it was part of a decades-long
campaign by P&G, along with some of the most innovative advertising
agencies of the early twentieth century, to convince Jewish women to
change their cooking fats of choice from butter and schmaltz, rendered
poultry fat, to Crisco. The effectiveness of this early instance of targeted marketing reveals a particular moment in the changing mores of
American Jews as religious practitioners and as consumers of commercial goods, identities that were often intertwined. Jewish home cooks,
generally women, were convinced to relinquish authority to corporate
experts not only in matters of cuisine and health but also regarding
religious practices related to food production and consumption. Over
the course of the twentieth century, for many American Jews, buying
packaged food products overseen by federal health regulators and Jewish religious organizations became an integral part of religious practice
throughout the twentieth century.

In the early twentieth century, as Americans generally moved toward
a more industrialized food system, embraced packaged foods, and

developed federal safety regulations, American Jews responded by standardizing and systematizing *kashrut*, the Jewish dietary laws of keeping kosher developed over two millennia of rabbinic interpretation. In the United States, *halakhah*, Jewish law, developed hand in hand with the creation of corporations—sometimes in tandem and sometimes in tension with one another—creating a particularly American system of religious practice. P&G's effort to induce Jewish women to embrace Crisco as a Jewish product essential to American Jewish cooking reveals a particular moment in the creation of an American religious system in which corporations became arbiters of religious authority. Within this advertising campaign, *kashrut*, a system of religious boundaries about what to eat and how to prepare food, became aligned with early twentieth-century language of health and food purity. As healthier and more stringently kosher food became associated with regulation, Crisco advertising campaigns conflated notions of religious permissibility, cleanliness, and food purity in ways that would continue to reverberate throughout the twentieth century. Due to the success of this campaign, Crisco became central to the creation of *parve* baked goods—breads and pastries than can be eaten with either dairy or meat items according to Jewish dietary laws. A century later, however, national ideas of health and American Jews' practice of *kashrut* have changed, reversing the industrial food trend that produced and sustained Crisco. Popular valorization of small-scale and homemade production rooted in images of female ancestry has allowed the use of schmaltz to come full circle.

BCE (Before the Crisco Era)

In the early twentieth century, as more than two million Jews entered the United States with the wave of European immigration between 1880 and 1924, there were no kosher certification agencies. On both of sides of the Atlantic, nineteenth- and early twentieth-century Jews bought food from butchers, bakers, and fishmongers whom they knew and trusted. Jews who kept kosher were expected to know the complex rules of which foods were permissible, and in large part, Jews viewed female home cooks as religious authorities in their own kitchens. Rabbis answered their congregants' questions as they arose, but there was no unifying system or authority determining which items were or were not kosher.[3]

Like other immigrant groups, Jewish immigrants from Central and Eastern Europe brought their foodways to the United States, including their use of schmaltz. *Kashrut* forbids certain foods, including pork products, and governs food preparation, including requiring the separation of foods made with meat and dairy products. Around the world, Jews have cooked in ways similar to their non-Jewish neighbors, adapting local foodways to *kashrut* regulations. Around the Mediterranean, Sephardi and Mizrahi Jews (those originally from the Iberian Peninsula and the Middle East) cooked with oil, which is *parve*, a neutral food that contains no meat or dairy ingredients that can be eaten with either meat or dairy meals. Ashkenazi Jews of Central and Eastern Europe, like their non-Jewish neighbors, tended to use butter and animal fats. Where non-Jewish Europeans (and later, Americans) used lard, Ashkenazi Jews used schmaltz. Schmaltz can be made from any poultry fat, but most Jews in Central and Eastern Europe and in the United States ate chicken schmaltz. Wealthier Jews might eat schmaltz made from goose fat, which is moister. Like lard, schmaltz can be used for both baking and frying, and like lard, it can be eaten as a spread on bread. Poorer Jews might smear schmaltz on a potato or an onion. The cracklings of schmaltz, *gribenes*, are also a treat, like pork rinds.[4]

Not all American Jews kept kosher, but many of those who did not strictly adhere to *kashrut* retained their preferences for Ashkenazi dishes, including schmaltz. For both American Jews who kept kosher and those who did not, the Central and Eastern European dishes that were once thought of as ordinary, lowly Jewish fare, including schmaltz, came to suggest group belonging and "tradition" for Jewish immigrants and their descendants.[5] In the United States, the way many of those dishes were made would change, even as they continued to represent a connection to Jewish heritage. In this context, P&G aimed to establish Crisco as a bridge between traditional European foodways and modern American consumer habits.

Though the centrality of schmaltz, a saturated fat, to Ashkenazi cooking should make it clear that *kashrut* and health concerns are unrelated, widespread American and European beliefs throughout the nineteenth and twentieth centuries incorrectly held that kosher food was healthier food. Pork was correctly held to be highly susceptible to contamination, but many Jewish apologists went further, inaccurately suggesting that Jewish slaughter practices were healthier and kinder to animals.[6] With its Crisco advertising campaign, P&G would draw together consumer concerns about industrial food production and long-standing ideas about *kashrut* and health.

Creating Crisco

Crisco is a quintessentially American item, the product of twentieth-century industry and commerce, and one that tells the story of American food industries. "Crisco may be understood as an artifact of a culture in the making," writes historian Susan Strasser, "a culture founded on new technologies and structured by new personal habits and new economic forms."[7] The development of American industrial *kashrut* followed America's technological and economic changes as well. The certification and advertisement of Crisco's kosher status demonstrate how the American *kashrut* system and American industry developed in tandem, both unique products of twentieth-century American commerce.

In the decades before and after the turn of the twentieth century, the United States saw enormous changes in population and in economics. Even as millions of immigrants almost doubled the American population between 1880 and 1910, the country completed a shift from an agricultural to an industrial society. Modern organizational systems and advanced technologies for production and distribution changed the way Americans worked and traveled. New products changed what Americans ate, drank, cleaned with, and wore. Techniques for national marketing developed alongside the products themselves, changing the way Americans learned about and made decisions about consumer goods.[8] P&G, the creator of Crisco, was at the forefront of changes in consumer goods and in advertising to immigrant groups.

Crisco was a new product marketed in new ways, but it has a pre-history dating back to the mid-nineteenth century. Cottonseed oil had been mixed with foods to create cheaper products since the 1860s, and American manufacturers turned to it increasingly in the 1880s.[9] At a time when hog prices were high and lard was expensive, American bakers mixed cottonseed oil with lard or other animal or vegetable fats to create "compound lard," a shortening that made breads light and flaky and might or might not contain lard. As an additive to compound lard, cottonseed oil softened the mixture and, more important, significantly reduced the cost.[10]

The general American public remained unaware of the additives to lard until an 1883 scandal suggested that much of Chicago's lard might have been adulterated. Widespread publicity about the adulterated lard boosted Americans' interest in the creation of "pure food" laws, as did two investigative studies. In 1890, the US Department of Agriculture commissioned *A Popular Treatise on the Extent and Character of Food Adulterations*. The treatise warned that food producers were cheating consumers and threatening Americans' health with adulterated food. "From the cheapest and most simple article of diet to the most expensive the art of the manipulator has been applied," the treatise decried.[11] Leaving food and food safety in the hands of manufacturers and advertisers left the American public vulnerable.

Several states instituted food-labeling laws, but federal food safety laws languished in Congress until the 1906 publication of Upton Sinclair's novel *The Jungle*. Sinclair's graphic depictions of the unsanitary meat-packing industry galvanized public attention. Horrified consumers demanded regulation and accountability in food production. Within a year, Congress passed the Meat Inspection Act and the Food and Drug Act, which prohibited misbranded and adulterated foods, drinks, and drugs.[12]

Crisco was developed in the midst of this national concern about the purity of shortenings and other foods. Though cottonseed oil was used in foods since the 1860s, a soap and candle company would bring the oil to its full potential as an independent comestible rather than an adulterant in other items. Brothers-in-law William Procter, a candlemaker, and James Gamble, a soapmaker, founded Procter & Gamble in Cincinnati in 1837.[13] By the 1870s, cottonseed oil had become an important raw material in soaps, and P&G competed with meat-packing companies for control of the industry. While P&G's soap line was successful, the candle business had declined with the advent of electrification. Searching for new industries, P&G looked for new ways to monetize their cottonseed oil. In the early twentieth century, as food production increasingly became the prerogative of manufacturers, P&G used its cottonseed oil to create the company's first edible product.[14]

Early shortenings and margarines made with cottonseed oil were excessively soft. In 1902, German chemist Wilhelm Normann developed a practical means of combining hydrogen with oils and fats, producing a fat that resembled lard.[15] P&G began its own research on hydrogenation in 1907. Three years later, the company had a patentable product, an edible shortening made of hydrogenated cottonseed oil mixed with cottonseed stearin.[16] They would convince the American market that this shelf-stable product was edible, that it was a "pure food" product, and that it was better than lard—or schmaltz.[17]

To convince American public that hydrogenated vegetable oil was a food it wanted, P&G needed the best advertisers. They turned to the enormously successful J. Walter Thompson (JWT) advertising agency, where adman Stanley Resor and copywriter Helen Lansdowne handled the P&G account. Together, Resor and Lansdowne (who later married) would become two of the most influential American advertisers of the twentieth century. They would develop many of their innovative techniques, including targeted marketing, in advertising Crisco.[18] Under Resor and Lansdowne, Crisco advertising was extraordinarily ambitious and meticulously planned.[19] They would sell Crisco as a "pure vegetable oil," responding to consumer concerns about industrial food by skillfully highlighting and dismissing the manufacturing process at once.

Under JWT's direction, P&G sent samples of Crisco to university-based food researchers, nutritionists, and home economists. Local Cincinnati hotels, railroad dining cars, and restaurants received samples and were solicited for endorsements and recipes. Across the country, Resor and Lansdowne experimented with advertising in newspapers, on streetcars, in store demonstrations, and with house-to-house samplings. They sent a case of Crisco to every grocer in the United States before the product's national launch in January 1912. To teach Americans how to use the new fat, P&G set up touring cooking schools. By April of that year, a small, round recipe booklet was packed inside the lid of every can, and several full-size recipe books were published over the next few years.[20]

"Truly Clean and Truly Kosher"

P&G's first ad campaign, led by Resor and Lansdowne at JWT in 1911 to 1912, advertised the all-vegetable shortening as healthy, clean, and cheap. The manufacturer and ad agency positioned the product to appeal to an American market still concerned about food purity, as consumer advocates and food chemists argued that the 1906 legislation failed to adequately protect consumers from food adulteration and misbranding.[21] In doing so, P&G took on a double competition of lard and butter—or for Jews, schmaltz and butter.

With the marketing of Crisco, the advertising agency JWT was an early adopter of targeted marketing, blending general marketing strategies with appeals to specific groups, including women in Vermont and Arkansas whose mothers had churned and rendered their own fats.[22] From the start, Crisco was also marketed toward Jews. P&G recognized kosher-keeping Jews, particularly the large immigrant population, as one of their most reliable potential markets. Crisco provided a *parve* alternative to butter or schmaltz, allowing the creation of *parve* baked goods that could be eaten with either dairy or meat meals. P&G would change how Jews cooked, what they ate, and how they viewed manufactured ingredients.

P&G was a pioneer in the integration of religious oversight and manufacturing, doing so as a matter of targeted advertising. The company consulted Yiddish newspapers, the experts on advertising to Jews, on the best way to attract the Jewish consumers. As the trade journal *Printers' Ink* reported, the newspapers "suggested as an indispensably necessity getting the endorsement of a well-known rabbi that the food was 'kosher'—pure"—a mistranslation underscoring advertisers' approach to *kashrut*. "When this was done," *Printers' Ink* continued, "large newspaper space was taken in the Jewish papers and Crisco was started on the highway to success."[23] Individual rabbis had given their approval to factory-produced foods for decades, including to Passover *matzah* beginning in the 1880s, a necessity that arose when Jewish consumers neither knew nor understood the production methods of packaged goods. By responding to the newspapers' suggestion about marketing Crisco, P&G became one of the first non-Jewish companies to bear a *heksher*, a symbol denoting the kosher certification agency attesting that it follows halakhah, Jewish law.[24] With this allegiance between rabbinic authority and manufacturing interests, American Jewish religion and American industry joined forces, indelibly influencing each other. With the advent of *hekshers*, kosher expertise became the prerogative of rabbis and food manufacturers alongside knowledgeable home cooks.[25]

P&G must have consulted the Jewish newspapers very early in their marketing process. In September 1911, P&G signed an agreement with Rabbi Moses S. Margolies of New York and Rabbi Sender Lifsitz of Cincinnati in which the rabbis certified that Crisco "contains no animal substance or other substance which is objectionable to the Mosaic Dietary Laws."[26] P&G allowed the rabbis the right to enter and inspect any or all parts of the factory in which Crisco was manufactured and to take samples of the raw materials from which Crisco was manufactured or from the finished product, modeling practices that would be continued in industrial *kashrut* certification.[27] At the same time, the agreement hints at P&G's confusion between scientific notions of food purity and cleanliness and *kashrut*: Margolies and Lifsitz are directed to have Crisco "chemically analyzed" to see if it conforms to the "Mosaic Dietary Laws." Though this would have been familiar language to the lab-oriented P&G marketers, it is unlikely that these congregational leaders had access to a laboratory (though later, some kosher certifiers would). It is far more likely that they reviewed the ingredients and manufacturing process.

P&G's choice of Lifsitz made sense, as he was a local rabbi who could regularly check on the production of Crisco. Margolies, in contrast, was a well-known national figure who would be trusted as an authority on Jewish law throughout the country. Described in his 1936 obituary in the *New York Times* as the "dean of the Orthodox Jewish rabbinate in this country," the Russian-born Margolies was the longtime leader of Congregation Kehilath Jeshrun on the Upper East Side of Manhattan. For many years, he was the president of the Orthodox Union (OU), the largest umbrella organization of Orthodox synagogues, created in 1899.[28] Beginning in the 1920s, the OU would turn its attention to industrial certification and would become the largest kosher certifying agency in the United States.[29] But in the 1910s, it was Margolies's name alone that provided Jews nationwide with the assurance that Crisco was kosher.

By 1912, *Printers' Ink* found Crisco displayed in grocery store windows in the Lower East Side alongside other "well-known package goods," including Ivory Soap, Uneeda Biscuit, and Kellogg's Toasted Corn Flakes. The advertising journal suggested that American advertisers considered recent immigrants, including Jews, to be a profitable, even gullible market, accustomed to heavily censored newspapers and advertisers held to accuracy: "Immigrants who come into this country bring along with them their respect for their newspapers—and they believe almost implicitly what they read in them, and do not distinguish between the news and advertising columns."[30] Whether or not immigrant consumers were any more susceptible to advertising than other Americans, P&G and other companies found them a fertile new market in the early twentieth centuries.

Following their initial impulse of contacting Jewish newspapers, JWT heavily advertised Crisco in the prominent Yiddish-language newspapers the *Jewish Morning Journal* and the *Jewish Daily Forward* in 1911 and 1912. Quarter-page ads contained eye-catching illustrations suggesting ways of using Crisco for the Yiddish-speaking housewife: feeding children and husbands by using Crisco as a shortening in cakes or, in an appeal to the foods eaten by Yiddish-speaking Jews, frying turnips or herring in it.

One full-page advertisement containing only text in the *Jewish Morning Journal* in December 1912 provides a window into JWT's approach to the Jewish market. The ad begins by explaining what the product was— "as Crisco is a new product and most Jewish readers will be unfamiliar with it"—and lays out the general arguments for using Crisco, "a new scientific product which will reduce food expenses and bring your cooking to the highest level," before turning to Jewish-specific concerns. As in the agreement with Lifsitz and Margolies, the ad aligns *kashrut* and scientific and legal food purity: "Following a rigorous investigation, lasting six months, and according to the scientific investigations of various chemists," Rabbis Margolies and Lifsitz "indicated that it is truly clean and truly kosher" and installed a permanent *mashgiach*, kosher supervisor, in the factory.[31] While a *mashgiach* would, in fact, only have jurisdiction over whether food was kosher—following ritual laws that have nothing to do with cleanliness—the ad suggests that the presence of authorized ritual experts assures not only Jewish religious observance but also health and food safety.

At the same time, only one paragraph of this full-page ad directly addresses Crisco's kosher status. The rest of the ad appeals to Jewish women in the context of the contemporary emphasis on home economics, the new field promoting rational and scientific approaches to domestic concerns.[32] The ad presents Crisco as modern, scientific, clean, elegant, and inexpensive. As the ad explains, "Cooking is a science today. Gone are the days when the kitchen was merely a 'place for the Jewess'" who learned to cook from her mother. Now women were obliged to keep up with the culinary advances of "the greatest scientific men." Jewish women could follow "the highest standards" of *kashrut* and establish themselves as economical housekeepers and forward-thinking Americans utilizing "one of the most important discoveries of these times."[33]

Crisco, the ad explains in detail, is better than both butter and schmaltz for cooking "a *latke, blintz,* or simply a herring."[34] According to the ad, Crisco is elegant and practical because it will leave a house odor-free; the smell of frying with butter or schmaltz is a hallmark of the old-fashioned. "It is especially unpleasant when there are guests visiting, because it gives the impression that the whole house is a kitchen." The ad explicitly describes Crisco as clean because it is derived from vegetable oil. "The Jewish law and the Pure Food Law guarantee that," the ad assures consumers, aligning modern refinement, *kashrut,* and the American legal system.[35]

Crisco's kosher status is also noted in a mainstream P&G recipe book, *The Story of Crisco* (1913), written by Marion Harris Neil, one of several well-known home economists employed to promote Crisco. *The Story of Crisco* contains 615 recipes, from lobster bisque to pound cake, all using Crisco.[36] Paralleling the Yiddish advertisements' injunctions against butter and schmaltz, this cookbook presents Crisco as healthier, more digestible, cleaner, more economical, and more modern than butter and lard. Crisco's kosher status appears in a list of "Brief, Interesting Facts," amid claims of Crisco's increasing use in "the better class hotels, clubs, restaurants, dining cars, ocean liners" and Crisco's handiness on camping trips because "hot climates have little effect upon its wholesomeness."[37] Within this miscellany, Neil explains that Crisco is a "neutral fat" that can be eaten with both "milk and flesh" foods. "Special

Kosher packages, bearing the seals of Rabbi Margolies of New York, and Rabbi Lifsitz of Cincinnati, are sold [to] the Jewish trade," she explains. "But all Crisco is Kosher and all of the same purity," she continues, again aligning *kashrut* and health purity and assuring Jewish consumers that they could purchase Crisco beyond the confines of Jewish neighborhood shops.

Neil's book includes the apex of Crisco's advertising to Jews: "Rabbi Margolies of New York, said that the Hebrew Race had been waiting 4,000 years for Crisco." P&G suggests that Crisco, as a parve cooking fat, is a solution to long-standing kosher rules of separating dairy and meat products.[38] In addition to being a modern, healthy, scientific product, Crisco has become a *Jewish* product. Crisco would simultaneously allow Jews to follow distinctive religious rules and eliminate the semblance of separation from their non-Jewish neighbors. While it is extremely unlikely that the serious Rabbi Margolies indeed quipped this witty advertising line, P&G had successfully integrated itself into Jewish history.

"It Fills a Great Need"

After a hiatus of two decades, P&G returned to promoting Crisco to Jews in 1933, this time working with the influential Jewish advertiser Joseph Jacobs to create the cookbook *Crisco Recipes for the Jewish Housewife*. As art historian Kerri Steinberg details, Jacobs transformed American Jews' consumption throughout the twentieth century. Established in 1919, the Joseph Jacobs Organization "played matchmaker, pairing mainstream companies with the Jewish market" throughout the mid-twentieth century. Jacobs's work as the media representative for three major Yiddish newspapers, the *Jewish Daily Forward*, the *Day*, and the *Jewish Morning Journal*, as well as his creative promotional products demonstrated the benefits of ethnic marketing before this approach became widespread after World War II. He was able to convince mainstream brands to pay attention to the Jewish market and, at the same time, convince Jewish consumers that mainstream products were Jewish products.[39]

By 1933, American industrial *kashrut* was in flux. The processed food industry was growing rapidly, but there were no universal *kashrut* standards in factories. In the 1920s, the OU attempted to create a kosher

Figure 8.1. Procter & Gamble Company, *Crisco Recipes for the Jewish Housewife*, Cincinnati, 1933

supervision and certification process that would be recognized by Jewish consumers throughout the country. Rabbis authorized by the OU would visit the plants to ensure that all the ingredients and equipment met the OU's *kashrut* requirements, and items produced by those factories would bear a symbol attesting to the OU's certification. This new system shifted authority from individual rabbis to the OU as a national, and later international, organization. In 1923, the H. J. Heinz Company's cans of vegetarian beans were the first product to carry the OU's national certification. The canned beans were labeled with a discreet Ⓤ symbol, an *O* circling a *U* for Orthodox Union. Jews looking for the symbol would know the factory-produced item was certified by a rabbinical organization they trusted, while non-Jews would remain ignorant of Jewish involvement in the manufacturing process and would not be scared away from buying a "Jewish" product.[40]

Jacobs, meanwhile, approached the kosher market differently. An observant Jew himself, the advertiser conducted market research demonstrating to companies that the Jewish market was a lucrative one.[41] But Jacobs encouraged food companies to ignore the OU and, later, other kosher certification agencies. In contrast to the OU's efforts, Jacobs maintained the older view that housewives, not rabbinical organizations, were the true arbiters of household *kashrut*. He believed that the Jewish woman "knows pretty well what is kosher and what is not," especially guided by ingredient labels required by federal law. If she had doubts, she could consult a rabbi, but according to Jacobs, the rabbi "has no power to decree the *Kashruth* of the product" and "merely expresses his opinion."[42] Jacobs advocated for placing *kashrut* in the hands of the lay female consumer—the target of his advertising—opposing the OU's consolidation of religious authority within an institution of male clergy.

At most, Jacobs encouraged food manufacturers to work with individual rabbis to certify their products as kosher rather than a certification agency and mark their products with a small *K* for "kosher." As a single letter, K was never trademarked. Any rabbi could use it to signify his supervision, and companies also used it to denote products that they deemed kosher without rabbinic supervision. This option gave companies more choice in determining how much and whether they wanted to pay for kosher supervision, and at times, rabbis using the K symbol were more lenient than the OU. Encouraging companies to use the K symbol and work with individual rabbis—who would certify a greater range of products for Jacobs to advertise—Jacobs clashed with OU's increasingly stringent goals of standardized national rabbinic supervision.[43] At stake were questions about which who could decide what was kosher and which products kosher-keeping consumers should purchase.

Jacobs had the dual goal of convincing companies to self-certify their products as kosher and convincing Jews to buy these products. To achieve the latter, the Joseph Jacobs Organization worked with companies to produce a number of promotional booklets to convince Jewish consumers to buy new products, including Yiddish and English promotional booklets for Jell-O, which bore Jacobs's signature K symbol based on some rabbis' approval of gelatin—made from animal bones—despite more stringent rabbinic opinions against its certification.[44] These books present modern, factory-produced items as Jewish products that fit easily alongside Jewish narratives and culinary histories.[45]

In some ways, Jacobs's *Crisco Recipes for the Jewish Housewife* continues the legacy of JWT's 1910s Crisco advertising with its messages of health and ease. At the same time, by the 1930s, the American Jewish market had changed. Now the target Jewish consumers were not only Yiddish-speaking immigrant women but also their daughters, who primarily read and spoke English. The book's English and Yiddish instructions and recipes are identical in order "to enable two people (as, for example, a Yiddish-reading mother and an English-reading daughter) to work together on any particular recipe."[46] According to P&G and Jacobs, Crisco, the all-purpose lubricant, would aid intergenerational relationships. Yiddish-reading mothers would share their experience preparing their traditional cuisine, while English-reading daughters would be more receptive to using the modern, manufactured fat.[47]

Crisco Recipes for the Jewish Housewife both links itself with Jewish culinary traditions and presents itself as elevating them. It presents Crisco as a Jewish product, announcing the Jewish consumers' acceptance of Crisco as a fait accompli: "Ever since it was put on the market, Crisco has been the principal cooking fat in many Jewish homes. It fills a great need, taking the place of heavy fats and oils which have been used in Jewish foods for hundreds of years." Moreover, P&G and the Jacobs organization have demoted schmaltz from a staple of Ashkenazi Jewish cooking to a mere necessity that was quickly abandoned with the advent of Crisco: "Goose-fat, chicken-fat, and olive-oil were good enough when there was nothing to take their place, but when it became possible to obtain a strictly Kosher and Parve fat in the form of Crisco, Jewish women quickly appreciated its merits."[48] Crisco, not schmaltz, according to them, is the true Jewish fat.

As in the advertising of the 1910s, Crisco's kosher status and its purported health benefits are presented as nearly one and the same. In Crisco, Jewish home cooks "find a pure, sweet-flavored fat which they can use for meat, dairy, and parve foods" as well as a cooking fat that "makes everything in which it used more digestible." While only cans of Crisco sold in Jewish markets were labeled "kosher" and "*parve*" in Yiddish, the book reassures readers that all Crisco cans are kosher, certified by "a prominent Orthodox rabbi," regardless of the label. At the same time, following Jacobs's view that the Jewish housewives were the true arbiters of *kashrut* and Jewish traditions, each of the recipes "has been thoroughly tested in a strictly Orthodox home."[49] It is not clear if Orthodox housewives have tested them for taste, health, or *kashrut*, as Crisco smoothly conflated these categories.

The recipes fill seventy pages, divided in categories from soup to cakes. Nearly all of the recipes are for traditional Ashkenazi dishes, including directions for using Crisco in blintzes, fried cabbage with *schlichkes* (potato-based dumplings), poppy-seed cookies, and apple cake. These recipes suggest that, rather than being new product, Crisco conserved Ashkenazi Jewish culture. Crisco was presented as a singular innovation within a cuisine that had otherwise been transmitted perfectly intact.

Jacobs's case against rabbinic *kashrut* organizations would not withstand the twentieth century. In the second half of the twentieth century, the OU would systematically convince manufacturers that the approval of a rabbinic organization was essential to capturing the Jewish market. It promoted the products that it certified to synagogues in its national network.[50] In 1956, the OU trademarked its packaging symbol and then convinced manufacturers that a nonprofit religious institution could do more for them than Jacobs's advertising agency.[51] In the following decades, the OU, OK, Kof-K, and Star-K—the "big four" kosher certifying agencies—expanded their reach as America's industrial food system grew and developed internationally.

Even as producers increasingly advertised their goods as "healthy" and "natural," Jewish and non-Jewish consumers remained skeptical that they could trust food manufacturers regarding health and food safety. The imprimatur of rabbinical organizations seemed more trustworthy than a firm's advertising—even though *kashrut* remained unrelated to health and safety.[52] Although Jacobs's nontrademarked K symbol continues to be in use, it becomes less popular every year as American Jews' religious standards began to grow stricter at the end of the twentieth century.[53] Crisco would not acquire an OU certification until 1985.[54] But long before then, thanks to the efforts of the JWT and the Jacobs agency, Crisco was firmly established in American Jewish kitchens as a Jewish product.

Return to Schmaltz

Jewish community cookbooks created by synagogues and Jewish women's groups would include recipes with Crisco throughout the twentieth century.[55] By the early twenty-first century, recipes containing Crisco were being published as heritage recipes, passed down from earlier generations.[56] Writing in *Jewish Woman* magazine in 2011, Jewish writer Meredith Lewis described turning to a box of her grandmother's recipes, handwritten on index cards. Sharing her "treasured recipes" of "Grandma Hilda's Carrot Ring" and "Grandma Hilda's Mandel

Bread," both of which call for Crisco, Lewis remarks, "Why do all of my Grandma's recipes start with ½ cup Crisco!?!"[57] The answer to her rhetorical question lies in the dedicated efforts of P&G, the JWT advertising agency, and the Joseph Jacobs Organization in the early twentieth century.

Nonetheless, in the early twenty-first century, some Jews have turned back to schmaltz, now a heritage food with older credentials than Crisco, guided by Jewish cultural trends, broader culinary trends away from "big food," and as in the turn to Crisco a hundred years earlier, scientific health claims. "Low fat" animal fat substitutes such as Crisco, margarine, and soybean oils remained popular through the late 1980s, when scientists began to associate heart disease with saturated fats. Americans turned to trans fats until the 1990s, when scientists raised alarms about them too, culminating in the FDA's steps to remove artificial trans fat from manufactured foods in 2015.[58] Though Crisco, now owned by the J. M. Smucker Co., has offered a version without trans fat since 2004 and no Crisco products have contained any trans fat since 2007, the public stigma of the unhealthiness of hydrogenated vegetable oil and trans fat remains.[59] Schmaltz offered access to an older, seemingly authentic culinary heritage of grandmotherly authority to those who wished to move away from overly processed consumer goods.

In 2014, the *New York Times* heralded the official return of schmaltz, announcing, "*Schmaltz* Finds a New, Younger Audience."[60] For some Jews, schmaltz has become a symbol of Jewish culinary heritage, part of a broader nostalgic resurgence of interest in Ashkenazi food. Jewish restaurateurs and entrepreneurs are following early twenty-first-century American culinary trends emphasizing sustainability, reliance on local goods, and the slow food movement, adapting these trends to interests in Jewish heritage. They see a decline of Jewish cuisine in the mid-twentieth century, as American Jewish food increasingly relied on manufactured goods, including Crisco. They are turning back to American Jewish fare from the early twentieth century and its roots in Central and Eastern Europe—itself now imagined as the "purer" tradition—and reimagining them in light of contemporary culinary trends. Like many American Jews in the early twentieth-first century, most of these culinary innovators do not keep kosher, eliminating much of the Jewish interest in Crisco and other *parve* fats.[61] As a *parve* fat, Crisco still holds some appeal for some traditionally religious-minded Jews, but its widespread hold on American Jews has weakened in the face of broader religious and culinary trends.

Restaurateur Noah Bernamoff, owner of the Jewish-themed Mile End restaurants in New York, views the use of schmaltz in his restaurants' dishes as a rebellion from the reliance on hydrogenated vegetable fats of his parents' generation. "They had a screwed-up idea of what was healthy and what wasn't," he told the *New York Times*.[62] Instead, he saw himself returning to the world of his grandmother. His wife and business partner, Rae Bernamoff, explains in *The Mile End Cookbook*, "Noah's Nana Lee was the ultimate homemaker, while my Grandma Bea was (and still is) a high-powered professional. . . . We wanted to take a cue from Nana's old-world, made-from-scratch ethic and meld it with the forward-thinking ambition of my own grandmother."[63] At Mile End, cooks fry with schmaltz, spread it on challah, blend it with chopped liver, and add it to soup, roasted vegetables, and chicken salad sandwiches with gribenes. "We use a disgusting amount of *schmaltz*," Noah Bernamoff enthusiastically told the *New York Times*. "It has a richness you don't get with vegetable oil."[64] For Bernamoff and others, schmaltz is both healthier and more authentically Jewish.

Interest in schmaltz parallels non-Jewish chefs' resurgence of interest in pork in "farm-to-table" establishments. In 2013, non-Jewish chef and cookbook author Michael Ruhlman published *The Book of Schmaltz: Love Song to a Forgotten Fat*.[65] Ruhlman's interest in schmaltz grew out of his long-standing interest in pig fat; he had encouraged Americans to dry-cure salami and prosciutto and to make their own sausage in earlier books.[66] Rallying against what he perceives as a "Fear of *Schmaltz*"—a fear of "clogged arteries and an early grave"—he resolves, "My goal here is not simply to give *schmaltz* back, guilt-free, to the Jews, but to give it to American home cooks far and wide." Schmaltz "doesn't make us fat," exhorts Ruhlman; "eating all that processed crap," overeating, and lack of exercise does.[67] Just as American Jews had entered mainstream American culinary and health trends by using Crisco and other manufactured vegetable fats, they can now follow American culinary trends favoring animal fats by returning to schmaltz, now seen as the purer and healthier option.

The Book of Schmaltz includes instructions on rendering homemade schmaltz and preparing both traditional Jewish recipes and contemporary innovations such as "Vichyssoise with Gribenes and Chives." Most but not all of these recipes are kosher. "Presumably, those who keep kosher know for themselves what they can and cannot eat," Ruhlman writes while dryly advising kosher-keeping readers to refrain from attempts to make vichyssoise and scones without dairy.[68] Following Joseph Jacobs's belief, religious authority rests solely with practitioners.

Just before Passover in April 2016, the Gefilteria, a purveyor of gefilte fish, horseradish, kvass, and other "Old World Jewish foods" made from sustainable ingredients, tweeted a picture of schmaltz and onions cooking on a stovetop with the caption "Rendering *schmaltz*. Because, Passover. Because, Jewish."[69] Once again, schmaltz has become a sign of Jewish culture and religion itself, just as Crisco once was. The relationship among American Jews, schmaltz, and Crisco throughout the twentieth and twenty-first centuries has articulated the location of religious authority and institutional power as well as the intertwined relationships among *kashrut*, American Jewish dietary habits, and popular conceptions of health. If Jews had waited four thousand years for Crisco, they enthusiastically returned to schmaltz a century later.

NOTES

1. Neil, *Story of Crisco*, 19. I am grateful to Shulamith Z. Berger, curator of Special Collections and Hebraica-Judaica at Yeshiva University, for sharing print advertisements from her personal collection with me as well as assisting my research in Yeshiva University's Special Collections.
2. *Crisco Recipes*.
3. Fishkoff, *Kosher Nation*, 46.
4. In the United States, even as Jews continued to cook with schmaltz, the word for the greasy cooking fat acquired a metaphorical meaning of excessive sentimentality, much like the word *cheesy*. Schmaltz does not have this connotation in Yiddish. Wex, *Rhapsody in Schmaltz*, 77–82.
5. Berg, "From Pushcart Peddlers," 73.
6. The 2008 Agriprocessors scandal widely revealed that kosher slaughter could be inhumane. See Gross, *Question of the Animal*. See also Sussman, "Myth of the Trefa Banquet," 38. For more on Jews and health, see Hart, *Healthy Jew*.
7. Strasser, *Satisfaction Guaranteed*, 5.
8. Strasser, 5–7.
9. King and Olejko, "Use of Cottonseed Oil," 273–75.
10. Wrenn, *Cinderella of the New South*.
11. Thomas, *In Food We Trust*, 17–18.
12. Wrenn, *Cinderella of the New South*, 78–79; Thomas, *In Food We Trust*, 18–21.

13. During the Civil War, contracts to supply candles and soap to the Union Army secured the P&G's success, and veterans returned home familiar with the brand. Dyer, Dalzell, and Olegario, *Rising Tide*.

14. Dyer, Dalzell, and Olegario, *Rising Tide*, 47; Forristal, "Rise and Fall of Crisco," B6.

15. Patterson, *Hydrogenation of Fats and Oils*, xiii.

16. Dyer, Dalzell, and Olegario, *Rising Tide*, 51.

17. P&G initially called the product Krispo, but a Chicago cracker manufacturer had already trademarked the name. They briefly renamed the product Cryst before realizing that it might be pronounced "Christ," which might alienate both Christian and Jewish customers. Eventually, P&G landed on Crisco, short for crystalized cottonseed oil. Forristal, "Rise and Fall of Crisco," B6.

18. P&G considered marketing Crisco so important that the company opened its board of directors meeting to a woman for the first time so that Lansdowne could "answer questions from the woman's point of view," as Crisco would be marketed primarily to housewives. Stanley Resor became president of JWT in 1916, and he and Lansdowne married in 1917. Together, they ran JWT for several decades; he focused on administration and she directed the preparation of ads. Dyer, Dalzell, and Olegario, *Rising Tide*, 52; "P&G Co"; "Resor, Helen Lansdowne (1886–1964)."

19. Dyer, Dalzell, and Olegario, *Rising Tide*, 52; Strasser, *Satisfaction Guaranteed*, 14.

20. Strasser, *Satisfaction Guaranteed*, 12.

21. Thomas, *In Food We Trust*, 24.

22. Strasser, *Satisfaction Guaranteed*, 17.

23. Hurd, "Oft Overlooked Market," 60–64.

24. Fishkoff, *Kosher Nation*, 48–50.

25. Horowitz, *Kosher USA*.

26. Photocopy of "copy" of agreement between P&G and Sender Lifstitz and M. S. Margolies, September 22, 1911.

27. Horowitz, *Kosher USA*.

28. The Upper East Side Jewish prep school Ramaz is named for Margolies, using a Hebrew acronym for his initials. "Rabbi Margolies Dies of Pneumonia," 21.

29. Fishkoff, *Kosher Nation*, 48.

30. Hurd, "Oft Overlooked Market," 192.

31. "Crisco," 2.

32. See Goldstein, *Home Economists*.

33. "Crisco."

34. "Crisco." A latke is a potato pancake traditionally prepared for Hanukkah. A blintze is a thin pancake wrapped around cheese or fruit, akin to a crepe.

35. "Crisco."

36. Stage, *Rethinking Home Economics*, 291.

37. Neil, *Story of Crisco*, 19.

38. Neil, 19. Though the advertising copy wittily traces this rule back to the biblical origins of Judaism, the Israelite religion of the second millennium BCE, the

separation of dairy and meat products is not nearly so old. The Jewish practice derives from the Torah's injunction not to cook a calf in its mother's milk (Exodus 23:19, 34:26; Deuteronomy 14:21). Ancient Jews took this instruction literally, refraining from cooking calves in the milk of their own mothers. It is not until the rabbinic period, following the destruction of the Second Temple in Jerusalem in 70 CE, that Jews took this law to be a metaphorical instruction to refrain from mixing meat and dairy products. Nonetheless, for two thousand years, this practice has set Jews apart from their neighbors. Kraemer, *Jewish Eating.*

39. Steinberg, *Jewish Mad Men*, 55–59.
40. Fishkoff, *Kosher Nation*, 48–50.
41. Yoskowitz, "American Processed Kosher," 74.
42. Horowitz, *Kosher USA*, 86–87.
43. Fishkoff, *Kosher Nation*, 50. See Horowitz, chap. 4, for a detailed account of conflicts between Jacobs and the OU in the 1940s and 1950s.
44. Although the product was created in 1897, at the time of this publication, Jell-O had not yet reached the height of its appeal as a quintessentially American product, reaching across regional and ethnic lines, as it would in the 1930s. Steinberg, *Jewish Mad Men*, 61–62. For the controversy over the kosher certification of Jell-O, see Horowitz, *Kosher USA*, chapter 3.
45. Steinberg, *Jewish Mad Men*, 64–65.
46. *Crisco Recipes*, 80.
47. Kirshenblatt-Gimblett, "Kitchen Judaism," 94.
48. *Crisco Recipes*, 82.
49. *Crisco Recipes*, 82.
50. Horowitz, *Kosher USA*, 89.
51. When Ⓤ symbol was created in the 1920s, US law would not allow "an 'association' that neither produces goods nor trades in them" to register a trademark. This changed with the 1946 Lanham Act. Horowitz, *Kosher USA*, 88–89.
52. Horowitz, 108.
53. Fishkoff, *Kosher Nation*, 50.
54. Brenner, "Super Mashgiach."
55. For example, Greenbaum, *International Jewish Cook Book.*
56. For example, Satz, *Heirloom Cookbook.*
57. Lewis, "Jewish Family Legacy."
58. US Food and Drug Administration, "FDA Cuts Trans Fat."
59. The FDA allows food manufacturers to list amounts of trans fat that are less than half a gram per serving as zero on the Nutrition Facts panel. Crisco, "Frequently Asked Questions."
60. Clark "*Schmaltz* Finds."
61. In 2013, 22 percent of American Jews reported keeping kosher in their home. Pew Research Center, *A Portrait of Jewish Americans.*
62. Clark, "*Schmaltz* Finds."

63. Bernamoff, *Mile End Cookbook*, 10.
64. Clark, "*Schmaltz* Finds."
65. Ruhlman, *Book of Schmaltz*.
66. Ruhlman, *Book of Schmaltz*; Ruhlman, *Salumi*; Ruhlman, *Charcuterie*.
67. Ruhlman, *Book of Schmaltz*, 3.
68. Ruhlman, 2–3, 6.
69. Gefilteria, "Rendering schmaltz."

BIBLIOGRAPHY

Berg, Jennifer. "From Pushcart Peddlers to Gourmet Take-Out: New York City's Iconic Foods of Jewish Origin, 1920 to 2005." PhD diss., New York University, 2006.

Bernamoff, Rae. Preface to *The Mile End Cookbook: Redefining Jewish Comfort Food From Hash to Hamantaschen*, by Noah Bernamoff and Rae Bernamoff. New York: Clarkson Potter, 2012.

Brenner, Bayla Sheva. "The Super Mashgiach: Rabbi Chaim Goldzweig." *Jewish Action*, May 26, 2011. https://jewishaction.com.

Clark, Melissa. "*Schmaltz* Finds a New, Younger Audience." *New York Times*, December 9, 2014.

Crisco. "Frequently Asked Questions about Crisco Shortening with 0 Grams Trans Fat per Serving." Archived on February 18, 2008. http://web.archive.org.

Crisco Recipes for the Jewish Housewife. Cincinnati: P&G, 1933.

Dyer, Davis, Frederick Dalzell, and Rowena Olegario. *Rising Tide: Lessons from 165 Years of Brand Building at P&G*. Boston: Harvard Business School Press, 2014.

Fishkoff, Sue. *Kosher Nation: Why More and More of America's Food Answers to a Higher Authority*. New York: Schocken Books, 2010.

Forristal, Linda. "The Rise and Fall of Crisco." *Epoch Times*, December 31, 2013.

Gefilteria. "About Us." http://gefilteria.com.

Gefilteria (@gefilteria). "Rendering schmaltz. Because, Passover. Because, Jewish." Twitter, April 18, 2016. https://twitter.com/gefilteria/status/722115368257462274.

Goldstein, Carolyn M. *Home Economists in Twentieth-Century America*. Chapel Hill: University of North Carolina Press, 2012.

Greenbaum, Florence Kreisler. *The International Jewish Cook Book: A Modern "Kosher" Cook Book*. New York: Bloch, 1918.

Gross, Aaron. *The Question of the Animal and Religion: Theoretical Stakes, Practical Implications*. New York: Columbia University Press, 2014.

Hart, Mitchell B. *The Healthy Jew: The Symbiosis of Judaism and Modern Medicine*. New York: Cambridge University Press, 2007.

Horowitz, Roger. *Kosher USA: How Coke Became Kosher and Other Tales of Modern Food*. New York: Columbia University Press, 2016.

Hurd, Charles W. "Oft Overlooked Market in the Tenements." *Printers' Ink* 81, no. 4 (1912): 60–64.

King, C. Clay, and John Olejko. "The Use of Cottonseed Oil in Vegetable Shortenings," *Cereal Foods World* 34, no. 3 (March 1989): 273–75.

Kirshenblatt-Gimblett, Barbara. "Kitchen Judaism." In *Getting Comfortable in New York: The American Jewish Home, 1880–1950*, edited by Susan L. Braunstein and Jenna Weissman Joselit, 77–105. New York: Jewish Museum, 1990.

Kraemer, David C. *Jewish Eating and Identity through the Ages.* New York: Routledge, 2007.

Lewis, Meredith. "A Jewish Family Legacy in Recipes." *JW Magazine*, February 23, 2011. www.jwmag.org.

Neil, Marion Harris. *The Story of Crisco.* Cincinnati: P&G, 1913.

"P&G Co." *Advertising Age*, September 15, 2003. http://adage.com.

Patterson, H. B. W. *Hydrogenation of Fats and Oils: Theory and Practice.* Champaign, IL: AOCS, 2009.

Pew Research Center. *A Portrait of Jewish Americans: Findings from a Pew Research Center Survey of U.S. Jews.* Washington, DC: Pew Research Center, 2013. www.pewforum.org.

Photocopy of "copy" of agreement between P&G and Sender Lifstitz and M. S. Margolies. Kehillath Jeshrun Collection, Box 78-001, Crisco folder, Yeshiva University Archives. September 22, 1911.

"Rabbi Margolies Dies of Pneumonia." *New York Times*, August 26, 1936.

"Resor, Helen Lansdowne (1886–1964)." *Advertising Age*, September 15, 2003. http://adage.com.

Ruhlman, Michael. *The Book of Schmaltz: Love Song to a Forgotten Fat.* New York: Little, Brown, 2013.

———. *Charcuterie: The Craft of Salting, Smoking, and Curing.* New York: W. W. Norton, 2013.

———. *Salumi: The Craft of Italian Dry Curing.* New York: Norton, 2012.

Satz, Miriam Lerner Satz. *Heirloom Cookbook: Recipes Handed Down by Jewish Mothers and Modern Recipes from Daughters and Friends.* North Minneapolis, MN: Kar-Ben, 2003.

Stage, Sarah. *Rethinking Home Economics.* Ithaca, NY: Cornell University Press, 1997.

Steinberg, Kerri P. *Jewish Mad Men: Advertising and the Design of the American Jewish Experience.* New Brunswick, NJ: Rutgers University Press, 2015.

Strasser, Susan. *Satisfaction Guaranteed: The Making of the American Mass Market.* New York: Pantheon Books, 1989.

Sussman, Lance J. "The Myth of the Trefa Banquet: American Culinary Culture and the Radicalization of Food Policy in American Reform Judaism." *American Jewish Archives Journal* 57, nos. 1–2 (2005): 29–52.

Thomas, Courtney I. P. *In Food We Trust: The Politics of Purity in American Food Regulation.* Lincoln: University of Nebraska Press, 2014.

US Food and Drug Administration. "FDA Cuts Trans Fat in Processed Foods." www.fda.gov.

Wex, Michael. *Rhapsody in Schmaltz: Yiddish Food and Why We Can't Stop Eating It*. New York: St. Martin's Press, 2016.

Wrenn, Lynette Boney. *Cinderella of the New South: A History of the Cottonseed Industry, 1855–1955*. Knoxville: University of Tennessee Press, 1995.

Yoskowitz, Jeffrey. "American Processed Kosher," *Gastronomica* 12, no. 2 (2012): 72–76.

Zarrow, Sarah, trans. "Crisco." *Jewish Morning Journal*, December 12, 2011.

9

The Search for Religious Authenticity
and the Case of Passover Peanut Oil

ZEV ELEFF

In Sidney Roth's home on Manhattan's Lower East Side, Passover preparation began months in advance. His mother started to plan for the springtime holiday in the winter season. As she shopped for her family's Sabbath meals, Mrs. Roth made sure to purchase the fattiest chickens "because now was the time to start saving 'Schmaltz for Pesach.'" At the turn of the twentieth century, chicken fat—schmaltz—was a critical ingredient for most Passover recipes: Jews used schmaltz to prepare potato fritters, fried matzah, and "even just to put on a slice of Matzo with a little bit of salt." For the Roths, Passover dining had to be basic. Available foods and ingredients were quite limited. As late as the 1920s, kosher food producers did not yet offer much beyond matzah and "kosher soap for washing dishes." Recalling the dire culinary situation many years later, Roth put it this way: "There were no 'Heshgochos' [kosher certifications] for canned foods. Chocolate candy was 'Avada Chomitz' [definitely leavened bread] and even butter was 'better not,' according to my father. So there was very little you could have with matzo except the schmaltz."[1] On any other occasion, households like Roth's would have relied on vegetable oil. On Passover, however, most religiously traditional Ashkenazic Jews withheld from consuming oils extracted from *kitniyot* (legumes) that might contain grain particles that leaven into Passover-proscribed *hametz* (leaven forbidden on Passover). Orthodox Jews therefore resorted to chicken fat to grease their pans and moisten their Passover desserts. That changed in the 1930s. By then, most American chefs had discovered peanut oil. Jews certainly noticed. Recalling their memories of Eastern Europe, America's Jews had never heard of a Passover ban on peanuts in association with forbidden kitniyot. They therefore began using that more appealing product in their kitchens rather than less appetizing, greasy schmaltz.

The history of the American Jewish encounter with peanut oil is a most intriguing case study to understand the flow of culture from Europe to the United States and how competing forces manifested themselves in new religious environs. This tracing of "foodways" offers a portal of entry to "lived religion."[2] In a word, anyone can play a role in the development of foodways culture. Especially for low-cost items, food is a cultural commodity available and used by all types of people, and their collective interactions inform an important component of religious history. The Passover peanut oil conflict was fiercely debated by rabbinic elites in Europe and then even more vociferously by scholars in the United States. Certainly, though, the issue was also controlled to a large extent by the everyday Orthodox Jewish consumer who elected whether to purchase the product from the grocer.[3]

Jewish consumption of peanut oil must have been significant since manufacturers took notice. Planters Peanut Company published a Yiddish-language recipe book, titled *46 Oyfanim far Besere Peyseh Maykholim [46 Ways for Better Passover Food]*, of forty-six Passover recipes that all utilized peanut oil. "Planters Hi-Hat Peanut Oil," the cookbook's editors boasted, "is the ideal oil for all your Passover cooking, baking, frying, salads and gravies."[4] Similar to other Passover publications of this sort, the thin cooking guide was a benchmark in the American Jewish experience.[5] For Orthodox Jews, the cookbook represented their community's embrace of all-American consumerism. To Planters, the publication was a prudent marketing strategy to keep its product on Jewish holiday shopping lists. Yet neither outlook lasted more than a few decades. In time, America's Orthodox Jews viewed peanuts like other legume products and avoided peanut oil during Passover. This chapter seeks to understand the cause for this change and how it betokened a broader religious transition in Orthodox Judaism.

Some might be tempted to explain this later move toward stringency as a function of what one noted scholar describes as the "disappearance of a way of life and the mimetic tradition" and the emergence of "text-based religiosity."[6] This outlook suggests that due to the devastation of the Holocaust, there was "little chance that the old ways would be preserved."[7] As a result, Orthodox Jews turned to more rigid texts to decide religious practice and, consciously or not, suppressed the opaque memories of their parents' and grandparents' conflicting religious norms. Maybe this was the case for Passover peanut oil. Perhaps American Jews looked into rabbinic literature and interpreted that peanuts should also be part of the kitniyot ban despite the decades-long tradition to the contrary.

But the later abandonment of peanut oil was not based on any sort of crisis and succeeding rereading of rabbinic texts. In fact, the debate over the *halakhic*—the rabbinic term for Jewish law—status of kitniyot on Passover postdates the Talmud. It emerged in Ashkenaz, in the French-German areas of Europe, probably a century or two before the tradition made its way into rabbinic writing in the thirteenth century.[8] For this reason, Sephardic Jews have never withheld from foods like beans and rice on Passover. In contrast, Ashkenazic Jews have constantly encountered new foods like corn, potatoes, peanuts, and most recently, quinoa with the same penetrating question: Is it permitted on Passover? Throughout the centuries, rabbinic writers developed tools to decide whether to broaden the Passover menu: they have considered how the food grows, whether it develops in isolation or in bunches, and researched how the food is baked or cooked.[9] Halakhists borrowed several of these lines of inquiry from other realms of Jewish law and justified others based on common sense. Their solutions were creative but fully removed from any learned reading of the Talmud. In all cases, therefore, authorities understood that their decisions were products of what we might describe as "religious intuition" rather than anything directly derived from rabbinic sources.[10]

No doubt, religious intuition has played a role in many aspects of Jewish law. Yet owing to its extratalmudic origins, kitniyot is a unique area of Jewish legal and religious culture determined by intuition and sensibilities. Jews with a more expansive interpretation of kitniyot held to a more stringent *halakhic* culture. Ashkenazic Jews inclined to permit newly encountered foods represented a culture denoted by its more lenient juridical tradition. The case of peanuts is not altogether exceptional in modern discussions of kitniyot. Jews faced similar dilemmas when assessing products derived from buckwheat, coffee, sesame seed, and cottonseed.[11] But unlike other questionable foods, peanuts offer insight into the migration of Jewish cultures from the Old World to the United States. The peanut's emergence as a major food product around the turn of the twentieth century coincided with the mass immigration of Eastern European Jews. As a result, the Jewish population in the United States grew from three hundred thousand in 1880 to nearly five million by 1940.[12] A disproportionate number hailed from Lithuania, where the Orthodox rabbinate was known for its lenient-leaning rabbinic culture.[13] Not surprising, then, peanut oil became a particularly precious item for Eastern European immigrants and their first-generation American children.

Then came another wave of Jewish migrants. In the mid-twentieth century, large numbers of other Jews from the Ukraine and Hungary settled in the United States. Foods preferences often divided Jews from different European enclaves, but there was something much deeper to the friction between the earlier Eastern European transplants and these newer Hungarian extracts.[14] Hungarian Jews arrived with luggage filled with a traditional culture known for its rigidness and stringency when compared to its Lithuanian counterpart.[15] Not surprisingly, Hungarian Jews cooked with schmaltz rather than peanut oil on Passover. The rise and fall of Passover peanut oil was therefore emblematic of the competition between multiple European folkways—Lithuanian and Hungarian—for cultural hegemony in the New World.[16] Evidence of this conflict can be derived from rabbinic literature as well as more popular forms.[17] Tracing this history through a variety of forms demonstrates the pervasiveness of this cultural battle. Consequently, peanut oil and the *halakhic* and cultural circumstances that surround its use on Passover serves as a clear example of how religious change in American Orthodox Judaism was as much a result of contending folkways from Europe as it was the product of cultural ruptures caused by the Holocaust and the subsequent reconstruction of religious life in the United States.

Kitniyot and Its Extratalmudic History

The Bible (Deuteronomy 16:3) proscribes consumption of "leavened bread" during the seven days of Passover. The Babylonian Talmud (Pesahim 35a) enumerates five specific grains that count as leavened bread once they came into close contact with water. Writing at the end of the twelfth century, Maimonides maintained the same list without any emendations. He also explicitly permitted eating kitniyot.[18] Subsequently, Sephardic Jews—hailing from Spain and other Mediterranean areas—have followed Maimonides's ruling. Ashkenazic Jews have not. The thirteenth-century scholar Yitzhak ben Yosef of Corbeil was one of the first to record the stringent tradition that forbade kitniyot.[19] In subsequent centuries, rabbinic writers in Ashkenazic territories like France and Germany offered two primary explanations for the stringency: First, the consumption of kitniyot products on Passover could confuse Jews and lead them to inadvertently eat bread on the holiday. Second, forbidden grains might be found in the same containers that held kitniyot.[20] By the 1500s, despite the Talmud's ruling to the contrary, virtually all Jews in Ashkenaz abstained from eating legumes on Passover.[21]

For centuries, the stringent custom persisted undisturbed. However, amid religious upheaval in Europe, kitniyot emerged as a major area of religious conflict in the nineteenth century. Since kitniyot stood out as an extratalmudic prohibition, its widespread observance represented Orthodox Jewry's fidelity to the "spirit" as well as the "letter" of the law.[22] Not everyone agreed. Owing to the financial burdens of their coreligionists, moderate reformers sought to suspend the kitniyot prohibition and allow European Jews to purchase more affordable foodstuff for Passover. In 1810, religious liberals in Westphalia attempted to abolish the prohibition, claiming that it lacked any basis in the Talmud. In turn, religiously conservative leaders responded, arguing that there was much more to traditional religion than what was explicitly handed down in the Talmud.[23] Likewise, in 1843 Samuel Adler's first reform as district rabbi of Alzey was to abolish the ban on legumes, to the chagrin of the Orthodox.[24] A final noteworthy incident took place in Palestine in 1909. In his rabbinical post in Jaffa, Rabbi Avraham Yitzhak Kook permitted the use of sesame seed oil on Passover. The Jaffa rabbi's decision was adamantly opposed by the leading rabbinic court in Jerusalem. In the end, Kook retreated, a decision that would do much to solidify the strict stance maintained by Orthodox Jews in Israel in subsequent decades.[25] All told, kitniyot stood out as a commitment to an Orthodox faith, no matter the financial hardships incurred by the punctilious observance of the custom.

The American Jewish Kitchen and Peanut Oil

Peanuts came to the New World aboard slave ships from Africa. It remained mostly a "slave food" until the Civil War, when Union and Confederate troops encamped in the South made use of peanuts as a substitute for their usual snack items. Other properties of the peanut proved beneficial. In response to Union blockades, Confederate forces and industrialists found peanut oil a satisfactory substitute for the whale oil used to lubricate machinery. Also short on supplies and funds, northerners tried peanut oil. After the war, the upper classes of American society regarded peanut consumption as "ungenteel." Yet peanuts were "almost universally liked" by the rank and file and spread throughout the country and into kitchen pantries.[26] Peanut oil was a different matter. After the Civil War, Americans dropped peanut oil for other types.[27] Peanut oil finally emerged as a major domestic product during World War II. In 1942, the United States restricted the commercial distribution of most lards, oils, and butters. To the great fortune of Planters Edible Oil Company (est. 1933), the federal government did not place limits on the sale of peanut oil. From then on, peanut oil was a staple in millions of American homes.[28]

American Jews were one of the first groups to embrace peanut oil. The US Department of Agriculture reported in 1941 that "a white form of refined peanut oil enjoys much popularity among the Jewish trade in several eastern cities."[29] Much of the Jewish consumption of peanut oil had to do with Passover. In 1936, Planters Peanuts announced a line of "kosher peanut-oil as well by retaining rabbis to inspect production."[30] Jewish newspapers and magazines around springtime featured advertisements for Planters' brand, as well as a peanut oil produced by Rokeach and Sons, a Brooklyn-based kosher food manufacturer.[31] Two reasons account for this. First, Jewish cooks happily greased their pans with peanut oil rather than less appetizing chicken fat during the holiday. Second, in contrast to vegetable oils, Orthodox Jews did not view peanut oil as falling under the Passover ban on kitniyot.

Lithuanian Foodways

Since peanuts did not enter the European diet until the very end of the 1800s, the vociferous debates that had ignited Jewish communities in the Old World involved neither the crop nor foods made from it.[32] When peanuts finally reached Eastern Europe, Jews freely ate them on Passover without concern that they might be kitniyot.[33] If there was any unease over peanuts, Jews in that region no doubt would still use peanut oil. It was consistent with the well-known ruling of one of the leading Lithuanian authorities on Jewish law. In a responsum that permitted Jews to consume products made from buckwheat, Rabbi Yitzhak Elhanan Spektor of Kovno ruled that in most cases, oils extracted from kitniyot could also be used on Passover—so long as the product was checked for grain prior to production.[34]

Eastern European Jews followed Spektor's decision and took it with them to the United States.[35] Any and all skeptics were silenced by several highly respected North American rabbis who put fears to rest. Rabbi Yosef Eliyahu Henkin of New York cited Spektor's ruling for good measure but held that there was no reason to count peanuts under the rubric of kitniyot.[36] In 1935, Toronto's Rabbi Yehudah Leib Graubart—his Polish hasidic followers referred to him as the "Stashever Rebbe"—permitted peanut oil.[37] In addition, Rabbi Shmuel Pardes of Chicago guaranteed the readers of his rabbinic journal that he could vouch for the reliability of the few manufacturers that produced Passover-approved peanut oil.[38] He reaffirmed his position the following year, this time with mention of Rokeach's brand of peanut oil, a line that Pardes personally supervised.[39] In 1948, the subsequent generation of mostly American-born clergymen who led the Rabbinical Council of America and the Orthodox Union formally offered their approval of peanut oil for Passover.[40] From that point onward, the Orthodox Union routinely listed peanut oil among the approved "consumer products" for Passover.[41] The Orthodox felt comfortable with that decision since they had the backing of a Lithuanian rabbinic tradition that so often sought out leniency wherever possible to make Jewish living easier.

The Orthodox laypeople were certainly grateful. Well into the 1960s, no one could object when a food columnist for Boston's Jewish weekly opined that "Jewish housewives . . . depend on Planters Peanut Oil for so much of their cooking and baking."[42] Planters advertised its oil each year in the spring as the solution to "better tasting Passover meals."[43] Often, Planters offered consumers a complimentary copy of its Passover recipe book. Each item of course included peanut oil among the ingredients.[44] By the end of the decade, the leading peanut product manufacturer published a new English-language cookbook that reinforced its wares as an approved alternative for a holiday when "everyday foods [are] forbidden."[45] Peanut oil, Planters once again claimed, was a key ingredient to "feather-light matzo balls."[46] All this would quickly change, however. By the 1960s, a far more stringent Hungarian folkway touched down on American soil. In short order, the Hungarian foodway established itself as a formidable rival to the Lithuanian brand that had peerlessly thrived in the United States for nearly a century.[47]

Hungarian Foodways

In 1966, Rabbi Yaakov Goldman wrote to Rabbi Moshe Feinstein about a "new custom" that he had observed in the Orthodox community. Goldman had recently moved from Manhattan's Lower East Side to Brooklyn.[48] The Hebrew book publisher maintained strong ties to leading Lithuanian rabbis like Feinstein in Manhattan as well as greener Hungarian scholars who inhabited various neighborhoods in Brooklyn.[49] Despite his familiarity with the Hungarian element, Goldman was taken aback to find that his new neighbors did not use peanut oil on Passover. He therefore wrote to Feinstein to seek clarification.

At the time that Goldman submitted his peanut query, Feinstein was already recognized as a leading rabbinic authority in the United States. Orthodox Jews hailed him as a "Torah giant," and more religiously liberal coreligionists at the very least acknowledged Feinstein as an undisputable "genius."[50] The publication of his responsa was considered by many a "major halachic event" in America.[51] Nevertheless, a Hungarian folkway proved persistent and agitating to Feinstein and like-minded Lithuanian rabbinical scholars in the United States. Feinstein's response revealed his utter frustration. As he understood it, the kitniyot prohibition was a ban that had always been governed by popular practice rather than any rabbinic ruling decided in a synod or court. Were it initiated by learned scholars, presumed Feinstein, there would have been a set of rules transmitted throughout generations to decide which foods were to be considered kitniyot on Passover. That there were no such guidelines tacitly implied that only those foods like rice, millet, and beans that were known to earlier Jews were off limits for Passover. Further, Feinstein recalled that Jews snacked on peanuts during Passover when he was a child in Belarus. He therefore saw absolutely no reason to refrain from peanuts and their oil during Passover.[52]

The Hungarian rabbinate could amply match Feinstein's childhood recollections with its own memories of a far more rigid but no less traditional *halakhic* culture.[53] In the mid-1800s, Rabbi Yekutiel Yehuda Teitelbaum, the Grand Rebbe of Sighet, prohibited all oils on Passover. In an undated letter to a rabbinic colleague, Teitelbaum refused to permit anything other than chicken fat, lest Jews accidentally use prohibited kitniyot oils on the holiday.[54] In all probability, the Grand Rebbe never came across peanuts during his lifetime. Therefore, the task of banning that food fell to his son and heir, Rabbi Hananya Yom Tov Lipa Teitelbaum. In a well-publicized discourse around the turn of the century, the son banned peanuts in a "Shabbat ha-Gadol" ("The Great Sabbath") discourse delivered directly before Passover.[55]

The decision held its own in the face of rabbinic opposition to Teitelbaum's restrictive ruling.[56] In one instance, a ranking scholar initially supported the use of peanuts on Passover in 1922 but quickly backpedaled from that lenient decision since the leading rabbis in Hungary did not agree with his conclusion.[57] That same year, when Rabbi Yehuda Leib Tsirelson in nearby Romania issued permission to his community to consume peanuts on Passover, his opinion was promptly challenged by neighboring rabbis.[58]

The Hungarian culture of halakhic stringency eventually migrated to the United States. In 1947, it was fortified with the arrival of Rabbi Yoel Teitelbaum, the scion of that hasidic dynasty from Sighet.[59] In the aftermath of the Holocaust, the so-called Satmar Rebbe restarted his family's hasidic court in the Williamsburg section of Brooklyn.[60] For Teitelbaum, Williamsburg was fertile soil and, according to one observer, "already the center of the more religious Hungarian Jews in America."[61] Agreeable adherents empowered their charismatic leader to offer up ideas and positions that challenged Feinstein and other Lithuanian-trained halakhists. Peanut oil on Passover was one of many points of disagreement between Teitelbaum and Feinstein, and the former's followers continued to abide by Teitelbaum's positions after his death in 1979.[62]

The Hungarian stringent-conforming intuition manifested itself in areas beyond the Satmar community.[63] In the 1950s, Rabbi Yonatan Steif of Williamsburg held firm to the stance on peanut oil that he had articulated earlier as a leading authority in Budapest.[64] Stationed in England, Rabbi Yitzhak Yaakov Weiss refused to budge from his Hungarian-learned stringent ruling on cottonseed oil. No matter how many reasons others offered to be lenient, Weiss believed that "the custom throughout the Diaspora was to rule stringently on all cases of oil that they be considered kitniyot on Passover."[65] Similarly, a Brooklyn-based rabbinic journal published several essays that called into question American Orthodoxy's long-standing tradition to consume products made from buckwheat and honey on Passover.[66] These rulings also implied to the followers of these Hungarian leaders that peanut oil was off limits as well.

The conflict left American Orthodoxy without a unified position. The Orthodox Union continued to certify peanut oil, but few others were of one mind.[67] In his popular 1977 Passover guidebook, Rabbi Shimon Eider acknowledged "various opinions" and that "one should conduct himself according to his minhag," the custom, or "consult" a rabbinic authority.[68] Another publication declared under the heading of "Please Read This Important Notice" that "there are Rabbis who permit the use of oils and syrups that are derived from *kitniyos*" while "there are other Rabbis who are more stringent concerning this and do not allow the use of these products on Pesach."[69]

The emergent equivocation frustrated the Orthodox establishment that grew up with peanut oil in their Passover pantries. Planters Peanuts also felt pressure to push the issue. In the 1970s, the snack and oil manufacturer rebranded its peanut oil as the "Passover Oil."[70] However, fewer Jewish consumers believed in that slogan. Instead, Orthodox Jews contacted kosher certification organizations to confirm that the "OK" symbol that appeared on the Planters label was indeed legitimate.[71] The head of the Organized Kashrus Laboratories that certified Planters' peanut oil lamented the "many inquiries" he received about peanut oil. To assure confused constituents, Rabbi Bernard Levy thought it best to print a personal correspondence with Rabbi Moshe Feinstein in his *Jewish*

Homemaker magazine. Levy published the letter yearly. In it, Feinstein assured both Levy and his readers that they "may give certification for peanuts and the oil derived from them."[72] But for a growing number, Feinstein's approval was no longer sufficient against the Hungarian form of Orthodox Jewish foodway culture.

What was it about the Hungarian folkway that enabled it to compete—and eventually topple—the Lithuanian establishment in the United States? Part of the answer is timing. In the 1970s, American Protestantism underwent a conservative upsurge, a reaction to the radical politics and social agendas of Christian denominations during the previous decade.[73] Much like evangelical leaders, Hungarian Jewish exponents offered their followers a more insular form of religious instruction that stressed moralism and conduct rather than social responsibility and tolerance.[74] Just as important, the Hungarians gained a level of "authenticity" through their separatism.[75] Unlike the Eastern European immigrants who happily partnered or assumed control of existing Jewish schools and organizations when they had arrived in the United States, the Hungarians preferred to furnish new institutions.[76] Moreover, Hungarian Jews in Brooklyn prided themselves on their unique dress. Men sported long beards and sidelocks. Some adorned fur hats as religious uniforms that they would not remove amid sweltering New York summers. As well, Hungarian women could be identified by their simple wigs and plain and modest dresses.[77] These features lent Hungarian Orthodoxy a level of perceived authenticity that could not be matched by the most pious Lithuanian Jews. As a result, to measure their own punctiliousness and levels of religious observance, Orthodox Jews—who did not necessarily dress like or identify with Hungarian Orthodox Jews—sought out the approval of this burgeoning Hungarian element. Questioning the halakhic veracity of peanut oil on Passover was just one small way Orthodox Jews interrupted the status quo.

Israeli Foodways

In time, the stringent Hungarian folkway overpowered the Lithuanian culture. At the outset of the 1980s, a shrinking but sizable number of Orthodox households retained peanut oil in their cooking repertoire.[78] This may have had just as much to do with the high costs of other approved Passover oils as it did with maintaining older *halakhic* traditions. Heavily burdened by the cost of Passover foods, Jewish homemakers looked wherever they could to relieve the onerous costs of holiday groceries. In fact, in April 1981 the president of the Rabbinical Alliance of America issued a statement deploring the high costs of Passover foods to the benefit of "money hungry store keepers and distributors."[79]

Eventually, most Orthodox Jews abandoned peanut oil. One Jewish woman in 1985 was very much unaware of a more lenient tradition when she wrote matter-of-factly that "Sephardim traditionally use rice, corn, peanuts and pulse and the Ashkenazim do not."[80] According to another observer who wrote about kitniyot at the end of the decade, "Items in that category include corn, rice and peanuts."[81] The disappearance of peanut oil from Orthodox Jewish life was very apparent in other ways too. In an Orthodox children's song, "Found Some Peanuts," a verse that specifically detailed the various uses of peanut oil listed its utility for lighting Hanukkah candles but failed to mention its place in the Passover kitchen. Decades ago, Planters had convinced so many Jewish consumers of its product's status as the premier "Passover Oil." But the image of peanut oil was no longer bound up with Passover when this lyricist composed his peanut song in 1982.[82]

The transition toward strictness was helped along by a like-minded Israeli folkway. There, Orthodox Jews did not eat peanuts or use peanut oil on Passover. In 1926, Rabbi David Zvi Hoffman reported that the rabbinic intuition ensconced in Jerusalem sided with the stringent Hungarian point of view.[83] That incorrigible culture emanated from Jerusalem and carried influence throughout the Holy Land. Rabbi Zvi Pesah Frank, a leading judge in Jerusalem, confessed a certain powerlessness to change the trend.[84] In 1966, resisters such as Rabbi Yehoshua Moshe Aaronson of Petah Tikva refused to budge from the established practice.[85] Two years later in nearby Tel Aviv, the local rabbinic establishment was met with great reservation by other rabbis and laypeople.[86] Eventually, Israel's Chief Rabbinate proscribed peanut oil for Ashkenazic Jews.[87] More recently, the late Rabbi Yosef Shalom Elyashiv reaffirmed the stringent practice for Jews living in Israel.[88]

An explanation for the successful transplant of the Israeli folkway is far less complex than the earlier Hungarian triumph. It had much to do with the passing of Rabbi Feinstein in 1986. In addition to Feinstein, another leading scholar, Rabbi Yaakov Kamenetsky, died in that year. But even before that date, Feinstein's health prohibited him from maintaining his station as American Orthodoxy's leading halakhist.[89] With no one in the United States deemed worthy of replacing Feinstein, his non-Hungarian followers looked to Israel to fill the vacuum.[90] This transition could only hurt the case of those who supported Passover peanut oil and the sympathetic type of rabbinic intuition that stood behind it. Sure enough, Planters discontinued its line of peanut oil in the early 1990s.[91] The Rokeach brand remained in circulation longer but with vanishing consumer interest. Rokeach finally dropped its Passover peanut oil product in 2002. Since then, the Orthodox Union's "Kosher for Passover" division has not certified peanut oil.[92]

An Epilogue on Rabbinic Intuition

The controversy that surrounded Passover peanut oil has an afterlife. Toward the end of the 1990s, more and more Jewish chefs discovered that they could do much with quinoa, a grain-like crop with edible seeds. Quinoa received Passover certification from one kosher certifier as early as 1997.[93] Before long, controversies reminiscent of the peanut oil debates appeared yearly in the Jewish press, always a few weeks before Passover. For one Orthodox woman, a rumor circulating in 2008 that several rabbis had considered whether "to ban quinoa has just sent me over the edge."[94] In 2012, a major kosher supermarket in Brooklyn "placed *all* quinoa in the kitniyot section" of its store.[95] A year later, the Orthodox Union's leading man in kosher certification told a reporter that he could not "certify quinoa." Rabbi Menachem Genack's reasoning echoed the same cautious refrain that Orthodox Jews had voiced ever since the more stringent Hungarian Jewish folkway made its way to the United States: "It's a disputed food, so we can't hold an opinion, and we don't certify it. Those who rely on the OU for a kashrut just won't have quinoa on Passover."[96]

Not everyone agreed, especially those who clung to the surprisingly resurging Lithuanian folkway and foodway. "Rav Moshe Feinstein said we weren't to add on to the rules of kitniyot, so I don't know why anyone would," offered a representative of another kosher agency, alluding to Feinstein's peanut oil responsum. "And what's more telling of this ridiculous debate," concluded the exasperated rabbinic writer, "is that quinoa is a seed not a legume."[97] Of course, that upset kosher certifier was correct. His and others' agitation paid off. In 2014, the Orthodox Union relented and listed quinoa in its annual Passover directory, a decision that was based more on cultural politics than rabbinics.[98] Peanut oil remained excluded. Like so many other areas of Jewish behavior, the battles over kitniyot had much more to do with cycles and clashes of cultures and religious intuition than with any sensible solution or reasonable reading of Jewish texts.

NOTES

1. Roth, "Reminiscence of Passover."
2. See Orsi, "Everyday Miracles," 3–21.
3. Certainly, many traditional-leaning Conservative Jews also held to much of the halakhic standards of kitniyot on Passover. For some insight into this matter, see Bergman, "New Look at Peanuts," 269–72.
4. *46 Oyfanim far Besere Peyseh Maykholim*, 1.
5. For another prominent example, see Balin, "'Good to the Last Night,'" 85–90.
6. See Soloveitchik, "Migration, Acculturation," 212; Soloveitchik, "Rupture and Reconstruction," 86; and Heilman, *Sliding to the Right*, 127–39.
7. Soloveitchik, "Migration, Acculturation," 201; Soloveitchik, "Rupture and Reconstruction," 70.
8. See Rosenstein, "Legumes on Passover," 33.
9. For a fuller treatment of the history of this stringency, see Zevin, *Ha-Mo'adim Bi-Halakhah*, 305–12. Zevin also discussed the rabbinic assumption that the oils and juices extracted from kitniyot receive the same stringent status as actual kitniyot. See also Medini, *Sdei Hemed*, 233–40.
10. Jacob Katz offered a similar theory in what he called "ritual instinct." See Katz, *Goy shel Shabbat*, 179–80. After I completed this chapter, Jonathan Sarna pointed out to me that Haym Soloveitchik used the same term that I have used. See Soloveitchik, "Religious Law and Change," 220–21.
11. See sources in Weinberg, *Sridei Eish*, 77–78. Before writing his responsa, Weinberg consulted another leading authority. See Breisch, *Helkat Yaakov*, 340.
12. Sarna, *American Judaism*, 375.
13. See Stampfer, "Geographic Background," 220–30.
14. Diner, *Hungering for America*, 202.
15. See Silber, "Emergence of Ultra-Orthodoxy," 23–84.
16. By folkways, I have in mind in the broadest sense the culture and customs of specific communities. See Fischer, *Albion's Seed*, 7–11.

17. There are a number of terms used for "peanuts" in the responsa literature. For Hebrew and Yiddish terms, see "She'elot un Teshuvot."

18. Moses Maimonides, Mishneh Torah, Laws of Hametz u-Matzah 5:1.

19. Yitzhak ben Yosef, *Sefer Mitzvot Katan*, no. 222.

20. Ta-Shma, *Minhag Ashkenaz ha-Kadmon*, 271–82. See also Cohen, "Kitniyot in Halachic Literature," 65–77.

21. See Moses Isserles's gloss on Joseph Karo, *Shulhan Aruch*, Orah Hayyim 453:1.

22. See Salmon, *Do Not Provoke Providence*, 11–49.

23. See Katz, *Divine Law in Human Hands*, 429–31. See also Leiter, "Issur Kitniyot bi-Pesah," 59–67.

24. See *Samuel Adler, 1809–1857*. See also Siegel, "War of the Kitniyot (Legumes)," 383–93.

25. See Ben-Artzi, *He-Hadash Yitkadesh*, 119–50; Gotel, *Innovation in Tradition*, 25–35.

26. "Pea-Nut," 449.

27. Smith, *Peanuts*, 68–70.

28. Smith, 101–7.

29. Clay, *Marketing Peanuts and Peanut Products*, 97.

30. "Prolific Peanuts," 42; and "Planters Hi-Hat Peanut Oil," 40. Planters' peanut oil line was initially certified by Rabbi Hersh Kohn.

31. It is probable that Rokeach also commenced production of peanut oil in 1936. See "Rokeach's Kosher and Pure Products for Passover," 46.

32. Smith, *Peanuts*, 66–68.

33. Feinstein, *Iggerot Moshe*, 370–71. One rabbinic scholar's extensive list of foods considered kitniyot makes no mention of peanuts. See Burstein, *Ma'adanei Shmuel*, 333–35. On numerous occasions, Eastern European Jews asked permission from leading rabbis to eat kitniyot during years of famine. For example, see "Rusland," 100.

34. Spektor, *Be'er Yitzhak*, 24a–25b.

35. On Spektor's influence on American émigrés, see "Last Gaon of Vilna," 116. See also Caplan, *Orthodoxy in the New World*, 72–74. Rabbinic authorities from Germany also ruled leniently on peanut oil. For this, see Hoffman, *Melamed Le-Ho'el*, 106. In addition to his own decision, Hoffman also testified to the lenient position of Rabbi Samson Raphael Hirsch.

36. See Henkin, "Piskei Halakhot bi-Inyanim Shonim," 6. See also Henkin, *She'elot u-Teshuvot Gevurot Eliyahu*, 242; Henkin, "'Mara De-Atra shel America,'" 126–39.

37. "Shemen shel Peanuts," 14–15. He offered a similar leniency regarding poppy seed oil. See Graubart, *Havalim Ba-Ne'imim*, 168–69.

38. "Shemen shel Peanuts," 15.

39. "Shemen shel Peanuts Le-Pesah," 7. For Pardes's supervision of Rokeach products, see "I. Rokeach & Sons, Inc."

40. See Max, "Report of Kashruth Commission," 57. It is therefore curious that one writer claimed that Rabbi Joseph B. Soloveitchik, the leading authority within

this organization, did not personally approve most cooking oils for Passover. See Meiselman, "Rav, Feminism and Public Policy," 12. See also, "Urge Caution in Purchase of Foods," 1.

41. See, for example, *Kosher for Passover Product Directory*, 10.

42. Jacobs, "Passover Suggestion from Planters Oil," 5.

43. See "Kosher Le-Pasah," A9; "Planter's [*sic*] Peanut Oil," A11.

44. See "For Passover Enjoyment," 20.

45. "New Planters Jewish Recipe Book," A1. The publication was first distributed in 1967.

46. *5 Great Cuisines with Planters Peanut Oil*, 21.

47. Thousands of Hungarian Jews settled in America during the nineteenth century but identified with their German coreligionists rather than maintaining a distinct culture in the New World. See Perlman, *Bridging Three Worlds*, 253–55.

48. "Oy Va-Voy," 26.

49. See "Ha-Shas He-Hadash," 32.

50. See Rackman, "Halachic Progress," 365; Elberg, "Rav Moshe," 2.

51. Kirschenbaum, "Rabbi Moshe Feinstein's Responsa," 369. For another understanding that dates Feinstein's emergence as American Orthodoxy's preeminent halakhist to the 1970s, see Mintz, "Chapter in American Orthodoxy," 21–59.

52. Feinstein, *Iggerot Moshe*, 370–71.

53. See Friedman, *Lekutei Maharyah*, 21b; Feldman, *Lekutei Maharmi*, 8a; and other sources listed in Zinner, *Nitei Gavriel*, 205. On the relatively cordial relationship between Hasidim and Mitnagdim in Hungary, see Silber, "Limits of Rapprochement," 124–47.

54. See letter published in Ashkenazi, *Haggadah shel Pesah*, 18.

55. "Le-Afrushei Me-Issurra," 196. See also Kahane, "Hashpa'ot Hitzoniyot be-Halakhot Pesah," 89–90.

56. See Trutzer, "Responsum no. 134," 155; Lemberger, "Responsum no. 145," 166.

57. See Lebovitch, "Bi-Inyan Gezerot Kitniyot Bi-Pesah," 13–14; Lebovitch, "Bi-Inyan Gezerot Kitniyot Bi-Pesah u-be-Sha'ar Yom Tov," 36–37.

58. See Tsirelson, *Atzi Ha-Livanon*, 15–16; Posek, *Divrei Hillel*, 13a–15a; Posek, letter to the editor, 50–51. See also Telushkin, "Minei Peirot She-Dineiheim Meyuhadim," 20.

59. See Rubenfeld, "Bi-Inyan Akhilat Shemen," 130–42.

60. See Mintz, *Hasidic People*, 27–42.

61. See Poll, *Hasidic Community of Williamsburg*, 29.

62. Tendler, *Responsa of Rav Moshe Feinstein*, 18. For one of the most strident oppositions to Feinstein's rulings, see Schwartz, *Ma'aneh Le-Iggerot*, 3–25. My thanks to Marc Shapiro for directing me to this source. See Roth, *Kuntres Lekutei*, 21.

63. See Horowitz, *Kosher USA*, 163–209.

64. On Steif, see Kranzler, *Hasidic Williamsburg*, 160. In Budapest, Steif's rabbinic journal, *Hachaim*, affirmed the stringent position toward peanut oil. See Lebovitch, "Bi-Inyan Gezerot Kitniyot Bi-Pesah u-be-Sha'ar Yom Tov," 37.

65. See Weiss, *She'elot u-Teshuvot Minhat Yitzhak*, 3:240–41; 4:248.

66. See Kohn, "Bi-Din Devash Devorim Mekhasemet," 6–7; Shuchatowitz, "Bi-Davar Devash Devorim," 14–15; and Leizer, "Min Dagan o Min Kitniyot," 20.

67. See *Kosher Directory*, 19.

68. Eider, *Summary of Halachos of Pesach*, 14.

69. Blumenkrantz, *Laws of Pesach*, 16.

70. See "Passover Recipe from the Passover Oil," 10; "Passover Recipe from the Passover Oil," 56; and "Passover Recipe from the Passover Oil," A5.

71. Later and fully unrelated to the above, the reputation of the "OK" and its administrator declined. See Lytton, *Kosher*, 70–71.

72. Levy, "Keeping Kosher," 19. See also Kraemer, *Jewish Eating*, 148.

73. See Boyer, "Evangelical Resurgence in the 1970s," 34–35.

74. See Dochuk, *From Bible Belt to Sunbelt*, 326–61. One writer who noticed the Hungarian Orthodox Jews' emergence at an early date offered a different explanation: "They are sustained by the aristocratic feeling of belong to 'the saving remnant.' With the growing appreciation in the sixties of the exotic and the nonconformist, they had others no longer view their basic posture as being somehow 'un-American.'" See Agus, "Jerusalem in America," 107.

75. On the pivotal role of "authenticity" in determining the contours of Orthodox Judaism and tradition-bound faiths in the United States, see my forthcoming *Authentically Orthodox: A Tradition-Bound Faith in American Life* (Detroit: Wayne State University Press, forthcoming).

76. See also Elberg, "Rav, Admor Hassidi, Rosh Yeshiva," 2–3; and Helmreich, *World of the Yeshiva*, 45–46.

77. Mayer, *From Suburb to Shtetl*, 72–80.

78. See, for example, "Perfect Dessert for Passover," A6.

79. Hecht, "Campaign to Reduce Price," 49.

80. Meisels, "Kosher Confusion," A23.

81. Dayanim, "Fewer Brand Names on Pesach" A6.

82. Kunda, "Found Some Peanuts"; Kunda, *Boruch Learns His Brochos*.

83. Hoffman, *Melamed Le-Ho'el*, 106.

84. Frank, *Mira'ei Kodesh*, 205.

85. Aaronson, *Yeshu'at Moshe*, 173–74.

86. See Tsorsh, "Shalosh She'elot," 20; "Le-She'elot Ha-Betanim bi-Pesah," 23–24. See also Aviner, *Am Ke-Lavi*, 131–33.

87. See Meisels, "Oil Turmoil," A14. See also Schwartz, *Kuntres "Hametz Mashehu,"* 59–60.

88. See Elyashiv, *Kovetz Teshuvot*, 97; Turetsky, *Yashiv Moshe*, 59.

89. See Liebb, "Rabbi Feinstein's Illness," 2.

90. See Kelman, "Moshe Feinstein," 173–87.

91. Bill Osey, e-mail message to author, December 12, 2013. Osey is a member and webmaster for the Peanut Pals Collectors Club. See also www.sadiesalome.com (accessed December 12, 2013). Special thanks to longtime Peanut Pals member Sherwin Borsuk for pointing out this online source.

92. The 2001 edition of the Orthodox Union's Passover food guide was the final directory that included peanut oil. See "Products Directory," 53. See also Blumenkrantz, *Laws of Pesach*, 24–25.
93. Vitello, "Something Tasty," A1.
94. Rosenstock, "Kitniyot Controversy Hits Home," 17.
95. Schockett, "Quinoa Broadens Pesach Menu," 16.
96. Lieber, "Is Quinoa Kosher for Pesach?" 48. See also, Blech, *Kosher Food Production*, 360.
97. Lieber, "Is Quinoa Kosher for Pesach?" 48.
98. See Nemes, "Quinoa Ruled Kosher for Passover."

BIBLIOGRAPHY

Archival Sources

Roth, Sidney. "Reminiscence of Passover as Celebrated on the Lower East Side of New York." SC-10468, American Jewish Archives, Cincinnati, OH.
Samuel Adler, 1809–1857: His Years in Germany. Translated by Agnes Goldman Sanborn. 21, MS-423, Samuel Adler Papers, American Jewish Archives, Cincinnati, OH.

Published Sources

Aaronson, Yehoshua Moshe. *Yeshu'at Moshe*. Petah Tikva, Israel: Y. M. Aaronson, 1967.
Agus, Jacob. "Jerusalem in America." In *The Religion of the Republic*, edited by Elwyn A. Smith, 94–115. Philadelphia: Fortress, 1971.
Ashkenazi, Ephraim Yosef Dov. *Haggadah shel Pesah im Peirush Divrei Yo'el*. Brooklyn: Jerusalem Book Store, 1984.
Aviner, Shlomo Hayyim. *Am Ke-Lavi*. Jerusalem: S. H. Aviner, 1983.
Balin, Carole B. "'Good to the Last Night': The Proliferation of the Maxwell House Haggadah." In *My People's Passover Haggadah: Traditional Texts, Modern Commentaries*, vol. 1, edited by Lawrence A. Hoffman and David Arnow. Woodstock: Jewish Lights, 2008.
Ben-Artzi, Hagi. *He-Hadash Yitkadesh: Ha-Rav Kook Ki-Posek Mi-Hadesh*. Tel Aviv: Yedi'ot Aharaonot, 2010.
Bergman, Ben Zion. "A New Look at Peanuts—from the Ground Up." In *Proceedings of the Committee on Jewish Law and Standards of the Conservative Movement, 1986–1990*, 269–72. New York: Rabbinical Assembly, 2001.
"Bi-Inyan Gezerot Kitniyot Bi-Pesah u-be-Sha'ar Yom Tov." *Hachaim* 1 (1922): 37.
Blech, Zushe Yosef. *Kosher Food Production*. Ames, IA: Blackwell, 2008.
Blumenkrantz, Avrohom. *The Laws of Pesach: A Digest*. Far Rockaway, NY: A. Blumenkrantz, 1981.
———. *The Laws of Pesach: A Digest*. Far Rockaway, NY: Bais Medrash Ateres Yisroel, 2001.
Boyer, Paul. "The Evangelical Resurgence in the 1970s: American Protestantism." In *Rightward Bound: Making America Conservative in the 1970s*, edited by Bruce J. Schulman and Julian E. Zelizer. Cambridge, MA: Harvard University Press, 2008.

Breisch, Mordecai Yaakov. *Helkat Yaakov: Helek Orah Hayyim*. Tel Aviv, 1992.

Burstein, Shmuel. *Ma'adanei Shmuel*. Petrikov, 1908.

Caplan, Kimmy. *Orthodoxy in the New World: Immigrant Rabbis and Preaching in America (1881–1924)*. Jerusalem: Zalman Shazar, 2002.

Clay, Harold J. *Marketing Peanuts and Peanut Products*. Washington, DC: US Department of Agriculture, 1941.

Cohen, Alfred S. "Kitniyot in Halachic Literature, Past and Present." *Journal of Halacha and Contemporary Society* 6 (1983): 65–77.

Dayanim, Behnam. "Fewer Brand Names on Pesach, but More Food in the Pantry." *Jewish Advocate*, April 13, 1989.

Diner, Hasia R. *Hungering for America: Italian, Irish, and Jewish Foodways in the Age of Migration*. Cambridge, MA: Harvard University Press, 2001.

Dochuk, Darren. *From Bible Belt to Sunbelt: Plain Folk Religion, Grassroots Politicians, and the Rise of Evangelical Conservatism*. New York: W. W. Norton, 2011.

Eider, Shimon D. *A Summary of Halachos of Pesach*. Lakewood, NJ: Shimon D. Eider, 1977.

Elberg, Simha. "Rav, Admor Hassidi, Rosh Yeshiva—Le-Mi Me-Heim yesh Hashpa'ah?" *Ha-Pardes* 37 (1963): 2–3.

———. "Rav Moshe." *Ha-Pardes* 39 (1965): 2.

Elyashiv, Yosef Shalom. *Kovetz Teshuvot*. Vol. 3. Jerusalem: Keren Re'em, 2012.

Feinstein, Moshe. *Iggerot Moshe*. Vol. 5. New York: Noble Book, 1973.

Feldman, Moshe Yisrael. *Lekutei Maharmi: Hilkhot Pesah*. New York: E. Grossman's Publishing House, n.d.

Fischer, David Hackett. *Albion's Seed: Four British Folkways in America*. New York: Oxford University Press, 1989.

5 Great Cuisines with Planters Peanut Oil. New York: Standard Brands, 1967.

"For Passover Enjoyment." *Jewish Exponent*, March 18, 1955.

Frank, Zvi Pesah. *Mira'ei Kodesh*. Vol. 2. Jerusalem: Mekhon Ha-Rav Frank, 1974.

Friedman, Yisrael Hayyim. *Lekutei Maharyah*. Vol. 3. New York: Avraham Yitzhak Friedman, 1965.

Gotel, Neirah. *Innovation in Tradition: The Halakhic-Philosophical Teachings of Rabbi Kook*. Jerusalem: Magnes, 2005.

Graubart, Yehudah Leib. *Havalim Ba-Ne'imim*. Vol. 1. Petrikov: Shmuel Pinski, 1901.

"Ha-Shas He-Hadash shel Ozer Ha-Sefarim." *Hamaor* 28 (1977): 32.

Hecht, Abraham B. "Campaign to Reduce Price of Kosher for Passover Products Bringing Beneficial Results." *Jewish Press*, April 3, 1981.

Heilman, Samuel C. *Sliding to the Right: The Contest for the Future of American Jewish Orthodoxy*. Berkeley: University of California Press, 2006.

Helmreich, William B. *The World of the Yeshiva: An Intimate Portrait of Orthodox Jewry*. New Haven: Yale University Press, 1982.

Henkin, Eitam. "'Mara De-Atra shel America.'" *Yeshurun* 20 (2008): 126–39.

Henkin, Yosef Eliyahu. "Piskei Halakhot bi-Inyanim Shonim." *Am ha-Torah* 10 (1979): 5–7.

———. *She'elot u-Teshuvot Gevurot Eliyahu*. Lakewood, NJ: Mahon ha-Rav Henkin, 2013.

Hoffman, David Zvi. *Melamed Le-Ho'el*. Vol. 1. Frankfurt: Hermon, 1926.

Horowitz, Roger. *Kosher USA: How Coke Became Kosher and Other Tales of Modern Food*. New York: Columbia University Press, 2016.

"I. Rokeach & Sons, Inc." *Ha-Pardes* 6 (1932): 1.

Jacobs, Ruth. "Passover Suggestion from Planters Oil." *Jewish Advocate*, March 25, 1965.

Kahane, Yitzhak Ze'ev. "Hashpa'ot Hitzoniyot be-Halakhot Pesah." *La-Mo'ed* 3 (1946): 89–90.

Katz, Jacob. *Divine Law in Human Hands: Case Studies in Halakhic Flexibility*. Jerusalem: Magnes, 1998.

———. *Goy shel Shabbat*. Jerusalem: Zalman Shazar, 1984.

Kelman, Wolfe. "Moshe Feinstein and Postwar American Orthodoxy." In *Survey of Jewish Affairs 1987*, edited by William Frankel. Cranbury: Associated University Presses, 1988.

Kirschenbaum, Aaron. "Rabbi Moshe Feinstein's Responsa: A Major Halachic Event." *Judaism* 15 (1966): 364–73.

Kohn, Zvi Hersh. "Bi-Din Devash Devorim Mekhasemet." *Hamaor* 6 (1956): 6–7.

The Kosher Directory: Passover Edition. New York: Union of Orthodox Congregations of America, 1985.

Kosher for Passover Product Directory. New York: Union of Orthodox Jewish Congregations of America, 1966.

"Kosher Le-Pasah." *Jewish Advocate*, March 31, 1960.

Kraemer, David C. *Jewish Eating and Identity through the Ages*. New York: Routledge, 2007.

Kranzler, George. *Hasidic Williamsburg: A Contemporary American Hasidic Community*. Northvale: Jason Aaronson, 1995.

Kunda, Shmuel. *Boruch Learns His Brochos*. Brooklyn: Shmuel Kunda, 2005.

———. "Found Some Peanuts." In *Boruch Learns His Brochos*. Brooklyn: Shmuel Kunda, 1982.

"The Last Gaon of Vilna." *Reform Advocate*, March 28, 1896.

"Le-Afrushei Me-Issurra." *Tal Talpiyot* 22 (1913): 196.

Lebovitch, Yitzhak Zvi. "Bi-Inyan Gezerot Kitniyot Bi-Pesah u-be-Sha'ar Yom Tov." *Hachaim* 1 (1922): 36–37.

Lebovitch, Zvi. "Bi-Inyan Gezerot Kitniyot Bi-Pesah." *Hachaim* 1 (1922): 13–14.

Leiter, Moshe. "Issur Kitniyot bi-Pesah." *Ha-Darom* 15 (1962): 59–67.

Leizer, Natan. "Min Dagan o Min Kitniyot." *Hamaor* 7 (1957): 20.

Lemberger, Yitzhak. "Responsum no. 145." *Tal Talpiyot* 22 (1913): 166.

"Le-She'elot Ha-Betanim bi-Pesah." *Halikhot* 38–39 (1968): 23–24.

Levy, Bernard. "Keeping Kosher: The OK Symbol of Kashruth." *Jewish Homemaker*, February–March 1978.

Liebb, Julius. "Rabbi Feinstein's Illness Remains Undiagnosed." *Jewish Press*, March 22, 1985.

Lieber, Chavie. "Is Quinoa Kosher for Pesach?" *Washington Jewish Week*, March 14, 2013.

Lytton, Timothy D. *Kosher: Private Regulation in the Age of Industrial Food*. Cambridge, MA: Harvard University Press, 2013.

Max, Morris. "Report of Kashruth Commission," In *Proceedings of the Twelfth Annual Convention of the Rabbinical Council of America*, 55–59. 1948.

Mayer, Egon. *From Suburb to Shtetl: The Jews of Boro Park*. Philadelphia: Temple University Press, 1979.

Medini, Hayyim Hezkiyahu. *Sdei Hemed*. Vol. 8. Bnei Brak: Beit Ha-Sofer, 1962.

Meiselman, Moshe. "The Rav, Feminism and Public Policy: An Insider's Overview." *Tradition* 33 (1999).

Meisels, Martha. "Kosher Confusion." *Jerusalem Post*, April 5, 1985.

———. "Oil Turmoil." *Jerusalem Post*, March 25, 1988.

Mintz, Adam. "A Chapter in American Orthodoxy: The Eruvin in Brooklyn." *Hakirah* 14 (2012).

Mintz, Jerome R. *Hasidic People: A Place in the New World*. Cambridge, MA: Harvard University Press, 1992.

Nemes, Hody. "Quinoa Ruled Kosher for Passover." *Forward*, December 23, 2013. Accessed January 5, 2014. http://blogs.forward.com.

"New Planters Jewish Recipe Book." *Jewish Advocate*, March 20, 1969.

Orsi, Robert. "Everyday Miracles: The Study of Lived Religion." In *Lived Religion in America: Toward a History of Practice*, edited by David D. Hall. Princeton: Princeton University Press, 1997.

"Oy Va-Voy al Avdan Ish Kasher Ha-Rav Yaakov Goldman Einenu." *Hamaor* 47 (April–May 1994): 26.

"A Passover Recipe from the Passover Oil." *Jewish Advocate*, April 13, 1978.

"A Passover Recipe from the Passover Oil." *Jewish Exponent*, March 18, 1977.

"A Passover Recipe from the Passover Oil." *Jewish Press*, March 25, 1971.

"Pea-Nut." *Harper's Weekly*, July 16, 1870.

"Perfect Dessert for Passover." *Jewish Advocate*, April 2, 1981.

Perlman, Robert. *Bridging Three Worlds: Hungarian-Jewish Americans, 1848–1914*. Amherst: University of Massachusetts Press, 1991.

"Planters Hi-Hat Peanut Oil." *Ha-Pardes* 10 (1936): 40.

"Planter's [*sic*] Peanut Oil." *Jewish Advocate*, March 24, 1960.

Poll, Solomon. *The Hasidic Community of Williamsburg: A Study in the Sociology of Religion*. New York: Free Press, 1962.

Posek, Hillel. *Divrei Hillel*. Vol. 1. Sinaia: Jacob Wider, 1925.

———. Letter to the editor. *Beit Va'ad Le-Hakhamim* 7 (1928): 50–51.

"Products Directory." *Jewish Action*, Passover 2001.

"Prolific Peanuts: 'Mr. Peanut' Grows Up, Becomes Symbol of Huge Industry." *Literary Digest*, March 6, 1937.

Rackman, Emanuel. "Halachic Progress: Rabbi Moshe Feinstein's Igrot Moshe on Even Ha-Ezer." *Judaism* 13 (1964).

"Rokeach's Kosher and Pure Products for Passover." *Ha-Pardes* 10 (1936): 46.

Rosenstein, Marc J. "Legumes on Passover." *Central Conference of American Rabbis Journal* 22 (1975).

Rosenstock, Natasha. "The Kitniyot Controversy Hits Home," *Washington Jewish Week*, April 17, 2008.

Roth, Yehezkel. *Kuntres Lekutei Halakhot al Hilkhot Hag ha-Pesah*. Borough Park: Beit Midrash Kahal Yirei Hashem, 1982.

Rubenfeld, Yaakov Shlomo Aryeh. "Bi-Inyan Akhilat Shemen Zayit bi-Pesah, u-Birur Da'at Maran Heitev Lev." *Kovetz Beis Vaad L'chachumim* (Nissan 2011): 130–42.

"Rusland." *Ha-Magid*, March 25, 1868.

Salmon, Yosef. *Do Not Provoke Providence: Orthodoxy in the Grip of Nationalism*. Translated by Joel A. Linsider. Boston: Academic Studies Press, 2014.

Sarna, Jonathan D. *American Judaism: A History*. New Haven: Yale University Press, 2004.

Schockett, Joni. "Quinoa Broadens Pesach Menu, but Sparks a Rabbinical Debate." *Jewish Advocate*, March 30, 2012.

Schwartz, Yoel. *Kuntres 'Hametz Mashehu': Madrikh Li-Inyani Ha-Kashrut bi-Pesah*. Jerusalem: Davar Yershalayim, 1988.

Schwartz, Yom Tov. *Ma'aneh Le-Iggerot*. New York: 1973.

"She'elot un Teshuvot." *Yidishe Shprakh* 33 (1974): 80.

"Shemen shel Peanuts." *Ha-Pardes* 8 (1935): 14–15.

"Shemen shel Peanuts Le-Pesah." *Ha-Pardes* 9 (1936): 7.

Shuchatowitz, Aharon. "Bi-Davar Devash Devorim." *Hamaor* 6 (1956).

Siegel, Seymour. "The War of the *Kitniyot* (Legumes)." In *Perspectives on Jews and Judaism: Essays in Honor of Wolfe Kelman*, edited by Arthur A. Chiel. New York: Rabbinical Assembly, 1978.

Silber, Michael K. "The Emergence of Ultra-Orthodoxy: The Invention of a Tradition." In *The Uses of Tradition: Jewish Continuity in the Modern Era*, edited by Jack Wertheimer. New York: Jewish Theological Seminary of America, 1992.

———. "The Limits of Rapprochement: The Anatomy of an Anti-Hasidic Controversy in Hungary." *Studia Judaica* 3 (1994): 124–47.

Smith, Andrew F. *Peanuts: The Illustrious History of the Goober Pea*. Urbana: University of Illinois Press, 2002.

Soloveitchik, Haym. "Migration, Acculturation, and the New Role of Texts in the Haredi World." In *Accounting for Fundamentalisms: The Dynamic Character of Movements*, edited by Martin E. Marty and R. Scott Appleby, 197–235. Chicago: University of Chicago Press, 1994.

———. "Religious Law and Change: The Medieval Ashkenazic Example." *AJS Review* 12 (1987): 205–21.

———. "Rupture and Reconstruction: The Transformation of Contemporary Orthodoxy." *Tradition* 28 (Summer 1994): 64–130.

Spektor, Yitzhak Elhanan ben Israel Isser. *Be'er Yitzhak*. Jerusalem: 1970.

Stampfer, Shaul. "The Geographic Background of East European Jewish Migration to the United States before World War I." In *Migration across Time and Nations:*

Population Mobility in Historical Context, edited by Ira A. Glazier and Luigi de Rosa. New York: Holmes & Meir, 1986.

Ta-Shma, Yisrael. *Minhag Ashkenaz ha-Kadmon*. Jerusalem: Hebrew University Magnes Press, 1992.

Telushkin, Nissan. "Minei Peirot She-Dineiheim Meyuhadim." *Or Ha-Mizrah* 1 (1954).

Tendler, Moshe David. *Responsa of Rav Moshe Feinstein: Care of the Critically Ill*. Hoboken: Ktav, 1996.

Trutzer, Avraham Lev. "Responsum no. 134." *Tal Talpiyot* 22 (1913).

Tsirelson, Yehuda Lev. *Atzi Ha-Livanon*. Klausenburg: Avraham Koyfman, 1922.

Tsorsh, Katriel Fishel. "Shalosh She'elot." *Halikhot* 37 (1937).

Turetsky, Moshe. *Yashiv Moshe*. Gateshead: M. Turetsky, 1989.

"Urge Caution in Purchase of Foods: Rabbi Soloveitchik Offers Suggestions for Passover Care." *Jewish Advocate*, April 8, 1938.

Vitello, Paul. "Something Tasty, Healthy, and Perfect for the Seder, Unless . . ." *New York Times*, April 18, 2011.

Weinberg, Yehiel Yaakov. *Sridei Eish*. Vol. 2. Jerusalem: Mosad Ha-Rav Kook, 2003.

Weiss, Yitzhak Yaakov. *She'elot u-Teshuvot Minhat Yitzhak*. Vols. 3–4. Jerusalem: 1973, 1975.

Zevin, Shlomo Yosef. *Ha-Mo'adim Bi-Halakhah*. Vol. 2. Jerusalem: Mekhon Ha-Talmud Ha-Yerushalmi Ha-Shalem, 1980.

Zinner, Gavriel. *Nitei Gavriel: Hilkhot Pesah*. Vol. 2. Jerusalem: Cong. Nitei Gavriel, 2002.

10

How Shabbat Cholent Became a Secular Hungarian Favorite

KATALIN FRANCISKA RAC

Cholent is one of the best-known Central and Eastern European (i.e., Ashkenazi) Jewish dishes associated with the weekly holiday of Sabbath that, as the Bible tells us, honors the day on which God rested after completing the creation of the world (Exodus 20:11). What is less well known, however, is that Jews all over the world consume different variations of this one-pot dish: Sephardi Jews in South and Southeastern Europe, the Middle East, and North Africa name their versions *adafina*, *scheena*, or *hamin*, while Iraqi Jews use the term *tebeet* or *tebit*.[1] The list goes on. These names express one of two qualities: being buried or hidden (*adafina*, *tebeet*) and warm (*hamin*, *scheena*), and not by coincidence. As the name of the holiday itself, Sabbath, means to cease work, which according to Jewish law (*halakhah*) includes the ban on kindling fire or cooking, the different names of the dish refer to the technical solution of how to prepare warm food when cooking is forbidden.[2] The cooking technique is referenced to in the earliest recorded collection of rabbinic legal prescriptions, the third-century CE Mishnah: it orders Jews to bury or cover the hot food (in the original Hebrew text, *tomnin et ha-hamin*) so that it remains warm for the Sabbath.[3] The Sephardi names echo the mishnaic phrase, while Yiddish- and German-speaking Ashkenazi Jewish communities named their dish cholent, *chunt*, *tshunt*, or *schalet*, terms that most probably originate from the French word for "warm," *chaud*, and thus follow the "logic" of the Sephardi etymology.[4] In addition to the linguistic connections, the similarity of ingredients (vegetables, grain, seasoned meat, and water combined in a well-sealed pot) and the mode of preparation (slow simmering overnight in a warm oven or in the ground) suggest that the dish originated in Sepharad and reached Ashkenaz via French mediation.[5] The belief that warm food lifts the holiday spirit, on the one hand, and the mode of its preparation that conforms to the ban on work on the Sabbath, on the other, allowed the different variations to become the ultimate warm holiday meal.[6] The ceramic or metal pots in which cholent was made were often embellished with quotes from the Torah, offering additional illustration of the close association between cholent and the Sabbath. The popularity of the different variations of this dish confirms the shared religious heritage of Jewish communities living in different geographical regions.

Through its election as a staple meal in Jewish cuisines all over the world, cholent and other variations have become tantamount to the culinary expression of Jewish identity. Through the centuries, rabbinic commentaries further elaborated the mishnaic precept and detailed the proper circumstances in which this dish should be prepared and served at the table. The Inquisition also recognized its consumption as a sign of Judaizing; in general, Christians viewed eating cholent as a Jewish act even as late as the nineteenth century.[7] As Marion A. Kaplan notes, a non-Jewish peasant in late nineteenth-century Hesse eating "a stew-like bean soup (probably a form of Schalet)" remarked, "Today, I am a Jew."[8] The peasant confirmed that consuming a Jewish dish expresses Jewishness—an illustration of the conventional wisdom that one is what one eats.[9]

The history of cholent, however, took a new trajectory in late nineteenth- and early twentieth-century Hungary. During this period, the connection between the consumption of Jewish food and Jewish identification loosened and finally dissolved. Whereas in modern Hungary, as part of the celebration of the Sabbath, practicing Jews continued to consume cholent, called *sólet* in Hungarian, non-Jewish Hungarians also incorporated the dish into their diet. Consequently, sólet assumed a non-Jewish, Hungarian identity. Perhaps the most suggestive illustrations of this new chapter in the history of cholent are the nonkosher sólet cans available in supermarkets all over the country. By the early 2000s, at least four different companies offered canned sólet for both domestic consumption and export. They symbolically replaced the cholent pots used in Jewish households. Restaurants in Budapest similarly offer nonkosher sólet as a Hungarian dish, testifying to its popularity beyond the Jewish community. Whereas the German peasant attributed proselytizing powers to the Jewish cholent, in Hungary consumers and cooks transformed it into a Hungarian dish. Thus sólet became fully integrated into modern Hungarian cuisine.

In addition to its culinary historical curiosity, the reconstruction of Hungarian sólet's history offers a unique perspective on the process of Jewish integration in modern Hungary. Here I interpret Jewish integration in nineteenth- and twentieth-century Hungary as a two-way process: as relations between the Jewish minority and the Christian majority intensified and became more diversified, the Christian majority's influence on Jewish life and Jews' influence on the development of modern Hungarian cultural, political, economic, and scholarly institutions simultaneously shaped the everyday Jewish experience in modern Hungary.[10] Examining the integration of the signature Jewish dish into Hungarian cuisine highlights both the modernization of the Hungarian kitchen (through the assimilation of foreign elements) and the evolution of Hungarian Jewish cuisine (which has always been shaped by Jewish households' material means, cultural values, and attitudes toward religious law—as well as by the available ingredients) and demonstrates how these processes intertwined.[11] Indeed, the evolution of the Hungarian non-Jewish cholent coincided with the inclusion of Hungarian dishes into the Jewish diet—a process briefly discussed at the end of this chapter. Analyzing Jewish cookbooks published in Hungary and the United States as well as modern Hungarian literary pieces (by Jewish and non-Jewish authors) demonstrates that the culinary historical approach contributes to the study of how Jews established themselves as Hungarian citizens. Consequently, culinary history advances our understanding of the transformations of Jewish cultural practices, identity discourse, and attitudes toward and relationships with the non-Jewish world.

The Linguistic Transformation: From Cholent to Sólet

Not only did German peasants use the word *schalet*, but it was famously immortalized by the German Jewish poet Heinrich Heine's poem "Shabbat Prinzessin," in which Heine described cholent as kosher ambrosia: "Cholent is the true God's kosher ambrosia."[12] In the light of Hungarian Jewry's modern history, the German *schalet* is likely the etymology of the Hungarian word sólet. German- and Western Yiddish–speaking

Jewish immigrants from German, Austrian, Bohemian, and Moravian regions begun to settle in Hungary in the late seventeenth and early eighteenth centuries, after Christian forces regained control over the lands of the Hungarian Crown formerly under Ottoman rule. Following Poland's first division in 1772, Jewish immigration from Galicia intensified.[13] Throughout the eighteenth and the first half of the nineteenth centuries, Jewish immigrants contributed to the linguistic heterogeneity of Hungary's multiethnic and religiously diversified population. However, from the 1840s, much to the Liberal political elite's approval, Jewish immigrants and their descendants proved to be one of Hungary's linguistically most intensively acculturating minorities. By 1910, 76.9 percent of Hungarian Jews, a community of about 910,000 that is 5 percent of Hungary's 18 million inhabitants, considered Hungarian their mother tongue, thus raising Hungarian speakers' proportion within the country's population to 54.5 percent.[14]

From the second half of the nineteenth century, the name of the dish in the form *scholet* appears in sources that testify to the language spoken by Hungarian Jews in the western part of the country. A well-known journalist contributing to German newspapers in Pest, Berlin, Munich, and mostly in Vienna, Moritz Gottlieb Saphir noted that, unlike Heinrich Heine, he called the dish *scholet*.[15] Likewise, in the second half of the century in western Hungary, the recipe collection of András Körner's great-grandmother listed the dish as *Bohnen Scholet* ("bean cholent"). Hungarian orthography corresponds with the pronunciation of the name *sólet*.[16] *Szakácskönyv vallásos izraeliták háztartása számára* (Cookbook for the households of religious Israelites) by Mrs. Rezső Rafael Hercz née Bauer Leonora was among the first Jewish cookbooks written in Hungarian.[17] Published in 1899, it used the Hungarian name sólet. The word *sólet*, thus, entered the Hungarian vocabulary through morphing a foreign word to fit Hungarian phonetics, not an unusual process in the history of the Hungarian language, which throughout centuries incorporated various other Hebrew and Yiddish as well as Turkish, Slavic, German, Spanish, and Italian phrases.[18] The continuous incorporation of foreign vocabulary into Hungarian amply illustrates the various cultural influences, including that of Jews, that shaped Hungarian culture before and after the advent of sólet.

Sólet Becomes a Hungarian Dish

One of the earliest Hungarian literary depictions of sólet, written as *schólet*, appeared in the novel *A barátfalvi lévita* (The Levi from Barátfalva) by the celebrated author and culinary expert Mór Jókai, who has been dubbed "the Hungarian Jules Verne." The novel appeared in 1896, three years prior to Mrs. Hercz's cookbook. Jókai describes sólet as *gölődény* with goose cracklings. The word *gölődény* (or *gölődin*) denotes a ball-like dumpling made of cooked and mashed potatoes mixed with flour (and occasionally eggs and some type of shortening), kneaded into balls, and cooked in boiling water. Similar dough is used for other dishes and in the surrounding countries as well. More important, gölődin is practically the same as the ball-shaped, flour-based potato *kugli* or *ganef* (outside of Hungary known as *kugel*), which in certain Jewish households was and still is an inseparable addition to the sólet.[19] Yet Hugó Veigelsberg, the editor of the progressive literary periodical *Nyugat* (West) and better known by his penname Ignotus, revealed in a 1925 editorial that Jókai did not mistake *kugel* for sólet. A Jewish family once invited him for dinner, and Jókai believed that the gölődin soup that he ate there must have been sólet.[20] Since Jókai knew that Jews ate goose cracklings, a food item that Hungarian peasants also favored and often consumed together with gölődin, he "figured" they would make a good sólet.[21] Jókai's culinary imprecision, however, rests on an ethnological observation that is validated by Jewish home cooks. András Körner's aforementioned recipe book and Tibor and Róbert Rosenstein's cookbook, both based on family recipes from the mid-nineteenth through the early twentieth centuries, likewise include recipes for goose cracklings and *nudli* with poppy seeds, made of the same dough as gölődin. Hence these recipe collections confirm that Christians and Jews in the Hungarian countryside consumed similar dishes that both complied with *kashrut* (rabbinic dietary laws) and fitted peasant cuisine.[22]

Despite his deep respect for the elder author, Ignotus could not bear to leave Jókai's uninformed claims about sólet without comment. Ignotus added that, in his understanding, sólet, "the Jewish national dish," was in fact a bean stew (*babfőzelék*). Equaling the two dishes, not unlike the Hessian peasant's association between the two, is significant considering that Ignotus was undoubtedly aware of the substantial differences between bean stew and sólet, despite their similarity in appearance and consistency. In contrast to the oven-baked bean sólet, Hungarian vegetable stews, including bean stew, are made of vegetables (sliced or cubed if needed), cooked in water on the stove, seasoned, and thickened with a mix of shortening and flour (*roux*), which is often seasoned with paprika and other spices. By defining sólet as a stew, even if it is a misleading classification, Ignotus fit sólet into one of Hungarian cuisine's basic food categories. In so doing, he went beyond merely acknowledging that certain dishes appeared on both Christian and Jewish tables; instead of viewing it as a foreign dish, he argued that sólet was part of Hungarian cuisine.

In fact, Ignotus's editorial repeated an earlier argument of his. In 1905, in the periodical *A Hét* (The week), writing under the pen name Emma Asszony (Madam Emma), Ignotus asked readers for their "favorite Hungarian recipes." Three years later, Madam Emma edited and published the readers' recipes in *A Hét szakácskönyve* (The week's cookbook). In contrast to the aforementioned Mrs. Hercz, who a decade earlier listed her sólet recipes among "original Israelite dishes," *A Hét szakácskönyve's* sólet recipe appeared among vegetable stews.[23] Already "Madam Emma" viewed sólet as a Hungarian dish, just like all the other dishes that came to Hungarian cuisine via foreign culinary influences. She emphasized that the readers' recipes directly reflected Hungary's cultural diversity. "In few countries people adhere to as many different cuisines as in our multiethnic country. . . . From this collection one can clearly see how all the cooking styles of East and West merge in our cuisine."[24] According to Madam Emma, the Jewish kitchen was just one among the many culinary cultures that shaped Hungarian cuisine. It introduced "the cured and onion-dishes of the Provence, the Rhineland, Venice, Spain as well as the Southwest's and Polish northeast's sugary and almond-filled meat dishes" to the Hungarian kitchen.[25] Reading Ignotus's interpretation of the broader implications of a Jewish dish's integration into Hungarian cuisine, it is hard to disregard the fact that he was not only the editor of a politically progressive literary magazine but also a Liberal Jewish public intellectual. Also, when in female literary disguise, he clearly distinguished between the foreignness of Jewish cuisine and the Hungarianness of the Jewish sólet, thus revealing a modern, multicultural concept of nationhood—which Jewish and non-Jewish Liberal intellectuals shared. Despite their firm support for Hungarian cultural hegemony within the country's borders, for them Hungarian nationhood was neither the product of the politicization of an ethnically homogeneous collective nor contrary to the heterogeneous ethnic and religious composition of Hungary's population. Hungarianness allowed Hungarian and Jewish dishes to form one culinary culture and Hungarian and Jewish identities to coexist.

The Liberal ideals represented by Ignotus and the *West* proved to be short-lived. In the 1930s, in two autobiographically inspired short stories, another literary giant and gourmand and a scion of a provincial lower noble family, Gyula Krúdy, described how the Hungarianization of sólet irreversibly forced its Jewishness into oblivion. He reminded his readers that Jewishness continued to have both ethnic and religious connotations while the culturally and politically dominating Hungarian element was never reduced to a religiously and ethnically neutral concept. The two stories, *A levegőváltozás öröme és szomorúsága* (The happiness and sorrow over the change of air) and *A pénteki vendég* (The Friday guest), tell the events of two consecutive days. The jovial and verbose Mr. Friday, who on Fridays dines at the restaurant Rózsacsokor (Rose Bouquet), invites the servile and curt chief waiter Mr. Kraut to eat sólet with him the next day in the restaurant Szegfűhöz (To the Carnation).[26] Mr. Friday learned to appreciate sólet while being married to a Jewish woman, who, though converted to Catholicism, continued to cook sólet at home every Saturday. Krúdy, himself a Christian who was twice married to Jewish women, describes Mrs. Friday as a (former) member of the Budapest Jewish upper-middle class through a collage of clichés.[27] Krúdy writes that she "even knew the Mendelssohns in Pest, who, despite all their European culture, golden-Spanish past, and Polish nobility could not give up eating one certain Jewish food once a week. This was none other but 'sólet' which especially women liked . . ."[28] After she divorced him, Mr. Friday, being accustomed to the Saturday sólet lunches, continued eating sólet on Saturdays at Szegfűhöz. Hearing Mr. Friday's sólet story, Kraut recalls a client at his former workplace, the Casino (gentlemen's club), a nobleman who occasionally ordered sólet from Braun's kosher restaurant for old times' sake.[29] Krúdy's description of converted and ennobled Jews' passion for sólet reveals the disparity between the public and private facets of Jewish assimilation and the role of conversion and intermarriage in Jewish integration—social phenomena thoroughly examined by scholars.[30] In Krúdy's stories, the acceptable public act of eating sólet contrasts with stories about *conversos* (Jewish converts to Catholicism) in early modern Iberia and Latin America who secretly followed Jewish customs. In modern Hungary, through familial interactions, the non-Jews, like Krúdy or Mr. Friday, even become experts on Jewish food and contribute to its inclusion into the Christian majority's cuisine.

On the next day, when he shares his sólet lunch with Kraut, Mr. Friday contends, "I reformed the 'Jewish sólet.' I invented the 'Hungarian sólet' when I divorced my wife."[31] The Hungarian sólet is not Jewish since it was not prepared in compliance with Jewish dietary rules or the prohibition of cooking on the Sabbath. Moreover, it includes ham, a nonkosher meat; both the Inquisition and medieval rabbis recognized the refusal to consume nonkosher meat as an important marker of Jewishness.[32] The rest of the original recipe remains intact: the Hungarian sólet contains beans and whole hard-boiled eggs and is seasoned with paprika. Just as Mr. Friday divorced his formerly Jewish wife, the nonkosher "Hungarian *sólet*" has severed all ties with Judaism. Its consumption has become disconnected from Jewish dietary laws and the celebration of the Sabbath, even if it is eaten on Saturday.

Krúdy's and Ignotus's sólet recipes list similar ingredients and cooking techniques that slightly differ.[33] According to Krúdy, the ingredients of sólet are to be assembled in one pot, enough water should be added to completely cover them, and it needs to be prepared in the oven for four hours. *A Hét szakácskönyve* recommends adding a tablespoon of flour to the water and stirring it while the sólet simmers in the oven; this clearly contradicts the prescriptions of medieval rabbis while also making the dish resemble a stew. From Madam Emma, the reader also learns that it is the main Sabbath holiday dish and that eggs or *ganef* (kugel) can be added to it.[34] Neither recipe details what type of meat should be used in the sólet except for mentioning that it needs to be smoked, which clearly contrasts with Mrs. Hercz's bean sólet recipe in which only "fatty breast meat" is listed.[35] Smoked meat is essential in several other famous Hungarian dishes, such as *rakott krumpli* (layered potato with smoked meat, sausage, and hard-boiled eggs), the meatless version of which is favored by the Satmar Jews of Williamsburg, New York City, or *Jókai bableves* (bean soup Jókai style)—named after Jókai the author. Often smoked bacon is used for both the fat and the taste—for example, in stuffed cabbage, the kosher version of which is known to Ashkenazi Jews as *holishkes*. As Hungarian and Hungarian Jewish cookbooks published in the twentieth century amply confirm, in addition to the generous use of paprika (and often goose fat), the smoked flavor is the key to sólet's ideal taste in both Jewish and non-Jewish households.[36] They also illustrate that, by the early twentieth century, bean sólet prevailed among the lentil, rice, and other types of sólet. Using smoked meat distinguished Hungarian bean cholent in the Ashkenazi world. Whereas Hungarian Jewish housewives who abided by *kashrut* may well have preferred smoked goose, for Christians, smoked ham and pork loin were available in Hungarian markets; therefore, they became the smoked meats in the (nonkosher) "Hungarian *sólet*." Three decades apart, Ignotus and Krúdy similarly demonstrated that, as Jews integrated into Hungarian society, sólet acclimatized to the Hungarian taste and became part of the national culinary landscape. During these decades, however, it also became clear that sólet's non-Jewish and Jewish identifications became irreconcilable; Christian Hungarians prepared and ate exclusively Hungarian sólet.

After World War II

Sólet remained on the Hungarian menu after the trauma of World War II and the Holocaust. Sólet at the Kádár restaurant, which opened in the 1950s, is a case in point. As one of the waitresses told me a few years ago, the founder and first owner was Jewish. Since its opening, the restaurant has changed ownership twice; nonetheless, its name and the menu remained the same. Kádár continues to entertain a clientele composed of the many different segments of the capital's population. In growing numbers, tourists also frequent the restaurant. As an American gastrotourist's blog notes, Kádár's sólet is so popular that, along with tables, clients also need to reserve servings of sólet on the phone.[37] Like the "Hungarian *sólet*" in Krúdy's story, Kádár's sólet and most of those offered in the city's other restaurants are not kosher. It is cooked on Saturdays (similarly to Szegfűhöz, Kádár is open on Saturdays), and one can have different kinds of sólet made with different types of meat products, including daisy ham (smoked pork shoulder). Kádár follows the practice of other restaurants and shortens the lengthy simmering time by first precooking the ingredients on the stove and then baking them in a moderately warm oven.[38] This modernized method of sólet's preparation further distances the Hungarian sólet from its Jewish origins.

The proliferation of canned nonkosher Hungarian sólet demonstrates how, in addition to the modernization of the preparation method, changing customer behavior strengthens sólet's non-Jewish Hungarian identity. Canned sólet is not produced under rabbinic supervision (*hashgachah*) or prepared in the traditional way, as it goes through an additional heat treatment. Moreover, as in restaurants, it is often offered with nonkosher meat products, such as pork sausage and ribs, taboo for religious Jews. Since canned sólet is always available and has a long shelf life, even if it complies with kosher style, its consumption is disassociated from the Sabbath holiday lunch. Modern sólet is in its "post-Judaic" phase: it is intensively shaped by the taste of the cook and the consumer while it is liberated from the bindings of traditional preparation methods, cooking styles, and Jewish culinary identity.

Hungarian Food in the Jewish Kitchen

Not only did sólet become a Hungarian dish, but Jews in Hungary also came to embrace modern Hungarian cuisine. As mentioned before, family recipe collections and most Jewish cookbooks written either in Yiddish, German, or Hungarian at the end of the nineteenth century reflect that Jews indulged in their non-Jewish neighbors' cooking.[39] American Jewish cookbooks offer further illustration. For example, one of the most authoritative sources on Jewish cuisine in the United States, Joan Nathan's *Jewish Holiday Cookbook*, records the following Hungarian Jewish Friday dinner menu: "Challah, Chicken Noodle Soup, Chicken Paprikash, Rice, Hungarian Cucumber Salad, Splendid Strudel."[40] Aside from challah, which, similarly to cholent, is eaten all over the Ashkenazic world, none of the dishes on the list is specifically Jewish in the Hungarian culinary context. Soups made with chicken or beef and different types of noodles are consumed everywhere in the Central European region and beyond, while chicken paprikash (chicken with paprika) has been considered a signature Hungarian dish since the second half of the nineteenth century.[41] In Hungary, neither cucumber salad nor strudel is associated with the Jewish kitchen.

Similarly, Gil Marks presents Hungarian Jewish cuisine through a characteristic Hungarian dish: beef goulash (using its Hungarian name *marha gulyás*). As a far echo of Madam Emma's observation, he argues that Hungary's numerous political changes exposed Hungarian culture to various influences and, as a result, "Hungarian-Jewish cuisine evolved into the liveliest Ashkenazic cooking, as exemplified by this dish."[42] Marks's goulash recipe matches the descriptions found in most Hungarian cookbooks. By attributing it to Hungarian Jews, he distinguishes their food traditions from those of other Ashkenazi Jewish communities in the United States through a recipe that in Hungary is recognized as a national staple dish, having no unique connection to Jewish cuisine. Nathan's menu and Marks's goulash recipe reveal that Hungarian Jews incorporated Hungarian dishes into their diet, but unlike Krúdy's Mr. Friday, they did not alter their recipes at all or invent a "Jewish goulash."[43] One would argue that they did not need to, given that these recipes comply with *kashrut*. Yet the consumption of "authentic" Hungarian food did not have the same transformative power on Hungarian Jews as cholent had on the German peasant. Eating across the religious boundary, at least in American Jewish cookbook authors' eyes, left their Jewishness intact.

Conclusion

This chapter describes how Ashkenazic cholent integrated into the Hungarian culinary culture due to the flexibility of Hungarian Jewish cuisine, through the usage of smoked meat and paprika, and thanks to Christian Hungary's culinary curiosity and cultural hegemonic drive. Cholent became sólet as Jews in Hungary became Hungarian speakers and their culinary culture acclimated to the Hungarian taste. Accordingly, the history of sólet illustrates the process through which Hungarian Jews distanced themselves from the Central European Ashkenazi communities and immersed themselves in Hungarian culture. The reconstruction of cholent's history allows the study of both premodern Jewish identities and the modern social and cultural processes that transformed them, altering the dynamics of Jewish-Christian relations. Formerly a social and cultural marker of Jewish exclusivity, cuisine became a channel of communication between Jews and their non-Jewish neighbors. The spread of sólet into Hungarian restaurants, its commercial trade in the form of cans, and the way in which Jews made native Hungarian dishes part of their diet all shed light on the mutual influence between majority and minority cultures—the central momentum of Jewish integration. It highlights how the modern Jewish cultural experience became gradually dissociated from earlier Jewish traditions and how different Jewish and non-Jewish responses to modernity influenced the interactions between the Jewish minority and the Christian majority.[44]

NOTES

1. The terminologies *Ashkenazi* and *Sephardi* refer to the different Jewish communities' geographical origins, German/Central and Eastern European and Iberian, respectively. Today these designations define different religious rituals.

2. *Jewish law* is a generic term that refers to rules established in the Hebrew Bible (written law) and binding enactments and legal interpretations by rabbinic authorities, often referred to as oral law, part of which were recorded in the Talmud and other rabbinical sources.

3. Mishnah Shabbat 2.7. Jewish families who lived in regions where the cooking method of burying food in the ground was not customary prepared the cholent in a sealed pot and placed it in a hot oven for the night between Friday and Saturday. Sealing ensured that no work was performed on the cholent. Some households were equipped with a special oven that was to be sealed with clay while the cholent was simmering during the night. Most families with meager means would bring their sealed pots on Friday afternoon to the local baker, whose oven remained hot during the night, and then collect it for the Sabbath festive lunch on Saturday.

4. Wexler, "Term 'Sabbath Food,'" 461–65. Marks points out that they also correspond with "medieval cooking methods of inserting the pot into a hole in the ground with embers or sealing it in an oven" (*Encyclopedia of Jewish Food*, 1).

5. The spread of the different names might indicate the history of how cholent spread all around the Jewish world. The forerunner of cholent, *adafina*, and *hamin* was *harisa*, a dish made of grain and meat that is still prepared and enjoyed by Yemenite Jews. Probably through the addition of vegetables and the perfection of different slow-simmering techniques, *harisa* evolved into *adafina* and *hamin*. Around the eleventh century, they spread northward through France to Germany and to the rest of Central Europe. See Cooper, *Eat and Be Satisfied*, 103. See different *adafina*, *hamin*, and cholent recipes in Marks, *Encyclopedia of Jewish Food*; Ansky, *Tscholent*.

6. Cooper, *Eat and Be Satisfied*, 101.
7. Cooper, 106, 184; Marks, *Encyclopedia of Jewish Food*, 127; Toaff, *Mangiare alla giudia*, 132–33.
8. Kaplan, *Making of the Jewish Middle Class*, 73.
9. Brillat-Savarin, *Physiology of Taste*, 13; Feuerbach, "Das Geheimnis des Opfers," 3, 5.
10. Katz, "Uniqueness of the Hungarian Jewry." There is a consensus among scholars that Jews adopted Hungarian cultural and political identity to a considerably higher degree than other national minorities in Hungary.
11. Barbara Kirshenblatt-Gimblett provides a similar list of influences on the evolution of Eastern European Jewish cuisine ("Kitchen Judaism").
12. Heine, "Prinzessin Shabbat." My translation. Original: "Schalet ist des wahren Gottes/Koscheres Ambrosia."
13. Frojimovics, *Szétszakadt történelem*, 30.
14. Frojimovics, 107; Konrád, *Zsidóságon innen és túl*, 76; Don, *A magyarországi zsidóság*, 13. At the threshold of the twentieth century, Hungarian Jewry formed the second largest Jewish community in Europe.
15. Saphir, "Die Gastronomie," 65. Körner notes that this writing by Saphir was published in 1856; see Körner, *A magyar zsidó konyha*, 340.
16. Körner, *Kostoló a múltból*, xiii, 239. Körner argues that he kept the original spelling of the recipe titles.
17. About Hungarian Jewish cookbooks, see Kiss, "A Zsidó szakácskönyvek története."
18. For example, the Hebrew word for luck, *mazal*, in Yiddish *mazel*, in Hungarian became *mázli*, and it is still used as slang parallel to the word *szerencse* (fortune or luck). Morvay, "A jiddis nyelv Magyarországon."
19. About kugel's symbolic position in the Hasidic Sabbath lunch, see Nadler, "Holy Kugel."
20. Gölődin soup is a vegetable soup with gölődin.
21. Ignotus, "Jókai."
22. Körner, *Kostoló a múltból*; Róbert Rosenstein and Tibor Rosenstein, *Rosenstein szakácskönyv*.
23. Mrs. Hercz, *Szakácskönyv*, 10.
24. Madam Emma, *A Hét szakácskönyve*, 5. All translations from Hungarian are mine.
25. Madam Emma, 6.
26. Both stories were reprinted in Krúdy, *Az emlékek szakácskönyve*, 89–106, 139–52. It features Krúdy's recipes as well.
27. I thank Katalin Fenyves for drawing my attention to this biographical detail.
28. Krúdy, *Az emlékek szakácskönyve*, 150.
29. Krúdy, 151.
30. See, for example, McCagg, *Jewish Nobles and Geniuses*; Konrád, "Zsidók és kitért zsidók"; Konrád, *Zsidóságon innen és túl*.
31. Krúdy, *Az emlékek szakácskönyve*, 151.

32. Homza, *Spanish Inquisition*.
33. Krúdy, *Az emlékek szakácskönyve*, 200.
34. Madam Emma, *A Hét szakácskönyve*, 192.
35. In the pot, Mrs. Hercz first placed a marrowbone. Mrs. Hercz, *Szakácskönyv*, 10.
36. Rosenfeld, *A zsidó nő szakácskönyve*, 126.
37. Emberling, "Magyar Food Tales."
38. A few years ago, I talked with the chief waiter of one of the restaurants in Budapest who confirmed that this is the method of preparation employed in Budapest restaurants. The journalist Gusztáv Megyesi confirms that indeed *sólet* at Kádár is not prepared in the traditional way ("Kádár kifőzde")
39. See, for example, Mrs. Ganz, *Ganz Ábrahámné Kóser szakácskönyve*; Kauders, *Erstes israelitisches*.
40. Nathan, *Joan Nathan's Jewish Holiday Cookbook*, 21.
41. See Kisbán, *Népi kultúra*.
42. Marks, *World of Jewish Cooking*, 118.
43. Save for those cases in which a kosher version was prepared and thus some ingredients from the original recipe had to be replaced or omitted. Mrs. Hercz's cookbook also includes recipes for goulash: Mrs. Hercz, *Szakácskönyv*, 66.
44. Biale, "Introduction to Part Three," 726–27.

BIBLIOGRAPHY

Ansky, Sherry. *Tscholent*. Jerusalem: Keter Books, 2008.

Asszony, Emma (Madam Emma) [pseud.]. *A Hét szakácskönyve* [The week's cookbook]. Budapest: Pytheas, 2008.

Biale, David. "Introduction to Part Three." In *Cultures of the Jews*, edited by David Biale, 725–29. New York: Schocken, 2002.

Brillat-Savarin, Jean Anthelme. *The Physiology of Taste*. Translated by Anne Drayton. New York: Penguin Books, 1970.

Cooper, John. *Eat and Be Satisfied: A Social History of Jewish Food*. Northvale, NJ: Jason Aronson, 1993.

Don, Jehuda. *A magyarországi zsidóság társadalom- és gazdaságtörténete a 19–20. században* [The social and economic history of Hungarian Jewry in the nineteenth and twentieth century]. Budapest: MTA Judaisztikai Kutatóközpont, 2006.

Emberling, Amy. "Magyar Food Tales—Story #1—Getting Acquainted with Sólet." Zingerman's. 2012. Accessed August 29, 2015. www.zingermanscommunity.com.

Feuerbach, Ludwig. "Das Geheimnis des Opfers oder der Mensch ist, was er isst" [The mystery of sacrifice or man is what he eats]. In *Sammtliche Werke X* [Collected works], 1–37. Leipzig: Otto Wigand, 1866.

Frojimovics, Kinga. *Szétszakadt történelem: Zsidó vallási irányzatok Magyarországon 1868–1950* [History torn apart: Jewish religious trends in Hungary, 1868–1950]. Budapest: Balassi Kiadó, 2008.

Ganz, Abraham, Mrs. *Ganz Ábrahámné Kóser szakácskönyve* [Mrs. Abraham Ganz's kosher cookbook]. Budapest: Gabbiano Print, 2007.

Heine, Heinrich. "Prinzessin Shabbat." In *Romanzero*, 205–12. Hamburg: Hoffmann und Campe, 1851. https://de.wikisource.org.

Hercz, Rafael Rezső, Mrs. (née Bauer Leonora). *Szakácskönyv vallásos izraeliták háztartása számára* [Cookbook for the households of religious Israelites]. Budapest: Schwarz, 1899.

Homza, Lu Ann, ed. *The Spanish Inquisition, 1478–1614*. Indianapolis, IN: Hackett, 2006.

Horowitz, Elliot. "Remembering the Fish and Making a Tsimmes: Jewish Food, Jewish Identity, and Jewish Memory." *Jewish Quarterly Review* 104, no. 1 (2014): 57–79.

Ignotus. "Jókai." *Nyugat* 3–4 (1925). Accessed August 29, 2015. http://epa.oszk.hu.

Jókai, Mór. *A barátfalvi lévita* [The Levi of Barátfalva]. Magyar Elektronikus Könyvtár [Hungarian electronic library]. 1896. Accessed August 29, 2015. http://mek.oszk.hu.

Kaplan, Marion. *The Making of the Jewish Middle Class: Women, Family, and Identity in Imperial Germany*. New York: Oxford University Press, 1991.

Katz, Jacob. "The Uniqueness of the Hungarian Jewry." *Moled* 6 (1974): 193–98. In English: *Forum* 2 (1977): 45–53. In Hungarian: *Múlt és Jövő* 3 (2001): 30–35.

Kauders, Marie. *Erstes israelitisches Kochbuch für böhmische Küche* [First Israelite cookbook for Bohemian cuisine]. Prague: Brandeis, 1886.

Kirshenblatt-Gimblett, Barbara. "Food and Drink." YIVO Encyclopedia of Jews in Eastern Europe. 2011. Accessed August 29, 2015. www.yivoencyclopedia.org.

———. "Kitchen Judaism." In *Getting Comfortable in New York: The American Jewish Home, 1880–1950, 77–105*. New York: Jewish Museum, 1990.

Kisbán, Eszter. *Népi kultúra, közkultúra, jelkép: A gulyás, pörkölt, paprikás* [Folk culture, popular culture, symbol: Goulash, pörkölt, paprika-meat]. Budapest: MTA, 1989.

Kiss, Bettina. "A Zsidó szakácskönyvek története" [History of Jewish cookbooks]. In *"A szívnek van két rekesze": Tanulmánykötet Prof. Dr. Schweitzer József tiszteletére, 90. születésnapja alkalmából*, edited by Kornélia Koltai, 327–39. Budapest: L'Harmattan, M. Hebraisztikai Társ, 2012.

Konrád, Miklós. "Zsidók és kitért zsidók a dualizmus korában. A kitérés okai zsidó szemmel" [Jews and Jewish converts in the dualist period: The reasons for conversion in the Jewish eye]. *Történelmi Szemle* [Historical review] 49, no. 3 (2007): 373–402.

———. *Zsidóságon innen és túl: Zsidók vallásváltása Magyarországon a reformkortól az első világháborúig* [On this side of Jewishness and beyond it: Jewish religious conversion in Hungary from the Reform Era until World War I]. Budapest: MTA Bölcsészettudományi Kutatóközpont Történettudományi Intézet, 2014.

Körner, András. *A magyar zsidó konyha: Kultúrtörténet 77 autentikus recepttel* [The Hungarian Jewish kitchen: Cultural history with seventy-seven recipes]. Budapest: Corvina, 2017.

———. *Kostoló a múltból: Egy XIX. századi magyar zsidó háziasszony mindennapjai és konyhája*. Budapest: Vince, 2005. In English: *A Taste of the Past: The Daily Life and Cooking of a Nineteenth-Century Hungarian Jewish Homemaker*. Hanover: University Press of New England, 2004.

Krúdy, Gyula. *Az emlékek szakácskönyve: Ízes írások és régi receptek* [The cookbook of memories: Tasty writings and old recipes]. Budapest: Táltos, 1983.

Magyar Szleng [Hungarian slang]. http://mnytud.arts.klte.hu.

Marks, Gil. *Encyclopedia of Jewish Food.* Hoboken, NJ: Wiley, 2010.

———. *The World of Jewish Cooking.* New York: Simon & Schuster, 1996.

McCagg, William. *Jewish Nobles and Geniuses in Modern Hungary.* Boulder: East European Monographs, 1986.

Megyesi, Gusztáv. "Kádár kifőzde" [Kádár cookshop]. *Hócipő* 24 (2010). www.hocipo .hu.

Morvay, Kinga. "A jiddis nyelv Magyarországon" [The Yiddish language in Hungary].

Nadler, Allan. "Holy Kugel: The Sanctification of Ashkenazic Ethnic Foods in Hasidism." In *Food and Judaism, edited by Leonard J. Greenspoon, Ronald A. Simkins, and Gerald Shapiro,* 193–214. Omaha, NE: Creighton University Press, 2005.

Nathan, Joan. *Joan Nathan's Jewish Holiday Cookbook: Revised and Updated on the Occasion of the 25th Anniversary of the Publication of the Jewish Holiday Kitchen.* New York: Schocken Books, 2004.

Rosenfeld, Márton, Mrs. *A zsidó nő szakácskönyve* [The Jewish woman's cookbook]. Subotica: Minerva, 193?.

Rosenstein, Róbert, and Tibor Rosenstein. *Rosenstein szakácskönyv—Minden kóser, ami jó* [Rosenstein cookbook: Everything good is kosher]. Budapest: Kossuth, 2014.

Saphir, Moritz Gottlieb. "Die Gastronomie der Juden oder Vogls Garküche. Eine Jugend-Erinnerung" [The gastronomy of the Jews or Vogl's cookshop: A memory from youth]. In *Ausgewählte Schrifte: 2. Serie 2* [Selected writings 2, series 2]. Brünn, Vienna, Leipzig: Karafiat, 1871.

Toaff, Ariel. *Mangiare alla giudia: La cucina ebraica in Italia dal Rinascimento all'età moderna* [To eat Jewish style: The Jewish cuisine in Italy from the Renaissance to the modern period]. Bologna: Il mulino, 2000.

Wexler, Paul. "The Term 'Sabbath Food': A Challenge for Jewish Interlinguistics (Yiddish čolnt, šalet = Moroccan Yahudic sxīna versus Judezmo adefina, adafina = Algerian, Tunisian Yahudic dfīna = Iraqi Yahudic t(ə)bīt = (?) Yemenite Yahudic kubânäh, gilläh)." *Journal of the American Oriental Society* 98, no. 4 (1978): 461–65.

PART 3

Ethics

Introduction to Part 3

AARON S. GROSS

The seven chapters of the ethics part show us examples of different ways that Jewish ethics and food have been and could be intertwined. These chapters are not an attempt to achieve a comprehensive approach to Jewish food ethics but an attempt to stimulate our appetite for engaging ethically with Jewish traditions about food.

The chapters of this part, like religious ethics more broadly, can be divided into *descriptive* approaches and *prescriptive* (also called *normative*) approaches. Since the rest of this volume is wholly descriptive in intent and because the issue attracted considerable energy in the editing process, it is worth taking a moment to clarify the descriptive/prescriptive line and its significance here. Descriptive approaches to ethics make a claim to objectivity in the same way historians or physical scientists make a claim to objectivity: by basing their argumentation on more or less undisputed data points and methods of reasoning that do not require the author and the reader to share an ethical worldview. Descriptive scholarship in both this part and previous ones is thus often described as "bracketing" the author's own ethical sensibilities and "beliefs" in order to help readers understand and assist them in forming their own conclusions. The metaphor of bracketing carries an important nuance: when something is in brackets, you can still see it, but it is set aside and not the main focus. Prescriptive chapters differ from descriptive ones by removing those brackets, putting the ethical intuitions of the author front and center. Descriptive scholarship on ethics, then, is not about the scholar pretending she has no ethical concerns—indeed, most scholars of ethics believe our language itself is unavoidably filled with ethical commitments and that ethical choices are implicit in even so small a thing as pronoun choice. Rather, descriptive chapters differ from prescriptive/normative ones in that they, insofar as possible, seek primarily to advance understanding. Prescriptive chapters in addition seek to persuade.

The descriptive chapters that make up the bulk of this part focus on how a particular community, text, or individual constructed their own moral ideas. A descriptive chapter often simply points out that a particular text or individual makes such and such a moral claim (e.g., "the Bible has such and such a portrayal of food laws") but does not take sides on whether that moral claim is true (e.g., "the Bible's food laws tell us that we *should* do such and such"). Thus when authors are sympathetic with an ethical view they attempt to describe, the difference between a descriptive and prescriptive approach will be harder to discern.

Overwhelmingly descriptive in orientation, this volume does not offer any singular diagnosis of what, if anything, is problematic about contemporary Jewish food practices. That said, the editors of this volume are conscious that many in the Jewish community and beyond believe that contemporary food systems and the values that undergird them are in some ways broken, insufficient, or outright dysfunctional. As detailed in all parts of this book—see especially the earlier chapters by Jody Myers in part 1 and by Rachel Gross in part 2—industrialization and increasing globalization of food production in particular have caused dramatic and rapid changes that have been both embraced and disparaged, or often both, by various segments of the Jewish community. My decision to co-edit a volume about food and Judaism at this historical moment is in part driven by the sense that something important is at stake in current social reflection on food. I sense that scholarship—mostly descriptive but also prescriptive—has something that can help aide this broader social reflection, making it both more critical and more sensitive to the diversity of views that always must be negotiated in societies like ours that produce food collectively.

My duty as editor of this part included an obligation to select chapters that I believe can help advance ethical debate and discernment in the contemporary Jewish context, something that cannot be done without some reliance on one's own ethical intuitions. To those who find their views less represented or unrepresented, I ask your forgiveness in advance. The intent has been to include chapters that address issues of concern to a considerable subset of contemporary Jews, not only scholars. I have also chosen to include authors committed to highlighting the *resources* of Jewish texts, tradition, and community in addressing the ethical issues connected with food they discuss. Those ethical issues range from the question of how we steward land (Thompson), to how we farm (Krone), to the problem of human violence as such (Weiss), to balancing traditional and liberal forms of Judaism (Ratzman), to how we treat the stranger (Pava), to how we find satisfaction (Crane), and to how we treat nonhuman others (Gross).

The first two chapters, primarily descriptive in nature, give special attention to a growing movement in North American Judaism to reconnect with food production by creating gardens and farms in Jewish settings that often become sites for community programming and holiday observance. The chapter by Thompson uses an Iowa synagogue's decision to create a food garden to illustrate a general method for identifying and analyzing ethical questions in a Jewish context, whether dealing with food or related issues. Her chapter has the additional virtue of pointing us toward comparative ethics by offering insight into how Jewish ethics is often in tension with the utilitarian ethical calculations that dominate public discourse.

The next three chapters of this part consider Jewish food ethics particularly in relation to the traditional dietary laws (kashrut). Daniel Weiss's chapter builds upon a history of scholarly interpretation of the biblical dietary laws in order to offer an original reconstruction of aspects of the symbolic, political, and ethical logic of the dietary laws found in the Hebrew Bible. Weiss is attempting not to take a stance on what should inform kosher practice today but rather to describe the biblical text on its own terms. He regards what he is doing as descriptive ethics, but his findings may also have important implications for normative understandings of Jewish or Christian ethics that value engagement with scholarly readings of the biblical text.

Unlike Weiss's interest in primarily describing ideas found in the biblical text, the next two chapters by Elliot Ratzman and Moses Pava take up prescriptive stances that in part return us to the issue of industrialization raised most pointedly by Myers and R. Gross in parts 1 and 2 respectively. Ratzman engages the contemporary kosher industry, making an untraditional argument for the value of keeping the traditional kosher laws. Ratzman's chapter steers between the liberal notion of adapting "old" laws to new contexts and a traditionalist call to continuity, considering how the Jewish ethical tradition known as *mussar* may inform Jewish food ethics today. Pava's chapter also raises normative concerns by considering a major scandal of worker and animal abuse at the Iowa-based Agriprocessors kosher abattoir. Pava reflects on how Jewish businesses navigate the weighty Jewish commandment to love not only one's neighbor but the stranger.

The next chapter by Krone sets the case study of the Iowa synagogue's garden in a wider context by surveying the contemporary movement to create and utilize Jewish community farms and how these farms become vehicles to express, enact, and transmit Jewish ethical values. In so doing, Krone also provides a model example of the value of qualitatively oriented ethnography in the study of Judaism.

The final two chapters of this part focus on how everyday food practices might inform Jewish ethical life. Jonathan Crane marshals traditional rabbinic sources to reflect on the ethics of the act of eating itself, regardless what the food may be. He begins by taking on the question of satiety—How much food is enough?—and concludes prescriptively with a case for moderation and attentiveness to internal bodily cues.

My closing chapter considers several Jewish responses to questions about what, or who, is eaten: Can one kill and eat animals without ethical compromise and, if so, how? I also illustrate how this study of Jewish food can inform studies of religion and food more broadly by first framing a basic human phenomenon (discomfort with killing animals) and then considering the specificity of Jewish responses. While primarily descriptive in nature, my chapter also dips into the prescriptive by noting my own normative concern with the question of animal suffering toward the end. As the final chapter in part 3 and the volume, it also attempts a closing observation about what it means to engage food ethics from Jewish perspectives.

Taken as a whole, these chapters offer an image of different ways to conceptualize ethics in the Jewish context and introduce the reader to a range of Jewish approaches to some of the most salient contemporary ethical questions about food. The ethics part also concludes this book for an important reason: whatever ethical commitments Jews may have or that readers of any religion or no religion bring to this book, it is likely that whether those values will be honored or trampled upon will be dramatically affected by the future of food. As the most basic act of living and a foundation of all economic activity, questions about the food in our mouths not only shape identities and world-views but materially impact virtually every ecosystem on the planet, the quality of life many humans will have, and many facets of all our daily lives. Our planet is, increasingly, a farm, and the only question is what kind of farm it will be. It is my hope that this final part will help read-ers comprehend the role that Jewish traditions—and religious traditions more broadly—could play in shaping the future of food and thus the future world in which life as we know it might suffer, struggle, or thrive.

11

Jewish Ethics and Morality in the Garden

JENNIFER A. THOMPSON

In a medium-sized midwestern city in 2011, liberal synagogue community Beth Shalom (a pseudonym) faced a question of financial, aesthetic,
relational, and ethical significance. The demolition of its dilapidated
historic synagogue building had created a rift within the congregation.
How could its members come together? They answered this question by
growing, harvesting, distributing, and celebrating with homegrown food.

The congregation responded creatively to the problem of hurt feelings created by its demolition and renovation project using a decision-
making process that accommodated both utilitarian and Jewish modes
of ethical thought. Following the congregation's decision-making process and its outcomes illuminates how to do applied Jewish ethics—that
is, the process of recognizing an ethical problem, understanding the
situation from multiple perspectives, and deciding on a course of action.
Because food is already a central focus of Jewish practices and ethical
thought and because models for growing food as part of congregational
life were already present in the surrounding community, focusing on
food helped Beth Shalom to move past deep tensions generated by the
demolition of its historic building to create new sites for relationship and
engagement with Jewish traditions.

Beth Shalom's impressive Moorish Revival synagogue had stood
since 1929 but by 2010 was in substantial disrepair. The local newspaper
reported that the cost to fix its leaky roof and ensuing water damage had
been estimated at $7 million, an enormous sum for this small congre-
gation to raise. The congregation's Building Committee evaluated its
options with utilitarian cost-benefit logic—that is, thinking about what
would produce the greatest good for the greatest number—and decided
that the best plan was to demolish the run-down building and renovate

a newer addition to it. The utilitarian approach feels natural and familiar for many Americans.[1] However, this solution failed to respond to congregants' values and emotional attachments to the old building, where their families had celebrated life-cycle events, observed holidays, and mourned their dead for generations. In order to heal deep fissures within the congregation, some approach other than utilitarianism was needed.

The story of Beth Shalom presented here is true, mediated by my perspective. From 2010 to 2012, I was a participant-observer there—a member of the synagogue, a lay leader, and an ethnographer all at once. Beth Shalom's decision-making process about its building and land shows how people understand and assess moral situations amid constraints and disagreements. As Beth Shalom members tried to determine which of their possible actions had the greatest moral worth, they considered how much Jewish values would determine the congregation's course of action and how much these values might have to be overridden by financial concerns. They had to engage their moral imaginations.

When we ask ourselves how we know whether our actions are right or good, we access our moral imaginations. Even though we may not always consciously register the ethical import of our choices, in nearly every facet of our lives—what we eat, the kind of transportation we use, the homes we live in, what we spend our money on—we regularly make choices about what is right or good. We do not do so from a set of unlimited possibilities, however. While we may wish to live our lives without contributing to the climate crisis, for example, it is unlikely that we could completely avoid contributing to greenhouse gas emissions. Given that a perfect option does not exist, we must choose from the imperfect options that do exist.

We can gain insight into the process of using moral imagination to make ethical choices by examining how others have done it. The womanist ethicist Stacy Floyd-Thomas explains that using a case study helps us recognize the roles of "the observable behavior of people, the meanings people assign to their behavior, and the secular and sacred forces that shape those meanings and actions."[2] Any given setting entails many perspectives because individuals have different experiences, even in a shared situation.

Because this ethnographic approach foregrounds differences of opinion and experience in the case study, it can help us understand applied

Jewish ethics. Jewish tradition encourages multiple perspectives on the sacred texts underlying Jewish values and ethics. Scholars of Jewish ethics Elliott Dorff and Jonathan Crane explain that "there are multiple approaches to ethics within Judaism," and "one can only describe how a particular Jew or community of Jews interprets and applies the tradition to [a] specific area of concern" rather than claiming that Judaism takes one clear stand on any given issue.[3] Some Jews apply *halakhah*, Jewish law, to specific areas of concern. For the roughly 80 percent of American Jews[4] who do not adhere to Jewish law, study of Jewish sacred texts may instead identify Jewish values and principles that suggest which actions would be the most beneficial for everyone or most exemplary of Jewish priorities and Jews' relationship with God. Jews (and others) may also make ethical decisions based on their feelings and what they might regard as common sense rather than any specific textual teachings or even any thoughts about God at all, although religious teachings often do lie unrecognized underneath their common sense. For anyone doing applied ethics, analysis of ethical issues can show us the advantages and disadvantages of different approaches, but usually no one approach can resolve an issue completely and perfectly. The action we take in the end is an attempt to do the best we can amid a situation's constraints.

A Brief History of the Congregation and Its Buildings

For years, synagogue members had entertained ideas about what should be done about the building and how to pay for it. By the time the historic building was demolished, the congregation's leaders were exhausted by the decision-making process leading up to it. Coordinating with architects, contractors, financial managers, board members, and the congregation as a whole had been an enormous undertaking.

From a utilitarian standpoint, demolition of the historic sanctuary and renovation of the newer building brought the greatest good for the greatest number in that the congregation could maximize its financial resources with the fewest hassles. A limited amount of money was available to the congregation, and Building Committee members were concerned about upholding their duties to their stakeholders—the rabbi, the staff, the elderly members for whom the synagogue was a key aspect of their social lives, the longtime members who had raised their children within the congregation, and the young families who sought a Jewish environment for their children. The Building Committee wanted to ensure that the congregation could meet in a building free of indoor rain or snow and prioritized educational programs, salaries, and religious items over preserving the historic sanctuary. Some congregants were excited about the project because they felt the historic building made the congregation look dated. The historic building had a formal, solemn atmosphere with a high-domed ceiling and a bimah that placed the officiants high above the rest of the congregation, who sat in stiff wooden pews. The smaller and newly renovated building that they would have after the project was completed would have a sleek, modern look. It would be intimate, egalitarian, and comfortable. They hoped that this new space would entice new members to join the congregation.

As the Building Committee opted for demolition and renovation, its utilitarian approach to stewardship of the synagogue's resources struck some congregants as insensitive. Some people felt that the building helped them maintain a strong connection to the past. They wanted the congregation to remain traditional, not to modernize, and they preferred the aesthetic qualities of the historic building. Further, many people did not know that the demolition was imminent until an article in the local newspaper announced it. An open letter voicing strong feelings of opposition to this major change to the congregation's physical home circulated among congregants. But the Building Committee did not consider this letter to be sufficient reason to derail its plans to demolish the building. A salvage company was brought in to purchase parts of the building that could be resold, and congregants were given the opportunity to purchase mementos such as pews. This opportunity was small comfort, though, for the contingent of the congregation that was deeply upset about this break from the synagogue's past.

While a utilitarian approach tries to yield the greatest good overall, it may do so at the cost of causing a smaller amount of harm. The Building Committee's decision to destroy the historic building and failure to communicate clearly about the timeline of the demolition provided for safer financial footing. However, it did so at the expense of considerable relational harm. The congregation drew upon its moral imagination to improve the situation.

Making Something from Nothing

At roughly the same time that the demolition was taking place, the rabbi had spoken with a few congregants about starting what he called a Tik-kun Olam Committee. *Tikkun olam* means "repair of the world." While originally used by Jewish mystics, it has become a common way for liberal Jews and Christians to refer to social justice work. Approximately ten congregants, including me, began meeting every two weeks at the synagogue to explore ideas about what this committee might do. The combination of our members' interest in environmentalism and our awareness of a new movement in the community to end local childhood hunger within the next few years inspired us. We had new land available to us because of the building demolition, and people in the congregation were still angry about the demolition. Perhaps there was a way to bring all these elements together productively.

We had already started down this path by fostering the congregation's interest in being "green." Jon, a Tikkun Olam Committee member, had recently worked with me and Beth Shalom's cantor to create and teach a workshop about the Jewish ethical principle of *bal tashchit* ("do not destroy"), which we connected with experiential learning about composting. The workshop addressed the amount of waste American communities generate, how much could be recycled but isn't, and why composting some waste is environmentally more beneficial than sending it to a landfill. The principle of *bal tashchit* arises from a passage in Deuteronomy concerning proper conduct during wartime that forbids cutting down trees during a siege: "You may eat of them, but you must not cut them down. Are trees of the field human to withdraw before you into the besieged city? Only trees that you know do not yield food may be destroyed. . . ."[5] Rabbinic elaboration on the *bal tashchit* passage in Deuteronomy forbids all pointless destruction in wartime, from the needless killing of trees to shifting the course of streams, stopping up wells, or killing or sickening animals. The rabbis also forbade unnecessary pollution or destruction of the environment or destruction of human-made products. "It is forbidden to destroy or to injure [*hamekalkel*] anything capable of being useful to men [*lehanot bo bnei 'adam*]"—even the object's owner may not destroy it.[6] However, this edict is subject to a kind of cost/benefit analysis just like the one performed in the decision-making process about Beth Shalom's building demolition. The rabbis explained that any given item, even a fruit tree, may not have to be preserved if doing so presents a hardship or if the item is causing damage to something else that is valuable. What *is* forbidden is destroying the item for convenience.[7]

With the newly empty land from the demolished building before us, this teaching about making good use of resources seemed to apply directly to our situation. The blueprints for the demolition and renovation project contained a plan to cover the empty land with sod—carpets of grass growing in thick strips of dirt. Jon and I pointed out to the Tikkun Olam Committee that sod would waste water through irrigation and contribute to greenhouse gas emissions through maintenance. An ardent environmentalist, Jon suggested that native grasses adapted to the local environment's water and soil conditions could be used instead of sod. They require much less human fuss to thrive and provide wildlife habitat that conventional lawns do not.[8] In contrast to the harmful outcomes for humans and other forms of life that the turf grass lawn could bring, the prairie or meadow grasses of the Midwest could create a more harmonious setting.

We also focused on food. I suggested that part of the land could be set aside for a garden to grow produce for food pantries. Unlike the native plant idea, a garden would be resource and labor intensive. We would need a team of volunteers to plant, water, weed, and harvest by hand. But the garden would be a labor of love, growing edible food, not just keeping grass alive.

The idea for the garden came from the example of several nearby Christian churches. They were already collaborating to raise fruits and vegetables on church land—formerly vast expanses of green lawn—in order to donate fresh produce to food pantries. One of the church gardens' leaders told me that when the Great Recession hit, many of their church's members realized how precarious their own economic situation was. They began to think of "the poor" as their actual neighbors rather than a more nebulous Other. That led them to action. They realized that people depending on food pantries received shelf-stable items like beans and rice but rarely fresh produce and even more rarely organic fresh produce. Meanwhile, their churches or their homes perched on well-kept lawns, watered and mowed regularly. Why waste the money and effort to maintain lawns, they wondered, when that land could feed vulnerable people? So they set to work.

The churches' effort was part of an ambitious project to end childhood hunger in the city. Leaders of several churches had pieced together a strategy using volunteer-run church, school, and community gardens as well as the resources of local government agencies and nongovernmental organizations. At an annual conference, these parties taught others how and why they went about their work and shared their strategies for making the best use of volunteer labor, choosing the right plants, and sizing the garden properly. Each year, the number of food pantry gardens expanded.

Beth Shalom's Tikkun Olam Committee chair Alisa and I attended sessions on "faith gardens" and "community gardens" at this conference in 2011. The founders of several local food pantry gardens taught us the lessons of their hard-earned experience: how to get free or cheap seeds, plant starts, and building materials and how to find Boy Scouts and Eagle Scouts to build raised garden beds, high school students and corporate volunteer teams to do community service hours, someone who would rototill our garden sites for free, a retired farmer able to provide guidance, and a volunteer garden expert willing to make presentations to congregations about starting their own food pantry gardens. We then reported back to the full committee. The Tikkun Olam Committee agreed with the advice of the garden representatives to start small. Often new gardeners full of enthusiasm planted a big garden the first year, quickly became overwhelmed by the hearty weeds and enormous yields of some plants, and later allowed the garden to die out. Starting small, in contrast, would ensure a manageable garden in the first year and the opportunity to build on its success in future years. The church garden representatives invited us to visit and volunteer in their gardens to learn from them.

The committee also discussed what form Beth Shalom's garden should take: community garden or faith garden. In the community garden model, interested families would be assigned plots of land to grow any produce they liked and donate some of their yield to the synagogue's kitchen for Shabbat lunches, to low-income seniors in the congregation who could not afford fresh produce, or to a local food pantry. The faith garden was a more cooperative model. There would be no separate plots of land; rather, a community of gardeners would work together toward the common purpose of growing food to donate. The committee felt most attracted to the faith garden model because it seemed to have a greater likelihood of building community among its participants. The rabbi suggested that we not use the term *faith garden* because it sounded too Christian. Instead, we settled on *garden*.

With the basic decision-making done, it was time to generate support for the idea from the congregation and make action plans. A garden had existed in the past on the synagogue's grounds, and the two former garden managers came to meetings to advise us. Two more members agreed to do an article for the synagogue newsletter to solicit support. Alisa presented the idea to the synagogue's board of directors. The rabbi was concerned that the acrimony surrounding the building demolition process would swallow our garden idea, and some board members were concerned that the garden would look ugly and set the synagogue apart from its pretty and polished upper-middle-class neighborhood. Ultimately, Alisa's negotiation skills and standing in the community won them over. As a former board member, committee chair, and regular volunteer for all kinds of the synagogue's needs, she commanded respect.

It took many meetings with many different people to get the project off the ground. The landscape architects who had worked on the building demolition and renovation project attended Tikkun Olam Committee meetings to hear our ideas, researching plants that would meet our needs and offering suggestions about hardscape materials. They found native grasses that could satisfy the board members' desire for a "normal" looking lawn rather than a billowy meadow. They also drew up formal plans for the garden, including a multistage plan for fruit trees, perennials, and annuals. Committee members did research to find out what kinds of materials we should use as well and determined that the most efficient strategy would be to spend a year gathering information and then build structures that fit our needs exactly. Alisa pointed out that we should ensure that at least one garden bed would be built tall, with a wide ledge around its perimeter to allow people to sit and work rather than stooping over the ground. This way, people of differing abilities could participate easily in the garden's upkeep.

As plans for the garden took shape, the congregation's enthusiasm for the project grew. Donations trickled in to fund trellises for climbing vines and compost and straw wattles for the garden beds. Alisa persuaded the president of the congregation to donate crushed limestone left over from projects undertaken by his construction firm. Another member donated the use of a Bobcat construction vehicle for a day to help transfer compost from an enormous pile into the garden beds. About fifteen people helped set up and plant the garden beds, from senior citizens to five-year-olds. Congregants signed up for volunteer shifts to water, weed, thin, and transplant the vegetables over the summer.

By June of the garden's first year, Alisa remarked that it was growing beautifully. Carrots, melons, pumpkins, squash, basil, and cherry tomatoes were bursting out of the space allotted to them. This was possible only through the interdependence among the congregants who created and supported it with their financial, logistical, intellectual, and aesthetic resources and energy. Where the building demolition project had divided the congregation, the garden knitted it together.

The garden became integrated into the congregation's weekly and yearly rhythm. Its ample basil harvest became pesto served at Shabbat kiddush (the light meal that takes place after Sabbath-morning worship services at many synagogues). Its zucchini were added to a vegetable tray for a meal cooked at the synagogue and delivered to a nearby women and children's shelter. Its cucumbers appeared at a young families' summer barbecue dinner, and its zinnias were cut for bouquets to decorate the synagogue. A variety of produce was featured in a congregation-wide dinner during the autumn holiday of Sukkot in the permanent sukkah built in the garden. Sukkot is a biblical pilgrimage holiday honoring the fall harvest. During Sukkot's eight days in the Diaspora or seven days in Israel, Jews build, decorate, eat meals in, and sometimes sleep in temporary huts called sukkot (plural of sukkah). A hallmark of the holiday is sharing meals in the sukkah with guests—both real and mystical. Beth Shalom's garden was a natural setting for a more permanent sukkah that the congregation could use every year to celebrate Sukkot with harvest meals.

Beyond Avoiding Waste

Although utilitarian considerations about resources played a part in the decision-making process, other ethical commitments were at least as important. The congregation had to consider the costs of the energy and time of volunteers and paid staff, money needed to buy supplies, and the congregation's programming priorities. Yet a religion cannot operate only on a utilitarian basis because it ultimately has different concerns. Judaism has different first principles from utilitarianism.

Relations among Humans, God, and the Earth

In Judaism, the relationship among humans, earth, and God matters. Jewish law emphasizes Jews' role as stewards of God's creation. Jews mark God's ownership of the earth and everything in and on it by observing Shabbat (the Sabbath), when they stop creating and interfering with nature.[9] The requirement of tzedakah, supporting the needy, emphasizes God's ultimate ownership of humans' wealth. Humans merely steward wealth; it is not theirs to use as they please. Similarly, requirements to grow food sustainably are based on God's ownership of the land, regardless of what the deed to the property might say.[10] The biblical practices of the jubilee year and sabbatical year are a kind of extended Shabbat, during which the earth is allowed to rest from cultivation and humans recognize through their stillness that the earth belongs to God.[11] Biblical ideas about land management are supported by the contemporary scientific knowledge that a seemingly mundane decision about what to plant in a yard can affect the lives of countless humans, animals, and plants. This is where we run into problems using utilitarian ethics. The greatest good for the greatest number is very simple, but it can ignore the more complex obligations and considerations that come with having a symbiotic society.

Feeding the Hungry

Laws concerning the sabbatical and jubilee year not only allow the earth to rest; they also set aside the produce of the land for only the poor and the stranger. Managers of the local interfaith food pantry regularly pointed out that writing a check was more helpful than donating food because the food pantry has access to much cheaper food than the average consumer does. A utilitarian analysis would urge us to focus on fundraising or on pursuing the most lucrative career we can manage in order to be able to donate the greatest amount of money to the food bank, which would then purchase the greatest amount of food.[12]

Nevertheless, congregations like Beth Shalom continue to hold canned food drives in addition to creating and expanding their food pantry gardens. These efforts do not necessarily supply food more cheaply. But in contrast to more strictly utilitarian reasoning, their efforts were not primarily about efficiency.

Covenant

Just as the garden evoked an ideal relationship between humans and the earth, it also evoked an ideal relationship among humans, lived out through and symbolized by food. Growing food to donate rather than writing a check for food to be purchased by someone else created a physical link between giver and recipient, even though they might never meet. Beth Shalom's gardeners explained how the garden helped their community, including beautification of the synagogue's outdoor environment and creation of the opportunity to teach about environmental issues. Researchers have found that community gardens help create and deepen relationships among people in non-Jewish and nonreligious settings as well, from Ohio to Alaska to the UK.[13]

By creating a new path into the community, the garden as a place for worship and a site for the growing of relationships responded to the idea of covenant. Ethicist Moses Pava, whose chapter in this volume explores ethical obligations to those we consider part of our community and those beyond it, explains covenant as primarily about "shared community" in which people together grow and develop understandings of "life's meanings."[14] To the extent that the Tikkun Olam Committee discussed feeding the hungry, the needs of both physically and spiritually hungry members of the synagogue were first in the committee's conversation. In a city with a limited number of Jewish institutional choices, the garden presented a new way to engage with Judaism. There were community members who cared about the environment, for example, and who did not have much interest in going to services. This was a way for them to engage with their environmentalist values in a Jewish context, to create a place for themselves in the community, and to have a place opened for them by the community. Garden work is hands-on, outdoors, fun, and communal, and it helps others. It can appeal to people who do not like to sit in pews. The garden provides an experiential component of Jewish life, particularly helpful in liberal settings where halakhic observance isn't emphasized.

Hiddur Mitzvah

With the garden, Beth Shalom had created a new sacred space, and the congregants took care to make it attractive, reflecting the concept of *hiddur mitzvah*, or "beautifying the commandment." This concept entails going beyond what Jewish law requires in order to make observance of a mitzvah aesthetically pleasing as well. It comes from a midrashic interpretation of Exodus 15:2: "This is my God and I will glorify Him." For rabbinic interpreters, this biblical verse provoked a question: If God is already as glorious as anything can be, then how can humans glorify God? The rabbis answered by developing the concept of *hiddur mitzvah*, which exhorts Jews to spend extra financial resources, time, and effort to not just fulfill a mitzvah but enhance and appreciate it and emphasize its significance.

Beth Shalom already had a history of beautifying its sacred spaces in this way. Its historic building had been a grand statement conveying the solemnity and dignity of the congregation. The historic building anchored a visual narrative of Beth Shalom's deep roots in the city, depicting Jews as insiders rather than a separate group. Demolishing the building demolished that visual narrative as well. The rabbi said that the historic building no longer reflected the contemporary congregation's sensibility or needs: rather than solemnity, they needed warmth and closeness.

Instead of the visual narrative demonstrating the congregation's link to its own past, the garden brought in a new visual narrative, one that also connected it with the community around it because other religious communities in the area were also doing vegetable gardens. It foregrounded a relationship with sustainability and the earth.

Hiddur mitzvah also undergirds an experiential approach to Judaism. Observance of Jewish law itself is an experiential approach to Judaism. However, the vast majority of American Jews do not take this approach, following instead the American religious pattern of understanding religion as a primarily individual and private matter to be experienced within one's own heart and mind. The garden brought Jewish experience out of the privacy of each individual's own heart and relocated it into a framework where religion is experienced as one's hands work in the dirt. The Tikkun Olam Committee was creating the possibility of sensory experiences of Judaism for all ages and creating a new path into the community.

Where Is God in Contemporary Jewish Ethics?

The ethical principles discussed earlier are firmly situated in the context of a relationship between Jews and God in the sacred texts from which they arise. Judaism provides plenty of opportunities for people to think about and talk about their relationship to God, as evidenced by the fact that there are blessings for almost anything and everything you could do on any given day. So in a contemporary religious institution like a synagogue, you might expect that people would talk about God, their relationship to God, or other aspects of theology. But discussions about demolishing the historic building and starting the garden rarely, if ever, explicitly mentioned God. At Tikkun Olam Committee meetings, people sometimes talked about their connections to other Jews and Jewish values, but not God. They may have believed in God, or they may not have. The topic simply did not come up. How, then, can we characterize the players in this story as doing applied *Jewish* ethics? Don't Jewish ethics imply the involvement, somehow, of God?

At Beth Shalom, and perhaps in other contemporary liberal Jewish communities, the God present in Jewish ethics is loosely defined, compared to the God who appears in the sacred texts. This newer understanding of God is implicit in community rather than commanding. The idea of God lurked in the congregation's discomfort with the utilitarian ethical approach used in the decision to demolish the historic building. The language and lens of utilitarian ethics left out the bonds among congregation members with each other, their past, and the community around them. By paying attention to the acrimony and anxiety within the congregation and the values behind those feelings, the Tikkun Olam Committee was able to engage its moral imagination to explore opportunities for new space and new relationships that implied God—feeding the hungry, covenant, *hiddur mitzvah*—while rarely evoking God directly. The meetings to plan and create the garden embodying these values were working meetings of the same kind you might have in a secular context. Even though the committee was deeply engaged in ethical inquiry, it was not holding explicitly ethics-focused discussions or debates. Growing food together created nonhierarchical, interdependent relationships between congregants.

Applied Jewish ethics need not happen only in the context of a synagogue or other religious settings. Just as Jewish law is designed to apply to every aspect of a Jewish person's life, one may also apply Jewish ethics to every aspect of his or her life outside the context of law. People who are not Jewish may also find Jewish ethics a helpful supplement to their own approaches to ethics. Whatever our reasons for applying Jewish ethics, Beth Shalom's decision-making processes help us identify how we can do so. We can start by recognizing the constraints amid which we do ethics—the conflicting values we bring to a situation, the limited financial resources, and the internal disagreements. We can begin to respond to ethical problems only when we have identified them. Jewish sources, combined with our own experiences, provide a wealth of starting points from which to engage our moral imagination in responding to these constraints.

NOTES

1. See Tipton, *Getting Saved from the Sixties*, chap. 1.
2. Floyd-Thomas, "Teaching for Conflict Resolution," 254–59.
3. Dorff and Crane, *Oxford Handbook*, 3.
4. According to the North American Jewish Data Bank's "Pocket Demographics: US Jewish Population" (2012), 21 percent of American Jews reported that they keep kosher at home. Kashrut observance was the most demanding of the Jewish ritual behaviors the survey asked about, so I use this as an index of observance of Jewish law overall; http://jewishdatabank.org.
5. Deuteronomy 20:19–20. *Tanakh: A New Translation of the Holy Scriptures According to the Traditional Hebrew Text* (Philadelphia: Jewish Publication Society, 1985).
6. Gordis, "Ecology and the Judaic Tradition," 332–33.
7. See Lamm, "Ecology in Jewish Law and Theology," 168.
8. Brittingham, "Meadows and Prairies."
9. See Lamm, "Ecology in Jewish Law and Theology," 163.
10. On land stewardship, see Gordis, "Ecology and the Judaic Tradition," 333.

11. Arthur Waskow, "Jewish Environmental Ethics: Intertwining *Adam* with *Adamah*," in *Oxford Handbook*, 405–9. See also Gordis, "Ecology and the Judaic Tradition," 333.
12. See Singer, "Logic of Effective Altruism."
13. Meadow, "Alternative Food Systems," 76–84; Flachs, "Gardening as Ethnographic Research," 97–103; Holland, "Diversity and Connections," 285–305.
14. See Pava, *Jewish Ethics as Dialogue*, 16.

BIBLIOGRAPHY

Brittingham, Margaret C. "Meadows and Prairies: Wildlife-Friendly Alternatives to Lawn." Pennsylvania Wildlife #5. PennState Extension. http://extension.psu.edu.

Dorff, Elliott, and Jonathan K. Crane, eds. *The Oxford Handbook of Jewish Ethics and Morality*. New York: Oxford University Press, 2013.

Flachs, Andrew. "Gardening as Ethnographic Research: Volunteering as a Means for Community Access." *Journal of Ecological Anthropology* 16, no. 1 (2013): 97–103.

Floyd-Thomas, Stacey M. "Teaching for Conflict Resolution: Metaethical Case Study Analysis as a Teaching Strategy." *Teaching Theology & Religion* 13, no. 3 (2010): 254–59.

Gordis, Robert. "Ecology and the Judaic Tradition." In *Contemporary Jewish Ethics and Morality: A Reader*, edited by Elliot N. Dorff and Louis E. Newman, 327–35. New York: Oxford University Press, 1995.

Holland, Leigh. "Diversity and Connections in Community Gardens: A Contribution to Local Sustainability." *Local Environment* 9, no. 3 (2004): 285–305.

Lamm, Norman. "Ecology in Jewish Law and Theology." In *Faith and Doubt: Studies in Traditional Jewish Thought*. Jersey City, NJ: Ktav, 2006.

Meadow, Alison M. "Alternative Food Systems at the Ground Level: The Fairbanks Community Garden." *Journal of Ecological Anthropology* 16, no. 1 (2013): 76–84.

Pava, Moses L. *Jewish Ethics as Dialogue: Using Spiritual Language to Re-imagine a Better World*. New York: Palgrave Macmillan, 2009.

Singer, Peter. "The Logic of Effective Altruism." *Boston Review*, July 6, 2015. https://bostonreview.net/forum/peter-singer-logic-effective-altruism.

Tipton, Steven M. *Getting Saved from the Sixties: The Transformation of Moral Meaning in American Culture*. Berkeley: University of California Press, 1982.

12

Ecological Ethics in the Jewish Community Farming Movement

ADRIENNE KRONE

Introduction

I was in the dining room at Eden Village Camp on the Saturday night of family camp when I first heard an announcement about tuna fish followed by raucous cheering and applause. Andrew Gurwitz, associate director of the camp, and Tom Hidas, the head chef—also both leaders in the Jewish community farming movement—introduced the meal so everyone in the room would know a little bit about what we would be eating and where it came from. At Eden Village, an overnight camp for students in third through eleventh grades, this is how every meal begins. I learned that Eden Village works with Oliver's Organic Eggs to offer organic, pasture-raised, higher-welfare local eggs in dishes like the egg salad they were serving that night. There was also tofu salad for people that don't eat eggs. All the mayonnaise was egg-free, so the coleslaw, potato salad, and tofu salad were vegan. The bread table was stocked and included vegan and gluten-free loaves. There were pickles from the on-site farm for everyone. And there was tuna fish for the first time ever at Eden Village. Andrew explained that they are intentional about what food they serve, and they had only recently found a tuna fish supplier that lived up to their standards.[1] The tuna fish enjoyed by the family camp attendees that evening was "100% pole and line caught by certified vessels operating from US ports."[2] The fish was certified kosher and certified sustainable by the Monterey Bay Aquarium. While Andrew and Tom explained that they cannot always meet every one of their values in the food they purchase, they do ensure that everything they serve at camp is "100% consciously sourced." At this Jewish camp, the kitchen meets Orthodox standards of kosher observance but also extends beyond the traditional laws of kashrut. Andrew and Tom review all their products "to ensure they meet our strict kosher, organic, fair-trade, welfare, local, and sustainability standards."[3] These reviews are ongoing, and at the end of each summer, Andrew and Tom sit down to talk about what foods they could source better. They acknowledge challenges, even if they can't always fix them. In the case of the tuna, after six years of seeking a kosher and sustainable source, they finally found one.

Food is central to the experience at Eden Village in part because the heart of camp is a two-acre farm on site. Many Jewish camps have gardens, and several have farms, but Eden Village is unique in being a camp based around a farm. Andrew clarified this point for me: "We are a farm-based summer camp. Everything is happening on the farm. It's not like a once-in-a-while activity."[4] Mornings at camp begin on the farm, and campers move through the farm throughout the day. The campers are involved in every step of food production. They plant, weed, water, harvest, chop, season, cook, and eat. All the food used for educational programs during camp comes from the farm. Ayelet Singer, the farm director, explained that they use about half of their growing space as a production vegetable farm for this purpose. They grow large amounts of cabbage and tomatoes so campers can make sauerkraut and salsa. There is a square designated for wheat that campers harvest, thresh, winnow, and grind to bake challah before Shabbat. A medicinal herb garden produces all the herbs used by the herbalists on staff in the camp's apothecary.[5] Centering Eden Village Camp on a farm enables campers and visitors to embrace the intentional approach to food utilized in the camp kitchens to reflect on and re-envision their own relationship with Judaism, the earth, and its inhabitants.

Jewish Community Farming

When I describe my research project, which focuses on Eden Village Camp and other organizations like it that together compose the Jewish community farming movement, a common response is some form of the question "Jews farm?"—often accompanied by a giggle. This response speaks to the real and perceived distance between most modern Jews and their agrarian ancestors. It surprises many Jews to learn that agriculture is central to many Jewish practices and holidays and a constant point of reference in Judaism's sacred texts. Jewish community farming organizations have a mission to educate people about the Jewish agricultural past while ensuring that there is also an agricultural Jewish present and future.

The methods the campers at Eden Village learn in order to process their wheat into challah form the basis of eleven of the thirty-nine categories of labor traditionally forbidden on Shabbat, a holiday of rest traditionally observed every Friday sunset to Saturday sunset. The earliest text of Rabbinic Judaism,[6] a law code known as the Mishnah compiled circa 200 CE that also incorporates narrative elements, identifies eleven labors—sowing, plowing, reaping, binding sheaves, threshing, winnowing, separating the inedible from the edible, grinding, sifting, kneading, and baking—as the work ancient Jews had to do in order to eat challah on Shabbat (Shabbat 73a). Many Jews today bake and consume challah, but only a small fraction of modern Jews engage in the agricultural labors related to growing and processing wheat. In fact, it has been hundreds of years since the majority of the Jewish people worked in agriculture.[7] Daron Joffe, also known as "Farmer D," worked as the director of Agricultural Innovation and Development at the Leichtag Foundation from 2014 to 2018. He sees this disconnection as something that can and should be rectified.[8] As we sat in his office, he reflected on this: "As Jewish people, we've been pushed off of land through the Diaspora. We've lost touch."[9] Joffe sees Jewish community farming as a path back. He explained that engaging in farming could move Jews toward reclaiming their "cultural identity and connection to the earth and seasons and social justice and stewardship."[10] At Leichtag they've dedicated sixty-seven and a half acres of their site in Encinitas, California, to Coastal Roots Farm. Coastal Roots is a community farm inspired by the Jewish tradition of agriculture.[11] Eden Village Camp, Coastal Roots Farm, and other Jewish community farming movement organizations are united by a shared commitment to engage Jews in nondenominational settings to reconnect them to Judaism, the earth, and its creatures through the revitalization of Jewish agricultural laws and traditions. In this chapter, I will explain how this movement interprets the often ancient Jewish agricultural laws, rituals, and values that they point to in describing the basis of an ecological ethic that guides North American Jews as they grow food in a diverse array of farms and gardens across the continent.

Jewish Agricultural Texts Reinterpreted

Daron Joffe had a solution to reconnect Jews to the land. He elaborated, "The guidebook back, in many ways, is the Jewish farmer's almanac in the Torah, like how we farm and how we care for animals and people."[12] The Torah, referred to hereafter as the Hebrew Bible (what Christians know as the Old Testament), is the most sacred text of Jewish traditions, and it assumes an agricultural setting.

Consider, for example, the opening creation narrative in the first chapter of Genesis that describes how the earth was created and how and when everything on it came to be. There is much debate in and outside of Jewish traditions over how to interpret Genesis 1:26 in particular, which grants humans "dominion" over the creatures of earth, specifically including livestock but says little about what this might mean. For some this dominion is understood as an almost unlimited license to use animals for human benefit, but others emphasize it is an obligation of stewardship. Either interpretation calls for humans to be intentional about their relationship with land, plants, and animals, and in the Jewish community farming movement, variations on the stewardship reading seem to be dominant. Continuing with agriculturally invested themes, in Genesis 3:17–19, Adam and Eve are banished from the Garden of Eden, and Adam's punishment is to toil and sweat—that is, to work the land through agriculture—in order to eat. Biblical narratives like this offer an explanation about the lives ancient Israelites were living that have also captured the imagination of the Jewish community farming movement. The "almanac" portions of the Hebrew Bible that Joffe mentioned offer guidelines for agriculture, including laws governing how to grow food and when to harvest it and troubleshooting advice for the times when animals were inflicted with disease or the rains didn't come. The question that the Hebrew Bible answers isn't *whether* humans should engage in agriculture but rather *how* humans, and the ancient Israelites (the ancestors of contemporary Jews) in particular, should engage in agriculture.

The agricultural laws were the first priority of the earliest rabbis, known as Tannaim, whose views are preserved in the Mishnah. Victor Raboy, author of an essay on Jewish agricultural law that echoes many of the ideas that I have heard in the Jewish community farming movement, offers a simple explanation for agriculture's prominent placement: "Farming was the primary occupation of the Jewish people when the Mishnah, the Jewish law code, was compiled in the second century C.E. So it is no surprise that the *first* volume of the Mishnah is called Zeraim or 'Seeds,' and it addresses the obligations of farmers."[13] The Mishnah prioritized agriculture because its audience, the Jewish people, were overwhelmingly farmers.

Five of the eleven tractates, or sections, of Zeraim deal specifically with farming and food, while the others are concerned with blessings, donations to the Temple, and tithing. These tractates attract considerable attention in the Jewish community farming movement. Leviticus 23:22 commands the ancient Israelites to leave the corner of one's field for the poor. Regulations based on this verse are the subject of tractate Pe'ah. Tractate Kil'ayim, which translates as "of two sorts," deals with the rules related to forbidden mixtures; laws discussed in this tractate forbid Jews from planting two kinds of seeds together and breeding between different types of animals. Tractate Orlah, "uncircumcised," is about the waiting period that must be observed before the fruit from trees can be consumed. This is based on Leviticus 19:23–25, which informs ancient Israelites that after a tree is planted, the fruit is forbidden for the first three years, in the fourth year it should be offered to God, and they may begin eating the fruits in the fifth year. The first fruits from the trees, and the first products of all harvests, are also meant for God. This is the topic of tractate Bikkurim, "first fruits." Tractate Shevi'it, "seventh year," describes the restrictions of the agricultural sabbatical year known as *shmita*, "release." This practice offers a sabbath for the land. The Hebrew Bible commands humans and land animals to rest after six days of work and commands shmita, a rest for the land, after six years of being worked. All forms of agricultural labor are forbidden in the seventh year, including plowing, seeding, reaping, and harvesting. Jews are permitted to eat perennial crops and to ensure that their animals and people without land are also fed. The shmita year also includes an economic component, which calls for Jews to release debts.

Each of these sections of the Mishnah includes detailed information that is meant to help Jews understand the intended relationship between humans and the earth, plants, animals, and God. Raboy argues that the prohibitions described in Zeraim reveal an underlying agricultural ethic: "We can surmise from its place in the Mishnah that the authors believed agriculture was one of the first activities requiring ethical standards. The fundamental agricultural principles expressed in Zeraim remain critical tenets today, and they can guide us as we strive to live more ethically with each other and the land."[14]

According to interpretations common in the Jewish community farming movement, these ancient laws encourage Jewish farmers to give their trees time to grow before they begin to harvest, and the best of their harvest is marked as sacred and offered to God. Similarly, forbidding the mixing of crops and animals is understood as calling Jews to be conscious of their power and wary of abusing it. Setting aside the corners of one's fields for the poor is understood as a reminder to Jews that the food they grow is meant to feed not just their family but all who are hungry. Finally, the sabbatical year prohibitions are understood as reminders to Jews that the land does not belong to them and that it deserves rest in the same way animals and humans do.

These agricultural laws are discussed further in the Talmuds, later but still canonical rabbinic texts that interpret the Mishnah, but less attention is paid to them there because these laws are understood to apply only within the boundaries of the land of Israel. As North American Jews return to the land seeking to revitalize these ancient practices, their enthusiasm for the ethical approach to agriculture and their desire to reconnect Jews to their roots in every sense of the word has resulted in a creative reimagination of these laws that transcends geographical location. These reimaginations are in-line and overlap with the ethical approaches to the traditional Jewish dietary laws described in Elliot Ratzman's chapter in this volume as "ecokosher" and "tzedek-kosher" approaches.

For example, in the shmita year 5775 on the Hebrew calendar (2014–15), at Pearlstone Center, they embraced the shmita year and applied it to their farmland and institutional structures in their Baltimore, Maryland, retreat center. They cover-cropped their fields, ended their apprenticeship program, and paused their community-supported agriculture (CSA) program for the year. All the employees were given additional days off work to volunteer in their community, and the staff spent time studying Jewish texts and traditions around shmita together. The farm staff used the year to rebuild physical structures, to strategize and plan for the future, and to revitalize local ecologies by eliminating invasive species and planting indigenous varieties. The staff of Pearlstone released their land for the year and reset their priorities and dedication to creating physical and mental space for Jewish agriculture in Baltimore.

Jewish Agricultural Holidays Reinterpreted

Those active in the Jewish community farming movement like to point out that agriculture provides the scaffolding for both the biblical and rabbinic constructions of time. The calendar found in the Hebrew Bible and expanded upon in rabbinic texts is organized by both growing seasons and agriculturally rooted pilgrimage festivals and four "new years" that mark key moments in the annual agricultural cycle. *Rosh Hashanah* is the new year most familiar to contemporary Jews and one of the most widely observed holidays in contemporary Judaisms. This is the *New Year of Seasons* and occurs in the late summer or early fall, and it marks the point when the Hebrew year changes. The seven-year shmita cycle is counted using Rosh Hashanah. *Tu B'Shevat*, traditionally the *New Year for Trees* and often described as an environmental holiday in the Jewish community farming movement, celebrates the end of winter and the first buds of spring. The *New Year for the Jewish People* falls on the first of *Nissan*, the spring month that contains contemporary Judaisms' most widely observed holiday, *Pesach* (Passover), which commemorates the transitional moment when the ancient Hebrews left Egypt and became the nation of Israel. The final new year is *Rosh Hashanah L'Behamot*, the *New Year for Animals*, which falls in the late summer. This new year was used to keep track of the age of one's cattle and size of one's herd during the sacrificial period of ancient Judaism so appropriate tithing could be calculated. Some within the Jewish community farming movement have promoted this as a time to consider ethical obligations to animals in partnership with the Jewish Initiative for Animals.

Three pilgrimage festivals also punctuate Jewish time. Each of these festivals began as an agricultural festival that was later imbued with historical significance.[15] Passover marked the beginning of the new planting season in ancient Israel and also became associated with the Exodus of the Jewish people from slavery in Egypt. Shavuot, which falls seven weeks after Passover, was an agricultural celebration of the spring harvest. After the biblical period, it also took on significance as a commemoration of the day that Moses received the Torah on Mount Sinai. *Sukkot* was the joyous celebration of the fall harvest, and over time, it also began to recall the forty years that the Israelites wandered in the desert after the Exodus.[16] As Jews moved off the land and away from agriculture, rabbinic Judaism often diminished the agricultural foundations of these holidays in favor of their historical significance.

The Jewish community farming movement and Jewish environmentalism broadly speaking seek to reconnect Jews to the rhythm of the seasons that is ingrained in the annual cycle of Jewish holidays. Debra Robbins, writing about the "ecological implications of the Hebrew calendar," suggests, "If we embrace it, the Jewish calendar can define the pattern of our lives. In cultivating a relationship with nature, we cultivate a relationship with the One who provides for us."[17] The Jewish community farming sites offer agricultural spaces where Jewish holidays can be celebrated in ways that better accord with their original intentions.

A *sukkah*, the temporary structure used for meals during the Jewish festival of Sukkot, occupies a prominent spot in the center of Abundance Farm year round. Similarly, Sukkot has become a popular event at Congregation B'nai Israel (CBI), the synagogue that houses Abundance Farm. The sukkah at Abundance Farm is composed of tree branches, and it predates the farm. It was built when a few members of the synagogue took over the area for a community garden that began as a small side project but grew into a full one-acre farm that offers agricultural space for CBI holiday celebrations, educational space for Lander Grinspoon Academy and the Jewish day school next door, and food for the Northampton Survival Center.

Grace, who runs teen programming for the farm, told me that having the farm space for holiday celebrations "provides this whole other layer of Judaism to people to connect with the land."[18] She continued, explaining that although these holidays were based in the land of Israel, they end up being relevant in their New England location as well. She reflected, "When *Tu B'Shevat* comes, it's actually pretty much right when the maple sap starts to flow in the trees, and being able to find new meaning for these old practices really imbues them with relevance."

Ellen Bernstein, editor of *Ecology & the Jewish Spirit*, is considered a foundational figure in Jewish environmentalism by many in the Jewish community farming movement. She suggests that knowledge and experience in an agricultural space is not only useful but necessary to truly understand the intention of these holidays: "Sukkot—as harvest holiday—first teaches that life is intimately tied to the cycle of nature. The holiday assumes we are ecologists, that we know the species and habitat of our home, and that we participate in the life of our ecosystem. An authentic celebration of Sukkot presupposes that we have been tending our crops all season; now is the time to reap what we have sown. It is also time to gather the four species and build a sukkah."[19] Now that Abundance has a farm on site, the staff is engaged in their ecosystem, and festivals like Sukkot enable them to celebrate the holidays in a manner they understand to be closer to their biblical origins.

Grace thinks that the festival is particularly meaningful for the teenagers who are part of the Food Justice Internship at the farm. She explained that by the time Sukkot comes, the teens have been through a farming season, so it matters more to them and makes the cycle of Judaism easier to understand and embrace.[20] Rabbi Jacob Fine, director of Abundance Farm, also highlighted the community building potential of using the farm to celebrate holidays like Sukkot. He works with local Christian communities to make the Sukkot festival an interfaith event that brings hundreds of people together to connect to each other, to their shared history, and to the land.

Jewish Agricultural Law and Jewish Values

The farms employ different approaches to "Jewish agriculture." The farms offer a diverse array of holiday celebrations and observe the agricultural laws to varying degrees. What binds these organizations together as a movement is their dedication to a set of values that undergirds the laws and holidays. At Shoresh Jewish Environmental programs, located in Toronto, Canada, these values guide their agricultural work around the city. On a sunny day in late June 2016, hundreds of people gathered in Erin, Ontario, for the grand opening of Bela Farm, a Shoresh project. During her opening remarks, Risa Alyson Cooper, executive director of Shoresh, explained that at Bela Farm, they "are manifesting a 114-acre centre for sustainable, land-based Judaism."[21] After her remarks and some more singing, we marched out onto that land led by a band, singing as we went. We walked by beds of garlic and soon entered a protected forest area. Then the band stopped playing so we could walk quietly through the apiary, where the Bela bee hives live. We headed past nine hives accompanied by the quiet hum of thousands of bees buzzing away as they went about their work.[22] This was not a traditional holiday but rather a celebration of the "land-based Judaism" that Risa described, which highlights an ecologically oriented interpretation of three traditional Jewish laws.

The first traditional law is *tzaar baalei chayim*, which translates literally to "the suffering of living creatures" and is understood by rabbinic Jewish traditions as a prohibition on unnecessarily causing animal suffering. *Tzaar baalei chayim* is often discussed in contemporary Jewish conversations around the ethics of contemporary animal agriculture and meat consumption as such. That conversation happens on Jewish community farms too, but on farms this traditional commandment is also understood as an ethical value applicable to animal husbandry. The animal husbandry work at Shoresh is focused on bees and other pollinators. Sabrina, the director of engagement, picked up an interest in beekeeping as a fellow at another Jewish farm, Adamah, and brought it with her back to Toronto, where she began to learn from a local master beekeeper. At Shoresh, Sabrina has set up a clear approach to protecting pollinators that gives high priority to the health of the bees and the restoration of native pollinator populations. First, the staff has worked hard to ensure the bees are fed a plentiful and diverse diet. At Bela Farm, they have set aside twenty acres as a bee sanctuary filled with indigenous wildflowers, but all Shoresh garden projects regardless of size always include a bee habitat. Second, they keep bees for honey, which they sell to the Jewish community. The honey harvest coincides nicely with Rosh Hashanah, a celebration that often includes honey, so Shoresh uses the sale of their honey to educate the community about the ecological, agricultural, and ultimately religious importance of pollinators. Third, they experiment with alternative materials and locations to see where and how the bees will thrive at the highest level.[23] For example, Shoresh has used the common Langstroth hives for the majority of their work. These hives are composed of stacked boxes with removable frames. Sabrina learned from a fellow beekeeper than there was another type of hive that may provide the bees with a structure that is closer to what they would encounter in trees. In 2018, Sabrina began to experiment with these Warre hives, which are boxes with removable bars that are designed so that bees can build their own comb.[24] Sabrina and the staff at Shoresh frequently revisit and revise their practices to ensure that the bees suffer as little as possible.

A second traditional law, *bal tashchit*, meaning "you shall not destroy," is based on Deuteronomy 20:19–20, which prohibits Jews from cutting down trees that bear fruit during times of war. This traditional commandment has been widely interpreted as an ecological value by Jewish environmentalist, including those active on Jewish community farms. In keeping with this value, Shoresh staff use and reuse materials in creative ways. I attended a honey harvest event in September 2017, and during a bottling break, Risa showed me their wax melters. These melters were made up of a quirky collection of buckets, Tupperware containers, pieces of metal mesh, and plastic sheeting. These makeshift melters ensure that nothing from the honey harvest is wasted. Next to the wax melters, there is a small hut that houses a compost toilet. Even human waste is not wasted at Shoresh.

The final traditional law that animates the work on Jewish community farms is *tzedakah*, which translates as "justice" or "righteousness" and is interpreted by many contemporary Jews as representing values related to social justice. All the Jewish community farms interpret this value and center it in their work. At Shoresh, in addition to their work with pollinators, they are also reforesting twenty acres of their land with native trees and planting twenty acres of perennial native fruit and nut trees, berry bushes, and native wildflowers.[25] Shoresh donates all the food they grow at their gardens in and around Toronto. They also offer garden programming with social service organizations like Jewish Family and Child and Baycrest, a geriatric center. The values that are embedded at Shoresh around animal husbandry, resource conservation, and justice similarly inform the work at other Jewish community farming organizations.

Conclusion

North American Jews can study Jewish texts and traditions around agriculture and embrace Jewish environmental values anywhere, but the Jewish community farming organizations enable a deeper level of connection. These Jewish farms reinterpret traditional Jewish agricultural texts, holidays, and laws to create spaces that are defined by a Jewish ecological ethic. These spaces allow Jews who may not be aware of the prominence of agricultural themes in Judaism to experience Judaism in a novel and compelling way. In a conversation with Risa and Sabrina at Shoresh, they reflected on the relief they felt when they each realized that their commitments to Judaism and to environmental justice could be understood as part of a larger whole. Sabrina described it as a "healing moment" when she realized that the two worlds did not have to be separate as previous experience in other Jewish contexts had made her think. She recalled a "moment of integration and realizing we can have them both." She is grateful for her job at Shoresh because it offers her "the opportunity to actually live Judaism."[26] Risa recalled a "radical ah-ha moment" where she connected these pieces as well: "Not only do these things . . . go together, but . . . [they] bridge these two worlds of Jewish tradition and environmental sustainability—they just strengthen one another in such deep and profound ways."[27] Jewish community farming organizations like Shoresh are currently a relatively small part of the Jewish infrastructure in North America, but they are growing in both size and number. Jewish community farms may play a bigger role in the future as they continue to make living out Jewish ecological ethics based on biblical texts and ancient traditions both possible and practical in innovative ways.

NOTES

1. Participant observation, Dining Hall, Eden Village Camp, June 4, 2016.
2. "Food at Eden Village," Eden Village Camp Website, accessed October 18, 2017, http://edenvillagecamp.org.

3. "Food at Eden Village."

4. Andrew Gurwitz, interview with author, Eden Village Office, June 4, 2016.

5. Ayelet Singer, interview with author, Eden Village Office, June 5, 2016.

6. See the opening of chapter 2 in this book for a definition of Rabbinic Judaism.

7. This shift that moved Jews off the land is the result of a number of factors including displacement, urbanization, prohibitions and restrictions on land ownership, and the increasing availability of opportunities in other industries.

8. The ethnographic research that forms the basis of this chapter was funded by a research grant from Farm Forward and the Leichtag Foundation.

9. Daron Joffe, interview with author, Leichtag Foundation Offices, July 7, 2016.

10. Joffe, interview with author.

11. "Homepage," Coastal Roots Farm Website, accessed October 18, 2017, https://coastalrootsfarm.org.

12. Daron Joffe, interview with author, Leichtag Foundation Offices, July 7, 2016.

13. Raboy, "Jewish Agricultural Law," 191.

14. Raboy, 191.

15. Morgenstern, *Two Ancient Israelite*, 39.

16. Troster, "'In Your Goodness,'" 111.

17. Robbins, "Sun, the Moon, and the Seasons," 99.

18. Grace Oedel, interview with author, Congregation B'nai Israel Library, June 15, 2016.

19. Bernstein, "Sukkot," 133.

20. Grace Oedel, interview with author, Congregation B'nai Israel Library, June 15, 2016.

21. "Bela Farm Grand Opening," Shoresh Website, accessed November 18, 2016, http://shoresh.ca.

22. Participant Observation, Bela Farm Grand Opening, June 26, 2016.

23. Sabrina Malach, interview with author, Shoresh Office, June 28, 2016.

24. Sabrina Malach, interview with author, Shoresh Bee Sanctuary, June 14, 2018.

25. "Bela Farm," Shoresh Jewish Environmental Programs Website, accessed October 19, 2017, http://shoresh.ca.

26. Sabrina Malach, interview with author, Shoresh Office, June 28, 2016.

27. Risa Alyson Cooper, interview with author, Shoresh Office, June 28, 2016.

SELECT BIBLIOGRAPHY

Bernstein, Ellen. "Sukkot: Holiday of Joy." In *Ecology & the Jewish Spirit: Where Nature and the Sacred Meet*, edited by Ellen Bernstein, 133–36. Woodstock: Jewish Lights Publishing, 1998.

Morgenstern, Julian. "Two Ancient Israelite Agricultural Festivals." *Jewish Quarterly Review* 8, no. 1 (1917): 39.

Raboy, Victor. "Jewish Agricultural Law: Ethical First Principles and Environmental Justice." In *Ecology & the Jewish Spirit: Where Nature and the Sacred Meet*, edited by Ellen Bernstein, 190–99. Woodstock: Jewish Lights Publishing, 1998.

Robbins, Debra J. "The Sun, the Moon, and the Seasons: Ecological Implications of the Hebrew Calendar." In *Ecology & the Jewish Spirit: Where Nature and the Sacred Meet*, edited by Ellen Bernstein, 98–106. Woodstock: Jewish Lights, 1998.

Troster, Lawrence. "'In Your Goodness, You Renew Creation': The Creation Cycles of the Jewish Liturgy." In *Ecology & the Jewish Spirit: Where Nature and the Sacred Meet*, edited by Ellen Bernstein, 107–11. Woodstock: Jewish Lights Publishing, 1998.

13

Bloodshed and the Ethics and Theopolitics of the Jewish Dietary Laws

DANIEL H. WEISS

There is no scholarly consensus about what, if any, ethical concerns seem to motivate the dietary laws articulated in the Hebrew Bible. Even among those who have argued for links between the ethical concerns of the Bible and the dietary practices it describes, the first associations that come to mind are typically not "opposition to individual and political bloodshed" or "an anticipation of future messianic peace." Yet this chapter will argue that a careful reading of the book of Leviticus points precisely to such conceptions.

As we will see, read from a literary-canonical perspective, the biblical text does indeed connect dietary practice and what we today consider to be ethical and political issues. It does so by setting up a parallel between biblical Israel's distinction from other nations—their status as "chosen" by God—and the command to the Israelites to distinguish the permitted, "kosher" animals, specifically quadrupeds and birds,[1] from the forbidden ones. The text suggests that just as God selected Israel among the nations, God commands Israel to select certain animals in relation to food. The permitted "pure" food animals' "way of life" is symbolically invested so that this parallel between Israel's being chosen by God and Israel's being commanded to eat only certain animals implies a broader ethical concern with killing and bloodshed.

This structural parallel stands alongside Leviticus's repeated prohibition against consuming blood, which in turn has close links to the prohibition of bloodshed in passages of the book of Genesis that have been linked to the Priestly school (one of the several groups identified by scholars as composing the texts later redacted together to become the Hebrew Bible). Taken together, these various textual patterns serve to illuminate the fact that the permitted birds and quadrupeds appear to be ones that do not "murder" other birds and quadrupeds. Conversely, all predatory birds and mammals are forbidden. This in turn points to a dynamic where Israel's distinction from the nations is likewise based on Israel's rejection of the willful use of human power and force in connection to its own "national sustenance": its survival as a collective group. Just as the permitted sheep, cows, goats, and deer depend on God for their sustenance and survival rather than using sharp teeth and claws to shed blood, so too the Bible portrays Israel's collective task as differentiating itself from the aggressive use of human power. In sum, the food laws symbolically call the Israelites to a unique ethics and theopolitics through their renunciation of bloodshed and their dependence on God.

Other biblical passages—such as Ezekiel 34, in which Israel is presented as sheep, while the nations are presented as predatory beasts—serve to reinforce this sensibility. While many present-day interpreters of the biblical dietary laws sometimes view them as arbitrary and unconnected to concrete ethical concerns, reading the dietary laws in connection with their broader textual setting within the book of Leviticus as a whole and within the biblical canon uncovers specifically ethical and theopolitical dimensions of the dietary laws, linked to the abhorrence of bloodshed and of violent human power. In a variation of "you are what you eat," the biblical text presents the permitted birds and quadrupeds in terms of "eat only what you ought to be."[2]

Significantly, this chapter does not seek to specify what normative implications for contemporary Jews or Christians ought to follow from this conclusion. This chapter only identifies noteworthy conceptual dynamics of the biblical text read as a literary and historical document. While the analysis here may be useful for others who wish to engage in constructive theological projects addressing contemporary ethical or political issues, the aims of this chapter are descriptive rather than prescriptive.

Earlier Academic Attempts to Interpret the Dietary Laws

The analysis in this chapter follows a now fifty-year-old scholarly trajectory that began, unexpectedly, when anthropologist Mary Douglas put forth a compelling and novel reading of the rationale for the Hebrew

Bible's dietary laws. In her treatment of the biblical dietary laws in her now classic book *Purity and Danger* (1966), she presented one of the first substantive modern scholarly attempts to analyze the forbidden and permitted animals in terms of a broader symbolic-structural social framework.[3] This approach was highly influential on a range of subsequent biblical scholars, inaugurating a range of "religioethical" explanations of the dietary laws in contrast to explanations that focused on hygiene or disgust or argued that the laws are deliberately arbitrary (for discussion, see Elaine Goodfriend's chapter in this book).[4] My argument here will be most closely in conversation with the work of Jacob Milgrom (a teacher of Goodfriend) and Howard Eilberg-Schwartz, who themselves both follow in the path of Douglas in discerning a structural parallel between the biblical presentation of permitted and forbidden animals and the biblical presentation of Israel's own social and political life.[5] Via this lens of analysis, the restrictions and permissions in terms of food can be understood as symbolizing and reinforcing in daily life the restrictions and permissions placed upon Israel in terms of ethical and political relations to other human individuals and groups.

While the general approach of reading Leviticus's dietary restrictions as reflecting aspects of Israel's social values has been widely viewed as a valid methodology, there has not yet been scholarly agreement as to *which* ethical, social, and theological aspects are being reflected in the animal divisions or *how* these aspects relate to the specific features of the permitted and the prohibited animals. Thus previous scholarly accounts have come under criticism for not constituting a consistent reading of the biblical texts. The present analysis takes into account previous scholarly criticisms to put forth a new, more persuasive reading. If the argument succeeds, it will demonstrate that in the world of the biblical text (if not always in later Jewish and Christian traditions), diet, politics, theology, and ethics are bound together in a specific configuration that calls for an end to bloodshed as a means of sustaining one's individual or collective existence.

Broader Biblical Themes as Background to the Dietary Laws

We begin our investigation with Leviticus 20, which links the election of Israel from the nations to the separation between pure and impure animals, in which the "pure" animals are those permitted for Israel's table:[6]

> [22] You shall faithfully observe all My laws and all My regulations, lest the land to which I bring you to settle in spew you out. [23] You shall not follow the practices of the nation that I am driving out before you. For it is because they did all these things that I abhorred them [24] and said to you: You shall possess their land, for I will give it to you to possess, a land flowing with milk and honey. I the Lord am your God who has set you apart from other peoples. [25] So you shall set apart the pure quadruped (*behemah*) from the impure, the impure bird (*'of*) from the pure. You shall not draw abomination upon yourselves through quadruped or bird or anything with which the ground is alive, which I have set apart for you to treat as impure. [26] You shall be holy to Me, for I the Lord am holy, and I have set you apart from other peoples to be Mine. (Lev. 20:22–26)[7]

Here, the text presents a relationship between God's actions and Israel's actions: just as God made a separation between Israel and "the nations," so too Israel makes a separation between the pure quadrupeds[8] and the impure quadrupeds and between the pure birds and the impure birds. The same verb (*lehavdil*) is used for both the divine and the human act of separating. Jacob Milgrom has highlighted this parallel to argue that the book of Leviticus seems to be working with a structural parallel between divisions or separations in the human realm and divisions in the animal realm.

In the current passage, Israel, as "chosen" by God, corresponds to the pure quadrupeds and birds as "chosen" by Israel. Moreover, in the book of Leviticus more broadly, a further subseparation is to be found within Israel, in which the priests are separated by God from the rest of Israel for a special role. Corresponding to this, a special set of quadrupeds and birds are likewise separated out as fit for sacrifice. In this theological account, then, we can discern a tripartite separation among groups of human beings that corresponds to a tripartite separation among groups of quadrupeds and birds, as illustrated in the following diagram based on one drawn from Milgrom.[9]

In the context of the divisions represented in the first two circles of this diagram, the *pure* quadrupeds and birds mentioned in Leviticus 20

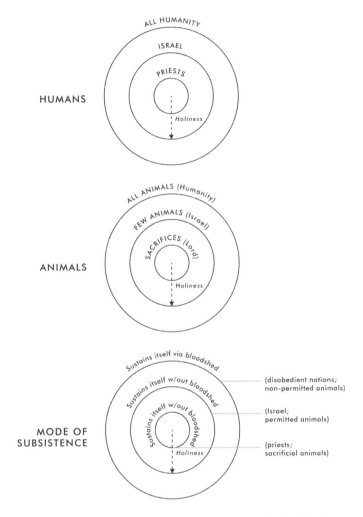

Figure 13.1. A revised version of Milgrom's diagram; the third circle has been added to Milgrom's original diagram to illustrate modes of subsistence

correspond to Israel as a subset of all humanity. The *sacrificial* quadrupeds and birds correspond to the priests as a subset of Israel. And the impure quadrupeds and birds correspond to the "other nations" from whom God has separated Israel.[10] The third circle in the diagram represents the additional observations I emphasize in the present chapter.

Holiness and Diet

In addition to highlighting these tripartite separations, Leviticus 20 presents social distinctions in terms of callings of holiness. After stating Israel's obligations to separate the pure quadrupeds and birds from the impure ones (in parallel to God's separating Israel from the nations), the text states, "You shall be holy to Me, for I the LORD your God am holy; and I have set you apart from the nations to be Mine" (Lev. 20:26). Israel is thus set apart from the nations in order to pursue a special task of holiness, just as the priests are set apart from the rest of Israel in order to pursue a special task of holiness. However, while both Israel (among the nations) and the priests (among Israel as a whole) have tasks of holiness, these do not appear to be identical tasks. The priests' holiness is manifested through service in the Tabernacle/Temple, whereas the rest of Israel does not serve in the domain of the Tabernacle/Temple. By contrast, the holiness of Israel as a whole appears to be linked to the commandments, to God's "statues and ordinances" (see Lev. 20:22), which are to be carried out in "common" life.[11] In this framework, God's "extra requirements" to Israel in the form of the commandments constitute the task of holiness that sets Israel apart from the rest of humanity. The priests are also obligated in the commandments of holiness incumbent upon all Israel and, in addition to these, engage in a distinctive form of holiness corresponding to the priestly requirements linked to the sacred space of the Tabernacle/Temple. As we shall see, these forms of "holiness in action" will play a key role in understanding the dynamics of permitted and forbidden animals in Leviticus 11 (cf. also Lev. 11:44–45).

Blood and Bloodshed

First, we must give attention to the significance of blood and bloodshed. Leviticus specifically prohibits eating blood in no less than four separate passages (Lev. 3:17, 7:26, 17:10–14, 19:26). This emphasis appears to be linked to the priestly theological conception that "the life (*nefesh*) of all flesh is its blood" (Lev. 17:14). That is to say, there is a prohibition on consuming blood because there is a prohibition on consuming the "life" of any fleshly being, and the blood is the "life."

In order to appreciate this notion, we need to look back to the first chapter of Genesis.[12] God, after creating the various types of living things, creates human beings as the "image of God" and places them in a position of rulership and responsibility over the other living things (Gen. 1:20–28).[13] Despite this authority, God does not give human beings the right to *eat* any of the animals. Instead, God communicates that He has specifically designated fruits and green plants to be their food and that He has likewise designated green plants to be the food for every other living thing (Gen. 1:29–30). Here, the plants are not designated as "living things" in the sense of a *nefesh hayah* but rather food for living things—that is, for animals and humans. The theology that appears to be expressed in this passage is that God is the creator of the life of animals and humans and that God retains authority over this life. Neither human beings nor animals are given the authority to consume "life" in order to sustain themselves. In this sense, the original commanded diet is specifically a nonviolent and nonbloodshedding diet.

Despite this initial set of authorizations, the subsequent creation narrative does not progress in accord with God's instructions. Instead, we read in Genesis 6 that by the time of the generation of Noah, "all flesh had corrupted its way upon the earth" and that "the earth was filled with violence" (Gen. 6:11–12). Here, the phrase "all flesh" is notable, as it appears to designate both animals and humans. Although bloodshed and violent eating are not specifically mentioned, the general description of violence (*hamas*) conceptually stands in sharp contrast to the peaceable diet described in Genesis 1. As Leon Kass has suggested, this passage may indicate the fact that some of the animals have now become carnivorous, violating the restriction put upon them in Genesis 1.[14] Thus God decides to destroy all flesh on earth, both humans and animals, apart from the few preserved by Noah and his family on the ark.

After the flood, God presents new commandments regarding food and eating. God now tells Noah and his descendants that "every moving things that lives shall be for you to eat; like the green vegetables, I give you all of these" (Gen. 9:3). While God permits human beings to kill animals for food, He puts in place a sharp restriction: "But you shall not eat flesh with its life, its blood" (Gen. 9:4). Here, human beings have been given an additional authorization to eat "flesh," but this still remains separate from an authorization to consume "life," which is linked to blood. Although flesh now becomes permitted, the separation of blood from the flesh is necessary in order to acknowledge that the "life" of the animal has still not been fully transferred over to human desires.[15] Thus the prohibition against eating blood corresponds to acknowledging that human beings continue to lack authorization in the realms of action that remain solely in God's domain.

In addition, the permission to eat the flesh of animals (but not their blood) is juxtaposed with a strong reinforcement of the prohibition against shedding the blood of human beings, who remain in the special position of rulership and governance as the image of God (Gen. 9:5–6). God has given human beings the authority to kill animals for sustenance; however, the authority to make such judgments about animal life does *not* carry over to an authorization of human beings to treat other human beings in such a manner. Human life remains fully under the authority of God, off-limits to "merely human" desires and judgments. Human beings have been granted authority over the flesh but not the blood of the nonhuman animals but do not have authority over *either* the flesh *or* the blood of other human beings.

Permitted Birds and Quadrupeds as Those That Do Not Shed Blood

With this religioethical orientation in mind, we can note that Leviticus's injunction against eating blood seems to link this prohibition specifically to quadrupeds and birds. Leviticus 7:26 states, "You shall eat no manner of blood, whether of quadruped or bird, in any of your dwellings," and Leviticus 17:3 states that "when you hunt any beast or bird that may be eaten, you shall pour out its blood and cover it with earth" rather than consuming the blood.[16] The text does not appear to talk about avoiding or pouring out the blood of permitted fish or locusts. It therefore appears that in the theological conceptuality of Leviticus, it is only quadrupeds and birds that fall under the category of "blood-containing animal." By contrast, the permitted fish and insects are not counted as containing "blood" (*dam*). This conceptuality is reinforced by the fact that only quadrupeds and birds are treated as eligible for sacrifice, since the atoning element in sacrifice is linked specifically to the pouring or sprinkling of blood on the altar (cf. Lev. 17:11). If fish or insects are not considered blood-containing animals, then it stands to reason that they would not be able to serve as animal sacrifices on the altar.

Given these various reflections on blood, we are now in a better position to reflect on God's commandment to Israel to separate out the pure quadrupeds and birds from the impure quadrupeds and birds. If, as we have seen in Leviticus 20, this act of separation parallels God's act of separating Israel from the nations, and if the pure quadrupeds and birds thus "correspond" to Israel, *what precisely is it about these animals that makes them a proper conceptual match for Israel?*

Let us begin with the birds. In the book of Leviticus, no general criteria are given for distinguishing the birds that are permitted for Israel to eat from those that are forbidden. Only a list of specific forbidden birds is presented (Lev. 11:13–19). However, as modern scholars as well as earlier commentators (see, e.g., Mishnah Chullin 3:6) have highlighted, the forbidden birds appear by and large to be predatory carnivores, including hawks, falcons, ravens, and owls, or scavenging carnivores, such as vultures.[17] In other words, the common characteristic of these birds, with their typical dietary pattern of killing and/or eating other birds and mammals through the use of their sharp talons and beaks, is that they *consume blood.* By contrast, the category of the remaining permitted birds would appear to encompass those that do not sustain themselves through bloodshed, such as pigeons, doves, chickens, and ducks.

In this regard, our discussion of what constitutes "blood" in Leviticus is crucial. To take the example of the duck, although much of its diet consists of fish and insects, we have seen that these latter are not classified as blood-containing animals. As such, in the framework of Leviticus, the duck would still not count as a "blood consumer," and the same goes for the insect-and-earthworm-eating chickens, pigeons, and doves. It is not the case that the permitted animals must be "vegetarian" in the sense of "eating no animals" but rather that they must refrain from eating *blood* and "blood animals," which do not include fish and insects.[18] Likewise, it is not that the permitted animals must refrain from "taking life" per se but that they must refrain from shedding blood—that is, committing "murder" by taking the life of other blood-containing animals.[19] In sum, the pure birds sustain themselves without bloodshed and without blood consumption, while the impure birds engage in bloodshed and blood consumption.

A similar pattern emerges regarding quadrupeds, although here the textual data are more complex. Rather than giving a list of forbidden quadrupeds, the text puts forth conceptual criteria: the permitted quadrupeds are restricted to those that both have cloven hooves and chew the cud (Lev. 11:3). This double criterion entails that Israel's quadruped diet will be restricted only to nonbloodshedding and non-blood-consuming species while encompassing both domesticated (cows, sheep, goats) and nondomesticated (deer, antelope, gazelle) animals. Not all non-blood-consuming animals are permitted (e.g., the camel, horse, and rabbit, having only one of the two criteria, are not permitted)—but all permitted animals are non-blood-consuming. Moreover, the physical features that distinguish permitted animals correspond to a nonbloodshedding form of sustenance: cloven hooves stand anatomically in contrast to sharp claws, while the flat teeth used for cud chewing stand in contrast to the sharp fangs of the predatory and carnivorous animals.[20]

Implications for Israel's Way of Life

Returning to the earlier diagram, we can construct the following account of the various separations: just as God has separated Israel from the nations, Israel is to separate the pure quadrupeds and birds from the impure quadrupeds and birds and is to restrict its diet only to the former. Thus Israel is to restrict its diet only to those quadrupeds and birds that correspond to Israel and is to refrain from consuming the quadrupeds and birds that correspond to the other nations. As we have seen, this restriction to the pure quadrupeds and birds simultaneously means that the only permitted animals are nonbloodshedding, and all bloodshedding animals are marked as forbidden. *This then raises the following question: What is implied by the fact that the animals that correspond to Israel are specifically the nonbloodshedding ones, while the bloodshedding animals are structurally presented as corresponding to the nations?*

We can view the permitted animals' refraining from shedding and eating blood as involving those animals' basic obedience to God's authority over all life, a core theological concept of Leviticus and of the Priestly school. By contrast, the forbidden animals include those who sustain themselves through bloodshed, thus distancing themselves from obedience to God as master of life and death. Likewise, Israel is called by God to a life of holiness through the commandments, which sets them apart from "the ways of the nations"—that is, from groups who, in the theological conception of Leviticus, refuse to align themselves with God's will for the postflood world. In this sense, Israel is to restrict its consumption only to "obedient" birds and quadrupeds as a symbolic means of reminding itself of its task of holiness and obedience to God via the commandments. By separating out the "obedient" birds and quadrupeds from the "disobedient" others, Israel's diet serves as a microcosm of its task to enact its ethical-behavioral separation from the "disobedient nations."

In addition, the restriction of Israel's diet only to nonbloodshedding birds and quadrupeds also appears to resonate with the commandment to refrain from human bloodshed and from the consumption of the blood of animals. While God has given human beings permission to eat animal flesh, human beings have not been given permission to consume the blood ("life") of animals or to take the life of human beings for their own purposes or desires. Yet in terms of the biblical narrative, the violence that we saw in Genesis 6 continued to mark the behavior of humans and human communities even after the flood. In particular, the theological framework of Leviticus may be working on the assumption, found elsewhere in the biblical text, that it is, unfortunately, typical of the nations of the world to engage in intra- and intergroup bloodshed. Thus on the collective or political level, bloodshed may constitute a core element of the "ways of the nations" and may represent a core practice by which a typical nation "sustains itself."

As such, by restricting Israel's diet only to birds and quadrupeds that refrain from sustaining themselves through spilling the blood of other birds and quadrupeds, the framework of Leviticus may be symbolically casting Israel's task as refraining from communal "means of sustenance" that involve committing bloodshed against other human groups.[21] For a nation to engage in such practices by means of its human judgment and deliberation constitutes a rejection of God's sole authority over human life and death. By contrast, Israel's communal task of holiness is founded upon an affirmation of God's mastery of life and death and of the human being as the image of God and thus involves a rejection of seeking to sustain itself through spilling the blood of other human groups or individuals.

As such, Israel's nonbloodshedding communal identity is reinforced by restricting its diet to nonbloodshedding birds and quadrupeds and by refraining from eating animals who engage in the symbolic equivalent of political bloodshed.[22]

Messianic and Historical Significance

This understanding of Israel's separation of the pure birds and quadrupeds from the impure is reinforced by Howard Eilberg-Schwartz's observation that throughout the Hebrew Bible, Israel is frequently collectively symbolized as a pure animal (often sheep or a cow), while the other nations are represented as predatory beasts.[23] Although Eilberg-Schwartz does not generally bring in the categories of blood and bloodshed, his basic observation stands in accord with my analysis here. Particularly in the prophetic texts of the Hebrew Bible, Israel is called to embody the nonviolent traits of the sheep, who, as in Psalm 23, trusts in "the Lord as its shepherd" for protection, even though this may involve suffering at the hands of the "predatory" other nations.

In this context of trouble and suffering, the texts also hold out hope for a future era in which Israel's faithfulness to God will be rewarded by restoration and peace. Thus in the book of Ezekiel, God describes the present situation of Israel's oppression and exile by declaring, "My flock is scattered all over the face of the earth, with none to take thought of them and none to seek them. . . . My flock has been a prey for all the wild beasts" (Ezek. 34:6–7). Here, Israel as God's sheep is ravaged by the "fangs" of those human beings whose behavior correlates them with the bloodshedding beasts. Later in the same chapter, God declares a coming time in which He will rescue and redeem His flock Israel: "They shall no longer be a spoil for the nations, and the beasts of the earth shall not devour them; they shall dwell secure and untroubled" (Ezek. 34:28).[24] In this latter verse, the conceptual juxtaposition of "the nations" with "predatory beasts" is spelled out explicitly.[25]

In the book of Isaiah, imagery of "the nations" likewise sits alongside animal imagery. The famous depiction of the messianic future in Isaiah 2:4 reads, "And He shall judge between the nations, and shall decide for many peoples; and they shall beat their swords into plowshares, and their spears into pruninghooks; nation shall not lift up sword against nation, neither shall they learn war any more."[26] A few chapters later, Isaiah 11:6–7 declares a coming time in which "the wolf shall dwell with the lamb, and the leopard shall lie down with the kid; and the calf and the young lion and the fatling together; and a little child shall lead them. And the cow and the bear shall feed; their young ones shall lie down together; and the lion shall eat straw like the ox." Here, just as the warlike nations will turn their implements of war and bloodshed into implements of vegetable cultivation, so too the predatory animals (who are correlated to those nations) will cease from their bloodshedding diets and will take up the vegetable-based dietary ways of the cow, sheep, and goat. In this sense, although those animals currently sustain themselves through bloodshed, they will ultimately, so to speak, beat their fangs into cud-chewing flat teeth and their claws into cloven hooves.

When set in this broader context, the theological framework in which the dietary laws of Leviticus are embedded takes on a messianic significance. By confining its diet only to the nonbloodshedding animals to which it "corresponds," Israel strives to align its communal life with the obedient antiviolence that stands in sharp contrast to the current bloodshedding practices of the other nations—an antiviolence that characterized God's initial plan for human beings and that will likewise characterize God's promised future redemption. Israel's dietary practices both symbolize and reinforce its task of communal holiness in the present, which entails upholding the human being as the image of God and rejecting ways of life that are structurally dependent on bloodshed, thereby anticipating and prefiguring the messianic future.

While the historical dating of the composition and redaction of the biblical books is a matter of much scholarly debate, we can nevertheless note that Leviticus's intertwining theological themes—of blood, bloodshed, dietary laws, Israel's task of holiness, and God's election of Israel from among the nations—would likely have been particularly resonant among an Israelite/Jewish community in the exilic or postexilic period. In a context in which violence-based political power was absent or unavailable, a community centered on a set of ethical and ritual commandments, seeking to maintain faith in God in a time of political oppression, could have found Leviticus's presentation of the dietary laws well suited to their situation.[27] By enacting a rejection of bloodshedding animals from their table and by "electing" only the nonbloodshedding animals, such a community could reinforce the idea that their own nonviolent communal structure brought them into closer alignment with the God of creation than did the violent communal structures of their political overlords.[28] This basic theological stance may likewise have continued in classical rabbinic Judaism, in which we also find comparisons of the nations oppressing Israel to the impure quadrupeds.[29] Thus, far from representing "merely ceremonial" legal injunctions, we can view the dietary laws of Leviticus as embodying a countercultural theological, ethical, and political framework in daily table practices that enact a communal opposition to bloodshed as well as a practical anticipation of the future messianic cessation of warfare.

NOTES

1. This chapter focuses specifically on the distinction between forbidden and permitted birds and quadrupeds. The reasons for permission and restriction with regard to animals *not* presented as linked with blood—such as fish and insects—may require different explanations.

2. While multiple different interpretations of the text are theoretically possible, the reading given here represents an attempt to make sense of a series of prominent and interconnected themes and emphases in the text, including blood, bloodshed, Israel's task of holiness, humanity as the image of God, and God's authority over life and death. Methodologically, the argument will focus on the form in which these laws are presented in the biblical text as we have it today, not on their extratextual historical origins; see Houston, *Purity and Monotheism*, 76–77, 123.

3. See Douglas, *Purity and Danger*, 51–71.

4. See also Kunin, *We Think What We Eat*, 29–103.

5. Milgrom, *Leviticus 1–16*; Milgrom, *Leviticus 17–22*; Milgrom, "Ethics and Ritual," 159–92; Eilberg-Schwartz, *Savage in Judaism*.

6. See Milgrom, *Leviticus 17–22*, 1763, on "pure" (*tahor*) in this passage as indicating "permissible for Israel to eat."

7. Biblical citations in the chapter, except where otherwise noted, are drawn from the New Jewish Publication Society translation, with slight modifications.

8. Throughout the chapter, I follow Jacob Milgrom's lead in translating behemah, in the context of Leviticus's dietary laws, as "quadruped."

9. See Milgrom, *Leviticus 1–16*, 721–22; Milgrom, *Leviticus 17–22*, 1718; Douglas, "Deciphering a Meal," 242–48; Douglas, "Looking Back," 311.

10. We can also note that in verse 25, the structural parallel is presented specifically as between Israel and the pure *quadrupeds and birds* rather than fish or insects (cf. Milgrom, *Leviticus 17–22*, 1763).

11. See Milgrom, *Leviticus 1–16*, 694–96; Milgrom, *Leviticus 17–22*, 1718, 1740–42.

12. These passages have been linked to the same Priestly school whose thought marks the book of Leviticus.

13. On this and other scholarly understandings of the meaning of "image of God" in Genesis 1, see Middleton, *Liberating Image*.

14. Kass, *Hungry Soul*, 211.

15. On Genesis 9 as making a distinction between "flesh" and "blood," see Soler, "Semiotics of Food," 128.

16. While Lev. 17:13 uses the term *hayah* rather than *behemah*, it seems clearly to be referring to the permitted wild quadrupeds such as the deer, gazelle, or antelope, as there do not seem to be any other type of animals that would fall under the combined category of "hunted animal" and "animal that may be eaten." In this regard, see Milgrom, *Leviticus 1–16*, 693.

17. See Milgrom, *Leviticus 1–16*, 661. Milgrom notes that not every single named bird on the list may fall under the category of predators or carrion-eating scavengers but that it nevertheless appears to be the strongly dominant feature.

18. Soloveichik ("Locusts, Giraffes," 73) points to the duck's diet in order to criticize those like Kass (in *The Hungry Soul*) who argue that the permitted animals are characterized by adherence to the plant diet of Genesis 1. A similar critique could be made of Soler ("Semiotics of Food," 134) or of Carroll ("One More Time," 342–44) for claiming that the permitted animals must be "vegetarian." Yet contra Soloveichik, scholars like Kass, Soler, and Carroll are correct in pointing to a connection to Genesis and to God's authority over life and over the order of creation—but the connection may be more to Genesis 9 (refraining from bloodshed and from consuming blood) than to Genesis 1 (eating only plants).

19. Cf. Leviticus 17:4, which describes an Israelite who slaughters blood animals improperly as having "shed blood" (*dam shafakh*), the same term used in the prohibition of murder in Genesis 9:6.

20. At the same time, we can also view the criteria for pure quadrupeds as constituting a conceptual extension from the three species of sacrificial animals—namely, cows, sheep, and goats. See Milgrom, *Leviticus 1–16*, 729. On the connection between animals that Israel may eat and animals Israel may sacrifice, see also Firmage, "Biblical Dietary Laws," 177–208; Houston, *Purity and Monotheism*, 114–20, 230–37. We have posited that the separation of pure quadrupeds from impure appears to correspond to Israel's separation from the nations and that this separation, as highlighted in the diagram in this chapter, also encompasses an internal separation of the priests from the rest of Israel. While the priests have an additional special role linked to the sacred space of the Temple/Tabernacle, they are also bound by the same basic pattern of behavioral holiness that is incumbent upon the rest of the Israelites. Likewise, through the double criteria of split hooves and cud chewing, we can arrive at a "middle category" of quadrupeds: ones that are structurally and behaviorally similar to the sacrificial (i.e., "priestly") animals but which are designated as not proper to the sacred space

of the altar (Milgrom, *Leviticus 1–16*, 729). Thus the sacrificial animals (sheep, goats, cows) are marked by nonbloodshedding features and diet and are *also* part of the Temple space, while the additional permitted animals (deer, antelope) are similarly marked by the same nonbloodshedding features and diet but live "in the wild" and do not participate in the sacrificial order of the altar. The latter thus correspond to Israel, who are marked by the task of holy behavior via the commandments but do not dwell within the special sacred confines of God's house and are thus less "domesticated" than are the priests. The double criteria for the pure quadrupeds enables them simultaneously to be part of the "same grouping" as the sacrificial quadrupeds while yet distinguished from them, just as the priests and the other Israelites are simultaneously part of the same community yet distinguished from one another. And although in Leviticus no general criteria are given for pure birds, we can likewise note that while only the pigeon and dove are designated for the altar (Leviticus 1:14), they share the same behavior of a nonbloodshedding diet with the other permitted birds such as the duck and chicken.

21. My account thus differs from that of Jacob Milgrom, who holds that the restriction to pure animals encourages Israel to uphold the value of "reverence for life," including animal life (*Leviticus 1–16*, 731–36; see also Milgrom, "Ethics and Ritual"). By contrast, while the general prohibition against eating animal blood may indeed be linked to something akin to "reverence for life," the commandments permitting only nonbloodshedding birds and quadrupeds to be eaten seems instead to correspond symbolically specifically to the prohibition of shedding the blood of *other human beings*. For related critiques of this aspect of Milgrom's argument, see Firmage, "Biblical Dietary Laws," 195; Wright, "Observations on the Ethical Foundations." Moreover, Milgrom does not assign symbolic or functional-behavioral value to the double criterion of split hoofs or chewing the cud and refers to these as "bizarre criteria" (*Leviticus 1–16*, 729). Likewise, in his commentary on Numbers (*JPS Torah Commentary*, 345), he describes these criteria as "arbitrary and meaningless in themselves." Thus while my argument follows Milgrom's in viewing the pure animals as corresponding to Israel in relation to his parallel tripartite structures and in assigning a broader "ethical" significance to the dietary laws, I depart from him in relation to the *reason* that only these specific animals are permitted, thus avoiding the critiques that Firmage and Wright direct at the "ethical" dimensions of Milgrom's claims.

22. Cf. Kass, *Hungry Soul*, 220.

23. In addition, Eilberg-Schwartz likewise notes the way in which these widespread metaphors correspond to criteria for permitted animals in the dietary laws: "Significantly, cloven hooves and chewing the cud are precisely the traits that distinguish the kind of animals that routinely serve as metaphors for Israelite society from those that generally do not. The flocks and herds which are the paradigmatic metaphors for Israelite society are also the model kind of food. Moreover, the animals that serve as metaphors for other nations, such as predatory animals,

are defined as unclean. Thus the dietary restrictions carve up the animal world along the same lines as Israelite thought." Eilberg-Schwartz, *Savage in Judaism*, 125; see also 118–22.

24. Cf. the similar mention of "evil beasts" in Leviticus 26:6.

25. For a good treatment of the use of animal imagery in the book of Ezekiel, see Galambush, "God's Land and Mine," 91–108.

26. Trans. King James Version, as with the subsequent citation from Isaiah 11.

27. Cf. Mein, *Ezekiel and the Ethics*.

28. While the presentation of the dietary laws given here may correspond well with the situation of a community in exile, it is also important to reflect on how the posited opposition to bloodshed meshes with the presence in the biblical text of practices such as the death penalty and warfare, both of which entail the taking of human life. See Weiss, "Direct Divine Sanction," 23–38.

29. See, for example, Leviticus Rabbah 13:5.

BIBLIOGRAPHY

Carroll, Michael P. "One More Time: Leviticus Revisited." *European Journal of Sociology* 19, no. 2 (1978): 339–46.

Douglas, Mary. "Deciphering a Meal." In *Implicit Meanings: Selected Essays in Anthropology*, 2nd ed., 231–51. London: Routledge, 1999.

———. "Looking Back at the 1970s Essays." In *Implicit Meanings: Selected Essays in Anthropology*, 2nd ed., 310–13. London: Routledge, 1999.

———. *Purity and Danger*. London: Routledge, 2002. First published 1966.

Eilberg-Schwartz, Howard. *The Savage in Judaism: An Anthropology of Israelite Religion and Ancient Judaism*. Bloomington: Indiana University Press, 1990.

Firmage, Edwin. "The Biblical Dietary Laws and the Concept of Holiness." In *Studies in the Pentateuch*, edited by J. A. Emerton, 177–208. Leiden: Brill, 1990.

Galambush, Julie. "God's Land and Mine: Creation and Property in the Book of Ezekiel." In *Ezekiel's Hierarchical World: Wrestling with a Tiered Reality*, edited by Stephen L. Cook and Corrine Patton, 91–108. Atlanta: Society of Biblical Literature, 2004.

Houston, Walter. *Purity and Monotheism: Clean and Unclean Animals in Biblical Law*. England: JSOT, 1993.

Kass, Leon. *The Hungry Soul: Eating and the Perfecting of Our Nature*. New York: Free Press, 1994.

Kunin, Seth Daniel. *We Think What We Eat: Structuralist Analysis of Israelite Food Rules and Other Mythological and Cultural Domains*. London: T&T Clark, 2004.

Mein, Andrew. *Ezekiel and the Ethics of Exile*. Oxford: Oxford University Press, 2001.

Middleton, J. Richard. *The Liberating Image: The Imago Dei in Genesis 1*. Grand Rapids: Brazos, 2005.

Milgrom, Jacob. "Ethics and Ritual: The Foundation of the Biblical Dietary Laws." In *Religion and Law: Biblical-Judaic and Islamic Perspectives*, edited by Edwin Brown Firmage, Bernard G. Weiss, and John W. Welch, 159–92. Winona Lake, IN: Eisenbrauns, 1990.

————. *The JPS Torah Commentary: Numbers*. Philadelphia: Jewish Publication Society, 1990.

————. *Leviticus 1–16: A New Translation with Introduction and Commentary*. Anchor Bible Series 3. New York: Doubleday, 1991.

————. *Leviticus 17–22: A New Translation with Introduction and Commentary*. Anchor Bible Series 3. New York: Doubleday, 2000.

Soler, Jean. "The Semiotics of Food in the Bible." In *Food and Drink in History*, edited by Robert Forster and Orest Ranum, 126–38. Baltimore: Johns Hopkins University Press, 1979.

Soloveichik, Meir. "Locusts, Giraffes, and the Meaning of Kashrut." *Azure* 23 (2006): 62–96.

Weiss, Daniel H. "Direct Divine Sanction, the Prohibition of Bloodshed, and the Individual as Image of God in Classical Rabbinic Literature." *Journal of the Society of Christian Ethics* 32, no. 2 (2012): 23–38.

Wright, David P. "Observations on the Ethical Foundations of the Biblical Dietary Laws: A Response to Jacob Milgrom." In *Religion and Law: Biblical-Judaic and Islamic Perspectives*, edited by Edwin B. Firmage, Bernard G. Weiss, and John W. Welch, 193–98. Winona Lake, IN: Eisenbrauns, 1990.

14

The Virtues of Keeping Kosher

ELLIOT RATZMAN

My Kosher Problem and Ours

The vast majority of Jews today do not keep kosher. Yet in the United States, intracommunal events are often held to the "frummest common denominator"[1]—that is, an Orthodox standard of kosher law is generally followed, although only about 10 percent of American Jews are Orthodox.[2] Typically Orthodox-certified kosher caterers are employed or carefully packaged kosher meals are specially ordered, sometimes at some expense and, if my experience is representative, usually with a diminished quality. The demands that the kosher-observant minority make on Jewish communal institutions in America are often, and dubiously, advocated in the name of pluralism. The argument goes like this: even unobservant Jews do not object to eating food that happens to be kosher, so why not simply have all food meet an Orthodox standard? In practice, however, such accommodation of Orthodox strictures often sidelines other Jews and Jewish concerns.

During my work in organizations committed to following Orthodox interpretations of kosher law, in my impatient moments, I and many others like me have sometimes found ourselves annoyed with the insistence on certain forms of kosher supervision where concern to meet Orthodox standards is undertaken *at the expense of justice and loving-kindness*. The attention to what is usually called the "ritual" dimension of kosher laws—for example, strictures separating dairy and meat, forbidding pork, or forbidding the consumption of almost invisible insects that often inhabit broccoli and lettuce—seem to take up all the available bandwidth that Jewish institutions are willing to put into food preparation. Such prioritization of the aspects of kosher law that have no obvious rational utility have made me and many others look unkindly on Orthodox practices, seeing their attention to kosher supervision as more often than not functioning at the expense of attention to intercommunal conduct, justice, and ethics. This would not be true of all Orthodox institutions and certainly not true of all Orthodox-identified Jews; it is perhaps better to speak of Orthodoxies. Yet rightly or wrongly, for many liberal Jews like myself, there is a strongly felt antipathy that arises from our ongoing experience of diverse ethical initiatives—from reducing packaging waste to reducing cruelty in meat production—being thwarted to accommodate the stringencies of contemporary kosher supervision.

Yet the strict tradition may be on to something. Rather than continuing this debate in its familiar form in which ritual and ethics are pitted against one another as competing concerns, the approach I advocate here reframes kosher observance as a unifying spiritual discipline. As we will see, approaching kosher observance as a spiritual discipline provides a model that could potentially appeal to the full range of Jewish communities from Orthodox to secular.

As demonstrated in the preceding chapters focused on history, kashrut (kosher law) has been one symbolic battleground on which different forms of Judaism (Judaisms) have fought. With modernity, attention to and anxiety over kashrut has intensified among many Orthodox Jewish communities.[3] For most non-Orthodox Jews, however, the meaning and substance of kosher has been bound up in the changing assessments of *halakhah* (Jewish law), especially regarding the ethical utility of specific burdensome strictures. What I will be calling "right" Jewish discourse emphasizes divine command, covenant, chosenness, and the priority of maintaining tradition against the headwinds of modernity; it is most commonly—but not exclusively—associated with Orthodoxies. What I will call "left" modern Jewish discourse emphasizes ethical reasoning about the meaning, essence, and practice of Judaism; it is most commonly—but not exclusively—associated with liberal, non-Orthodox Judaisms.[4]

I argue that the practice of kashrut in the modern context—whether by the right or the left—has neglected to incorporate an indispensable version of this ethical recasting, the *language of virtue* in the pursuit of character cultivation. It is my contention that the recent revival of the

Jewish ethical self-reform movement known as *mussar* (ethical discipline) allows for a new way of understanding and justifying the practice of kashrut. This understanding appeals to the ethical sensibilities of modern Jews and many others who do not observe traditional Jewish law *while also honoring the traditional forms and rigor*, which so often get neglected or watered down by non-Orthodox Jews. Further, this neomussar framing of kashrut can be a bridge discourse between Orthodox and the non-Orthodox Jewish majority, between "right" and "left" styles of framing *halakhah*.

Left Recasting and Right Justification

To better appreciate the left recasting of kosher law, consider Arthur Waskow, one of the leading thinkers of the Reconstructionist movement and the Jewish Renewal style who has much to say about Jewish dietary practices in his definitive *Down to Earth Judaism: Food, Money, Sex and the Rest of Life*.[5] Waskow, a radical in the 1960s who was one of the first to "return" to the left-wing liberatory potential of Jewish tradition, set out a number of now-familiar proposals for expanding kosher laws to include ecokosher and tzedek kosher. In this seminal text, Waskow highlighted the interpersonal and social dimension of food, eating together, and attending to workers and to the earth. Waskow noted the liberationist use for fasting and of living within (environmental) limits. However, Waskow's artful discussion of kashrut says nothing about the possibility of kosher practice as traditionally conceived, and the Jewish food practices he advocates would seem foreign to most Orthodox Jews.

Waskow's orienting kashrut toward left-political projects has by now peppered progressive Jewish discourse and informed several generations of non-Orthodox rabbinic students. Waskow's own pioneering *Freedom Seder* Haggadah was followed by the Passover *Haggadah for the Liberated Lamb*, a vegetarian's meditation on a central carnivorous ritual. Vegetarian and vegan Jews have recast religious rituals—and offered religious justifications—for these left, nontraditional practices.[6]

Ecokosher, tzedek kosher, and other overlays of valid but nontraditional, agendas are the dominant left adaptions of kashrut. Most Jews who would be attracted to these projects will most likely forego adhering to the traditional separation of plates, of the concern with ritual purity and cleanliness of the preparation of foods, of the long list of restrictions that traditional Jews have to worry about. These traditional practices are most often dismissed as having little to do with social justice or inter-personal ethics and thus are thought to be unimportant.[7]

Representatives of "right-wing" Jewish discourse have been less appealing to non-Orthodox Jews, generally speaking to and for other already kosher-observant Jews. Yet recent traditionalist thinkers have contributed to a legacy of rational reflection on the meaning and logic of specific practices. One such attempt is the Orthodox Rabbi Meir Soloveichik's fine attempt to devise a reflection that is informed by both Jewish theology and secular scholarship.

Soloveichik's argument is that previous attempts by traditional Jews—from medieval authority Maimonides to neoconservative author Leon Kass—to explain the meaning of the specific biblical dietary rules are inadequate. For Soloveichik, the meaning of the specific biblical rules are important and hinted at in the Bible's explanation of their func-tion in Leviticus 20: the separation of Jews from gentiles. The Jewish diet is "utilized as an expression of the Jewish relationship with God"[8]— that is, the God that seeks to forge Israel as a holy people. As also dis-cussed in Daniel Weiss's chapter in this volume, the people separate foods just as God has separated Israel from all other nations. "God wishes for the Jew, in encountering creation, and most specifically created life, to be confronted constantly by his Jewishness," and yet "he remains mysti-fied by the method of expression."[9] For Soloveichik, "particular animals have been chosen for the Jewish diet in order to serve as an expression of Jewish chosenness."[10] That is, "just as God can choose a minority of the animals for the Jewish table, the Jews, despite being a persecuted and exiled minority, can remain the chosen of God."[11] However, there will always be some dimension of mystery in the biblical kosher laws, and thus they "inspire not arrogance, but humility."[12]

While Soloveichik offers a stimulating interpretation of the biblical strictures, he does not explain why Jews should strive to observe kashrut in its current elaborated versions. For his observant audience, he simply does not need to do this. What rankles me and many other nontradi-tional Jews is less, for example, the prohibition of pork (though some object to even that) and more the insistence that a *mashgiach* (kosher supervisor) needs to verify the compatibility of this or that specific food arrangement with an Orthodox interpretation of Jewish law. Why should the fussy details, often including strictures adopted quite recently, be attended to with such rigor while biblical injunctions to labor justice receive far less communal attention? Traditional*ism*, that ideological commitment to reifying traditional practice as a bulwark against social and moral declension, is one possible argument that sidesteps the question of the meaning of specific practices. Kosher practice continues simply because "it is commanded" and the accepted communal norm. Of course, within the Orthodox world, not all discourse is about defending the traditional status quo. The scandal over the labor practices at the Agriprocessors slaughterhouse discussed in this book in the chapter by Moses Pava, himself an Orthodox Jew, has both captured the attention of non-Orthodox observers and inspired an Orthodox social justice movement around labor and environmental aspects of kashrut.[13] A mussar approach potentially reduces the distance between left-wing approaches of adaption, like Waskow's, and more right-wing approaches of traditionalism, like Soloveichik's.

Mussar and the Neomussar Movement

The mussar movement began as a movement of observant Jews in tension with the ecstatic, mystical, and pietist trends of Hasidism in the eighteenth and nineteenth centuries. Mussar often embraced an austere style that sought to strengthen character through an eclectic mix of self-examination, group criticism, intersocial experimentation, and practical tracking of character traits.[14] Mussar pulled from eclectic sources but was firmly grounded in—indeed, it assumed—a traditionally Jewish-observant environment.

This movement—unlike the ecstatic Hasidism—focused on the observance of Jewish law, on the examination of one's intentions, and on the minute details of customary practices. To the modern mind, it was not "ethical" but another version of pious austerity or "moralism" dedicated to rooting out masturbation and unclean thoughts.[15] By the beginning of the twentieth century, the mussar movement created a subculture of near-ascetic yeshivas, wrapped up with the discourse of anxiety. This movement was largely unknown to the non-Orthodox Jewish world until recent decades.

What I call the "neomussar" movement emerged in Philadelphia in the 2000s through the organization of Rabbi Ira Stone, a Conservative denomination pulpit rabbi who also taught Jewish thought and mussar at the Jewish Theological Seminary and Reconstructionist Rabbinic College seminaries.[16] Stone's experimental mussar groups entail a collective study of traditional mussar texts, weekly meetings, journaling, and other accoutrements adapted from the original movement. In contrast to the traditional emphasis on ritual purity, Stone's account of mussar is refracted, in part, through the teachings of the influential French Jewish philosopher Emmanuel Levinas.[17] Levinas, who is attributed with catalyzing an "ethical turn" in continental philosophy in the 1990s, was himself inspired by the historical mussar movement.

Levinas's ethical discourse entails the centrality of "the Other" as the object of one's concern. Levinas's phenomenology of ethics is a discourse of radical responsibility in which one is drawn out of the concerns of the self toward the "needs of the Other."[18] Given that there are always many "others"—not just one—Levinas asserts that one's "infinite responsibility" to the Other is always mediated. Mediation, at its best, avoids arbitrariness through the mechanisms of reasons embodied in law, specifically Jewish law. In sum, Jewish law is the appropriate format by which one figures out, through the community and with the tradition, what one's responsibilities are to the numerous "others" in the world.[19] For Levinas, Jewish law—its process, interpretation, and customary practice—is the model for truly human life.[20] Not that Levinas—or any of these thinkers, for that matter—believe that merely observing Jewish law makes for ethical perfection. Indeed, the emphasis in the mussar movement is on the specific procedural virtues—including supererogation (going beyond one's duty), intention, and character structure—that keep the otherwise obligatory forms of Jewish law from becoming ossified. For Levinas, it is the reminder of the actual human Other—a sort of microcosmic reflection of God, the superhuman Other—that disrupts any staid system of law or routinized ethics. The Other disrupts but disrupts within a framework of ethics, a scaffolding that keeps the traditional Jew along the path of piety but also with built-in opportunities for reflection, revision, perfectionist striving, and supererogatory acts.

The traditional mussar movement was most often framed in the language of piety—oriented toward one's duties to God by upholding

Torah and halakhah. Neomussar is first and foremost concerned with the Other. Stone's theology of the *mitzvot*/commandments holds that God's law is—or ought to be—always already subordinated to the "needs of the Other." Living a Jewish life is essentially one dedicated to "bearing the burden of the Other."

In short, for Stone keeping Jewish law—like kashrut—is not about divine command in itself but has as its rationale an *ethical-practical* reason. As Levinas notes, "No intrinsic power is accorded to the ritual gesture, but without it the soul cannot be raised up to God."[21] To put it more directly, by taking ritual law as "divine command," our attention is reoriented to the needs of the Other, providing strong roots that make possible the fruits of ethical living.

Beyond the Ritual-Ethical Binary: A Neomussar Kashrut

At this point, we might recall the modern distinction between ethical and ritual commandments. In brief, the largest Jewish movements, from Reform to revolutionary and secular, have been highly critical of the "ritual" commandments—especially Sabbath strictures and dietary practices—and looked favorably upon the ethical: the imperative to do justice, show mercy, attend to the poor and downtrodden, and so forth. In Stone's neomussar system, this negative assessment of "ritual" law is profoundly challenged. Stone redescribes ritual law as the ingenious technique for the development of virtuous agents. That is, Jewish ritual is a tool for making practitioners ethical through the cultivation of character. How does this work? Let me briefly explain four interconnected ways that the ritual practice of keeping kosher helps create character.

Interruption

First, mitzvot—biblically commanded practices as distilled, explained, and expanded by the rabbis—is an *interrupting practice*. For Stone, "interruption" means that our quotidian mind-set, which is mostly concerned with the needs of the self, is disrupted by Judaism's regulated series of prescribed imperatives. Jews are always "on the clock," having certain responsibilities—from prayer quorum, to holidays, to dietary regulations—that interrupt modern life's obscuration of the needs of the other. Every prayer and every traditional, nonutilitarian practice is a reminder of one's imperative to serve the other, to attend to the other. Stone also uses Levinas's language of "awakening" oneself to the other. Other attending is a familiar moral descriptor; dietary decisions are the mechanism for punctuating a day with reminders to live a "responsible life."

Training Attention

Second, keeping kosher is *training for attention*. For the modern Jew, choosing to engage in nonutilitarian behavior is a moment-to-moment decision. This is, perhaps, strictly a modern phenomenon in that most Jews today do not live in contexts in which kashrut observance is expected, assumed, and enforced. To keep kosher is a daily choice, a radical choice, in modern contexts. Some other recent theologians, such as Michael Fishbane, have framed the observance of mitzvot as a means of "attunement"—calibrating one's being toward cosmic holiness.[22] Stone's neomussar is attunement made actionable through a concern not with the holiness of the world but with one's obligations to the Other.

A set of regulations, prohibitions, and themes such as the system of kashrut is one such form of training. It is not about the specific kosher customs but the entire process of regulating attention. In actual practice, such systems do not automatically create humans more attentive to those who suffer. However, from a neomussar perspective, training for attention through whatever means ought to be "bent" toward the Other, directed toward responsibility toward others as the highest form of holy activity.

Symbolism

Third, a neomussar perspective sees the *important symbolism of the kosher practice as themed toward mortality, holiness, and ethics.* Along with its use value as a mindfulness practice, the symbolism of kosher—the meaning one can make of the system—is also relevant. Stone's early writings on kosher emphasized the degree to which food reminds us of our mortality.[23] Stone writes that kashrut functions as "life-giving death" that "reduce[s] the weight of death" by an "arbitrary disciplining of the urge to eat," making "us aware that we are dealing with death" as a "method for introducing compassion."[24] Kosher eating inculcates an attention to mortality and thus, ideally, compassion for others.

Offsetting Vices

Fourth, the mussar and neomussar tradition sees kosher eating *as a means of offsetting other readily identifiable "vices" and encouraging other "virtues."* As with many practices in Judaism, kosher eating is seen as a means—symbolically and practically—of curbing appetite, of regulating nature tooth and claw, overlaying human's eating-in-the-state-of-nature with normative limits. For example, as discussed further in Aaron Gross's chapter in this volume, ideally, animals are killed with a minimum of cruelty. In addition, food is separated, and appetites are disciplined. For neomussar, it is precisely the nonutility of the tradition that serves as the special mechanism for "interrupting" modern life, for training the moral agent, for cultivating character traits through symbol, and for the disciplining of appetites.

To come full circle, I wish to note that overcoming the ritual-ethical binary in this way has distinct advantages over other "religioethical"[25] interpretations of the biblical dietary laws, such as the descriptive interpretation presented by Weiss in this volume. These interpretations have typically focused exclusively on the Hebrew Bible and failed to take into account the long history of interpreting these laws found in rabbinic Judaisms. Consider the work of the influential anthropologist Mary Douglas, who in 1993 proposed a novel account of the dietary laws of the Hebrew Bible.[26] She revised her earlier theory developed in the 1960s (discussed in Weiss's chapter) and explored the relationship of the biblical dietary laws and biblical ethics. She argued that the modern—and often Protestant—distinction between, on the one hand, the ethical concerns of the Bible as exemplified by the biblical prophets (the "ethics of the prophets") and, on the other hand, the dietary laws found especially in the Levitical holiness codes was a bankrupt distinction, one too often deployed to devalue biblical dietary laws specifically and the holiness codes in general. Douglas argued that the dietary laws were both symbolic presentations of holiness *and* actual practices of justice and honor.

Douglas argued that the biblical authors forbid consumption of certain classes of animals because these animals *exemplified vulnerability*. Forbidden animals, at least some of them, were the "widows, orphans, and strangers" of the animal kingdom. If her reading or similar religioethical readings like Weiss's are correct, the ethics of the prophets permeates even the seemingly arbitrary holiness codes and kosher laws.

Douglas's, Weiss's, and similar religioethical readings can be persuasive attempts to dissolve the pernicious distinction between "ritual laws" and "ethical laws" in the Bible, thereby restoring the law in general and biblical dietary practices in particular to a place of respect among antinomians from Reform Jews to Reformist Christians. However, they still neglect the robust development of kosher laws initiated by the rabbinic tradition in the first centuries of the Common Era and continued in today's detailed Orthodox practices. It is here that Stone's vision of neomussar can do for the rabbinic tradition—and thus do for Jews committed to traditional kashrut observance—what Douglas and other religioethical interpreters do for the biblical tradition: dissolve the distinction between ritual and ethical law. This takes us beyond both left recasting of the dietary laws and right justification of them, redescribing kosher law as a sort of mindfulness discipline that helps form the contours of a responsible life.

NOTES

1. *Frum* = observant of traditional Jewish law.
2. For discussion, see "What We Talk about When We Talk about the Menu," *New York Jewish Week*, May 12, 2016, http://jewishweek.timesofisrael.com.
3. For an overview, see chapter 4 in this collection.
4. This distinction between left and right is a rough heuristic. Certain modern traditional Jewish thinkers have combined both "left" and "right" aspects in explicating how and why modern Jews should abide by halakhic strictures. The Orthodox voices calling for the logical extension of kashrut to questions of worker and animal suffering are two such examples.
5. Waskow, *Down-to-Earth Judaism*.
6. Notably, philosopher Steven Schwarzschild argued that vegetarianism (and pacifism and socialism) were inseparable from the "messianic ethics" incumbent on all Jews.
7. See, for example, Ellen Posman's findings on the class profile of Jewish vegetarians in "Veggieburger in Paradise: Food as World-Transforming in Contemporary American Buddhism and Judaism," in *Eating in Eden: Food and American*

Utopias, ed. Etta M. Madden and Martha L. Finch (Lincoln: University of Nebraska, 2006).

8. Soloveichik, "Locusts, Giraffes, and the Meaning of Kashrut."

9. Soloveichik, 14.

10. Soloveichik, 19.

11. Soloveichik, 20.

12. Soloveichik, 14.

13. For a broad overview, see Maria Diemling, "The Politics of Food: *Kashrut*, Food Choices, and Social Justice (*Tikkun Olam*)," *Jewish Culture and History* 16, no. 2 (2015): 178–95.

14. One such technique was drawn from Benjamin Franklin's auditing of various character traits. He created a worksheet for attending to the virtues that can be seen in his autobiography. While the tactic may have been drawn from the ancient Greeks, the list of virtues and their auditing sheet found its way into the mussar movement. On Franklin's influence on the mussar movement, see Nancy Sinkoff, "Benjamin Franklin in Eastern Europe: Cultural Appropriation in the age of Enlightenment," *Journal of the History of Ideas* 61, no. 1 (2000): 133–52.

15. See the infamously negative portrait of mussar culture in Chaim Grade's *The Yeshiva*, trans. Curt Leviant (Indianapolis: Bobbs-Merrill, 1976).

16. See Stone, *A Responsible Life*. See also Ira Stone, "From Middot to Mitzvot," *Conservative Judaism* 57, no. 4 (2005): 18–25.

17. Levinas is perhaps the foremost continental philosopher of ethics—ethical phenomenology—of the second half of the twentieth century, influencing thinkers as diverse as Simone DeBeauvoir, Gustavo Gutierrez, and Jacques Derrida. Levinas's advocacy of halakha as an ethical discipline has been largely overlooked by his philosophical fans.

18. For Stone's reading of Levinas's hermeneutics, see *Reading Levinas/Reading Talmud: An Introduction* (Philadelphia: Jewish Publication Society, 1998).

19. Levinas sketches his position that ritual law is an ethical discipline only in various interviews. For example, "The law is effort. The daily fidelity to the ritual gesture demands a courage that is calmer, nobler and greater than that of the warrior"; *Difficult Freedom*, 19.

20. Levinas writes, "And Rabbi Meir, one of the chief Doctors of the Law, has ventured to say that a pagan who knows the Torah is the equal of the High Priest. This indicates the degree to which the notion of Israel can be separated, in the Talmud, from any historical, national, local or racial notion"; *Difficult Freedom*, 22. Israel's ritual law is one tool for managing a community's responsibilities but not a method that all peoples should adapt wholesale. Levinas elsewhere acknowledges various legal systems and "national literatures" present in the cultures of other peoples. On this, see his discussion with Phillipe Nemo in *Ethics and Infinity* (Pittsburgh: Duquesne University Press, 1985), 21–23.

21. Levinas is here commenting on ritual regulations regarding touching a corpse. *Difficult Freedom*, 18.

22. Fishbane's beautiful theology of Judaism lacks—but is compatible with—a thoroughgoing ethical project. See Fishbane, *Sacred Attunement*.

23. Compare with the ethical symbolism found by Daniel Weiss in chapter 13 in this volume.

24. Stone, *Seeking the Path to Life: Theological Meditations on God and the Nature of People, Love, Life and Death* (Burlington, VT: Jewish Lights, 1995), 82, 83.

25. For discussion of religiopolitical interpretations of the biblical dietary laws, see chapter 1 in this book.

26. Douglas, "Forbidden Animals of Leviticus." Compare her chapter "Abominations of Leviticus" in *Purity and Danger* (London: Routledge, 1966), 42–58.

SELECT BIBLIOGRAPHY

Douglas, Mary. "The Forbidden Animals of Leviticus." *Journal Study of Old Testament* 59 (1993): 3–23.

Fishbane, Michael. *Sacred Attunement: A Jewish Theology*. Chicago: University of Chicago Press, 2008.

Levinas, Emmanuel. *Difficult Freedom: Essays on Judaism*. Baltimore: Johns Hopkins University Press, 1990.

Soloveichik, Meir. "Locusts, Giraffes, and the Meaning of Kashrut." *Azure*, no. 23 (2006). http://azure.org.il.

Stone, Ira. *A Responsible Life: The Spiritual Path of Mussar*. New York: Aviv, 2006.

Waskow, Arthur. *Down-to-Earth Judaism: Food, Money, Sex, and the Rest of Life*. San Francisco: HarperCollins, 1997.

15

Jewish Ethics, the Kosher Industry, and the Fall of Agriprocessors

MOSES PAVA

Imagination over dogma, vulnerability over serenity, aspiration over obligation, comedy over tragedy, hope over experience, prophecy over memory, surprise over repetition, the personal over the impersonal, time over eternity, life over everything.
—Roberto Mangabeira Unger[1]

The dignity of difference is at the heart of the Bible's command to love the stranger.
—Rabbi Jonathan Sacks[2]

In Leviticus, the Bible directs us to "love your neighbor as yourself" (19:18). This is a difficult principle to achieve. It is useful to conceive of this more as an aspiration and a promise about human potential than as a specific rule of behavior. It points us in the right direction, but it does not necessarily tell us how to get there.

Loving one's neighbor also implies not just a change in behavior but a change in attitude as well. To love someone is to respect and trust that person, to care and feel compassion for him or her, and to open oneself up to him or her. In the Jewish tradition, it is understood by some as the single most encompassing principle of the entire Torah. The great sage Hillel famously summarized this two thousand years ago: "That which is hateful to you, do not do to your neighbor. That is the whole Torah; the rest is commentary. Go and study it."

Just a few verses later, however, the Bible points us in a different direction: "The stranger that sojourns with you shall be unto you as the homeborn among you, and you shall love him as yourself; for you were strangers in the land of Egypt" (Leviticus 19:34).[3] This principle too is better thought of as an aspiration rather than as a simple rule of behavior. But this mitzvah is considerably more radical and demanding than the first one. Through loving one's neighbor, community is strengthened as existing interpersonal relationships become more deeply felt. Loving the stranger, however, challenges the very notion of a static and unchanging community. Who is this stranger who is neither friend nor enemy? To love the stranger requires an imaginative leap of faith into unknown and uncharted territories.

As we contemplate the meaning of loving the stranger, perhaps it strikes us as an odd and paradoxical call. How can one love a stranger who by definition is unknown to us? It asks us to cross an ambiguous and mysterious boundary that most of us, most of the time, are not especially comfortable or inclined to traverse. It not just demands a thickening of already familiar community ties but promises the possibility of a broadening and an enlarging of community. It is not simply context preserving, but it is context transforming.[4] We are asked to bring the outsider inside and thus to transform and to transcend our current conceptions of who "we" are.

We experience a constant tension between the centrifugal pull of loving one's neighbor and the centripetal push of learning to love the stranger. This chapter suggests that although it once made sense to think of the love of one's neighbor as a nearly all-encompassing view of ethics, as Hillel did, the call of contemporary life and its complexities demand a tilt in our perception toward an enhanced appreciation of our differences.

The contemporary rabbi Irwin Kula puts this newly emerging view of ethics as follows: We need to "see as many sparks as possible, to sink into the messiness, to fall in love with multiplicity. We need to tune in to the conversation that is always going on among our many selves, and the dialogue, the contradictions, the harmony, and the dissonance that fills the world."[5] He calls this evolving attitude "sacred messiness." And the call of this hour, more often than not, is to immerse ourselves in this sacred messiness and not to run away from it, Jonah-like, toward safety prematurely.[6]

This chapter immerses us in this messiness by considering how we might go beyond more traditional interpretations of the mitzvah (commandment) to love the stranger. To help bring this potentially abstract injunction down to earth, I ground this exploration in the pragmatic world of business ethics. I consider two cases, one in the textile industry and the other in the kosher meat industry. The ethical issues I raise are not unique to the food industry; that said, as we will see, these questions hit especially hard in the contemporary food industry, including the kosher industry, where immigrant labor often plays an outsized role.

Moving beyond the Traditional Interpretation of Loving the Stranger

The mitzvah of loving the stranger has been officially on the books in Judaism from time immemorial; however, its traditional meaning has been (perhaps not surprisingly) limited dramatically. From a traditional Jewish point of view, the term for stranger used in this biblical verse (*ger* in Hebrew) has been almost universally translated as a proselyte or convert to Judaism. The mitzvah has therefore historically been understood as a special case of the broader principle of loving ones neighbor and not as a separately identifiable push into uncharted territories.

The rabbis of the Talmudic era (roughly the beginning of the Common Era to 600 CE) understood this verse as a special obligation to treat newcomers to Judaism in a favorable way. Although these same rabbis argue that converts in Judaism possess nearly the exact same rights and obligations as born Jews, they were nevertheless especially concerned about the process of assimilation, warning explicitly, for example, that you should not remind the convert about his or her "idolatrous background."

My point in this chapter is not that this traditional interpretation is wrong. It remains a creative, appropriate, and timely understanding of the biblical material given the cultural demands of antiquity and the Middle Ages.[7] The point here is that we should not let the heavy weight of this authoritative insight obscure our own contemporary ability to create meaning with this text. What else might this text say to us today?

Balancing the Needs of Neighbors and Strangers
in the Real World: The Case of Aaron Feuerstein

It is relatively easy to make the theoretical point that we need to balance the needs of our own community against the needs of others outside of our community. But how does one proceed in practice? Consider the case of textile entrepreneur Aaron Feuerstein and his management of Malden Mills, which I will shortly contrastwith the main case study of this chapter, the rise and fall of Agriprocessors, one of the nation's largest purveyors of kosher meat.[8]

By anyone's definition, Aaron Feuerstein has spent most of his life as a successful entrepreneur. In 1995, his company, Malden Mills, employed 3,100 union workers and generated $400 million in revenue. Malden Mills owned the patent on Polartec Fleece, an extremely lightweight synthetic fiber, made primarily from recycled products, that keeps wearers warm and dry. This product was so innovative that *Time* magazine named Polartec one of the greatest inventions of the twentieth century. At the same time that General Electric (GE) and other well-known companies were terminating employees and relocating overseas in search of cheap labor, Malden Mills was increasing its workforce in Lawrence, Massachusetts, one of the most depressed areas of the country, and paying its employees above average wages.

Tragedy struck on the very same night Feuerstein was joyously celebrating his seventieth birthday with relatives and friends. On December 11, 1995, the worst industrial fire in Massachusetts history almost completely destroyed his manufacturing facilities. Feuerstein now faced one of the most excruciatingly difficult decisions of his long business career. He could pocket the $300 million in insurance and retire. He could use the insurance money and relocate the business overseas. Or he could recommit himself to Lawrence and to the guiding principles of his long and successful business career.

Less than a week after the fire, Feuerstein publicly committed himself to remaining in Lawrence and rebuilding the factory. Later, explaining his actions, he paraphrased the Talmud: "When all is moral chaos, this is the time for you to be a mensch [honorable, decent person]."

In the end, it cost Feuerstein $25 million to keep his employees on the payroll. He invested $400 million to build a state-of-the-art factory, the first new textile mill in New England in more than one hundred years. But by 2001, Feuerstein could not make the payments on his borrowed funds, and he was forced into bankruptcy. In July 2004, Malden Mills Industries, now controlled by creditors, replaced Aaron Feuerstein as CEO of the company.

Looking back at the history of Malden Mills and Aaron Feuerstein, one is at pains to draw an easy lesson from all this. What does it mean when we read and reread Feuerstein's words in the midst of the battle? "We insist the business must be profitable. . . . But we also insist a business must have responsibility for it workers, for the community. It has a social obligation to figure out a strategy, which will be able to permit workers to make a living wage. There's a responsibility to the workforce, to this community."

Some have argued that Feuerstein abandoned his own entrepreneurial instincts. He failed to view business decision-making "solely on a perception of market opportunities."[9] I suggest, however, an altogether different interpretation. Feuerstein, in deciding to keep the factory open, continued to rely on his imagination, playfulness, creativity, risk taking, alertness to new opportunities, realism, efficiency, singleness of purpose, and independence of thought—all those essential values that constitute the spirit of entrepreneurship. But he exploited these characteristics in an attempt to deconstruct our conception of business success and failure. He tried to balance and integrate his traditional business acumen with other important social values. In doing so, he provided us with a deeper, messier, and more complex model of entrepreneurship, one that emphasizes social responsibility, community, compassion, interconnectedness, and a sense of wholeness.

In his seventieth year, Feuerstein was not invoking an ancient but outmoded set of religious values—*in fact I know of no Jewish source or rabbinic authorities that demand the kind of superogatory actions he chose to engage in*. Rather, Feuerstein is as much an innovator and an iconoclast in ethical life as he is in business life.

Aaron Feuerstein clearly sees the long-term dangers that injustice, poverty, and inequity pose to our economy and our country. He has identified the failure of traditional business answers, and he is searching, in the most noble spirit of entrepreneurship, for new and alternative solutions. In this sense, Aaron Feuerstein represents the best of the spirit of Jewish entrepreneurship.

Agriprocessors and the Tragedy of Moral Myopia:
The Case of Aaron Rubashkin

Aaron Feuerstein's case provides an example of ethical heroism. Feuerstein's example shatters our conventional understanding of morality and raises the bar for the rest of us. This second case, about another and very different Aaron, demonstrates what happens when sympathy and concern for strangers is completely missing.

Aaron Rubashkin moved to Brooklyn, New York, in 1952 and opened a butcher shop on Fourteenth Avenue in the heart of Boro Park. With his hard work, competitive spirit, dedication, skill, friendly demeanor, charm, and good luck and with the help from nearly everyone in his family, the shop prospered and grew into a Boro Park institution. As the business grew and diversified, the Rubashkin family became one of the most respected and honored Chabad Lubavitch families in Boro Park.

In 1987, Aaron Rubashkin purchased an abandoned meat-processing plant in Postville, Iowa. Under Rubashkin's direction and encouragement and his son Sholom's management, the business grew exponentially. The Rubashkins introduced modern, industrial practices and a new business model to a traditional and sleepy industry that had until then little or no apparent concern for efficiency and technology improvements. Under the aptly named business, Agriprocessors, they developed new ways for packaging meat to keep it fresh for longer periods of time. They introduced new and innovative ways of marketing and distributing their products. And they used a new technology for streamlining and speeding up the kosher slaughtering process. Agriprocessors kept overhead and costs low and was able to pass on some of its cost savings to the kosher consumer, especially in small Jewish communities that had, until then, not been able to get kosher meat. Interestingly, the majority of their output was sold as nonkosher.

According to *Cattle Buyers Weekly*, in 1997 Agriprocessors generated $80 million in sales. On November 6, 2008, the *New York Times* reported annual sales of $300 million. At its height, Agriprocessors provided 60 percent of all US kosher beef and 40 percent of kosher poultry.

Trouble in Iowa

Troubling reports about Agriprocessors' business practices first surfaced in 2000 with the publication of Stephen Bloom's *Postville: A Clash of Cultures in Heartland America*. In response to these early criticisms, Sholom Rubashkin explained to the author tersely, "We have stayed on this planet longer than anyone else because we believe our way is the right way. You start slipping, making changes here and there, and then you have nothing. We live by our rules here and they've got to understand that."

Agriprocessors, however, did learn an important lesson from this episode and began to actively manage its reputation and its business environment in a serious and purposeful way. The Rubashkins became large campaign donors to many politicians and befriended Postville town council members. They hired public relations experts and high-priced and well-placed attorneys.

As Agriprocessors continued to grow, however, it began to make news again. This time it was accused by PETA (People for the Ethical Treatment of Animals) for its inhumane slaughtering practices. PETA's 2004 accusations were buttressed by hours of videotapes documenting a highly unusual method of ritual slaughter and showing animals surviving for several minutes after the slaughter took place. In some cases, the animals got up and walked around while bleeding profusely with torn tracheas dangling from their necks.

Many diverse voices were raised in protest. According to Dr. Bernard Rollin, an animal expert at Colorado State University, "What was depicted on this video tape is one of the most atrocious incidents I have ever witnessed." Rabbi Ezra Raful of Israel's Chief Rabbinate stated, "You see there, it looks like he ripped out the trachea and esophagus. We do not allow the animal to be touched after the shehita [ritual slaughter] until the main part of the bleeding stops." Even according to Rabbi Tzvi Hersh Weinreb, the executive vice president of the Orthodox Union, the kashrut agency in charge of assuring kosher standards are being strictly enforced (they currently oversee over a half a million products), Agriprocessors slaughtering practices were "especially inhumane" and "generally unacceptable."

More Trouble in Iowa

The accusations of inhumane slaughtering practices, which were startling to kosher consumers and others, receded into the background as new allegations concerning the company's unfair treatment of foreign workers gained force. In May 2006, the *Forward*, a weekly Jewish newspaper, first broke the new story. The long list of allegations against Agriprocessors and Rubashkins included

- the lowest hourly wages of any slaughterhouse in the nation;
- workers' pay being shortchanged three or four hours per week regularly;
- exploitive rental agreements;
- several Occupational Safety and Health (OSHA) violations;
- environmental pollution;
- a supervisor alleged to be demanding bribes from workers;
- no pay to workers for preparation and cleanup time as required by an earlier Supreme Court decision;
- little or no safety instructions;
- widespread fear among the approximately eight hundred undocumented immigrant workers, mostly Latino and Latina, of being fired or reported to authorities; and
- financial fraud.

Executives at Agriprocessors denied any wrongdoing, but concerns about abuses persisted, ultimately attracting the attention of federal authorities.

In May 2008, US immigration agents entered the Postville plant and arrested more than three hundred Agriprocessors' workers on charges of using false social security numbers in what was described by the *Des Moines Register* as the "largest workplace raid in Iowa history."[10]

Despite this major setback and a slight fallback in demand on the part of kosher consumers, Agriprocessors continued its production for the next several months, finding and hiring new workers to replace those who were arrested.

Intense debates about the appropriate relationship between the ritual aspects of kosher law and ethics reemerged as several groups in the

Jewish community responded to growing allegations against Agriprocessors. Although Agriprocessors did have its defenders, most voices seemed to accept the basic veracity of the charges, expressed deep concern, and called for action to be taken.

Agriprocessors and Rubashkin's legal and ethical troubles, however, did not end with the May workplace raid and arrests. On September 9, 2008, Iowa's attorney general charged Aaron and Sholom Rubashkin and several other executives with more than nine thousand child labor law violations. The complaint stated that the company not only knowingly hired illegal immigrant workers but also knowingly hired minors to operate conveyor belts, meat grinders, circular saws, power washers, and power shears. There were thirty-two children under the age of eighteen working at the plant, and seven of these were younger than sixteen years of age.

On October 30, 2008, Aaron and Sholom Rubashkin were arrested on federal charges of immigration-related offenses. On November 14, 2008, Sholom Rubashkin was arrested again on charges of a multimillion-dollar bank fraud and was subsequently found guilty. He was sentenced to twenty-seven years in prison.

But the story doesn't end there. In late December 2017, after serving more than eight years in prison, President Donald Trump commuted Rubashkin's sentence, citing bipartisan support from congressional leaders across the political spectrum. This decision does not vacate Rubashkin's original conviction and leaves intact his term of supervised release and his restitution obligation.

Conclusion

This case is a complex ethical maze. It raises a host of difficult issues and questions with no obvious answers. There are conflicting versions of the story, many different interests among the various stakeholders (economic and otherwise), and several questions about the significance of the ritual aspects of kosher observance and its relation to ethical behavior. It raises deep questions about immigration policy and the appropriate role of business in society. In addition, I think the Jewish community *needs* to ask ourselves at the outset, How much of our emotional reactions and intuitive ethical responses to this scandal are based on our uneasiness regarding our own consumption of meat and our own responsibility as consumers, always demanding the lowest possible prices, in supporting the entire production process?

The fact is that the Rubashkins are part of a larger culture that is today uncertain about the best way to deal with immigrants. Should we adopt stricter immigration controls as many political conservatives and political liberals suggest? Should we adopt easier immigration policies and tightly monitor and control immigrant workers while they are here? What kind of rights should we grant to the temporary workers who live among us? How extensive should these rights be? None of these questions will be answered satisfactorily by expressing indignation and throwing the book at a single company.

The Jewish tradition recognizes the need for both the pull of loving your neighbor and the push of loving the stranger. Jewish ethics is about the ability to balance these forces against one another to create the energy to live meaningful and holy lives in the present moment. This was, no doubt, the aspiration of Aaron Feuerstein and Malden Mills. In striving to live an ethical life, we are like the captain of a yacht playing off the power of the wind against the opposite power of the keel to keep the boat moving in a straight line.

Most of us easily recognize that there is a kind of absurdity in loving the stranger but not loving one's neighbor. What kind of love would this really be? This chapter suggests, through the use of the Agriprocessors case, that there is another kind of absurdity, one more difficult to recognize but equally impossible. In the end, it is not possible to truly love one's neighbor (in the deepest sense) in the absence of loving the stranger. While the Rubashkin family, on the surface, was seemingly a model for loving one's coreligionists, in the long run, their love of their neighbor was itself tainted.

Just as there can be too little love, there can be too much love. If love is only directed to those already in one's closest orbit, it is a deficient and dangerous kind of love. The Rubashkin family, in this instance, has brought shame not only to themselves but to the Jewish people, whom they profess to love with such abundance. It does make sense to talk of love of one's neighbor as distinct from the love of the stranger, but we should never forget that these two kinds of love are really two sides of the same coin.

Shalom Rubashkin's behavior demonstrates a profound moral myopia. Not only does he fail to "love the stranger"; he seemingly doesn't even see the stranger. The philosopher John Dewey was surely correct when he noted that "it is sympathy which carries thought out beyond the self and which extends its scope till it approaches the universal as its limit. It is sympathy which saves consideration of consequences from degenerating into mere calculation, by rendering vivid the interest of others and urging us to give them the same weight as those which touch our own."[11] Where was this kind of sympathy demonstrated at Agriprocessors?

The case of Shalom Rubashkin demonstrates what can go wrong when there is a lack of moral imagination, too much love turned inward, little self-awareness, a good dose of greed, poor public policy, and a complete insensitivity to the needs of both animals and those members of society who are least well off. In their initial alleged mistreatment of animals, perhaps louder alarm bells should have been raised by the Jewish community. The Jewish tradition prohibits causing pain to animals for no reason, and perhaps those that break this commandment are already in more danger to cut corners in other domains as well.

Loving the stranger is not a panacea, nor is it a substitute for good federal regulations, but it is a necessary ingredient to help build a just and caring food system and ultimately a just and caring society. In a world of increasing migration and of broken public policy, Jewish ethical sources remind us of our inherent responsibility to continually broaden the circle of ethics, even as we continue to strive to love our neighbor.

NOTES

1. Unger, *Self Awakened*, 237.
2. Saks, *Dignity of Difference*.
3. This mitzvah is reiterated in the Bible in slightly different language as "Love you therefore the stranger; for you were strangers in the land of Egypt" (Deuteronomy 10:19).
4. Unger, *Self Awakened*.
5. Kula with Lowenthal, *Yearnings*, 303.

6. For an extended and insightful literary and psychological analysis of Jonah's flight, see Zornberg, "Jonah."

7. Unfortunately, even today this highly constrained reading of the text is particularly apt in some situations. For example, the National Council of Young Israel, an organization whose goal is "to foster and maintain a program of spiritual, cultural, social and communal activity towards the advancement and perpetuation of traditional Torah-true Judaism" (www.youngisrael.org), issued a memorandum on August 1, 2007, to its member synagogues banning converts from serving as synagogue presidents (see http://yucommentator.com). Such a ban is an unfortunate but explicit violation of the traditional understanding of loving the stranger despite the organization's professed goal of perpetuating "traditional" Judaism.

8. The material on Aaron Feuerstein has been adopted from Pava, *Jewish Ethics*.

9. Formaini, "Engine of Capitalist Process," 2.

10. Duara, Schulte, and Petroski, "Meatpacking Plant."

11. Garrison, *Dewey and Eros*, 38.

BIBLIOGRAPHY

Bonder, Nihon. *Our Immoral Soul: A Manifesto of Spiritual Disobedience*. Boston: Shambhala, 2001.

Duara, Nigel, Grant Schulte, and William Petroski. "Meatpacking Plant Raid Rattles Postville." *Des Moines Register*, May 13, 2008.

Formaini, Robert I. "The Engine of Capitalist Process: Entrepreneurs in Economic Theory." *Economic and Financial Review* Q IV (2001): 2–11.

Garrison, Jim. *Dewey and Eros*. New York: Teachers College Press, 1997.

Hartman, David. "Religious Diversity and the Millennium." *Jerusalem Post*, December 3, 1999.

Hertz, J. H., ed. *The Pentateuch and Hafiorahs*. London: Soncino, 1969.

Kula, Irwin, with Linda Lowenthal. *Yearnings: Embracing the Sacred Messiness of Life*. New York: Hyperion, 2006.

Marcano, Donna-Dale. "The Strangeness of the Racialized Subject: Confronting Kristeva's Foreigner." *Philosophy Today* 47 (2003): 161–67.

Pava, Moses L. *Jewish Ethics in a Post-Madoff World: A Case for Optimism*. New York: Palgrave Macmillan, 2011.

———. "The Spirit of Jewish Entrepreneurship." In *Entrepreneurship: Values and Responsibility*, edited by W. Gasparski and L. Ryan, 211–20. New York: Routledge, 2009.

Riskin, Shlomo. "Love the Stranger." *Jewish News* 61, no. 7 (2007): 53.

Sacks, Jonathan. "The Chief Rabbi's New Year Message BBC Online Religion and Ethics." 2001. Accessed November 11, 2008. www.chiefrabbi.org.

———. "The Dignity of Difference: 2007 Kenan Institute for Ethics Distinguished Lecture." 2007. Accessed August 2, 2018. http://rabbisacks.org.

Sarasvathy, Saras D. "Entrepreneurship as Economics with Imagination." *Business Ethics Quarterly* 11 (2001): 10–25.

Unger, Roberto Mangabeira. *The Self Awakened: Pragmatism Unbound*. Cambridge, MA: Harvard University Press, 2007.

Zornberg, Avivah Gottlieb. "Jonah: A Fantasy of Flight." *Psychoanalytic Dialogues* 18 (2008): 271–99.

16

A Satisfying Eating Ethic

JONATHAN K. CRANE

Eating well has long been a Jewish concern. From the earliest stories of the Bible, through the prophets and early rabbis, to medieval sages and commentators, and on to the modern period, Jews have wrestled with what eating well means.[1] They often urged eating practices that would promote health, not deteriorate it.[2] In evolutionary terms, Jews were to habituate themselves to proadaptive eating strategies instead of maladaptive ones. Though of course pre-nineteenth-century sources did not speak in evolutionary terms, they nonetheless discouraged such maladaptive eating strategies as continuous fasting for fasting's sake and, at the other extreme, feasting for feasting's sake.[3] Rather, Jews were to fast and feast only sparingly. They were to be done on certain holidays and were circumscribed by clear but not inflexible rules. For example, Yom Kippur is a day of complete fasting during which Jews are to consume neither liquid nor solid. These rules do not apply if one is ill, a minor, or pregnant or if one feels that fasting would be unreasonably deleterious to one's well-being. Conversely, Jews are to feast at Passover's Seder; they are to enjoy the bounty of the season, but only until midnight, when eating the *afikomen* signals the conclusion of consumption. By mandating a stopping point to the meal, it means that ceaseless eating is not only prohibited; it is to be abjured.

If extreme eating—too little or too much—is meant to be both highly regulated and only occasional, how are Jews to eat during the rest of the calendar year when no special celebrations require peculiar eating practices? What is a Jewish eating ethic that applies to everyday life? As this chapter will show, the Jewish textual tradition offers many and nuanced perspectives about an eating ethic that revolves around the notion of satisfaction.

Satiation, Satiety, and *Sove'a*

There are two aspects to satisfaction in relation to eating. The first, satiation, is inversely related to hunger. At the beginning of a meal, one's hunger is at its peak, and one's satiation is negligible. As one consumes and the belly fills, satiation increases and hunger depletes. Imagine these sensations plotted on a graph; as time passes, hunger curves down and satiation curves up. Where these two lines meet is called the satiation point. The other aspect to satisfaction is satiety. This is the state of being sated between meals. It begins when one stops eating one meal and ends when one begins the next. Though satiety diminishes over time as one's gut digests its contents and the body expends energy, it nonetheless is the state of noneating. If satiety is a state of being, or noun, satiation is a process, or verb. One *is* sated whereas one *satiates* oneself.[4]

Eating well, Judaically construed, involves paying attention to both aspects of satisfaction. It requires attending to satiation within a meal as well as to satiety between eating events. *Sove'a* is typically the Hebrew term for eating until one is satisfied.

In the Torah, Moses discusses this concept at length. He begins by reminding the Israelites of their radical dependence upon God: "God subjected you to the hardship of hunger and then gave you manna to eat, which neither you nor your fathers had ever known, in order to teach you that man does not live on bread alone, but that man may live on anything that Adonai decrees."[5] Just as they had relied upon God when they were struggling through the wastelands of the desert, so too were they to receive God's largess when they uphold God's commandments and enter the promised land: "For Adonai your God is bringing you into a good land, a land with streams and springs and fountains issuing from plain and hill; a land of wheat and barley, of vines, figs, and pomegranates, a land of olive trees and honey; a land where you may eat food without stint, where you will lack nothing; a land whose rocks are iron and from whose hills you can mine copper. When you have eaten and are sated, give thanks to Adonai your God for the good land which God has given you."[6] This last phrase—*achalta, sava'ata, uverachta* (literally, you [singular] will eat, you [singular] will be satisfied, and you [singular] will bless)—is the textual foundation for the *birkat hamazon*, the blessings Jews say after meals. Proper consumption requires each person to acknowledge that one's nourishment comes from the world beyond one's control; none other than God provides that which sustains each person.

Improper consumption, by contrast, is not humble but haughty:

> Take care lest you forget Adonai your God and fail to keep God's commandments, rules and laws, which I enjoin upon you today. When you have eaten your fill (*tochal v'sava'ata*), and have built fine houses to live in, and your herds and flocks have multiplied, and your silver and gold have increased, and everything you own has prospered, beware lest your heart grow haughty and you forget Adonai your God—who freed you from the land of Egypt, the house of bondage; who led you through the great and terrible wilderness . . . and you say to yourselves, "My own power and the might of my own hand have won this wealth for me." Remember that it is Adonai your God who gives you the power to get wealth, in fulfillment of the covenant that God made on oath with your fathers, as is still the case.[7]

Such hubris would eclipse God insofar as it would cause the consumer to forget God's liberating activities that brought the people out from Egypt. Worse, this self-congratulatory eating attitude would only lead to the grave, for it embodied the depravity and disobedience God abhorred and would eradicate.[8] In this kind of eating, because one is so full of oneself, there is no room to remember or acknowledge God.

Eating from self-satisfaction is thus a maladaptive and damned eating strategy. Eating to be sated is a proadaptive and theologically commendable eating strategy. Eating well requires each individual to situate oneself within a larger context, much of which transcends one's control.

Eating Well

As clear as Moses is about these kinds of alimentary satisfaction, however, he does not provide much concrete instruction about how to eat well on a daily basis. Perhaps we can gain insight from a different prophet, this time Elisha, who was known for enacting miracles, many of which involved food. For example, we read in 2 Kings that Elisha once neutralized a poisonous stew with flour.[9] The next miracle story in 2 Kings is most relevant here:

A man came from Baal-Shalishah and he brought the man of God [Elisha] some bread of the first reaping—twenty loaves of barley bread, and some fresh grain in his sack. And [Elisha] said, "Give it to the people and let them eat (*vayochelu*)." His attendant replied, "How can I set this before a hundred men?" But he said, "Give it to the people and let them eat (*vayochelu*). For thus said Adonai: They shall eat and have some left over (*achol v'hoter*)." So he set it before them; and when they had eaten, they had some left over (*vayochlu vayotru*), as Adonai had said.[10]

Elisha hereby feeds a multitude with just twenty loaves of bread and some kernels of grain, a feat Jesus would copy centuries later with bread and fish and five thousand people.[11] That so little food could feed so many is, indeed, miraculous. This opinion stems from looking at the story from the perspective of the provider, however. If we switch vantage points to that of the consumers, something different becomes apparent. The eaters did not consume everything provided them. Because they held themselves back from eating all that they could, leftovers remained. When eaters collectively eat less than they bodily can, more people can enjoy the repast.

According to the Babylonian Talmud, Elisha's immediate predecessor, Elijah, would teach this lesson of consumptive restraint to Rabbi Nathan in the second century CE.[12] Elijah says to Nathan, "Eat a third, drink a third, and retain a third." This could mean several things. It could mean to eat and drink a third of what is served, save a third, and eventually discard a third. It could also mean consume a third of what is served to allow others to consume a third each; that is, a meal of any size should or could satisfy several people. Such lessons orient the eater to respond to such external cues as the size of the meal and other potential eaters. The medieval rabbinic commentator Rashi would later explain, though, that it means to fill one's belly a third with food and a third with drink and leave a third of it empty.[13] For Rashi and probably for Elijah himself, eating well is not determined by what one sees on one's plate but rather solely by internal cues.

Elijah's lesson did not end there, however. Eating until one is two-thirds full has a rationale: "For when you become angry you will be filled to your capacity."[14] Elijah hereby speaks in terms Rabbi Nathan would understand. Rabbi Nathan, like many other rabbis until about the nineteenth century, understood the human body according to the prevailing Hippocratic and Galenic theories of human physiology—that is, a humoralist conceptualization. The dynamic balance of the four basic humors (black bile, yellow bile, phlegm, and blood) determined each person's temperament and health. Any imbalance of these humors would manifest personality disorders and fleshy ailments. Emotions too were physical things, a momentary sloshing of the humors that require physiological processing by the body. So when Elijah warns to leave room in one's belly, it is to allow room for the emotions to be metabolized, literally, alongside the ingested foodstuff. Rashi concurs, adding this graphic detail: "Anger fills your belly to its utmost capacity. So if you fill your innards with food and drink, when you become angry you will be split asunder."[15] Insofar as emotions are part and parcel of who one is, filling one's stomach with biology leaves insufficient room for biography. The consequence of stuffing oneself would be lethal.

Moses Maimonides, the great medieval legist and physician, ruled in his circa 1180 CE *Mishneh Torah* that "one should not eat until one's stomach is [very] full, but one should [only] eat until one's stomach is three-quarter's full."[16] Though Maimonides disagrees with Elijah's comparatively stringent two-thirds rule, they nevertheless agree that optimal eating is achieved by eating less than all that one can consume. In a letter to al-Malik al-Afdal Nfir al-Din 'Ali, the son of Saladin, sometime after 1193, Maimonides wrote, "Physicians all agree that taking a little food of bad quality is less harmful than taking much good and laudable food. This is because when a man takes bad foods and does not over-eat, they are digested well, and the organs derive from them all that is beneficial. . . . But in repletion, even if it is with well-prepared bread and laudable meat, the digestion will in no wise progress well."[17] Though ease of digestion and bodily health are compelling reasons to eat less than one's fullest capacity, in his earlier work, Maimonides offered another rationale: being healthy enough to know and understand God. "Since maintaining a healthy and sound body is among the ways of God—for one cannot understand or have any knowledge of the Creator, if he is ill—therefore, he must avoid that which harms the body and accustom himself to that which is healthful and helps the body become stronger. They are as follows: a person should never eat unless he is hungry, nor drink unless thirsty. . . ."[18] First among the ways that ensure one's being healthy enough to know God is the practice of refraining from eating between meals. Put in contemporary terms, when sated, don't eat, and conversely, eat only when no longer sated.

Sage eating also requires careful attention within meals too. As Maimonides says, "A learned sage should not be a glutton, but should eat foods according to the health of his body, and should not eat overly large meals, and should not rush to fill his belly as do those who fill themselves with food until they burst."[19] Rushing, perpetually eating and drinking, and glutting guts—such are the ways wicked people eat.[20] Sage eating, by contrast, is idiosyncratic (appropriate for an individual's body), modest (not filled to the brim), and spread out (meals are reasonably paced and spaced). Again, put in contemporary terms, eating well requires each individual to eat per his or her body's needs and only to the point of satiation.

Eating Ethically

These sources, among many others, depict an ongoing Jewish concern about eating and eating well in particular.[21] They promote both features of alimentary satisfaction: stopping consumption when one reaches the satiation point within a meal and not eating while sated between meals. Though these sources were composed in different geohistorical periods by authors concerned about different issues, they nonetheless share a common trope: eat more than nothing, but less than what one bodily can. Exceptions, of course, exist: as noted earlier, fasting and feasting punctuate the Judaic calendar. This proposed eating ethic thus applies for the rest of the year.

A question may arise whether eating and especially eating well is some form of ethics at all. I contend it is. Consider the fact that, for the most part, eaters today eat maladaptively. People are eating themselves to death, either by eating things that are inherently bad for them or eating badly (too much, too frequently, too little, and so on). Many lament the evidence of such poor eating habits: soaring weight-related illnesses, loss of productivity, and others, as well as the sequelae the contemporary food environment causes, like ecological degradation, extraordinary animal suffering, and perverse economic incentives. Contemporary eating harms eaters themselves as well as societies, animals, the environment, and so much more. Eating is no solipsistic activity occurring in a moral vacuum. As Maimonides discusses in his *Guide for the Perplexed*, eating's repercussions are fast, vast, and morally complex.[22] From every angle, eating is an ethically fraught enterprise. Ignoring this fact is itself a kind of ethical failure.[23]

The contemporary food environment inculcates inattention to our personal eating. Ads everywhere urge us to buy something to consume. Technology makes it possible for us to eat and drink anywhere anytime. Architecture and zoning enable us to get access to consumables quickly and conveniently. Manufactured foodstuffs are often substantially cheaper than unmanipulated ones, and they are often hyperpalatable, pumped full of kinds and quantities of salt, sugar, and fat our bodies do not need. In these and so many other ways, we live in a food environment that orients our eating to external cues. These cues, moreover, encourage us to eat nonstop until we are full and beyond. When others ask, "Are you full?" we worry when the answer is negative, and so we lift the fork again to our mouths. We eat despite and too often to spite ourselves.

Eating well, or at least the eating well I see Judaism endorsing, breaks dramatically from such outwardly oriented maladaptive eating strategies. The eating well Judaism promotes orients consumers to pay attention to internal cues. One is to eat more than nothing but less than what one bodily could consume. This involves stopping eating once the satiation point has been achieved, which is easily sensed by paying attention to the stomach's distension. Only individual eaters can pay attention to that. One is to eat what is appropriate for one's own peculiar body. No external authority—no diet guru, governmental agency, or giant corporation—can dictate or predict what any particular body needs; individual eaters are to discern this. One is to eat when hungry. The digestive track works best when given the opportunity to digest and evacuate its contents; constantly filling it with snacks and small meals undermines its effectiveness and efficiency. Knowing the features of one's own hunger requires listening to one's body, not to industries plying snacks.

Eating well, or until one is satisfied, reclaims and celebrates an internally oriented eating ethic. Ancient and modern philosophies as well as the cutting-edge science of metabolism corroborate that this eating strategy is as healthy for individuals as it is for civilizations generally.[24]

So a better question for us to ask than whether eating is a kind of ethics is whether anyone can afford—in any sense of that term—to continue to ask, "Am I full?" instead of "Am I satisfied?"

NOTES

1. In his 1991 interview, Derrida offers the most succinct version: "*How*, for goodness sakes, should one *eat well*?" Derrida, "'Eating Well,'" 115.

2. Maimonides's 1193 "Regimen of Health" is one of the clearest articulations of and directions for eating well in the medieval world. Maimonides, "Regimen of Health," 3–49.

3. Regarding fasting for fasting's sake, see Isaiah 58:3–5; Babylonian Talmud Ta'anit 11a; Babylonian Talmud Nedarim 10a. Regarding feasting for feasting's sake, see Numbers 11:3–36; Proverbs 23:1–3; Mishneh Torah, De'ot 4.15.

4. On the incredible contemporary science of satisfaction, see Blundell and Bellisle, *Satiation, Satiety and the Control of Food Intake*.

5. Deuteronomy 8:3. Biblical translations follow, for the most part, the New Jewish Publication Society (JPS) translation.

6. Deuteronomy 8:7–10.

7. Deuteronomy 8:11–18.

8. Deuteronomy 8:19–20.

9. 2 Kings 4:38–41.

10. 2 Kings 4:42–44.

11. John 6:11–13.

12. Babylonian Talmud Gittin 70a. See also Tosafot, Babylonian Talmud Niddah 24b, s.v. *achilato merubah mishetayato*.

13. Rashi, Babylonian Talmud Gittin 70a, s.v. *achul shalish*.

14. Babylonian Talmud Gittin 70a.

15. Rashi, Babylonian Talmud Gittin 70a, s.v. *ulchashteka'os*.

16. Mishneh Torah, De'ot 4.2. This ratio will be echoed later in Muslim circles, in such hadiths as Ibn Maajah, 3349, and al-Tirmidhi, 2380.

17. Maimonides, "Regimen of Health," 17.

18. Mishneh Torah, De'ot 4.1.

19. Mishneh Torah, De'ot 5.1.

20. Mishneh Torah, De'ot 5.1. See also Proverbs 13:25; Ibn Ezra on Proverbs 13:25.

21. For a more thorough examination of these and many other Jewish, Christian, and Islamic sources, see Crane, *Eating Ethically*.

22. *Moreh Nebukim*, 3:12.

23. On the moral vices of inattention, especially to food-related issues, see Jenni, "Vices of Inattention," 279–95.

24. See Crane, *Eating Ethically*.

BIBLIOGRAPHY

Blundell, John E., and France Bellisle, eds. *Satiation, Satiety and the Control of Food Intake*. Cambridge: Woodhead, 2013.

Crane, Jonathan K. *Eating Ethically: Religion and Science for a Better Diet*. New York: Columbia University Press, 2017.

Derrida, Jacques. "'Eating Well,' or Calculation of the Subject: An Interview with Jacques Derrida." In *Who Comes after the Subject?*, edited by Eduardo Cadava, Peter Connor, and Jean-Luc Nancy, 255–87. New York: Routledge, 1991.

Jenni, Kathie. "Vices of Inattention." *Journal of Applied Philosophy* 20, no. 3 (2003): 279–95.

Maimonides, Moses. "Regimen of Health / Fī Tadbīr Al-Ṣiḥḥah." Translated by Ariel Bar-Sela, Hebbel E. Hoff, and Elias Faris. *Transactions of the American Philosophical Society* 54, no. 4 (1964): 3–49.

17

The Ethics of Eating Animals

AARON S. GROSS

Eating Animals as Universally Fraught

A basic fact of human religious life is that killing and eating animals for food is not taken lightly. It is invariably the subject of intense regulations and often the subject of energetic disagreement.[1] Cross-cultural anthropological studies have revealed that of all known human activities regarding food, none generate more taboos than the consumption of meat, especially the meat of larger animals.[2] If you doubt the strength of these meat taboos today or think we have moved past such thinking, imagine inviting your neighbors over to barbecue a dog or cat and the reactions you might get.

If we have learned through our study of the Jewish case in this volume that food in general is always bound to identity, not all foods are of equal importance to human identities. Meat consistently influences people's sense of identity more than other foods.[3] As we will see, Jewish traditions are no exception.

The fact that meat plays an outsized role in human identity is one of the most secure facts of food studies, but explaining why this is so is more complicated. Much of the answer lies in the fact that meat comes from beings who share important similarities with humans, especially the capacity to suffer in many of the same ways humans do. There is widespread evidence of a general human discomfort with killing animals.[4] Seeing animals in pain is difficult for most humans, and one doesn't need to look far to see numerous examples of people moved to action by witnessing the plight of a suffering animal.[5] Humans may often choose to close off empathy with the animals we eat, but except for sociopaths, that empathy for animal others is always there as a potentiality.[6] It is simply a fact of human physiology that we have the brain structures and observational capacities to accurately identify some forms of animal suffering, to relate to them, and to care about them.

The spontaneous nature of human empathy for animals and the inevitable suffering bound to meat, even if it is minimized, makes meat *fraught* in culture generally and religion in particular. Unsurprisingly, in all the so-called world religions[7]—Judaism, Christianity, Islam, Hinduism, Buddhism, Daoism, and so forth—passionate human disagreements and ethical debates continue to shape the practices that allow or restrict eating animals in the lives of particular communities today. These disagreements and ethical concerns show no sign of fading anytime soon.[8]

The recent advent of factory farming has perhaps aggravated the tension between different human moral intuitions about the rightness or wrongness of eating animals. The practices of factory farming pose serious challenges to traditional ideas about how animals should be treated that are only now being realized, let alone responded to, by religious institutions. This chapter will not detail the nature of factory farming since good information is readily available, but as we turn to how Jews respond to this basic human predicament, it is worth noting that we do so in an era where animals arguably suffer more acutely than ever before and in numbers that few could conceive a generation ago.[9] As Yuval Noah Harari frames it, "If we accept a mere tenth of what animal-rights activists are claiming, then modern industrial agriculture might well be the greatest crime in history."[10] In the US alone, we consume nearly nine billion chickens annually—more than one hundred times what Americans ate per capita roughly a century ago.[11]

How do contemporary Jewish traditions respond to this universally common and fraught activity—eating animals—especially in an ethical register? Let us sketch a partial answer to this question by considering two stories: first, one told by contemporary Jewish novelist Jonathan Safran Foer in his 2009 nonfiction book critiquing the meat industry, *Eating Animals*, and second, the biblical narrative about eating animals found in Genesis 1 and 9, what I will call the biblical story of meat. These two stories straddle an immense territory from the popular appeal of contemporary nonfiction to the authoritative density of the Bible, from the private sphere of one Jewish-American family's history to the communally held narratives of the Jewish textual tradition. These stories can provide us a feel for how Jews explore ethical questions, in this case about eating animals, through sharing and interpreting *stories*.

A Family Story: Foer's Opening to *Eating Animals*

Foer built his international reputation through his first novel, *Everything Is Illuminated* (2002), which alternated between a fancifully imagined Eastern European Jewish past and a semiautobiographical account of Foer's real-life confrontation with his past as the grandchild of a Holocaust survivor. The book was translated into more than thirty languages and won him the National Jewish Book Award. Foer's second novel, *Extremely Loud and Incredibly Close* (2005), also chose the fictionalized autobiography as a vehicle and explored the psychological aftermath of the September 11 terrorist attack in New York City, where Foer still lives. Both books were published before Foer was thirty, leading *Newsweek* in 2006 to consider him one of a handful of young authors who serve as a "voice of this generation."[12] Both these books also contained sympathetic vegetarian characters, based in part on Foer himself, foreshadowing Foer's more serious turn to the issue of eating animals in his third book, also his first work of nonfiction, *Eating Animals*, in 2009.

Like his two previous novels, *Eating Animals* examined a form of distinctly modern, globally significant mass violence, in this case factory farming, which Foer describes as follows: "Like pornography, factory farming is hard to define but easy to identify. In a narrow sense it is a system of industrialized and intensive agriculture in which animals—often housed by the tens or even hundreds of thousands—are genetically engineered, restricted in mobility, and fed unnatural diets (which almost always include various drugs, like antimicrobials). . . . Ninety-nine percent of all land animals eaten or used to produce milk and eggs in the United States are factory farmed. So although there are important exceptions, to speak about eating animals today is to speak about factory farming."[13] *Eating Animals* is part memoir, part exposé of the meat industry, and part philosophical reflection on the topic named in its title. Unlike most nonfiction books addressing the situation in contemporary agriculture today, however, Foer did not begin or end his book with an argument critiquing agriculture today (though he certainly gets to that in between). He opens and closes the book with chapters of the same title, "Storytelling," and it is stories, not the many important facts and arguments that Foer also relays, that dominate its opening.

Specifically, Foer opens with stories about his family life, especially his grandmother, a survivor of the holocaust, and the tales she related to the family of her survival. "Then it all changed," his grandmother tells him, referring to the rise of Nazism. "During the War it was hell on earth. . . . I was always running, day and night, because the Germans were always right behind me. If you stopped, you died. There was never enough food. I became sicker and sicker from not eating, and I'm not just talking about being skin and bones. I had sores all over my body. It became difficult to move." These stories were the sacred stories of his family, and by sharing them in this internationally bestselling book, they became sacred stories for many more. "Even at the worst times, there were good people, too," his grandmother continued. "Someone taught me to tie the ends of my pants so I could fill the legs with any potatoes I was able to steal. I walked miles and miles like that, because you never knew when you would be lucky again. . . . You had to have luck and intuition." The story of his grandmother's survival in Nazi Europe reaches its crescendo at the end of the first chapter in the following exchange between Jonathan and his grandmother:

> "The worst it got was near the end. A lot of people died right at the end, and I didn't know if I could make it another day. A farmer, a Russian, God bless him, he saw my condition, and he went into his house and came out with a piece of meat for me."
>
> "He saved your life."
>
> "I didn't eat it."
>
> "You didn't eat it?"
>
> "It was pork. I wouldn't eat pork."
>
> "Why?"
>
> "What do you mean why?"

"What, because it wasn't kosher?"

"Of course."

"But not even to save your life?"

"If nothing matters, there's nothing to save."

The point of this story as Foer wields it is not a return to traditional, ritually oriented kosher practice, in which Foer shows little interest. Rather Foer utilizes the story to address the importance of drawing lines, drawing lines about the ultimate question of who we are and drawing those lines not abstractly in our minds but in the choices we make in the material world. What Foer takes from this story as he then takes the reader on a tour of the dismal state of contemporary animal agriculture throughout the rest of the book is that food matters. Food is one location where we draw the lines that decide who we are. In the Jewish context, as in so many others, food's importance is amplified through the transmission of food practices in families and communities and across generations. Foer's point in telling this story and mine in repeating it is, at minimum, to insist that food, ethics, and identity go together at the deepest conceivable level.

Eating Animals goes on to engage a tremendous volume of factual information about the state of contemporary animal agriculture and invites the readers to follow Foer in trying to come to more firm ethical conclusions about the question of eating animals, a question that, for Foer, felt especially urgent after he had had his first child and started to make eating decisions for someone else. Foer passionately argues for the significance of eating animals as a moral issue, documenting the massive scale of human and animal suffering and ecological degradation that have been associated with factory farming. He ultimately concludes he and his children will be vegetarian but doesn't call on everyone to follow him, instead prioritizing an opposition to factory farming as the common ground that should unite public action.

Throughout *Eating Animals*, Foer makes multiple biblical allusions, and he disproportionately engages a number of Jewish thinkers over the course of his book, including Franz Kafka and Jacques Derrida. In addition to frequent personal stories that mention his Judaism, he explicitly speaks about his own disappointment with the state of kosher slaughter, but *Eating Animals* is not an explicitly Jewish or religious book. I have presented it here in a volume about *Jewish* food, in a section on food, Judaism, and ethics, but admittedly, Foer presents himself as just an ordinary American (who happens to be of Jewish decent) speaking about issues of universal concern. Despite the neutral presentation, I am indeed suggesting, for all the reasons listed at the opening of this paragraph, that his book *can* be read as distinctly Jewish, as one recent installment in a long line of *Jewish* reflection on the ethics of eating (among other things). Let us turn to, however, a more explicitly Jewish book: the biblical book of Genesis, specifically the (Priestly source) narrative found in Genesis 1 and again in Genesis 9. According to the dominant contours of classical rabbinic commentary, Genesis 1 and 9 provide the core narrative about eating animals found in the Hebrew Bible.[14]

A Biblical Story: From Eden to Sacrifice

For most Americans, including Jewish Americans, the simple fact that God commands humans to be vegetarian in Genesis is often a surprising discovery, so let us start with this fact. In the first chapter of Genesis, we have the famous narrative of creation that is structured around the seven days of the week—six for the creation of the world and the seventh during which God rests, the archetype of the Sabbath Jews celebrate every Friday to Saturday evening. On the sixth day of creation, God creates both humans and land animals (birds and sea animals have already been created), and according to this passage, God sets humans in relation to the rest of creation through two commands. The first command is more well known: human beings are granted dominion and told to not only be fruitful and multiply (which the animals are told to do as well) but *rule* creation. This verse, Genesis 28, is arguably the most famous verse in the whole of Genesis, and most people who know little else about the Bible are aware that it articulates some kind of human rule over creation. What is noteworthy for our purposes is that the immediately following verses, Genesis 29–30, as interpreted virtually unanimously by Jewish (and Christian) exegetes, declare that humans and animals must eat only plants. If you read closely, it appears that humans and animals are given slightly different vegan fair—humans are given plants "with seeds," but the animals receive only the leafy parts of plants, which perhaps points to the distinctly human aspects of seed-based agriculture. It is only after this command to eat only plants in Genesis 31 that God famously pronounces creation "very good," whereas each previous time creation was praised only as "good."

The biblical story of meat at first appears to end there, but as happens frequently throughout the Bible, it is picked up later in a process of intrabiblical exegesis. That is, later on in Genesis, the Bible returns to this story and interprets it further (much like the ancient rabbis, who founded Judaism as we know it, themselves did with biblical stories in the sacred texts they penned in the first six centuries of the Common Era, the Talmud and Midrash).[15] In Genesis 9, Noah and his family have just emerged from the arc after surviving the punishing flood God had sent to destroy his corrupted creation, and at the moment of this refounding of human civilization, God creates a new covenant with Noah, his family, and all creation—and this covenant explicitly reverses the command to eat only plants given in Genesis 29–30. God now allows humans to eat animals, but not in a casual manner. As God declares meat acceptable food, God insists that blood must be drained from animals first—the blood cannot be eaten. This is so because, we are told, the blood contains the life of the animals, and now interpreting the symbolism of the text, the life of the animals is not given to humans but is the sole property of God.[16] In other words, even when permission is given to eat meat, there is a qualification and restriction (as explored extensively in Weiss's chapter in this volume). Indeed, the blood prohibition is just the beginning of the massive complex of restrictions placed on consuming meat in the Bible, which ultimately constitute the core of the biblical system of animal sacrifice.

While the details of this biblical story are not frequently repeated in public today, virtually all Americans who eat meat—religious and secular—continue to follow the prohibition against consuming blood, which I mention here by way of suggesting that these stories continue to have real power in ways that are unexpected. So normal has the blood prohibition come to be seen that many seem to have made the assumption that blood is simply inedible (something I discovered when I started teaching the text in undergraduate courses). Blood, however, is a common food source cross-culturally and is known as quite tasty by those who consume it. Most Americans have a taboo on consuming blood not because there is any insurmountable pragmatic barrier to using it as food but because it violates a symbolically charged biblical mandate. We have simply forgotten this.

So if the example of the persistence of the blood prohibition tells us that, often unconsciously, we are still in the grip of the biblical narrative, what has the narrative about eating animals I just reviewed meant to Jews historically and what does it mean now? A truly detailed, historically rich answer is beyond the scope of this short chapter (one study of Genesis 1:28, a single verse, fills an entire book[17]), but there are at least two discernable streams of interpretation in the Jewish context. One stream of interpretation takes the fact that God originally planned a world without meat eating, along with other details, to mean that the "permission" given to eat meat in Genesis 9 is really a *concession*. Jews who have followed this stream of interpretation tend to view vegetarianism as a desirable ethical ideal. Vegetarianism here is a choice for lesser violence, a precursor to the messianic age that will reflect the perfect nonviolence of Eden. The first prestate, Ashkenazic rabbi of Israel, Rav Kook, is a notable recent representative of this view and was famously known to eat almost exclusively vegetarian fair.

Another stream of interpretation simply does not dwell on the distance between Edenic life and life as we know it in this regard and emphasizes instead the important role meat, often along with wine, can play in creating social cohesion and joy. In this second stream, the tradition can be read as greatly encouraging or even requiring the consumption of meat in celebration of the Sabbath and sometimes other holidays as a vital part of what makes these days special. Rav Kook famously honored this stream, even as the force of his teachings emphasize vegetarianism as an ultimate ideal, by consuming a small amount of meat on the Sabbath as an exception to his usually scrupulous vegetarianism.

In other words, far from telling Jews whether or not it is ethical to eat meat and how, the narratives of the Bible have instead given Jews (and others) a vocabulary to discuss the ultimate questions of meaning associated with meat. Working in community, specific answers have been given to these questions by Jews over the millennia, but the open-endedness of the Jewish textual interpretation is a counterweight to the creation of a final Jewish position on the question of eating animals.

Most Jewish communities and individuals have decided, unlike Foer, that eating animals is ethically acceptable (or even desirable) and have gone on to articulate various anticruelty measures that are meant to address the moral dangers of meat. This fits a broader pattern in which Jewish canonical texts evidence a "simultaneous insistence on both the value of animal lives and the greater value of human well-being," which is communicated "by juxtaposing countervailing principles of, on the one hand, kindness to animals (often coupled with an emphasis on human creatureliness), and, on the other hand, human ascendancy (often coupled with an emphasis on human distinctiveness)."[18] After all, meat may be acceptable in this dominant view, but cruelty to animals must be prevented. The classical rabbinic tradition reflected in the Talmud named this prohibition on "unnecessary suffering to animals" *tzaar ba'alei chayim*, and the prohibition and its implications are detailed in every subsequent Jewish legal code.

Conclusion

Bringing these two stories together, we can note that contemporary Jews like Foer who are concerned with raising the profile of attention to animal suffering and Jews with opposite or different concerns about eating animals not only have the previous biblical narrative available to them as a starting point to discussions of the ethics of eating animals but millennia of commentary on these narratives and, in addition, the various discussions of the principle of compassion for animals, *tzaar ba'alei chayim*, in the Talmud and beyond. However, Jews with concerns like Foer's will be frustrated by many (not all!) of the ways these ideas have developed. For example, at first glance, *tzaar ba'alei chayim* would seem a strong basis for opposing the cruelty of factory farming (say, for example, a basis to oppose breeding chickens to grow so fast that it hurts for them to move much of their lives, a ubiquitous practice Foer documents). However, in many cases, the ability of this principle to actually protect animals has been eviscerated by expansive interpretations of what counts as "necessary" suffering (recall that *tzaar ba'alei chayim* only prohibits *unnecessary* suffering). For some legal authorities in the Jewish tradition, any human interest whatsoever, no matter how trivial (say earning one cent more), is sufficient justification for animal suffering (i.e., any benefit whatsoever means the suffering was necessary). Most of the American Jewish leaders who run today's kosher meat industry adopt in practice something like this later view and therefore support raising animals in the same industrial settings that produce the rest of meat in America. A small minority of kosher businesses, most notably the kosher meat purveyor KOL Foods, has attempted to increase animal welfare standards in the kosher industry, a task also pursued by several nonprofit organizations, including Shamayim: Jewish Animal Advocacy, founded by the Orthodox Rabbi Shmuly Yanklowitz, and the Jewish Initiative for Animals (JIFA), a project of a secular nonprofit group, Farm Forward, that works in tandem with the Humane Society of the United States, the nation's largest humane organization, and Hazon, the nation's largest Jewish environmental group.[19]

Speaking from my own perspective as a Jew who cares about animal suffering, I find the limitations of this venerable ban on cruelty that dominate the conventional kosher industry today offensive to my Jewish sensibilities (and I'm not alone), but as a scholar who has and is primarily attempting to give you a more neutral picture of the tradition in this chapter, I have attempted to bracket my own view *to the extent possible*. And just as I explicitly inserted my own view into this chapter in the preceding sentence, mingling it with the reflections of Jews past and present, so do all Jews who care to insert their voices into the tradition and tell their own story. Let's return to our question: How do contemporary Jewish traditions respond to this universally common and fraught activity—eating animals—especially in an ethical register? A pithy answer is now possible: They—we—tell stories. We pass them from grandparent to child, we tell them at home and sometimes in best-selling books, and we often have the audacious hope that these stories could change the actual world. Foer, after opening *Eating Animals* with the story of his grandmother, closes his book with an invitation: he invites his readers to tell a new story of eating animals at our own dinner tables. He suggests that storytelling might be a way to resist all the steel and concrete of the factory farm.

So to answer standing on one foot (i.e., to answer in brief), How do contemporary Jewish traditions respond to the question of eating animals? We listen to and tell stories of all kinds, and we invite others to join. This is perhaps one of the most characteristic marks of what it means to respond "Jewishly" to any ethical question about food. Among other things, making food a *Jewish* ethical issue means to bring Jews in conversation with each other and with the inherited textual tradition. Everything else—from activism, to identity, to law—follows.

NOTES

1. Ingold, *What Is an Animal?*
2. Fessler and Navarrete, "Meat Is Good to Taboo."
3. Belasco, *Food*, 11–12.
4. For example, see Serpell, *In the Company of Animals*. For discussion, see Burkert, *Homo Necans*, 12–22; *Creation of the Sacred*, 150; Frazer and Gaster, *New Golden Bough*, 471–79; Ingold, "From Trust to Domination," 69; Milgrom, *Leviticus 1–16*, 712–13.
5. For an example in the Jewish case, see Jewish responses to an undercover video showing animal abuse at the Agriprocessors slaughterhouse (now AgriStar), a kosher abattoir in Postville, Iowa. See Gross, *Question of the Animal*, chap. 6.
6. On empathy, See Gross, "Animals, Empathy, and Rahamim."
7. Although I use the category "world religions" because of its general familiarity, the category is problematic and bound to a colonialist legacy. See Masuzawa, *Invention of World Religions*, for discussion.
8. On Jewish vegetarianism, see Labendz and Yanklowitz, *Jewish Vegetarianism*.
9. On factory farming, see Foer, *Eating Animals*.
10. Harari, *Sapiens*, 379.
11. Striffler, *Chicken*.
12. Grossman, "Who's the Voice?"
13. Foer, *Eating Animals*. I have a special relationship with this book; I am mentioned in its prose, including a short monologue, and am thanked in the acknowledgments.
14. I will not here attempt the tedious but important task of explicitly tracing the historical continuities between the concerns of contemporary Jewish writers like Foer (sometimes producing deceivingly secular-looking texts) and more traditional Jewish content, but such would be a desideratum.
15. For more on intrabiblical exegesis and its parallels with rabbinic commentary, see Fishbane, *Biblical Interpretation*.
16. On the meaning of the blood prohibition, I follow the work of Jacob Milgrom discussed in the chapters in this volume by Goodfriend and by Weiss.
17. Cohen, *Be Fertile and Increase*.
18. Gross, "Jewish Animal Ethics," 2.
19. I helped start JIFA in 2015.

BIBLIOGRAPHY

Belasco, Warren James. *Food: The Key Concepts*. Oxford: Berg, 2008.

Burkert, Walter. *Creation of the Sacred: Tracks of Biology in Early Religions*. Cambridge, MA: Harvard University Press, 1996.

———. *Homo Necans: The Anthropology of Ancient Greek Sacrificial Ritual and Myth*. Berkeley: University of California Press, 1983.

Cohen, Jeremy. *Be Fertile and Increase, Fill the Earth and Master It: The Ancient and Medieval Career of a Biblical Text*. Ithaca, NY: Cornell University Press, 1989.

Fessler, Daniel M. T., and Carlos David Navarrete. "Meat Is Good to Taboo." *Journal of Cognition and Culture* 3, no. 1 (2003): 1–40.

Fishbane, Michael. *Biblical Interpretation in Ancient Israel*. Oxford: Oxford University Press, 1989.

Foer, Jonathan Safran. *Eating Animals*. New York: Little, Brown, 2009.

Frazer, James George, and Theodor Gaster. *The New Golden Bough: A New Abridgment of the Classic Work*. New York: Criterion Books, 1959.

Gross, Aaron S. "Animals, Empathy, and Rahamim in the Study of Religion: A Case Study of Jewish Opposition to Hunting." *Studies in Religion/Sciences Religieuses* 46, no. 4 (2017): 487–88.

———. "Jewish Animal Ethics." In *The Oxford Handbook of Jewish Ethics and Morality*, edited by Elliot Dorff and Jonathan Crane, xx, 514. Oxford: Oxford University Press, 2013.

———. *The Question of the Animal and Religion: Theoretical Stakes, Practical Implications*. New York: Columbia University Press, 2014.

Grossman, Lev. "Who's the Voice of This Generation?" *Time*, July 2, 2006.

Harari, Yuval Noah. *Sapiens: A Brief History of Humankind*. New York: HarperCollins, 2015.

Ingold, Tim. "From Trust to Domination: An Alternative History of Human-Animal Relations." In *The Perception of the Environment: Essays in Livelihood, Dwelling and Skill*, edited by Tim Ingold, 61–76. London: Routledge, 2008.

———, ed. *What Is an Animal?* London: Unwin Hyman, 1988.

Labendz, Jacob, and Shmuly Yanklowitz, eds. *Jewish Vegetarianism and Veganism: Studies and New Directions*. Albany, NY: SUNY Press, 2019.

Masuzawa, Tomoko. *The Invention of World Religions: Or, How European Universalism Was Preserved in the Language of Pluralism*. Chicago: University of Chicago Press, 2005.

Milgrom, Jacob. *Leviticus 1–16: A New Translation with Introduction and Commentary*. Anchor Bible Series 3. New York: Doubleday, 1991.

Serpell, James. *In the Company of Animals: A Study of Human-Animal Relationships*. Cambridge: Cambridge University Press, 1996.

Striffler, Steve. *Chicken: The Dangerous Transformation of America's Favorite Food*. New Haven: Yale University Press, 2005.

Afterword

JONATHAN SAFRAN FOER

I became a vegetarian when I was nine years old. A babysitter persuaded me that it is wrong to hurt animals unnecessarily, and that meat production hurts animals. I saw no way to refute that logic and no reason not to change my life in response—save for my love of hot dogs at ball games with my dad, sushi with my mother on Wisconsin Avenue, burgers at barbecues with friends, chicken and carrots at my grandmother's house on Shabbat, brisket at Passover, lox at Yom Kippur breakfast, and fried chicken whenever and wherever it was served.

I became a vegetarian again when I was eleven, this time in response to a visit to the National Zoo with my family.

I became a vegetarian again when I was thirteen—a personal vow I made on the occasion of my bar mitzvah.

I became a vegetarian when I entered high school, and again when I entered college, and again upon becoming engaged to marry.

And several times since then.

The last time I became a vegetarian was right around the birth of my first son. I assume that last time will be my *last time*, but I've assumed that many times before.

Does the frequency with which I have made my decision not to eat meat suggest a lack of commitment or a commitment? Is my concern about the meat industry—which has developed, over the years, from being only about animal cruelty to include issues such as species extinction, global hunger, air and water pollution, the lives of farmers, and climate change—flimsy or steadfast? I have been unable to be a consistent vegetarian, but perhaps more important, I have been unable to be a consistent omnivore. My struggle with animal products has sustained itself over my life in a way that few other ethical concerns have. And I have come to understand that struggle not as an expression of my uncertainty about the right way to treat animals—despite my changing habits, my beliefs have held pretty constant—but as the complexity of eating.

This book reminds us that we do not simply feed our bellies and we do not simply modify our appetites in response to a few consciously held beliefs; we eat to forge identities, find out who we are, realize community, and manage the immense messiness of being human. All my different identities (father, son, American, New Yorker, progressive, Jew, writer, environmentalist, traveler, hedonist) are present when I eat, and so is my history. When I first chose to become vegetarian, my motivation was simple: do not hurt animals unnecessarily. Over the years, my motivations changed—because the available information changed, but perhaps more important because my identities changed. (It's not a coincidence that so many of my positive meat associations as a child involved eating with loved ones, and it's not a coincidence that so many of the times I became vegetarian were tied to life changes.) As I imagine is the case for most people, growing older has meant a proliferation of identities and a softening of ethical binaries in favor of a greater appreciation of what might be called the messiness of life. (As life becomes messier, so does the understanding of life.) Sometimes—as when I first visited the kind of family farm that gives its animals good lives and painless deaths or the first time I was able to travel to Japan, where it is virtually impossible to experience the culture without eating fish—that messiness has made it more difficult to see vegetarianism as the only option for me. Sometimes—as when I learned about the profound connection between meat eating and climate change or as I've had amazing meat-free culinary experiences—it has made it easier.

How one weighs one's human nature against the consequences of meat eating is, to some extent, one's own business, because it has to be one's own business, as each eater arrives at the table with his or her own set of identities. But we do have a responsibility to be informed eaters, and self-questioning ones. The messiness of life is real and not to be underestimated. But it is not an excuse to withdraw oneself from the struggle. We do not need to come up with the same answers, but in a world whose survival depends on how we eat, it has never been more important to ask the questions—and to keep asking them.

ACKNOWLEDGMENTS

As the editor of the volume as a whole, I am above all grateful to my wonderful co-editors and to each of this volume's fine contributors. It has been an honor to work with such insightful, interesting, and kind scholars. The volume owes a very special debt to the Leichtag Foundation, especially Charlene Seidle and Jim Farley, for their support of the initial conference that allowed most of the contributors of this volume to gather in person at the lovely Leichtag Commons in Encinitas, California, in July 2016. This volume might never have happened without their early support, and many of its best features are directly influenced by that 2016 meeting. The whole volume has also benefited from the support of Hasia Diner and Jonathan Safran Foer and their contributions of a foreword and afterword and from the support of the Department of Theology and Religious Studies at the University of San Diego. As editor of the ethics part, I also want to acknowledge the financial support of the nonprofit Farm Forward and its Jewish Initiative for Animals, especially Melissa Hoffman and Ilana Braverman, which helped cover the cost of course release to edit the ethics part; to thank the Jewish nonprofit Hazon, especially Nigel Savage and Judith Belasco, for numerous opportunities to discuss these issues at their annual Jewish food conference; and to thank the Society of Jewish Ethics for providing an ideal venue to present early versions of several of the ethics chapters. Finally, I thank Jennifer Channin and Fletcher for all the conversations and shared meals and their generative contributions to my scholarship.

—Aaron S. Gross

The keen intelligence and great wit of my co-editors made this project intellectually stimulating and a great pleasure. As editor of the history part and author of one of its chapters, I benefitted greatly from Hasia Diner's guidance and her crucial insights on gender and labor. I learned much from the other authors of the history chapters and am grateful for their gracious willingness to agree to my editorial guidance. Elizabeth Say, now retired dean of the College of Humanities at my university, California State University, Northridge (CSUN), enabled me without hesitation to devote time to research and writing. Finally, I owe a debt to the Los Angeles Jewish community members whose gifts to the CSUN Foundation provided essential financial support for this volume's publication.

—Jody Myers

I thank all the contributors for writing wonderful chapters. Most importantly, I thank my fellow editors, with whom it has been a pleasure to work. I have enjoyed our many conversations. Finally, I thank Josiah and Valerie, who make every day better.

—Jordan D. Rosenblum

Aaron S. Gross is Associate Professor of Jewish Studies in the Theology and Religious Studies Department at the University of San Diego. Dr. Gross is a historian of religions who focuses on modern and contemporary Jewish thought and ethics, especially Jewish food and animal ethics. Gross is Past President of the Society for Jewish Ethics, founding Cochair of the American Academy of Religion's Animals and Religion Group, and Founder and CEO of the nonprofit advocacy organization Farm Forward. He is the author of *The Question of the Animal and Religion: Theoretical Stakes, Practical Implications* (2014) and the co-editor of *Animals and the Human Imagination: A Companion to Animal Studies* (2012).

Jody Myers is Professor of Religious Studies and Director of the Jewish Studies Interdisciplinary Program at California State University, Northridge. She has written on modern religious thought and expression. She is the author of *Seeking Zion: Modernity and Messianic Activism in the Writings of Tsevi Hirsch Kalischer* (2004) and *Kabbalah and the Spiritual Quest: The Kabbalah Center in America* (2007), as well as more than two dozen articles. She is currently working on a study of contemporary Orthodox foodways, titled *Eating at God's Table: Purity, Charity, and Community in an Orthodox Jewish Community.*

Jordan D. Rosenblum is the Belzer Professor of Classical Judaism at the University of Wisconsin-Madison, where he is also the Director of Religious Studies. He holds a PhD in religious studies from Brown University and has been a Starr Fellow at Harvard University. His research focuses on the literature, law, and social history of the rabbinic movement in general and, in particular, on rabbinic food regulations. He is the author of *The Jewish Dietary Laws in the Ancient World* (2016; paperback edition, 2019) and *Food and Identity in Early Rabbinic Judaism* (2010; paperback edition, 2014) as well as the co-editor of *Religious Competition in the Third Century C.E.: Jews, Christians, and the Greco-Roman World* (2014). His latest book, titled *Rabbinic Drinking: What Beverages Teach Us about Rabbinic Literature*, is forthcoming in 2020.

Jonathan Brumberg-Kraus is Professor of Religion at Wheaton College (Massachusetts) and a Reconstructionist rabbi and regularly teaches the undergraduate seminar Rituals of Dinner. He has published extensively on Rabbenu Bahya ben Asher's eating manual *Shulhan Shel Arba* and is the author of *Gastronomic Judaism as Culinary Midrash* (2019).

Jonathan K. Crane is the Raymond F. Schinazi Scholar in Bioethics and Jewish Thought at Emory University Center for Ethics. Dr. Crane addresses pressing moral concerns in this quickly changing world by developing cutting-edge research in ethics and religion. He is the author of *Eating Ethically: Religion and Science for a Better Diet* (2018), *Narratives and Jewish Bioethics* (2013), and *Ahimsa: The Way to Peace* (2007, with Jordi Agusti-Panareda); co-editor with Elliot Dorff of *The Oxford Handbook of Jewish Ethics and Morality* (2012); and editor of *Beastly Morality: Animals as Ethical Agents* (2016) and of the forthcoming volume *Race with Jewish Ethics* (2019). While president of the Society of Jewish Ethics, he founded and continues to co-edit the *Journal of Jewish Ethics*.

Zev Eleff is Chief Academic Officer of Hebrew Theological College. He is also Associate Professor of Jewish History at Touro College. His *Who Rules the Synagogue?* and *Modern Orthodox Judaism* were both finalists for the 2016 National Jewish Book Award. Eleff's latest book, *Authentically Orthodox: A Tradition-Bound Faith in American Life*, is forthcoming.

David M. Freidenreich is the Pulver Family Associate Professor of Jewish Studies at Colby College, where he serves as Director of the Jewish Studies Program and Associate Director of the Center for Small Town Jewish Life. As a member of the Religious Studies Department, he teaches a wide range of courses on Judaism, Jewish history, and comparative religion. After receiving a BA from Brandeis University, he earned his PhD at Columbia University and rabbinic ordination from the Jewish

Theological Seminary. His award-winning first book, *Foreigners and Their Food: Constructing Otherness in Jewish, Christian, and Islamic Law*, explores attitudes toward adherents of foreign religions expressed in ancient and medieval laws about sharing food. He currently studies the ways Christians have used ideas about Jews to think about Muslims.

Elaine Adler Goodfriend received her PhD in Near Eastern studies from University of California, Berkeley, in 1990. She has taught at several universities in Southern California, including American Jewish University and Loyola Marymount University. She has been teaching Bible and Jewish studies at California State University, Northridge, since 1998. Her scholarly interests include Biblical law and the history of Ancient Israel.

Rachel B. Gross is the John and Marcia Goldman Professor of American Jewish Studies in the Department of Jewish Studies at San Francisco State University, where she teaches a course on American Jewish food history as well as other courses on American Jewish history. She is currently working on a book on American Jewish nostalgia, including a study of the Jewish deli revival in the twenty-first century. She received her PhD in religion from Princeton University.

David Kraemer is Joseph J. and Dora Abbell Librarian (Director of the Library) at the Jewish Theological Seminary, where he has also served as Professor of Talmud and Rabbinics for many years. As librarian, Prof. Kraemer is at the helm of the most extensive collection of Judaica—rare and contemporary—in the Western Hemisphere. On account of the size and importance of the collection, Prof. Kraemer is instrumental in setting policy and establishing vision for projects of international importance. Prof. Kraemer is a prolific author and commentator, with interest in rabbinic religion, the history and culture of Jews in late Antiquity, Jewish food and eating, and the history of Jewish books.

Adrienne Krone is Assistant Professor of Religious Studies and Director of Jewish Life at Allegheny College. She holds a PhD in American religion from Duke University. Her research focuses on religious food justice movements in North America. In her manuscript "American Manna: Religious Responses to the American Industrial Food System," she investigates the religious complexity present in contemporary food justice movements. Her current research project is an ethnographic and historical study of the Jewish community farming movement.

Susan Marks is the Klingenstein Professor of Judaic Studies at New College of Florida, the honors college of the state of Florida, where her courses include Meals in Jewish Tradition. She holds a PhD in religious studies from the University of Pennsylvania. She is the author of *First Came Marriage: The Rabbinic Appropriation of Early Jewish Wedding Ritual* (2013). Her work on weddings and wedding banquets led her to explore the ritual practices of other rabbinic meals in a number of articles and as co-editor (with Hal Taussig) of *Meals in the Early Judaism: Social Formation at the Table* (2014).

Moses Pava is the Alvin H. Einbender University Professor in Business Ethics at Yeshiva University. Dr. Pava is the former Dean of the Sy Syms School of Business at Yeshiva University and has been teaching there since 1988. He has published numerous books, including *Jewish Ethics in a Post-Madoff World, Business Ethics: A Jewish Perspective*, and *Jewish Ethics as Dialogue*. He lectures across the country and around the world on Jewish business ethics, spirituality in business, and corporate accountability. He serves on the editorial board of *Journal of Business Ethics* and is a former treasurer of the Society of Jewish Ethics.

Katalin Franciska Rac is Library Coordinator for Jewish Heritage in the Isser and Rae Price Library of Judaica at the Department of Special and Area Studies Collections of University of Florida's George A. Smathers Libraries. Rac holds a doctorate from the University of Florida and is a historian of modern European and European Jewish cultural and intellectual history, focusing on East-Central Europe, particularly Hungary. Her interest in Hungary's culinary history stems from her readings on national identity discourse, which from the nineteenth century until today continues to rely on a culinarily inspired language. As modern Hungarian national cuisine evolved throughout the nineteenth century, public discourse over Jewish integration likewise involved discussions on foodstuffs. Part of this process is captured in her chapter appearing in this volume.

Elliot Ratzman is a Fellow in Jewish Studies at Lawrence University. Elliot Ratzman holds a PhD in religion, ethics, and politics from Princeton's Religion Department and has been a Posen Fellow in Jewish Culture at Temple University. Ratzman has taught courses on modern religious thought, politics, ethics, and culture around the Philadelphia area. His current book project, *Between Precarity and Power: A Jewish Reckoning with Race*, engages Jewish ethics and critical race theory, addressing controversies of racism and antiracism in America, Israel, and Europe. His research interests include congregation-based community organizing, comparative ethical practices, and modern Jewish thought.

Jennifer A. Thompson is the Maurice Amado Professor of Applied Jewish Ethics and Civic Engagement at California State University. Dr. Thompson's research focuses on contemporary Jewish life. Her book *Jewish on Their Own Terms: How Intermarried Couples Are Changing American Judaism* uses ethnography to contrast the experiences of rabbis, Jewish educators, and intermarried couples with Jewish public discourses about intermarriage. Her other publications address women's religious leadership, the ethics of public discourse, and boundaries between Jews and non-Jews. Her current research concerns Jewish diversity, unconventional forms of Jewish affiliation, and women scholars' experiences in Jewish studies. She teaches courses that include Applied Jewish Ethics, American Jewish Experience, and Sociology of Jewish Families and Communities.

Daniel H. Weiss is Polonsky-Coexist Senior Lecturer in Jewish Studies in the Faculty of Divinity at the University of Cambridge. His research examines the intersection between classical Jewish texts and ethical, political, and philosophical thought as well as intersections between

Jewish and Christian thought and theology. He is the author of *Paradox and the Prophets: Hermann Cohen and the Indirect Communication* (2012) and co-editor of *Purity and Danger Now: New Perspectives* (2016). He is actively involved in the Cambridge Interfaith Programme and in Scriptural Reasoning.

INDEX